OTHER
PEOPLE'S
MONEY

OTHER PEOPLE'S MONEY

Debt Denomination and Financial Instability in Emerging Market Economies

EDITED BY

Barry Eichengreen

AND

Ricardo Hausmann

The University of Chicago Press

Chicago and London

Barry Eichengreen is the George C. Pardee and Helen N. Pardee Professor of Economics and Political Science at the University of California, Berkeley. His recent books include *Capital Flows and Crises; European Monetary Unification: Theory, Practice, Analysis;* and *Financial Crises and What to Do about Them.* Ricardo Hausmann is professor of the practice of economic development at the John F. Kennedy School of Government at Harvard University.

The University of Chicago Press, Chicago 60637
The University of Chicago Press, Ltd., London
© 2005 by The University of Chicago
All rights reserved. Published 2005
Printed in the United States of America

14   13   12   11   10   09   08   07   06   05   1   2   3   4   5

ISBN: 0-226-19455-8 (cloth)

Library of Congress Cataloging-in-Publication Data

Other people's money : debt denomination and financial instability in emerging market economies / edited by Barry Eichengreen and Ricardo Hausmann.
    p. cm.
    Includes bibliographical references and index.
    ISBN 0-226-19455-8 (cloth : alk. paper)
    1. Capital movements—Developing countries.   2. Debts, External—Developing countries.
3. Finance—Developing countries.   4. Monetary policy—Developing countries.   I. Eichengreen, Barry J.   II. Hausmann, Ricardo.
    HG3891.O84   2005
    332'.042'091724—dc22

                                                                        2004015213

♾ The paper used in this publication meets the minimum requirements of the American National Standard for Information Sciences—Permanence of Paper for Printed Library Materials, ANSI Z39.48-1992.

Contents

Acknowledgments

THE PROCESS of assembling this book has resulted in a decided imbalance in the credit and debit sides of our personal balance sheets. The papers were presented at an authors' meeting at the Kennedy School of Government, Harvard University, in Cambridge and at a public conference at the Inter-American Development Bank in Washington, DC. At these meetings, detailed commentaries were provided by Martin Anidjar, Howard Bodenhorn, Jorge Braga de Macedo, Guillermo Calvo, Eliana Cardoso, Kevin Cowan, Paul Denoon, Martin Eichenbaum, Eduardo Fernández-Arias, Morris Goldstein, Ben Heller, Jonathan Kelly, Michael Kumhoff, Enrique Mendoza, Michael Mussa, Arturo Porzecanski, Carmen Reinhart, Roberto Rigobon, Nouriel Roubini, Ernesto Stein, Federico Sturzenegger, Richard Sylla, and Philip Turner. Financial support was provided by the Center for International Development and the David Rockefeller Center for Latin American Studies, both of Harvard University; the Institute of European Studies at the University of California, Berkeley; and the Inter-American Development Bank. The Cambridge seminar was organized by Aaron Jette, while the Washington conference was arranged by Norelis Betancourt and Maria Helena Melasecca. Sibani Michael Bose in Berkeley carefully assembled the manuscript, while Alex Schwartz and Catherine Beebe in Chicago shepherded it into print. We are grateful to them all.

OTHER
PEOPLE'S
MONEY

Introduction

Debt Denomination and Financial Instability in Emerging Market Economies

Barry Eichengreen and Ricardo Hausmann

ONE OF the most momentous developments of the last ten years has been the liberalization of international financial markets. Much was promised on behalf of this policy. External finance was supposed to supplement domestic savings and support faster rates of capital formation in low- and middle-income countries, stimulating development and growth. Foreign borrowing was supposed to smooth consumption in the face of business cycles and commodity price fluctuations. International portfolio diversification was supposed to allow investors to share risk more efficiently across borders.

If much was promised, less was delivered. Rather than smoothing consumption and production, capital flows seem only to have accentuated their volatility. Models of the intertemporal approach to the balance of payments (e.g., Cole and Obstfeld 1991) are now supplemented by a darker literature on capital-flow reversals and sudden stops (Calvo 1998; Milesi Ferretti and Razin 1998). In practice, capital-flow reversals have been associated with disruptive crises in Mexico, Thailand, Indonesia, Korea, Russia, Brazil, Ecuador, Turkey, Argentina, and Uruguay, prompting the development of a literature on how capital flows and their composition can be an engine of instability (Frankel and Rose 1996; Rodrik and Velasco 1999; Stiglitz 2002). The markets have not comfortably digested these events. Rather than experiencing rising net flows of financial capital across borders in response to incentives to smooth consumption, encourage capital formation, and diversify risks internationally, we have now seen net private debt flows decline from an annual average inflow of US$95 billion in 1992–96 to an annual average *outflow* of $88 billion in 1998–2002 (World Bank 2003).

It would be an oversimplification to suggest that these problems have a single cause. The weakness of macroeconomic and financial policies and the underdevelopment of market-supporting institutions undoubtedly constitute part of the explanation for the skittishness of international investors and the tenuous capital market access of developing countries. At some level, the volatility of capital flows is just a specific manifestation of the general tendency for financial

markets to display high levels of volatility in an environment of insecure contract enforcement—which is necessarily the environment in which financial
transactions between distinct sovereign nations take place. Moreover, problems
in the capital-exporting countries of the North add to the volatility of flows; a
well-known example is the near failure of long-term capital management in
1998, which led to a reduction in leverage and a flight to quality, and specifically
to a flight away from emerging market debt.

But there is also another theme running through recent work on capital flows,
their volatility, and their potentially destabilizing impacts that distinguishes it
from previous research on this subject. This theme is balance-sheet effects. When
international financial markets are liberalized and international debt transactions are deregulated, making it possible for countries to borrow and lend
abroad, virtually all of these transactions turn out to be of a specific type. They
take place in a world in which the vast majority of international debt obligations
are denominated in the currencies of the principal creditor countries and financial centers: the United States, Japan, Great Britain, Switzerland, and the members of the euro area. Consequently, emerging market countries that effectively
make use of international debt markets by accumulating a net foreign debt will
necessarily assume a balance-sheet mismatch, since their external obligations
will be disproportionately denominated in dollars (or yen, euros, pounds, and
Swiss francs), unlike the revenues on which they rely to service those debts,
which are typically denominated in the local currency. Exchange rate changes
will then have significant wealth effects. In particular, the currency depreciation
that is the standard treatment for an economy with a deteriorating balance of
payments may so diminish the country's net worth that adjustment of the currency is destabilizing rather than stabilizing: the dollar value of its GDP declines, while the dollar value of its debt service does not. Aware that the normal
adjustment mechanism has been disabled, investors will be alarmed rather than
reassured by the change in the exchange rate, heightening the volatility of capital flows and giving rise to the possibility of sudden stops, current account reversals, and self-fulfilling currency and debt-sustainability crises.

There is now a considerable literature on balance-sheet factors in open-
economy macroeconomics (see, e.g., Krugman 1999; Razin and Sadka 1999;
Aghion, Bacchetta, and Banerjee 2000; Céspedes, Chang, and Velasco 2002;
Jeanne 2002). But there is less than complete agreement on the mechanisms
through which they influence the economy and less than full understanding of
their consequences for economic outcomes.

In part, this lack of consensus reflects incomplete understanding of why so
many international obligations are denominated in the currencies of a handful
of advanced economies. To put the point another way, we do not fully understand why emerging markets find it so difficult to borrow in their own currencies. And as long as this understanding eludes us, we will not be able to limit

this source of fragility, short of preventing capital-scarce developing countries from borrowing externally, which would seem perverse from the standpoint of the efficiency with which the global capital stock is allocated.

To some, why emerging markets cannot borrow abroad in their own currencies is self-evident. Foreign investors are reluctant to hold claims on countries with poor policies and weak market-supporting institutions: one should not expect foreigners to do things that even residents are unwilling to do (see, e.g., Reinhart, Rogoff, and Savastano 2003). There may be something to this view. But there are reasons to think that the problem is more complex than this explanation would suggest. The weakness of institutions of contract enforcement and the instability of macroeconomic and financial policies may help to explain why some countries cannot borrow at all, but this is not the same as explaining why many countries that can in fact borrow nonetheless find it so hard to borrow in their own currencies. And while histories of high inflation and fiscal profligacy can explain the reluctance of international investors to hold claims denominated in the currencies of some developing countries, investors seem equally reluctant to hold claims denominated in the currencies of emerging markets with respectable records of fiscal and monetary performance. If the issue is fear that borrowers may be tempted to inflate away debt denominated in their own currency, then we should observe inflation-indexed debt, not dollar-denominated debt.[1] In fact, all countries that are able to borrow abroad in their own currencies are also able to borrow at long maturities and at fixed rates in their domestic markets. The converse, however, is not true: a significant number of countries are able to convince local investors to purchase long-term obligations in nominal or inflation-indexed terms but are still unable to get foreigners to hold these claims—consider, for example, India, Israel, and Chile.

This suggests that there may be something about concentration of external debt in a handful of currencies that is associated with more than just fear of inflation and expropriation. To put the point another way, while the quality of policies and strength of institutions vary markedly across emerging markets, virtually all of them must borrow in foreign currency. At the end of 2001, according to estimates assembled by the U.S. Treasury, Americans held $84 billion of developing-country debt, but less than $3 billion of that total was denominated in the currencies of the developing countries in question. Of the $648 billion in overseas debt held by Americans at the end of 2001, fully 97 percent was denominated in five currencies: the U.S. dollar, the euro, the British pound, the Japanese yen, and the Canadian dollar. Of the average of $434 billion of debt securities issued by developing countries in international markets that was outstanding between 1999 and 2001, less than $12 billion was denominated in the currency of the issuing countries.[2]

The disproportion between these figures suggests that the problem is too widespread to be entirely explicable in terms of the weakness of policies and institutions. It is as if emerging markets suffer from an inherited burden, almost irrespective of the policies of their governments. This is why the difficulty they face in borrowing abroad in their own currencies is sometimes referred to as "original sin" (see Eichengreen and Hausmann 1999).[3] It is why some authors have sought causes of the problem in the structure of the international financial system and suggested international initiatives for solving it.[4]

The idea that the difficulty that emerging markets encounter when attempting to borrow abroad in their own currencies, and hence their susceptibility to exchange-rate-related balance-sheet effects, reflects not just weaknesses of their own policies and institutions but also something about the structure of the international financial system, has not sat well with some observers.[5] In part the controversy stems from the questions raised in this literature about the role of institutions in economic growth. The "original sin hypothesis" (that the difficulty emerging markets experience in attempting to borrow abroad in their own currencies has something to do with the structure of the international system) does not imply that policies and institutions are irrelevant. How could it, when there is so much evidence that institutions are important for economic growth? In the present context there is also the fact that only a handful of advanced industrial countries, who have achieved their high-income status in the course of a long period of institutional development, have managed to escape the problem of original sin and acquire the ability to issue substantial amounts of external debt denominated in their own currencies.

There is no question, then, that the dramatic changes in the strength and quality of institutions needed to transform emerging markets into advanced industrial countries would also enhance their ability to borrow abroad in their own currencies.[6] This is how we understand the fact that the advanced economies have both stronger institutions and lower levels of original sin. But once we limit our attention to developing countries, there is little evidence that the standard institutional reforms will redeem them from original sin. While the quality of institutions and policies varies enormously among developing countries, the extent of original sin does not. It is as if the foreign-currency denomination of their external debt consigns them to a kind of low-level equilibrium trap. Institutional reform promotes development—economic and financial development alike. But what it does not seem to promote over the time frame relevant for practical policy analysis is the ability to borrow abroad in the local currency. Hence, developing countries suffer higher levels of macroeconomic and financial volatility as a result of their exposure to exchange-rate-related balance-sheet effects. And the macroeconomic and financial disruptions caused by those balance-sheet effects make it correspondingly harder to sustain the process of institutional development and reform. This is not to say that institutional reform is irrelevant to economic growth; to the contrary, it is critically important. But it may not be sufficient if the structure of international finance heightens volatility in a way that handicaps efforts at institution building, effectively creating a low-level equilibrium trap.

WHILE THESE issues have begun to attract attention, they have yet to receive systematic treatment. The contributors to this volume aspire to provide just this. They provide new information on the extent to which foreign debt is denominated in foreign currency; that is, they attempt to measure the incidence of original sin. They analyze the consequences of original sin for the economic performance and prospects of emerging markets. They investigate the underlying sources of the problem. And they propose an international initiative to ameliorate it. Each goal is pursued with both theory and empirical analysis.

Chapters 1–4 attempt to measure original sin and analyze its consequences. The first chapter, by Ugo Panizza and the editors, quantifies the incidence and extent of original sin for a sample of developed and developing economies. The authors use these indicators to show that the composition of external debt—and specifically the extent to which that debt is denominated in foreign currency—is a key determinant of the stability of output, the volatility of capital flows, the demand for foreign reserves, the choice of exchange rate regime, and the level of country credit ratings. Their results show that original sin has statistically significant and economically important implications for these variables even after controlling for other more conventional determinants of macroeconomic outcomes. They demonstrate that the macroeconomic policies on which stability and creditworthiness depend, according to conventional wisdom, are themselves importantly shaped by the currency denomination of external debt.

The following three chapters explore the channels through which macroeconomic outcomes are affected by the currency denomination of the external debt. Chapter 2, by Luis Céspedes, Roberto Chang, and Andrés Velasco, augments a mainstream model of macroeconomic fluctuations in open economies to include a role for debt denomination. It uses this model to demonstrate how the presence of original sin makes monetary policy less effective and output stabilization more difficult. The authors also show how a sufficiently high level of foreign-currency debt can render an economy crisis-prone. Chapter 3, by Giancarlo Corsetti and Bartosz Maćkowiak, analyzes how the currency composition of the government's debt obligations can render that debt unsustainable when the economy is buffeted by shocks. The authors show how, as the share of dollar-denominated or short-term debt increases, the fiscal accounts become less flexible, and expected inflation and depreciation become more responsive to anticipated shocks. Hence, original sin may explain why inflation and currency depreciation are more sensitive to shocks in countries that are otherwise identical in terms of the magnitude of the debt and the disturbances they suffer.

Chapter 4, by Olivier Jeanne and Jeromin Zettelmeyer, demonstrates that balance-sheet mismatches of the sort that are a consequence of original sin when a country has a net foreign debt, as a developing country is expected to have, create scope for self-fulfilling crises in a large class of crisis models. Their analysis implies that no exchange rate arrangement may suffice to prevent the emergence of crises in the presence of original sin. Central bankers thus face an unsavory choice of channeling external pressure into higher interest rates or a weaker exchange rate, both of which weaken balance sheets. In principle, fiscal policymakers can help, but fiscal policy is itself subject to a financing constraint that will tighten just when expansionary policies might be warranted. In such circumstances, international rescue lending by an organization such as the International Monetary Fund may make countries with a fundamentally sound fiscal position but a temporary financing constraint less crisis prone.

The importance of original sin having been established, chapters 5 and 6 seek to identify its sources. Historical evidence is useful here, since the developed countries that are now able to borrow abroad in their own currencies have not always enjoyed this privilege. It should be illuminating, in other words, to understand what institutional developments and policy measures allowed them to gain this capacity. Chapter 5, by Michael Bordo, Christopher Meissner, and Angela Redish, focuses on the overseas regions of British settlement—the United States, Canada, Australia, New Zealand, and South Africa—which have some of the deepest and best-developed financial markets in the world, and the last of which has recently joined the short list of emerging markets able to fund themselves abroad by issuing securities denominated in their own currencies. The authors show that the U.S. government was able to issue and market dollar-denominated bonds abroad from the beginning of the nineteenth century, although the amounts involved were small and U.S. sovereign debt had gold clauses (effectively indexing it to foreign currency) until 1933. The British Dominions, in contrast, shifted to domestic-currency external sovereign debt only after 1973. The authors link cross-country differences in these developments and their timing to the soundness of financial institutions, the credibility of monetary regimes, and the state of financial development. In addition, they invoke an element of path dependence: these institutional factors mattered because of the superimposition of major shocks, like the two world wars, that effectively closed down international markets, in turn encouraging the development of domestic borrowing capacity and a constituency for creditor-friendly policies. In the U.S. case, in addition, the development of the ability to borrow abroad in the domestic currency was linked to the size and importance of the country, which by the end of the nineteenth century had made the dollar into a key currency. In the other countries considered, this capacity was linked to membership in the British Empire, which limited the fears of British investors about the stability of domestic-currency bonds and the intentions of their issuers.

In chapter 6, Marc Flandreau and Nathan Sussman also explore the idea that redemption from original sin has involved an element of path dependence.

They argue that redemption was related, in the continental European cases they consider, to the presence of a liquid market in that currency, acquisition of which tended to be correlated with a country's involvement in international trade and finance. They show that Russia, in spite of weak institutions, had less original sin than the Scandinavian countries, reflecting the legacy of these commercial and financial factors. They establish that relatively few countries lost or gained original sin over time. One exception is the United States, whose presence in world trade and investment changed in the course of its early history, with implications for its ability to borrow abroad in its own currency.

Chapters 7 and 8 train theoretical light on these issues. In chapter 7, Olivier Jeanne explores the implications of poor monetary-policy credibility for the currency denomination of private debts. He associates low credibility with the probability that the central bank may opt for a burst of inflation. The lower the credibility, the higher the ex post real interest rate in case the central bank keeps inflation low. This confronts the firm with a Hobson's choice between borrowing in dollars and going bankrupt if a massive depreciation takes place, versus borrowing in pesos and going bankrupt if things turn out well. The author demonstrates that as credibility declines, dollar borrowing becomes the safer option. The implication is that liability dollarization may not be the consequence of moral hazard and that taxing or restricting foreign-currency borrowing would not be welfare enhancing.

In chapter 8, Marcos Chamon and Ricardo Hausmann model the interaction of private borrowers' choice of debt denomination and the central bank's choice of monetary policy. In their model, the central bank faces a shock that can be accommodated through either changes in the exchange rate or changes in the interest rate. Borrowers seek to minimize the likelihood of bankruptcy and must choose between short-term peso or dollar liabilities. If bankruptcies are costly, the central bank may seek to avoid them by stabilizing the variable that is relevant given the private-sector choice of debt denomination. If the central bank stabilizes the exchange rate by letting the interest rate vary more with the shocks, dollar debt will be safer. If, on the other hand, it stabilizes the interest rate while letting the exchange rate go, peso debt will be preferred. The authors show that the externality that a private borrower's choice exerts on the other borrowers through the effect on the resulting monetary policy allows multiple equilibria to occur. In addition, if interest rates have small (large) demand effects and exchange rates have large (small) inflationary consequences, the central bank has a stronger a priori willingness to choose to stabilize the exchange rate (the interest rate). If those effects are sufficiently large, a private borrower will choose dollar (peso) debt even if all others choose peso (dollar) debt, thus eliminating the multiple equilibria. The implication is that original sin may be more prevalent in countries where the pass-through is high and the financial system is shallow.

Ultimately, the relevance of these theoretical perspectives can only be determined empirically. In chapter 9, Eichengreen, Hausmann, and Panizza therefore provide an empirical analysis of the sources of original sin. They explore whether low levels of development, weak institutions, low monetary-policy credibility, weak fiscal fundamentals, low trade openness, and a small proportion of domestic lenders relative to foreign lenders can explain the phenomenon. The authors find that these conventional hypotheses have surprisingly little explanatory power. In other words, the standard policy and institutional variables turn out to shed strikingly little light on why many emerging markets find it so difficult to borrow abroad in their own currencies, and they offer little in the way of an explanation for why a small number of countries have been able to escape this plight.

This leads the authors to pursue the possibility that original sin has as much to do with the structure and operation of the international financial system as with the weaknesses of policies and institutions at the national level. They find a robust relationship between the absence of original sin and the size of the economy as measured by the magnitude of its GDP, its trade, or the size of its financial system. This would be the predicted result if economies of scale, network externalities, or liquidity effects are important for the willingness of foreign investors to hold a national currency (as suggested by Flandreau and Sussman in chapter 6). The authors also find that emerging markets that have achieved redemption from original sin have often overcome the obstacles posed by the structure of the international system with help from foreign entities—multinational corporations and international financial institutions—that have found it attractive, for their own reasons, to issue debt in the currencies of these countries.

This leads in the final chapter of the book to proposed solutions. In chapter 10, the editors build on the fact that countries that have achieved redemption from original sin have overcome the obstacles posed by the structure of the international system with the help of foreign entities to propose an initiative for addressing original sin. They recommend that the international policy community commit to an initiative to develop an emerging-market index and a market in claims denominated in it. The index would be composed of an inflation-indexed basket of currencies. By having international investors hold long positions in this basket, it is then easy—through simple financial engineering—to allow each index member to borrow in terms of its own inflation-indexed currency. The editors offer detailed recommendations for how the international financial institutions and the governments of the advanced countries might go about this.

No single change in the international financial architecture, by itself, will eliminate financial crises or solve all the problems of developing countries. But neither will initiatives at the national and international levels limit the financial fragility of emerging markets and the instability of international capital flows if they fail to address the systemic problems that help to give rise to original sin. We hope that the contributions to this volume, which document the problem, analyze its sources, and propose solutions, will draw wider attention to this fact.

Notes

1. Or short-term debt, which is harder to inflate away. Of course, relying on short-term debt creates other problems; effectively, it substitutes a maturity mismatch for the currency mismatch on the books of the country that cannot borrow abroad, long-term, in its own currency. Subsequent chapters explore this trade-off.

2. These numbers are from tables 1.1 and 1.3 in chapter 1.

3. Currency mismatches, balance-sheet effects, and original sin are often referred to interchangeably. This makes it important to emphasize how they differ. Original sin refers to the inability of countries, typically emerging markets, to borrow abroad in their own currencies. This inability may result in a currency mismatch on the national balance sheet; indeed, it necessarily will if the country in question incurs a net foreign debt. But countries characterized by original sin that do not borrow abroad will not have a currency mismatch. Neither will countries that accumulate foreign reserves to match their foreign liabilities. But, then again, these countries will not have a net foreign debt. More generally, countries may wish to limit borrowing without prohibiting it or to accumulate reserves to offset some fraction, generally less than one, of that foreign borrowing. In their case, some degree of currency mismatch will result, but there will still be no direct mapping between original sin and the extent of the mismatch (appropriately scaled, say, by GNP). Still other countries may be able to substitute the placement of short-term domestic-currency debt for issuance of long-term foreign-currency debt. They too will suffer balance-sheet effects, in this case if the interest rate moves, but the balance-sheet effect will have nothing to do with the currency denomination of the foreign debt. Balance-sheet effects, currency mismatches, and original sin are all relevant to the discussion, but it is important to clearly distinguish them from one another.

4. Thus, the title of our volume is consciously a play on the title of Brandeis (1913), who similarly argued that unfettered financial markets could produce inefficient outcomes, albeit in a different context and for different reasons.

5. For a flavor of the controversy, see Reinhart, Rogoff, and Savastano 2003 and Goldstein and Turner 2003.

6. Eichengreen, Hausmann, and Panizza present evidence to this effect in chapters 1 and 9.

References

Aghion, Philippe, Philippe Bacchetta, and Abhijit Banerjee. 2000. "Currency Crises and Monetary Policy in an Economy with Credit Constraints." Manuscript, University College, London.
Brandeis, Louis. 1913. *Other People's Money and How the Bankers Use It.* New York: McClure Publications.

Calvo, Guillermo. 1998. "Capital Flows and Capital-Market Crises: The Simple Economics of Sudden Stops." Manuscript, University of Maryland, College Park, July.

Céspedes, Luis Felipe, Roberto Chang, and Andrés Velasco. 2002. "IS-LM-BP in the Pampas." Manuscript, Harvard University, Cambridge, MA.

Cole, Harold L., and Maurice Obstfeld. 1991. "Commodity Trade and International Risk Sharing: How Much Do Financial Markets Matter?" *Journal of Monetary Economics* 28:3–24.

Eichengreen, Barry, and Ricardo Hausmann. 1999. "Exchange Rates and Financial Fragility." In *New Challenges for Monetary Policy,* 329–68. Kansas City, MO: Federal Reserve Bank of Kansas City.

Frankel, Jeffrey, and Andrew Rose. 1996. "Currency Crashes in Emerging Markets: An Empirical Treatment." *Journal of International Economics* 41:341–66.

Goldstein, Morris, and Philip Turner. 2003. "Controlling Currency Mismatches in Emerging Market Economies: An Alternative to the Original Sin Hypothesis." Manuscript, Institute of International Economics, August, Washington, DC.

Jeanne, Olivier. 2002. "Monetary Policy and Liability Dollarization." Manuscript, International Monetary Fund, Washington, DC.

Krugman, Paul. 1999. "Balance Sheets, the Transfer Problem, and Financial Crises." Manuscript, Massachusetts Institute of Technology, Cambridge, MA.

Milesi-Ferretti, Gian Maria, and Assaf Razin. 1998. "Current Account Reversals and Currency Crises: An Empirical Treatment." NBER Working Paper no. 6620, National Bureau of Economic Research, Cambridge, MA, June.

Razin, Assaf, and Efraim Sadka. 1999. "Country Risk and Capital Flow Reversals." Manuscript, Tel Aviv University.

Reinhart, Carmen, Kenneth Rogoff, and Miguel Savastano. 2003. "Debt Intolerance." *Brookings Papers on Economic Activity* 1:1–74.

Rodrik, Dani, and Andrés Velasco. 1999. "Short-Term Capital Flows." In *Annual World Bank Conference on Development Economics,* 59–90. Washington, DC: World Bank.

Stiglitz, Joseph. 2002. *Globalization and Its Discontents.* New York: Norton.

World Bank. 2003. *Global Development Finance.* Washington, DC: World Bank.

The Pain of Original Sin

Barry Eichengreen, Ricardo Hausmann,
and Ugo Panizza

IF A COUNTRY is unable to borrow abroad in its own currency—if it suffers from the problem that we refer to as "original sin"—then when it accumulates a net debt, as developing countries are expected to do, it will have an aggregate currency mismatch on its balance sheet. Of course, such a country can take various steps to eliminate that mismatch or prevent it from arising in the first place. Most obviously, it can decide not to borrow. A financially autarchic country will have no currency mismatch because it has no external debt, even though it still suffers from original sin as we define it. But this response clearly has costs; the country in question will forgo all the benefits, in the form of additional investment finance and consumption smoothing, offered by borrowing abroad. Alternatively, the government can accumulate foreign reserves to match its foreign obligations. In this case the country eliminates its currency mismatch by eliminating its net debt (matching its foreign-currency borrowing with foreign-currency reserves). But this too is costly: the yield on reserves is generally significantly below the opportunity cost of funds.

All of this might seem relatively inconsequential. The currency denomination of the foreign debt has not, until recently, figured prominently in theories of economic growth and cyclical fluctuations. Macroeconomic stability, according to conventional wisdom, reflects the stability and prudence of a country's monetary and fiscal policies. The rate of growth of per capita incomes depends on rates of human and physical capital accumulation and on the adequacy of the institutional arrangements determining how that capital is deployed. Fine points like the currency in which a country's foreign debt is denominated, by comparison, are regarded as specialized concerns of interest primarily to financial engineers.

In this chapter we show that neglect of this problem constitutes an important oversight. In particular, we show that the composition of external debt— and specifically the extent to which that debt is denominated in foreign currency—is a key determinant of the stability of output, the volatility of capital flows, the management of exchange rates, and the level of country credit ratings. We present empirical analysis demonstrating that this "original sin" problem has statistically significant and economically important implications, even after controlling for other conventional determinants of macroeconomic outcomes. We show that the macroeconomic policies on which growth and cyclical stability depend, according to conventional wisdom, are themselves importantly shaped by the denomination of countries' external debts.

Establishing the importance of original sin for the macroeconomic outcomes of interest requires a precise measure of the phenomenon. Indeed, one reason that the problem of debt denomination has not received the attention it deserves may be that adequate information on its incidence and extent are not readily available. Thus, a contribution of this chapter is to develop a series of numerical indicators of original sin. In addition to demonstrating their importance for the macroeconomic variables relevant to our argument, we present the indicators themselves, country by country, so they can be used by other authors to analyze still other problems.

In the first two sections of this chapter, we quantify the problem and characterize its incidence. The next section analyzes its effects—what we characterize as the pain of original sin. This is followed by a brief conclusion and an appendix where we report the results of a battery of sensitivity analyses and present the underlying indicators.

Facts about Original Sin

Of the nearly US$5.8 trillion in outstanding securities placed in international markets in the period 1999–2001, $5.6 trillion was issued in five major currencies: the U.S. dollar, the euro, the yen, the pound sterling, and the Swiss franc. To be sure, the residents of the countries issuing these currencies (in the case of Euroland, of the group of countries) constitute a significant portion of the world economy and hence form a significant part of global debt issuance. But while residents of these countries issued $4.5 trillion of debt over this period, the remaining $1.1 trillion of debt denominated in their currencies was issued by residents of other countries and by international organizations. Since these other countries and international organizations issued a total of $1.3 trillion of debt, it follows that they issued the vast majority of it in foreign currency. The measurement and consequences of this concentration of debt denomination in few currencies is the focus of this chapter.

Table 1.1 presents data on the currency composition of bonded debt issued cross-border between 1993 and 2001. "Cross-border" means that table 1.1 excludes local issues. We split the sample into two periods, demarcated by the introduction of the euro. The figures are the average stock of debt outstanding during each subperiod. The information is organized by country groups and currencies of denomination. The first country group, financial centers, is composed of the United States, the United Kingdom, Japan, and Switzerland; the second is composed of the Euroland countries; the third contains the remaining developed countries; and the fourth is made up of the developing countries; we also report data on bond issues by the international financial institutions (since these turn out to be important below).

Column (1) presents the amount of average total stock of debt outstanding issued by residents of these country groups. Column (2) shows the corresponding percentage composition by country group. Columns (3) and (4) do the same for debt issued by residents in their own currency, while columns (5) and (6) look at the total debt issued by currency, independent of the residence of the issuer. Column (7) is the proportion of the debt that the residents of each country group issued in their own currency (the ratio of column [3] to column [1]), while column (8) is the proportion of total debt issued in a currency relative to the debt issued by residents of those countries (the ratio of column [5] to column [1]).

Notice that while the major financial centers issued only 34 percent of the total debt outstanding in 1993–98, debt denominated in their currencies amounted to 68 percent of that total. In contrast, while other developed countries outside of Euroland issued fully 14 percent of total world debt, less than 5 percent of debt issued in the world was denominated in their own currencies. Interestingly, in the period 1999–2001—following the introduction of the euro—the share of debt denominated in the currencies of other developed countries declined to 1.6 percent. Developing countries accounted for 10 percent of the debt but less than 1 percent of the currency denomination in the 1993–98 period. This, in a nutshell, is the problem of original sin.

When we look at the currency denomination of the debt issued by residents, we see that residents of the major financial centers chose to denominate 68.3 percent of it in their own currency in 1999–2001, while the residents of Euroland used the euro in 56.8 percent of their cross-border bond placements. This figure is substantially higher than the 23.2 percent that they chose to denominate in their own currency in 1993–98, before the introduction of the euro. In that earlier period, the other developed countries issued 17.6 percent of their debt in their own currencies, a number not too different from that for the Euroland countries; in the recent period, however, this number has declined to 9.6 percent. The number for developing countries is an even lower 2.7 percent.

It is sometimes possible for countries to borrow in one currency and swap their obligations into another. Doing so requires, however, that someone actually issue debt in the domestic currency (otherwise there is nothing to swap). Column (8) takes this point on board and is therefore a better measure of a country's ability to borrow abroad in its own currency than column (7), in the sense that when the ratio in column (8) is less than one, it indicates that there are not enough bonds to do the swaps needed to hedge the foreign-currency exposure of residents.

Table 1.1. International bonded debt in billions of U.S. dollars, by country groups and currencies

	Total debt instruments issued by residents		Total debt instruments issued by residents in own currency		Total debt instruments issued in group's currency		Share of own currency (%)	Share of group's currency (%)
	(1)	(2)	(3)	(4)	(5)	(6)	(7)	(8)
				1993–98				
Major financial centers[a]	939.1	34%	493.6	64%	1,868.4	68.1%	52.6	199.0
Euroland	855.9	31%	198.4	26%	647.5	23.6%	23.2	75.7
Other developed countries	390.1	14%	68.6	9%	128.2	4.7%	17.6	32.9
Developing countries	269.0	10%	6.3	1%	16.8	0.6%	2.3	6.3
International organizations	289.7	11%	0.0	0%	0.0	0.0%	0.0	0.0
European currency unit	0.0	0%	0.0	0%	82.8	3.0%	0.0	0.0
Total	2,743.7	100%	766.8	100%	2,743.7	100.0%	27.9	100.0
				1999–2001				
Major financial centers[a]	2,597.7	45%	1,773.6	61%	3,913.8	67.8%	68.3	150.7
Euroland	1,885.6	33%	1,071.5	37%	1,722.2	29.8%	56.8	91.3
Other developed countries	477.6	8%	45.9	2%	89.9	1.6%	9.6	18.8
Developing countries	434.0	8%	11.6	0%	47.4	0.8%	2.7	10.9
International organizations	378.4	7%	0.0	0%	0.0	0.0%	0.0	0.0
European currency unit	0.0	0%	0.0	0%	0.0	0.0%	0.0	0.0
Total	5,773.3	100%	2,902.5	100%	5,773.3	100.0%	50.3	100.0

Source: Authors' calculations based on unpublished data from the Bank for International Settlements.

[a]The United States, Japan, the United Kingdom, and Switzerland.

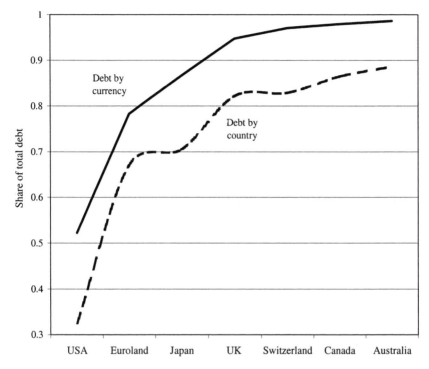

Figure 1.1 Distribution of debt by issuers and currencies, 1999–2001

Column (8) reveals that in 1999–2001 the ratio of debt in the currencies of the major financial centers to debt issued by their residents was more than 150 percent. (This, in a sense, is what qualifies them as financial centers.) This ratio drops to 91.3 percent for the Euroland countries, to 18.8 percent in the other developed countries (down from 32.9 percent in the previous period), and to 10.9 percent for the developing nations. Notice that after the introduction of the euro, Euroland countries narrow their gap with the major financial centers while other developed countries converge toward the ratios exhibited by developing nations.

Figure 1.1 plots the cumulative share of total debt instruments issued in the main currencies (the solid line) and the cumulative share of debt instruments issued by the largest issuers (the dotted line). The gap between the two lines is striking. While 87 percent of debt instruments are issued in the three main currencies (the U.S. dollar, the euro, and the yen), residents of these three countries issue only 71 percent of total debt instruments. The corresponding figures for the top five currencies, 97 and 83 percent, respectively, tell the same story.

Table 1.2 presents similar information for cross-border claims by interna-

18   Barry Eichengreen, Ricardo Hausmann, and Ugo Panizza

Table 1.2. Cross-border bank claims

	Total bank debt of residents (US$ billions)		Total debt in major five currencies (US$ billions)		Share in major five currencies (%)
	1995–98				
Major financial centers[a]	3,141	44.9%	2,448	44.02%	77.9
Euroland	1,637	23.4%	1,479	26.60%	90.3
Other developed countries	263	3.8%	167	3.00%	63.5
Offshore	502	7.2%	434	7.80%	86.4
Developing countries	1,305	18.7%	995	17.89%	76.2
International organizations	23	0.3%	17	0.31%	71.4
Unallocated	127	1.8%	22	0.40%	17.7
Total	6,998	100.0%	5,561	100.00%	79.5
	1999–2001				
Major financial centers[a]	3,691	47.3%	3,146	49.59%	85.2
Euroland	2,263	29.0%	2,080	32.79%	91.9
Other developed countries	356	4.6%	223	3.52%	62.8
Offshore	458	5.9%	381	6.01%	83.1
Developing countries	887	11.4%	673	10.61%	75.8
International organizations	18	0.2%	17	0.27%	93.7
Unallocated	134	1.7%	19	0.30%	14.5
Total	7,808	100.0%	6,344	100.00%	81.3

Source: Authors' calculations based on unpublished data from the Bank for International Settlements.
[a]The United States, Japan, the United Kingdom, and Switzerland.

tional banks reporting to the Bank for International Settlements. These data distinguish only the five major currencies (U.S. dollar, euro, Swiss franc, British pound, and Japanese yen) and an "other currency" category. The table shows that of $7.8 trillion in cross-border bank claims, 81 percent are denominated in the five major currencies. While we cannot know how much is actually issued in each borrower's currency, we can safely say that the bulk of the debt in the developing world and in the developed countries outside the issuers of the major currencies is also in foreign currency.

One possible problem with the data in table 1.1 is that they only capture cross-border bond issuance and do not capture the nationality of the bond-*holder,* only the place of issue. So it may be that countries do their local-currency funding in the local market and their foreign-currency funding abroad. Foreigners willing to hold domestic-currency bonds would just purchase them in the local markets. These domestically issued but foreign-owned domestic-currency bonds would not be included in table 1.1. To address this issue, we look at the currency composition of the international securities held by U.S. residents, independently of the place of issue.

According to the U.S. Treasury (table 1.3), these securities amounted to US$647 billion at the end of 2001. Of these securities, however, US$456 billion

Table 1.3. Composition of outstanding international securities (in billions) issued by non-U.S. residents and held by U.S. investors, 2001

	USD	EUR	JPY	GBP	Own[a]	Other	Total	Share of total (%)	Share of international securities (%)[b]	Securities by currency[c]	Currency share (%)[c]
Financial centers	137.4	5.1	32.5	16.1	0.1	0.3	191.6	29.57	19.45	511.8	79.00
Euroland	81.8	87.9	1.9	1.0	0.0	0.3	172.8	26.68	6.74	97.3	15.02
Other developed countries	115.3	1.0	0.7	0.5	34.1	0.3	151.8	23.44	29.91	34.1	5.26
Offshore	32.7	1.8	0.5	0.5	0.5	0.0	36.1	5.57	69.73	0.5	0.08
Developing countries	80.0	0.9	0.2	0.1	2.6	0.1	84.0	12.96	17.09	2.6	0.41
International organizations	9.0	0.6	0.8	0.6	0.0	0.6	11.5	1.78	3.05	0.0	0.00
Other and unallocated										1.5	0.23
Total	456.0	97.3	36.7	18.9	37.4	1.5	647.8	100	13.01	647.8	100

Source: Authors' calculations based on tables 16 and 17 in "Report on U.S. Holdings of Foreign Securities," U.S. Treasury, http://www.treas.gov/tic/shc2001r.pdf.

[a]The Own currency column is set equal to zero for Euroland (everything is reported under the euro column) and in the case of financial centers, for Japan, and United Kingdom. The value reported under Own for financial centers corresponds to issues in Swiss francs.

[b]Share of international securities held by U.S. investors over total international bonds issued in 2001 by non-U.S. residents.

[c]International securities (and their share) held by U.S. investors in each of the currency groups (for instance, at the end of 2001, U.S. investors held US$97.3 billion worth of international securities denominated in euro; this corresponds to 15 percent of the total international securities held by U.S. investors).

or 70.4 percent were denominated in U.S. dollars. This indicates that the willingness of U.S. investors to expose themselves to foreign credit risk is significantly higher than their willingness to expose themselves to foreign-currency risk: they hold more claims on foreigners than claims in foreign currency. Moreover, if we include the exposure to the euro, the yen, the British pound, and the Canadian dollar, the total foreign exposure of U.S. investors denominated in major currencies amounts to 97 percent of the total. In the case of developing countries, while U.S. investors held US\$84 billion in securities issued by developing countries, only \$2.6 billion (or 3.1 percent) was denominated in local currency. The message of table 1.3 is similar to that of table 1.1: global investors denominate their claims predominantly in very few currencies. The willingness to hold foreign securities is significantly larger than the willingness to hold them in foreign currency, except for a few major currencies.

All this points to the fact that original sin is a global phenomenon. It is not limited to a small number of problem countries. It seems to be associated with the fact that the vast majority of the world's financial claims are denominated in a small set of currencies. In turn this suggests that the problem may have something to do with observed patterns of portfolio diversification—or its absence. We develop this point in chapter 9.

Measuring Original Sin

To construct indexes of original sin, we use the data on securities and bank claims used to construct tables 1.1 and 1.2. We start with the securities data set, which provides a full currency breakdown.

Our first indicator of original sin (OSIN1) is one minus the ratio of the stock of international securities issued by a country in its own currency to the total stock of international securities issued by the country. That is,[1]

$$\text{OSIN1}_i = 1 - \frac{\text{Securities issued by country } i \text{ in currency } i}{\text{Securities issued by country } i}.$$

Thus, a country that issues all its securities in own currency would get a zero, while a country that issues all of them in foreign currency would get a one (the higher the value, the greater the sin). We also compute a variant of OSIN1 by using the data on security holding by U.S. investors (USSIN1).

OSIN1 has two drawbacks. First, it covers only securities and not other debts. Second, it does not take account of opportunities for hedging currency exposures through swaps. We deal with these issues next. Consider the following ratio:

$$\text{INDEXA}_i = \frac{\text{Securities } + \text{ Loans issued by country } i \text{ in major currencies}}{\text{Securities } + \text{ Loans issued by country } i}.$$

INDEXA has the advantage of increased coverage. (It also has the disadvantage of not accounting for the debt denominated in foreign currencies other than the majors; we address this problem momentarily). To capture the scope for hedging currency exposures via swaps, we also consider a measure of the form

$$\text{INDEXB}_i = 1 - \frac{\text{Securities in currency } i}{\text{Securities issued by country } i}.$$

INDEXB accounts for the fact, discussed above, that debt issued by other countries in one's currency creates an opportunity for countries to hedge currency exposures via the swap market. Notice that this measure can take on negative values, as it in fact does for countries such as the United States and Switzerland, since there is more debt issued in their currency than debt issued by nationals. However, these countries cannot hedge more than the debt they have. Hence, they derive scant additional benefits from having excess opportunities to hedge. We therefore substitute zeros for all negative numbers, producing our third index of original sin:

$$\text{OSIN3}_i = \max\left(1 - \frac{\text{Securities in currency } i}{\text{Securities issued by country } i}, 0\right).$$

We are now in a position to refine INDEXA. Recall that INDEXA understates original sin by assuming that all debt that is not in the five major currencies is denominated in local currency. This may be a better approximation for countries with some capacity to issue debt in their own currencies. If this is so, however, it should be reflected in OSIN3 because it means that someone— either a resident or a foreign entity—might have been able to float a bond denominated in that currency. If this is not the case, this provides information about the likelihood that the bank loans not issued in the five major currencies were denominated in some other foreign currency. We therefore replace the value of INDEXA by that of OSIN3 in those cases where the latter is greater than the former.[2] Hence we propose to measure OSIN2 as

$$\text{OSIN2}_i = \max(\text{INDEXA}_i, \text{OSIN3}_i).$$

Notice that OSIN2 $\geq$ OSIN3 by construction and that, in most cases, OSIN1 $\geq$ OSIN2.

Table 1.4 presents the average of these four indexes for the different country groupings and different parts of the developing world. (The individual country values can be found in appendix table 1A.1.) As before, we observe the lowest numbers for the major financial centers, followed by Euroland countries (which exhibit a major reduction in original sin after the introduction of the euro). Other developed countries exhibit higher values, while the highest values are for the developing world (fig. 1.2). The lowest values in the developing world are in eastern Europe, while the highest are in Latin America.

Table 1.4. Measures of original sin by country groupings (simple average)

	OSIN1 1993–98	OSIN1 1999–2001	OSIN2 1993–98	OSIN2 1999–2001	OSIN3 1993–98	OSIN3 1999–2001	USSIN1 2001
Financial centers	0.58	0.53	0.34	0.37	0.07	0.08	0.63
Euroland	0.86	0.52	0.55	0.72	0.53	0.09[a]	0.56
Other developed countries	0.90	0.94	0.80	0.82	0.78	0.72	0.66
Offshore	0.98	0.97	0.95	0.98	0.96	0.87	0.90
Developing countries	1.00	0.99	0.98	0.99	0.96	0.93	0.96
Latin American countries	1.00	1.00	1.00	1.00	0.98	1.00	0.99
Middle East and Africa	1.00	0.99	0.97	0.99	0.95	0.90	0.99
Asia and Pacific	1.00	0.99	0.95	0.99	0.99	0.94	0.96
Eastern Europe	0.99	1.00	0.97	0.98	0.91	0.84	0.91

[a] In the 1999–2001 period, it is impossible to allocate the debt issued by nonresidents in euros to any of the individual member countries of the currency union. Hence, the number here is not the simple average, but is calculated taking Euroland as a whole.

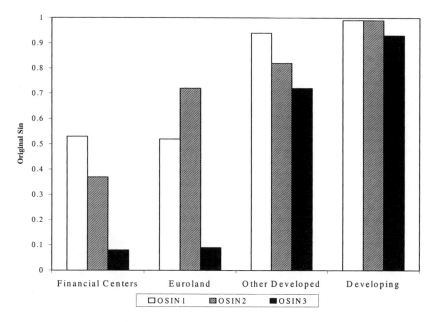

Figure 1.2 Original sin by country groups

Original sin from the perspective of U.S. investors (USSIN1) is similar to that we observe with the data from the Bank for International Settlements. There is a strong positive correlation between USSIN1 and each of OSIN1 (0.64, p-value 0.00) and OSIN3 (0.50, p-value 0.00). As in the case of OSIN3, the developing countries with the lowest values of USSIN1 (below 0.9) are South Africa, Czech Republic, Poland, and Taiwan (Hungary has a low value of USSIN1 but a high value of OSIN3).

Table 1.5 lists countries with measures of OSIN3 below 0.8 in 1999–2001, excluding the financial centers. Among the countries with the least original sin are several future eastern European accession countries and overseas regions of European settlement (Canada, Australia, New Zealand, and South Africa). Notice further that both fixed-rate Hong Kong and floating-rate Singapore and Taiwan appear on this list, raising questions about whether any particular exchange rate regime poses a barrier to redemption.[3] In fact, the countries listed in table 1.5 are equally distributed among fixers, floaters, and countries with an intermediate regime (fig. 1.3).

Original sin is also persistent, to a surprising extent. Flandreau and Sussman in chapter 6 present a three-way classification of original sin circa 1850, based on whether countries placed bonds in local currency, indexed their debt to gold (included gold clauses in their debts), or did some of both. Table 1.6 shows the

Table 1.5. Countries with OSIN3 below 0.8, excluding financial centers

	Non-Euroland			Euroland	
	1993–98	1999–2001		1993–98	1999–2001
Czech Republic	0.00	0.00	Italy	0.00	0.00
Poland	0.82	0.00	France	0.23	0.12
New Zealand	0.63	0.05	Portugal	0.42	0.24
South Africa	0.44	0.10	Belgium	0.76	0.39
Hong Kong	0.72	0.29	Spain	0.59	0.42
Taiwan	1.00	0.54	Netherlands	0.64	0.47
Singapore	0.96	0.70	Ireland	0.94	0.59
Australia	0.55	0.70	Greece	0.93	0.60
Denmark	0.80	0.71	Finland	0.96	0.62
Canada	0.55	0.76	Austria	0.90	0.68

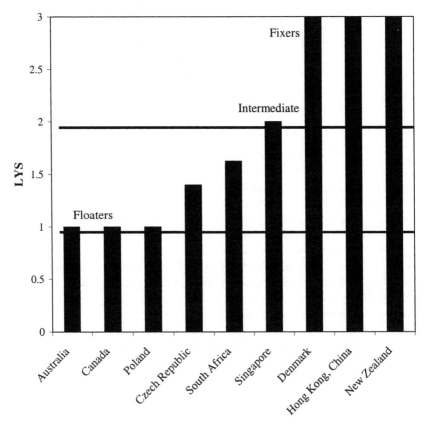

Figure 1.3 Original sin and exchange rate regime. The exchange rate regime is measured using the index developed by Levy Yeyati and Sturzenegger (2000), averaged over the 1992–98 period. One corresponds to a floating rate, and three corresponds to a fixed rate.

Table 1.6. OSIN3 in 1993–98 and the Flandreau-Sussman
classification, circa 1850

	Mean	St. dev.	N	Difference with respect to gold clauses
Gold clauses	0.86	0.28	31	0.00
Mixed clauses	0.53	0.39	6	0.36 (0.016)*
Domestic currency	0.34	0.36	5	0.52 (0.000)**
Total	0.75	0.35	42	

Note: p-values of the mean comparison test in parentheses.
*Significant at 5%. **Significant at 1%.

mean value of OSIN3 in the 1993–98 period for each of the three groups distinguished by Flandreau and Sussman. OSIN3 is highest today in the same countries that had gold clauses in their debt in the nineteenth century (average 0.86), lowest for countries that issued domestic debt (average 0.34), and intermediate in countries that issued both gold-indexed and domestic-currency debt (average 0.53); hence, there is a high correlation between original sin then and now. The standard t-test suggests that countries that exclusively issued debt with gold clauses in the 1850s suffer from significantly higher levels of original sin today than either countries that issued both gold-indexed and domestic-currency debt (p-value 0.016) or those that issued exclusively in local currency (p-value 0.000).

In their original formulation, Eichengreen and Hausmann (1999) defined original sin as "a situation in which the domestic currency cannot be used to borrow abroad, or to borrow long term, even domestically" (emphasis added). While the focus of this book and this chapter is the inability to borrow abroad in domestic currency (what we call *international* original sin), we also computed an index for the capacity of a country to borrow at long maturities domestically (which we refer to as domestic original sin). There are two reasons for deriving such an index. First of all, it would be important to know to what extent these two issues are related or are in fact two different types of issue. Second, it has been argued that creating a domestic market in a country's own currency is a necessary condition for inducing foreigners to use a country's currency (Tirole 2002). We would like to shed some light on these issues both here and in chapter 9.

Our main source of information is J. P. Morgan's *Guide to Local Markets* (2002, 2000, 1998), which reports detailed information on domestically traded public debt for twenty-two emerging market countries. J. P. Morgan also provides information on the presence of domestic private debt instruments and shows that in most countries (the exceptions being Singapore, South Korea, Taiwan, and Thailand) this is a negligible component of traded debt.

J. P. Morgan reports data on total outstanding domestic government bonds and the main characteristics (total amount, maturity, currency, and coupon) of the various government bonds present in each market. We classify the bonds listed by J. P. Morgan according to their maturity, currency, and coupon (fixed and indexed rate). In particular, we divide outstanding government bonds into five categories: (1) long-term domestic-currency fixed rate (DLTF); (2) short-term domestic-currency fixed rate (DSTF); (3) long-term (or short-term) domestic-currency floating-rate debt, that is, indexed to an interest rate (DLTII); (4) long-term domestic-currency debt indexed to the price level (DLTIP); and (5) foreign-currency debt (FC). Using the above information, we compute the following indicator of domestic original sin:[4]

$$\text{DSIN} = \frac{\text{FC} + \text{DSTF} + \text{DLTII}}{\text{FC} + \text{DLTF} + \text{DSTF} + \text{DLTII} + \text{DLTIP}}.$$

Our definition of domestic original sin focuses on both foreign-currency debt and domestic-currency short-term debt (or long-term but floating so that it has very little duration risk). It should be clear that while the definition focuses on total debt, we only have information on traded debt (and mostly public debt). Hence, our index does not include information on bank loans. Table 1.7 ranks countries according to the domestic original sin index. We find that more than half of the countries in our sample have indexes that are above 50 percent. Only five out of the twenty-two countries of table 1.7 have more than three-quarters of their public debt in long-term fixed-rate domestic-currency bonds.

Figure 1.4 organizes the twenty-one countries for which we have measures of their ability to borrow internationally in local currency (OSIN3) and domestically at long maturities and fixed rates in local currency (DSIN). It is clear that the two concepts are rather poorly correlated, indicating that they are not just two sides of the same coin. Looking in more detail at the data, we split the sample according to whether the respective values of these two variables are above or below 0.75. The resulting four quadrants are telling. The first quadrant is empty: there are no countries that can borrow abroad in local currency and have small long-term fixed-rate domestic markets. This suggests that domestic market development is a necessary condition for redemption from original sin. However, the graph also shows that it is not a sufficient condition: while there are eight countries that suffer from both types of sin (second quadrant) and six countries have achieved redemption in both dimensions (fourth quadrant), seven countries suffer from international original sin, while having been redeemed on the domestic front (third quadrant).[5] In chapter 9 we discuss the causes of this pattern and the unconventional role played by capital controls.[6]

Table 1.7. Measures of domestic original sin by country

	DSIN		DSIN
Taiwan	0.011	Czech Republic	0.588
India	0.036	Hong Kong	0.621
South Africa	0.052	Egypt	0.790
Slovak Republic	0.133	Mexico	0.837
Thailand	0.135	Greece	0.880
Singapore	0.275	Brazil	0.915
Israel	0.288	Argentina	1.000
Hungary	0.296	Venezuela	1.000
Poland	0.300	Turkey	1.000
Philippines	0.358	Indonesia	1.000
Chile	0.545	Malaysia	1.000

Source: See text.

Note: DSIN measures the share of domestic bonded debt that is in
foreign currency, short term, or indexed to inflation.

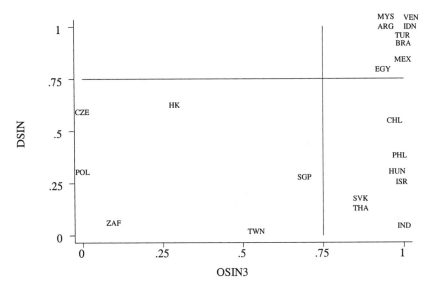

Figure 1.4 Domestic and international original sin. DSIN is the share of domestic bonded debt that
is in foreign currency, short term, or indexed to the interest rate.

The Pain

Original sin has important consequences. Countries with original sin that have
net foreign debt will have a currency mismatch on their national balance sheets.
Movements in the real exchange rate will then have aggregate wealth effects.[7]
This makes the real exchange rate a relevant price in determining the capacity
to pay. Since the real exchange rate is quite volatile and tends to depreciate in

bad times, original sin significantly lowers the creditworthiness of a country. Moreover, the wealth effects limit the effectiveness of monetary policy, as expansionary policies may weaken the exchange rate, cause a reduction in net worth, and are thus either less expansionary or even contractionary (Aghion, Bacchetta, and Banerjee 2000; Céspedes, Chang, and Velasco in chapter 2 of this volume). This renders central banks less willing to let the exchange rate move, and they respond by holding more reserves and aggressively intervening in the foreign exchange market or adjusting short-term interest rates (Hausmann, Panizza, and Stein 2001; Calvo and Reinhart 2002). The existence of dollar liabilities also limits the ability of central banks to avert liquidity crises in their role as lenders of last resort (Chang and Velasco 2000). And dollar-denominated debts and the associated volatility of domestic interest rates heighten the uncertainty associated with public debt service, thus lowering credit ratings.

Given these facts, it is no surprise that countries afflicted by original sin have a hard time achieving domestic economic stability. Their incomes are more variable and their capital flows more volatile than those of countries free of the phenomenon. Since financial markets know that inability to borrow abroad in the domestic currency is a source of financial fragility, developing countries burdened with original sin are charged an additional risk premium when they borrow, forcing them to skate closer to the edge of solvency. A shock to the exchange rate can then cause asset prices to move adversely, tipping them over the precipice. But if countries attempt instead to minimize these risks by limiting their recourse to foreign sources of funding, they may then be starved of the finance needed to underwrite their growth. The process of economic and financial development will be slowed. Countries in this situation thus face a Hobson's choice.

Original Sin and Fiscal Solvency

It has been amply recognized that developing countries tend to be more volatile than industrial countries in the sense that they have a more unstable rate of GDP growth (Inter-American Development Bank 1995; Hausmann and Gavin 1996). Table 1.8 shows that their GDP growth is more than twice as volatile as that of industrial countries: 5.8 percent per annum instead of 2.7. However, if a country's debt is denominated in foreign currency—say U.S. dollars—its capacity to pay will be related, not to the value of its GDP in constant local-currency units, but to the value of its GDP in U.S. dollar terms. Table 1.8 shows that the volatility of changes in real U.S. dollar GDP is almost three times as high as changes in real GDP in local-currency units for developing countries. Hence, the typical industrial country without original sin would face a relevant volatility of 2.7 percent per annum, while the typical developing country with original sin would face a relevant volatility of 13 percent.

The greater relevant volatility in the capacity to pay comes from the fact that

Table 1.8. Volatility of GDP growth, 1980–99

	All countries	Industrial countries	Developing countries
Real GDP growth	5.0%	2.7%	5.8%
Real dollar GDP growth	12.3%	10.3%	13.0%
Gap in 5-year moving average of the real exchange rate	49.7%	18.1%	61.2%
Number of countries	43	11	32

Table 1.9. Volatility of the real exchange rate

	1-year volatility	5-year volatility	1-year volatility 1980s	5-year volatility 1980s	1-year volatility 1990s	5-year volatility 1990s
Developing countries	1.292	1.283	1.327	1.321	1.234	1.249
Industrial countries	0.506	0.513	0.471	0.473	0.565	0.545
Difference	0.786	0.770	0.855	0.848	0.669	0.703
t statistics	4.262	4.818	3.769	3.689	3.176	4.130
p-value[a]	1.000	1.000	1.000	1.000	0.999	1.000

[a] p-value for the test that the mean of volatility in developing countries is greater than the mean of volatility in industrial countries.

original sin makes the real exchange rate matter for debt service, and this variable is very volatile in developing countries. Table 1.9 presents the volatility of the real exchange rate for a sample of developed and developing countries. The volatilities are normalized to be equal to one for the sample as a whole. The table clearly shows that the volatility of the real exchange rate is two to three times higher in developing countries. Hence, not only does the real exchange rate matter for debt service in countries with original sin, but in addition, the real exchange rate in these countries tends to be significantly more volatile.

Analysts often argue that a volatile real exchange rate does not matter if the debt is sufficiently long term. If purchasing-power parity holds in the long run, then deviations of the real exchange rate should not be very long-lived, and a country's solvency should not be much affected by temporary movements in the real exchange rate. Markets will not change their minds about the solvency of a country based on short-term movements of the real exchange rate. However, table 1.8 shows that the volatility of movements in the five-year moving average of the real multilateral exchange rate is very high. The table calculates the percentage gap between the maximum and the minimum value of a five-year moving average of the real exchange rate for a sample of developed and developing countries for the period between 1980 and 2000. The table indicates that the five-year moving average moved by more than 60 percent in the average developing country, more than three times the magnitude of industrial countries.[8] Said differently, the five-year average value of the debt to GDP ratio would have moved by more than 50 percent in the typical developing country through valuation changes in real exchange rate alone! Table 1.9 shows that the greater volatility of the real exchange rate in developing countries is as much of a feature at five years as at one year and that it remained the same in the 1980s and 1990s.

Another way to look at this data is by studying the events in which there has been a large decline in the capacity to pay foreign debt. Table 1.10 shows the occasions in which the dollar value of GDP over a two-year period fell by more than 30 percent.[9] Two facts clearly emerge from the table. First, the events identified tend to capture many of the recent debt crises. More important, while the average decline in dollar GDP for this sample of countries was 46 percent, the decline in GDP in local-currency units was less than a twentieth of that. The collapse in the capacity to pay is related more to real exchange rate movements than to output declines.

One implication of this analysis is that countries suffering from original sin should be significantly riskier than countries without this burden, after controlling for other determinants of creditworthiness such as debt ratios. This may help explain the poor predictive capacity of fiscal fundamentals such as the ratio of debt to tax revenue as a determinant of credit ratings, as is clear from figure 1.5.[10] Countries like Brazil, Argentina, Turkey, and Mexico had a debt to tax ratio that was broadly similar or in fact lower than those of the Italy, Belgium, the United States, Canada, or Spain, while their credit rating could not be more different.[11] Original sin lowers evaluations of solvency because it heightens the dependence of debt service on the evolution of the exchange rate, which is more volatile and may be subject to crises and crashes.

To test this hypothesis, we regress the foreign-currency credit rating of countries on two standard measures of fiscal fundamentals—public debt as a share of GDP and public debt as a share of tax revenues—on the level of development, on the magnitude of the foreign debt (SHARE), and on original sin. The equations are estimated by weighted double-censored Tobit. The results, in table 1.11, show a large and statistically significant effect of original sin on credit ratings.[12] Redemption (the total elimination of original sin) is associated with an improvement of ratings by about five notches. This effect is strong and present even though we control for the level of economic development, as captured by the real GDP per capita, and for the magnitude of the public debt measured either as a share of GDP or as a share of tax revenues.[13]

Hence, original sin helps explain why countries suffer from creditworthiness problems. It is not due to their incapacity to limit debt accumulation; it is that

Table 1.10. Large drops in dollar GDP

	Year	Change in dollar GDP (%)	Change in real GDP (%)		Year	Change in dollar GDP (%)	Change in real GDP (%)
Suriname	1995	−94	−7	Jordan	1990	−40	−19
Iran, Islamic Republic	1994	−93	21	Guatemala	1987	−40	3
Suriname	1994	−91	−35	Syrian Arab Republic	1988	−40	−13
Iran, Islamic Republic	1993	−91	23	Trinidad and Tobago	1987	−38	−20
Nigeria	1999	−74	−2	Togo	1982	−38	−15
Nigeria	1987	−68	28	Mexico	1982	−38	8
Uruguay	1984	−67	−8	South Africa	1985	−38	4
Egypt, Arab Republic	1991	−63	4	Ecuador	1987	−38	1
Indonesia	1998	−60	7	Egypt, Arab Republic	1992	−37	6
Sierra Leone	1986	−57	−10	Indonesia	1999	−37	−7
Mexico	1983	−56	−9	Egypt, Arab Republic	1990	−36	10
Uruguay	1983	−55	−17	Trinidad and Tobago	1986	−36	−13
Costa Rica	1982	−54	−10	Swaziland	1985	−36	2
Nigeria	1986	−52	1	Namibia	1985	−35	15
Syrian Arab Republic	1989	−48	9	Paraguay	1985	−35	13
Jamaica	1985	−46	4	Ecuador	1999	−33	−2
Honduras	1991	−46	−4	Jamaica	1984	−33	12
Dominican Republic	1985	−46	4	Papua New Guinea	1999	−33	−5
Togo	1994	−45	−12	Mexico	1995	−33	1
Chile	1983	−45	−13	Sierra Leone	1998	−31	−22
Sierra Leone	1990	−44	−15	Sweden	1982	−31	−1
Dominican Republic	1986	−44	10	Papua New Guinea	1998	−31	−4
Senegal	1994	−43	−4	Madagascar	1988	−31	7
Korea, Republic	1998	−41	−5	Jamaica	1992	−30	−10
Jordan	1989	−41	−20	Morocco	1982	−30	1
Thailand	1998	−41	−12	Venezuela	1984	−30	4
Honduras	1990	−40	0	Average		−46	−2

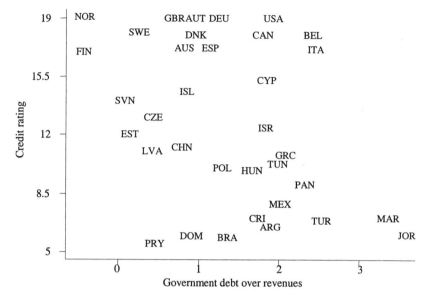

Figure 1.5 Credit rating and debt to revenue ratios

the structure of that debt makes them risky at low levels of debt that are consistent with a AAA rating in other countries.

Original Sin and Nominal Exchange Rate Volatility

We now explore the relationship between the management of monetary and exchange rate policy and the presence of original sin. We posit that countries that suffer from this phenomenon will be less willing to allow their exchange rate to fluctuate. There are no widely accepted indicators of exchange rate flexibility. We will therefore employ three alternative measures to make sure that any results are not excessively dependent on particular definitions. First, we use the de facto classification of Levy Yeyati and Sturzenegger (2000) (LYS). This is a discrete variable that equals one for countries with a flexible exchange rate regime, two for countries with intermediate regimes, and three for countries with a fixed exchange rate regime; we therefore expect original sin to be positively correlated with LYS. Our second measure of exchange rate flexibility (following Hausmann, Panizza, and Stein 2001) is international reserves over M2 (RESM2), the motivation being that countries that float without regard to the level of the exchange rate should require relatively low levels of reserves, while countries that want to intervene in the exchange rate market need large war chests. Again, we expect a positive correlation. Finally, following Bayoumi and Eichengreen (1998a, 1998b), we examine the extent to which countries actually

Table 1.11. Original sin and credit ratings

	RATING1 (1)	RATING1 (2)	Dropping financial centers	
			RATING1 (3)	RATING1 (4)
OSIN3	−5.845	−5.644	−5.214	−4.955
	(4.08)**	(4.01)**	(3.31)**	(3.21)**
DE_GDP[a]	−2.421		−2.285	
	(2.50)*		(2.32)*	
DE_RE[b]		−0.999		−0.975
		(2.49)**		(2.39)*
LGDP_PC[c]	2.916	2.670	2.976	2.729
	(8.48)**	(6.16)**	(8.36)**	(5.97)**
SHARE2	2.187	2.787	1.810	2.405
	(1.43)	(1.52)	(1.09)	(1.18)
Constant	−8.058	−5.962	−9.119	−7.037
	(2.12)*	(1.28)	(2.29)*	(1.44)
Observations	56	49	53	46

Note: t statistics in parentheses (weighted Tobit estimates).
[a]Public debt/GDP.
[b]Public debt/government revenues.
[c]Log of GDP per capita.
*Significant at 5%. **Significant at 1%.

use their reserves to intervene in the foreign exchange market, comparing the relative volatility of exchange rates and reserves (RVER).[14] RVER will be high in countries that let their currencies float and low in countries with fixed exchange rates; thus, we anticipate negative correlation with original sin.

In all regressions, original sin is measured as the average value for 1993–98, while all other dependent and explanatory variables are measured as 1992–99 averages. We focus on this period because most of our dependent variables are not available after 1999. Table 1.12 reports regressions using OSIN3 to measure original sin. (The results are robust to using OSIN2, as shown in appendix table 1A.2.) Because OSIN3 captures only one part of the currency composition of the foreign debt (it does not include information on bank loans), its precision depends on how representative bonded debt is of total external liabilities. To take account of this fact, we weight all observations by the share of securities in total foreign debt.[15]

All regressions control for the level of development (LGDP_PC, which denotes the log of GDP per capita), the degree of openness (OPEN), and the level of foreign debt (SHARE2, which denotes total debt instruments plus total loans divided by GDP). We do not have much guidance regarding the expected signs of these controls. Although the theory of optimum currency areas suggests that there should be a negative association between exchange rate volatility and openness, previous empirical studies (e.g., Honkapohja and Pikkarainen 1992;

Table 1.12. Original sin and exchange rate flexibility

	LYS (1)	RESM2 (2)	RVER (3)	Dropping financial centers LYS (4)	RESM2 (5)	RVER (6)
OSIN3	1.503	0.248	−0.801	1.112	0.339	−0.598
	(3.56)***	(3.74)***	(2.02)**	(2.45)**	(3.10)***	(1.33)
LGDP_PC	0.302	−0.053	0.026	0.285	−0.052	0.025
	(2.89)***	(1.85)*	(0.61)	(2.77)***	(1.81)*	(0.56)
OPEN	0.198	−0.014	1.017	0.153	−0.014	1.021
	(0.92)	(0.41)	(2.88)***	(0.72)	(0.41)	(2.93)***
SHARE2	0.290	−0.036	−0.570	0.297	−0.030	−0.544
	(0.96)	(0.66)	(2.36)**	(0.98)	(0.54)	(2.29)**
Constant	−2.188	0.531	0.104	−1.644	0.435	−0.084
	(1.94)*	(1.73)*	(0.17)	(1.46)	(1.35)	(0.13)
Observations	75	65	65	71	62	62
R^2		0.37	0.62		0.34	0.65

Note: Robust t statistics in parentheses (weighted ordinary least squares for RESM2 and RVER, weighted Tobit for LYS).
*Significant at 10%. **Significant at 5%. ***Significant at 1%.

Bayoumi and Eichengreen 1998a; Eichengreen and Taylor 2003) have not found much support for this hypothesis. They tend to find that any effect of openness is dominated by the effect of country size; in other words, the empirically relevant corollary of the theory of optimum currency areas is that small countries prefer to peg. The recent literature on fear of floating (Calvo and Reinhart 2002) suggests that there should be a negative correlation between level of development and desired levels of exchange rate volatility—although it also suggests that less developed countries may sometimes be less successful at limiting volatility in practice. We of course expect a negative correlation between exchange rate flexibility and share of foreign debt, on the grounds that exchange rate variability will then wreak havoc with debt service costs. This is because the share of foreign debt should amplify the negative effect of original sin. In fact, we do find some evidence that the interaction between original sin and share of foreign debt amplifies the effect of original sin on exchange rate flexibility (the results, however, are not very robust).

As expected, original sin is negatively correlated with exchange rate flexibility. The coefficients are always statistically significant when we run regressions using the full sample of countries. In the case of RVER, the coefficient is not significant (with a p-value of approximately 0.19) when we exclude financial centers from the regression.[16]

The coefficients are also economically important. Column (1) of table 1.12, for instance, suggests that complete elimination of original sin is associated with a jump of 1.5 points in the Levy Yeyati and Sturzenegger three-way exchange rate classification. Countries previously inclined to peg will move to an intermediate regime (to limited flexibility), while countries previously following policies of limited flexibility will be inclined to float. Viewed in this way, original sin provides an explanation for the fear-of-floating phenomenon. In the case of reserves over M2, redemption from original sin would move a country from the 75th percentile to the 25th percentile of the distribution of this ratio.

Here it is important to worry about reverse causality. Whereas we have argued that more original sin leads to less exchange rate variability, authors like Burnside, Eichenbaum, and Rebelo (2001) argue that less exchange rate instability leads to more original sin. Stabilizing the exchange rate, in their view, creates moral hazard; it conveys the impression that the government is socializing exchange risk, encouraging the private sector to accumulate unhedged exposures. In fact, many analysts have argued that original sin (or liability dollarization) is caused mainly by fixed exchange rates. The problem should go away with the recent move toward floating rates. However, our data should dispel this hope. Of the twenty-five developing countries with the most flexible exchange rate regimes during the 1993–98 period, according to the average value of the LYS index, twenty-two of them had a value of OSIN3 equal to one. The time-series evidence points in the same direction: there has been movement to greater flexibility of exchange rates but scant movement out of original sin except for countries that are in line to join the euro.[17]

The fact that original sin is associated with less exchange rate flexibility has the implication that interest rates have to do more of the work when the country is hit by shocks, making monetary policy less accommodating and domestic interest rates more volatile.[18] Prudent borrowers will therefore prefer dollar debts, since the alternative will be riskier (see Chamon and Hausmann, chapter 8 of this volume). Moreover, a volatile interest rate will tend to limit the development of the market in long-term debt.

Original Sin and Output and Capital-Flow Volatility

We now explore the correlation between original sin and the volatility of growth and capital flows. There are several reasons for anticipating that the phenomenon will be associated with relatively high levels of volatility. For one thing, original sin limits the scope and effectiveness of countercyclical monetary policies. In addition (as already noted), dollar liabilities limit the ability of central banks to avert liquidity crises in their role as lenders of last resort. Finally, dollar-denominated debts and real exchange rates interact to create uncertainty over the cost of dollar debt service while the associated volatility of domestic interest rates heighten the uncertainties associated with local debt service, thus lowering credit ratings and making capital flows more fickle and volatile (Hausmann 2003).

Table 1.13 examines the correlation between original sin and the volatility of output and capital flows. We measure output volatility as the standard devia-

Table 1.13. Original sin and volatility

	VOL_GROWTH (1)	VOL_FLOW (2)	Dropping financial centers VOL_GROWTH (3)	VOL_FLOW (4)
OSIN3	0.011	7.103	0.015	7.498
	(1.96)*	(3.58)***	(2.45)**	(2.69)**
LGDP_PC	−0.012	−3.214	−0.012	−3.322
	(2.14)**	(2.56)**	(2.09)**	(2.40)**
OPEN	−0.001	−4.181	−0.000	−4.333
	(0.12)	(1.20)	(0.08)	(0.83)
VOL_TOT	−0.000	0.223	−0.000	0.223
	(0.86)	(1.08)	(0.89)	(1.02)
SHARE2	−0.014	0.147	−0.015	0.949
	(1.72)*	(0.04)	(1.51)	(0.14)
Constant	0.135	32.825	0.131	33.282
	(2.25)**	(2.39)**	(2.15)**	(2.22)***
Observations	77	33	73	29
R^2	0.40	0.64	0.40	0.62

Note: Robust t statistics in parentheses.
*Significant at 10%. **Significant at 5%. ***Significant at 1%.

tion of GDP growth over the period 1992–99 and capital flow volatility as the standard deviation of capital flows (as a share of domestic credit) over the same period. We control for the level of development, openness, foreign debt, and volatility of terms of trade (VOL_TOT). Again, all equations are estimated by weighted least squares.[19]

Original sin is associated with relatively high levels of output and capital-account volatility. It accounts for a quarter of the difference in output volatility between developed and developing countries; in a horse race between original sin and terms-of-trade volatility, only original sin remains statistically significant. It is equally important in explaining capital-flow volatility: original sin again explains approximately a quarter of the difference in volatility between developing and OECD countries.

Conclusion

This chapter has developed and used a series of numerical indicators of the incidence of original sin. These are designed to capture both its international and domestic dimensions, both bank debts and securitized obligations, and both hedged and unhedged exposures. This is a more comprehensive set of measures than has been available to investigators before. These indicators and the methods we use to construct them should be of interest quite independently of the particular uses to which we put them.

These indicators allow us to establish the importance of original sin for the macroeconomic problems afflicting emerging markets. We show that countries suffering from original sin have found it difficult to participate in the movement toward greater currency flexibility or to exploit its benefits. Because exchange rate movements imbue monetary policy with wealth effects that limit its effectiveness, interest rates must do more of the work when the economy is buffeted by shocks. It follows that interest rates are more volatile and procyclical in such countries, and more volatile interest rates and fragile financial positions imply correspondingly greater macroeconomic volatility. Output fluctuations are wider in countries with original sin. Capital flows are more volatile and prone to reversal. Countries burdened by original sin have lower credit ratings and hence more tenuous access to international capital markets than their levels of indebtedness and other creditworthiness indicators would lead one to predict.

Thus, the fact that the external debts of emerging markets are disproportionately denominated in foreign currency goes a long way toward explaining why their economies are more volatile and crisis-prone than those of their advanced-country counterparts. A key challenge is thus to identify and distinguish the channels and mechanisms through which inability to borrow in the domestic currency creates this additional volatility. It is this issue that is taken up by chapters 2–4 in this volume.

Appendix

Table 1A.1. Measures of original sin by country

	OSIN1 1993–98	OSIN1 1999–2001	OSIN2 1993–98	OSIN2 1999–2001	OSIN3 1993–98	OSIN3 1999–2001	USSIN1 2001
Algeria	1		1		1		
Argentina	0.98	0.97	0.98	0.97	0.98	0.97	0.98
Aruba	1		1		1		1
Australia	0.69	0.82	0.63	0.7	0.55	0.7	0.79
Austria	0.95	0.7	0.9	0.69	0.9	0.69	0.74
Bahamas	1	1	1	1	1	1	0.99
Bahrain	1	1	1	1	1	1	
Barbados	1	1	1	1	1	1	1
Belgium	0.88	0.46	0.79	0.56	0.79	0.39	0.23
Bolivia	1		1		1		
Brazil	1	1	1	1	1	1	0.99
Bulgaria	1	1	1	1	1	1	1
Canada	0.78	0.85	0.76	0.83	0.55	0.76	0.8
Chile	1	1	1	0.98	1	0.98	1
China	1	1	1	1	1	1	0.99
Colombia	1	1	1	1	1	1	
Costa Rica	1	1	1	1	1	1	0.92
Cyprus	0.95	0.96	0.95	0.96	0.95	0.96	1
Czech Republic	1	1	0.88	0.84	0	0	0.71
Denmark	0.92	0.95	0.8	0.74	0.8	0.71	0.43
Dominican Republic	1	1	1	1	1	1	
Ecuador	1	1	1	1	1	1	
Egypt, Arab Republic		1		0.94		0.94	1
El Salvador	1	1	1	1	1	1	1
Estonia	1	1	1	0.95	1	0.83	1
Finland	0.98	0.65	0.96	0.62	0.96	0.62	0.78
France	0.59	0.35	0.52	0.42	0.23	0.12	0.46
Germany	0.69	0.37	0.67	0.48	0	0	0.35
Ghana	1	1	1	1	1	1	1
Greece	0.99	0.78	0.93	0.6	0.93	0.6	
Guatemala	1	1	1	1	1	1	0.98
Hong Kong, China	0.89	0.81	0.89	0.82	0.72	0.29	0.96
Hungary	1	1	1	0.98	1	0.98	0.44
Iceland	1	1	1	0.99	0.99	0.99	
India	1	1	1	1	1	1	1
Indonesia	0.98	0.99	0.94	0.98	0.94	0.98	0.98
Ireland	0.98	0.6	0.94	0.59	0.94	0.59	0.79
Israel	1	1	1	1	1	1	0.93
Italy	0.86	0.37	0.65	0.51	0	0	0.27
Jamaica	1	1	1	1	1	1	0.96
Japan	0.64	0.53	0.25	0.35	0	0	0.1
Jordan	1	1	1	1	1	1	1
Kazakhstan	1	1	1	1	1	1	1
Kenya	1		1		1		1

(continued)

Table 1A.1. (continued)

	OSIN1 1993–98	OSIN1 1999–2001	OSIN2 1993–98	OSIN2 1999–2001	OSIN3 1993–98	OSIN3 1999–2001	USSIN1 2001
Korea, Republic	1	1	1	1	1	1	0.95
Latvia	1	1	1	0.96	1	0.96	
Lebanon	1	1	1	1	1	1	1
Lithuania	1	1	1	1	1	1	1
Luxembourg	0.66	0.44	0.58	0.47	0	0.25	0.92
Malaysia	1	1	0.99	1	0.99	1	0.99
Malta	1	1	1	1	1	1	1
Mauritius	1	1	1	1	1	1	
Mexico	1	1	1	1	1	1	0.99
Moldova	1	1	1	1	1	1	1
Morocco	1	1	1	1	1	1	1
Netherlands	0.76	0.51	0.64	0.48	0.64	0.47	0.76
Netherlands Antilles	1	1	1	1	1	1	1
New Zealand	0.93	0.98	0.62	0.56	0.62	0.05	0.36
Nicaragua	1	1	1	1	1	1	1
Norway	0.99	0.99	0.98	0.89	0.98	0.89	0.93
Oman	1	1	1	1	1	1	
Pakistan	1	1	1	1	1	1	1
Panama	1	1	1	1	1	1	1
Papua New Guinea	1	1	1	1	1	1	
Peru	1	1	1	1	1	1	1
Philippines	0.99	1	0.98	0.99	0.98	0.99	1
Poland	0.97	0.99	0.95	0.89	0.82	0	0.69
Portugal	0.97	0.44	0.42	0.59	0.42	0.24	0.68
Qatar	1	1	1	1	1	1	
Romania	1	1	1	1	1	1	
Russian Federation	1	1	1	0.98	1	0.98	1
Singapore	0.97	0.94	0.96	0.78	0.96	0.7	0.97
Slovak Republic	1	1	0.96	0.97	0.87	0.85	1
Slovenia	1	1	1	1	1	1	1
South Africa	0.99	0.88	0.91	0.76	0.44	0.09	0.59
Spain	0.96	0.52	0.59	0.61	0.59	0.42	0.19
Sri Lanka	1	1	1	1	1	1	1
Suriname	1	1	1	1	1	1	
Sweden	0.98	0.98	0.95	0.91	0.95	0.91	0.68
Switzerland	0.84	0.8	0.29	0.25	0	0	0.89
Taiwan	1	0.99	1	0.62	1	0.54	0.52
Thailand	0.99	0.88	0.98	0.87	0.98	0.87	0.96
Trinidad and Tobago	1	1	0.99	1	0.66	1	1
Tunisia	1	1	1	1	1	1	1
Turkey	1	1	1	1	1	1	0.99
Ukraine	1	1	1	1	1	1	1
United Kingdom	0.56	0.64	0.26	0.31	0.26	0.31	0.89
United States	0.3	0.17	0.65	0.44	0	0	
Uruguay	1	1	1	1	1	1	1
Venezuela	1	1	1	1	1	1	
Zimbabwe	1		1		1		1

Table 1A.2. Original sin and exchange rate flexibility

| | LYS (1) | LYS (2) | Dropping financial centers | | RESM2 (5) | RESM2 (6) | Dropping financial centers | | RVER (9) | RVER (10) | Dropping financial centers | |
			LYS (3)	LYS (4)			RESM2 (7)	RESM2 (8)			RVER (11)	RVER (12)
OSIN2	1.401		0.230		0.415		0.733		−1.820		−1.229	
	(1.83)*		(0.24)		(3.54)***		(4.26)***		(3.04)***		(1.87)*	
OSIN3		1.503		1.112		0.248		0.339		−0.801		−0.598
		(3.56)***		(2.45)**		(3.74)***		(3.10)***		(2.02)**		(1.33)
LGDP_PC	0.143	0.302	0.105	0.285	−0.002	−0.053	0.005	−0.052	−0.093	0.026	−0.078	0.025
	(1.25)	(2.89)***	(0.93)	(2.77)***	(0.13)	(1.85)*	(0.27)	(1.81)*	(1.62)	(0.61)	(1.33)	(0.56)
OPEN	0.094	0.198	0.042	0.153	0.049	−0.014	0.048	−0.014	0.743	1.017	0.751	1.021
	(0.43)	(0.92)	(0.20)	(0.72)	(1.15)	(0.41)	(1.13)	(0.41)	(1.98)*	(2.88)***	(1.99)*	(2.93)***
SHARE2	0.344	0.290	0.351	0.297	0.000	−0.036	−0.003	−0.030	−0.305	−0.570	−0.310	−0.544
	(1.86)*	(0.96)	(1.98)*	(0.98)	(0.00)	(0.66)	(0.08)	(0.54)	(1.82)*	(2.36)**	(1.89)*	(2.29)**
Constant	−0.764	−2.188	0.710	−1.644	−0.132	0.531	−0.503	0.435	2.215	0.104	1.513	−0.084
	(0.52)	(1.94)*	(0.44)	(1.46)	(0.54)	(1.73)*	(1.70)*	(1.35)	(2.64)**	(0.17)	(1.71)*	(0.13)
Observations	75	75	71	71	65	65	62	62	65	65	62	62
R^2					0.18	0.37	0.14	0.34	0.52	0.62	0.51	0.65

Note: Robust t statistics in parentheses (weighted ordinary least squares for RESM2 and RVER, weighted Tobit for LYS).

*Significant at 10%. **Significant at 5%. ***Significant at 1%.

Table 1A.3. Original sin and macroeconomic volatility

| | VOL_GROWTH (1) | VOL_GROWTH (2) | Dropping financial centers | | | | Dropping financial centers | |
			VOL_GROWTH (3)	VOL_GROWTH (4)	VOL_FLOW (5)	VOL_FLOW (6)	VOL_FLOW (7)	VOL_FLOW (8)
OSIN2	0.016*		0.026		11.194		12.937	
	(1.68)		(2.10)**		(3.25)***		(2.78)**	
OSIN3		0.011		0.015		7.103		7.498
		(1.96)*		(2.45)**		(3.58)***		(2.69)**
LGDP_PC	−0.006	−0.012	−0.006	−0.012	−3.191	−3.214	−3.242	−3.322
	(2.02)**	(2.14)**	(1.85)*	(2.09)**	(2.69)**	(2.56)**	(2.38)**	(2.40)**
OPEN	0.005	−0.001	0.005	−0.000	−6.320	−4.181	−7.062	−4.333
	(1.15)	(0.12)	(1.14)	(0.08)	(2.00)*	(1.20)	(1.58)	(0.83)
VOL_TOT	−0.000	−0.000	−0.000	−0.000	0.393	0.223	0.382	0.223
	(0.39)	(0.86)	(0.46)	(0.89)	(2.32)**	(1.08)	(2.18)**	(1.02)
SHARE2	−0.003	−0.014	−0.003	−0.015	5.074	0.147	5.609	0.949
	(1.14)	(1.72)*	(1.11)	(1.51)	(2.32)**	(0.04)	(1.70)	(0.14)
Constant	0.070	0.135	0.058	0.131	26.478	32.825	25.758	33.282
	(1.88)*	(2.25)**	(1.43)	(2.15)**	(1.97)*	(2.39)**	(1.57)	(2.22)**
Observations	77	77	73	73	33	33	29	29
R^2	0.21	0.40	0.19	0.40	0.65	0.64	0.61	0.62

Note: Robust t statistics in parentheses.

*Significant at 10%. **Significant at 5%. ***Significant at 1%.

Table 1A.4. Original sin and credit rating

	RATING1 (1)	RATING1 (2)	RATING1 (3)	RATING1 (4)	RATING1 (5)	RATING1 (6)	RATING1 (7)	RATING1 (8)	RATING1 (9)	Dropping financial centers		
										RATING1 (10)	RATING1 (11)	RATING1 (12)
OSIN2	−15.252 (4.35)***	−12.718 (3.78)***			−9.497 (1.70)*	−11.078 (1.81)*			−14.487 (4.03)***	−11.874 (3.46)***		
OSIN3			−5.845 (4.08)***	−5.644 (4.01)***			−5.470 (2.24)**	−4.147 (1.84)*			−5.214 (3.31)***	−4.955 (3.21)***
DE_GDP[a]	−2.981 (3.22)***		−2.421 (2.50)**		7.352 (0.91)		−1.837 (0.57)		−2.969 (3.20)***		−2.285 (2.32)**	
DE_RE[b]		−0.736 (2.14)**		−0.999 (2.49)**		0.445 (0.12)		−0.346 (0.37)		−0.775 (2.25)**		−0.975 (2.39)**
LGDP_PC[c]	2.392 (7.10)***	2.273 (5.63)***	2.916 (8.48)***	2.670 (6.16)***	2.302 (6.84)***	2.247 (5.48)***	2.906 (8.36)***	2.621 (5.99)***	2.389 (7.10)***	2.235 (5.54)***	2.976 (8.36)***	2.729 (5.97)***
DE_GDPSIN2					−11.011 (1.28)							
DE_RE_SIN2						−1.232 (0.32)						
DE_GDPSIN3							−0.673 (0.19)					
DE_RE_SIN3								−0.732 (0.77)				
SHARE2	1.501 (2.66)**	1.589 (2.36)**	2.187 (1.43)	2.787 (1.52)	1.569 (2.83)***	1.597 (2.38)**	2.213 (1.44)	3.013 (1.64)	1.518 (2.69)***	1.656 (2.47)**	1.810 (1.09)	2.405 (1.18)
Constant	6.174 (1.09)	4.723 (0.77)	−8.058 (2.12)**	−5.962 (1.28)	1.450 (0.22)	3.372 (0.45)	−8.315 (2.06)**	−6.950 (1.45)	5.435 (0.95)	4.248 (0.69)	−9.119 (2.29)**	−7.037 (1.44)
Observations	56	49	56	49	56	49	56	49	53	46	53	46

Note: t statistics in parentheses (weighted Tobit estimates).

[a]Public debt/GDP.

[b]Public debt/government revenues.

[c]Log of GDP per capita.

*Significant at 10%. **Significant at 5%. ***Significant at 1%.

Table 1A.5. Robustness analysis (including developing-country dummy)

	LYS3 (1)	LYS3 (2)	RESM2 (3)	RESM2 (4)	RVER (5)	RVER (6)	VOL_GROWTH (7)	VOL_GROWTH (8)	VOL_FLOW (9)	VOL_FLOW (10)	RATING1 (11)
LGDP_PC	0.271	0.265	−0.029	−0.031	−0.100	−0.118	−0.014	−0.015	−2.817	−3.058	1.937
	(1.74)*	(1.72)*	(0.61)	(0.65)	(1.31)	(1.55)	(1.60)	(1.60)	(1.67)	(1.61)	(4.02)***
OSIN3	1.535	1.136	0.205	0.286	−0.577	−0.236	0.013	0.019	6.894	7.306	−4.760
	(3.48)***	(2.39)**	(3.40)***	(2.61)**	(1.45)	(0.68)	(2.52)**	(2.94)***	(3.35)***	(2.48)**	(3.49)***
OPEN	0.199	0.153	−0.013	−0.013	1.012	1.016	−0.001	−0.000	−4.016	−4.287	
	(0.92)	(0.72)	(0.38)	(0.38)	(3.14)***	(3.26)***	(0.10)	(0.05)	(1.12)	(0.81)	
SHARE2	0.289	0.298	−0.047	−0.041	−0.511	−0.468	−0.015	−0.016	0.241	1.060	1.752
	(0.96)	(0.99)	(0.89)	(0.76)	(2.42)**	(2.36)**	(1.84)*	(1.65)	(0.07)	(0.16)	(1.23)
DEVELOPING[a]	−0.105	−0.069	0.095	0.083	−0.507	−0.578	−0.009	−0.010	1.095	0.722	−3.006
	(0.26)	(0.17)	(1.11)	(0.92)	(2.05)**	(2.38)**	(0.59)	(0.68)	(0.30)	(0.19)	(2.71)***
VOL_TOT							−0.000	−0.000	0.221	0.222	
							(0.82)	(0.85)	(1.06)	(1.00)	
DE_GDP[b]											−2.458
											(2.73)***
Constant	−1.888	−1.450	0.299	0.250	1.338	1.210	0.159	0.157	28.750	30.633	1.595
	(1.17)	(0.91)	(0.61)	(0.52)	(1.75)*	(1.54)	(1.70)*	(1.68)*	(1.57)	(1.51)	(0.32)
Observations	75	71	65	62	65	62	77	73	33	29	56
R^2	0.39	0.35	0.39	0.35	0.65	0.69	0.41	0.41	0.64	0.62	

Note: t statistics in parentheses.

[a] Dummy variable that has a value of 1 for developing countries.

[b] Public debt/GDP.

*Significant at 10%. **Significant at 5%. ***Significant at 1%.

Table 1A.6. Robustness analysis (regressions without weights)

	LYS3 (1)	LYS3 (2)	RESM2 (3)	RESM2 (4)	RVER (5)	RVER (6)	VOL_GROWTH (7)	VOL_GROWTH (8)	VOL_FLOW (9)	VOL_FLOW (10)	RATING1 (11)
LGDP_PC[a]	0.180	0.175	−0.006	−0.006	−0.023	−0.036	−0.006	−0.006	−3.271	−3.388	2.815
	(1.70)*	(1.70)*	(0.31)	(0.33)	(0.44)	(0.74)	(2.01)**	(2.02)**	(2.50)**	(2.27)**	(8.82)***
OSIN3	1.149	0.789	0.230	0.252	−0.560	−0.051	0.012	0.015	6.432	7.101	−4.879
	(2.78)***	(1.78)*	(3.10)***	(1.79)*	(1.37)	(0.14)	(2.39)***	(2.58)***	(2.43)***	(1.87)*	(3.68)***
OPEN	0.103	0.040	0.055	0.055	0.713	0.744	0.005	0.005	−1.838	−1.927	
	(0.49)	(0.20)	(1.21)	(1.19)	(1.79)*	(1.93)*	(1.15)	(1.17)	(0.49)	(0.29)	
SHARE2	0.327	0.339	−0.002	−0.002	−0.328	−0.326	−0.003	−0.003	1.242	1.460	1.387
	(1.82)*	(1.92)*	(0.05)	(0.05)	(1.85)*	(1.92)*	(1.32)	(1.24)	(0.43)	(0.28)	(2.35)**
VOL_TOT							−0.000	−0.000	0.361	0.356	
							(0.39)	(0.44)	(2.07)**	(1.97)*	
DE_GDP[b]											−2.484
											(2.59)**
Constant	−0.765	−0.337	0.078	0.061	0.453	0.040	0.071	0.070	31.213	31.693	−7.673
	(0.68)	(0.31)	(0.37)	(0.25)	(0.71)	(0.07)	(2.17)**	(2.09)**	(2.16)**	(1.81)*	(2.20)**
Observations	75	71	65	62	65	62	77	73	33	29	56
R^2			0.19	0.11	0.44	0.49	0.22	0.20	0.65	0.61	

Note: t statistics in parentheses.

[a]Log of GDP per capita.

[b]Public debt/GDP.

*Significant at 10%. **Significant at 5%. ***Significant at 1%.

Notes

We are grateful to the Bank for International Settlements and to J. P. Morgan and in particular to Rainer Widera, Denis Pêtre, and Martin Anidjar. We are grateful to Frank Warnock for pointing us to the U.S. Treasury data, to Ernesto Stein for very useful collaboration in the early stages of this project, and to Alejandro Riaño for excellent research assistance.

1. We follow Hausmann, Panizza, and Stein (2001) but extend their sample from thirty to ninety countries and update it to the end of 2001.

2. If the composition of the bank debt were the same as that of securities, then OSIN3 should be smaller than INDEXA, since it includes not only debt issued by residents but also that issued by foreigners. When OSIN3 is greater than INDEXA, it is informative of a potential underestimate of original sin.

3. We return to this issue in chapter 9.

4. Hausmann and Panizza (2003) discuss alternative indicators of domestic original sin.

5. In the rest of this chapter, we will refer to original sin as referring exclusively to its international dimension, that is, to the ability to borrow abroad in local currency.

6. A more in-depth discussion can be found in Hausmann and Panizza 2003.

7. Governments can, of course, close the economy to foreign borrowing or accumulate international reserves sufficient to match the foreign-currency obligation (in which case the country will also not have a *net* foreign debt). Our point is that an aggregate mismatch is unavoidable when a country suffers from original sin and there is a *net* foreign debt. Note also that the wealth effect may be smaller in countries with a larger tradable sector; this is why most of our regressions control for openness.

8. The multilateral exchange rate tends to be smaller than the bilateral real exchange rate vis-à-vis the U.S. dollar, especially for industrial countries.

9. We use a two-year period in order to take account of the fact that a large depreciation will have a different impact on the one-year decline in GDP depending on the month in which it takes place. A two-year period helps smooth out this effect.

10. The debt to GDP ratio is an even worse predictor. However, it can be argued that public debt is serviced out of the portion of GDP that the government can tax. Since tax revenue to GDP ratios are lower in developing countries, they should therefore have a lower debt to GDP ratio for the same rating.

11. We used the ratings from Standard and Poor's. We converted the S&P rating into a numerical variable by adopting the following criterion: Selective default = 0, C = 2, CC = 2.5, CCC = 3, B− = 4, and each extra upgrade one point. The maximum is 19, which corresponds to AAA.

12. These results are robust to alternative definitions of original sin, as shown in appendix table 1A.4.

13. We tested whether the effect of credit rating was due to nonlinearities around the investment grade threshold but found no evidence for this hypothesis.

14. RVER is equal to the standard deviation of exchange rate depreciation divided by the standard deviation of the reserves over M2 ratio. Hausmann, Panizza, and Stein (2001) provide further details on the construction of this index.

15. Formally, the weight is equal to (total debt instruments)/(total bank loans +

total debt instruments). In appendix table 1A.6, we show that the results are robust to dropping the weights.

16. However, doing so involves eliminating the bulk of the contrast between low and high measures of original sin. In contrast, the results are robust to the addition of a developing-country dummy (appendix table 1A.5) and to dropping the weights (appendix table 1A.6).

17. We also experimented with instrumental variables, for example, using country size as an instrument for original sin, and they left our results unchanged.

18. The relationship between original sin and interest rate volatility is documented in Hausmann, Panizza, and Stein 2001.

19. These results are robust to dropping the weights and using alternative measures of original sin, as shown in appendix table 1A.3.

References

Aghion, Philippe, Philippe Bacchetta, and Abhijit Banerjee. 2000. "Currency Crises and Monetary Policy in an Economy with Credit Constraints." Manuscript, Harvard University.

Bayoumi, Tamim, and Barry Eichengreen. 1998a. "Exchange Rate Volatility and Intervention: Implications from the Theory of Optimum Currency Areas." *Journal of International Economics* 45:191–209.

———. 1998b. "Optimum Currency Areas and Exchange Rate Volatility: Theory and Evidence Compared." In *International Trade and Finance: New Frontiers for Research,* ed. Benjamin Cohen, 184–215. Cambridge: Cambridge University Press.

Burnside, Craig, Martin Eichenbaum, and Sergio Rebelo. 2001. "Hedging and Financial Fragility in Fixed Exchange Rate Regimes." *European Economic Review* 45:1151–93.

Calvo, Guillermo, and Carmen Reinhart. 2002. "Fear of Floating." *Quarterly Journal of Economics* 117:379–408.

Chang, Roberto, and Andrés Velasco. 2000. "Financial Fragility and the Exchange Rate Regime." *Journal of Economic Theory* 92:1–34.

Eichengreen, Barry, and Ricardo Hausmann. 1999. "Exchange Rates and Financial Fragility." In *New Challenges for Monetary Policy,* 329–68. Kansas City, MO: Federal Reserve Bank of Kansas City.

Eichengreen, Barry, and Alan Taylor. 2003. "The Monetary Consequences of a Free Trade Area of the Americas." NBER Working Paper no. 9666, National Bureau of Economic Research, Cambridge, MA, May.

Hausmann, Ricardo. 2003. "Good Credit Ratios, Bad Credit Ratings: The Role of Debt Denomination." In *Rules-Based Fiscal Policy in Emerging Markets: Background, Analysis, and Prospects,* ed. G. Kopits. London: Macmillan.

Hausmann, Ricardo, and Michael Gavin. 1996. "Securing Stability and Growth in a Shock-Prone Region: The Policy Challenge for Latin America." In *Stability and Growth in Latin America.* Paris: OECD.

Hausmann, Ricardo, and Ugo Panizza. 2003. "The Determinants of 'Original Sin': An Empirical Investigation." *Journal of International Money and Finance* 22:957–90.

Hausmann, Ricardo, Ugo Panizza, and Ernesto Stein. 2001. "Why Do Countries Float the Way They Float?" *Journal of Development Economics* 66:387–414.

Honkapohja, Seppo, and Pentti Pikkarainen. 1992. "Country Characteristics and the Choice of Exchange Rate Regime: Are Mini-Skirts Followed by Maxi?" CEPR Discussion Paper no. 774, Centre for Economic Policy Research, London, December.

Inter-American Development Bank. 1995. *Economic and Social Progress in Latin America 1995: Overcoming Volatility.* Baltimore: Johns Hopkins University Press for Inter-American Development Bank.

Levy Yeyati, Eduardo, and Federico Sturzenegger. 2000. "Classifying Exchange Rate Regimes: Deeds vs. Words." Manuscript, Universidad Torcuato di Tella.

Tirole, Jean. 2002. "Inefficient Foreign Borrowing." Invited lecture, Latin American and Caribbean Economic Association, Madrid, October.

Must Original Sin Cause
Macroeconomic Damnation?

Luis Felipe Céspedes, Roberto Chang,
and Andrés Velasco

ORIGINAL SIN, defined as a country's inability to borrow abroad in its own currency, is arguably the biggest obstacle that emerging markets face today as they endeavor to become more integrated into the world economy. Original sin is increasingly blamed for a host of macroeconomic ills: volatility of capital flows, vulnerable fiscal balances, and instability of investment and output.[1] The basic story is simple enough. Having to borrow in dollars or other major currencies leaves local residents open to exchange rate risk. When the real exchange rate depreciates, for whatever reason, domestic balance sheets suffer. Locals with lower net worth find it harder to borrow abroad, and investment consequently goes down, perhaps pulling output down with it. If the shock is big enough, default and bankruptcy can take place. Understanding how vulnerable domestic corporations and banks are, foreign lenders are jittery, running for the exits at the first sign of trouble. This closes the circle, making both capital movements and exchange rates volatile, and exacerbating domestic exposure to currency risk.

The story is plausible, but it raises as many questions as it answers. First, what exactly is the link between exchange rates, balance sheets, and the capacity to borrow and invest? In the textbook IS-LM-BP model with well-functioning financial markets and perfect international capital mobility, only expectations of future returns, properly arbitraged, guide capital flows and investment; corporate balance sheets and current output levels are irrelevant. This suggests that other financial imperfections must be added to original sin to cause macroeconomic damnation.

Second, how do these assorted financial imperfections interact with exogenous shocks? Does the response depend on the exchange rate regime in place, and how? A plausible conjecture is that the imperfections magnify the effects of shocks, but that the precise magnification mechanism depends quite crucially on the accompanying exchange rate movements.

A third issue has to do with the effects of exchange rates on aggregate demand and output. Even if balance-sheet effects are contractionary, standard expenditure switching effects, which obviously have an expansionary effect, are still present. Which one prevails and when?

This chapter investigates these issues.[2] For that purpose we develop a simple general equilibrium open-economy model in which real exchange rates play a central role in the adjustment process, wages and prices are sticky in terms of domestic currency, liabilities are dollarized, and the country risk premium is endogenously determined by the net worth of domestic entrepreneurs, in the manner postulated by Bernanke and Gertler (1989). Hence, all the basic building blocks are there for unexpected real exchange rate movements to be financially dangerous under original sin. In spite of the model's apparent complexity, we obtain an analytic solution for all variables of interest, which can be depicted in terms of three familiar schedules: the IS and the LM, which correspond to equilibrium conditions in the goods and money market, and the BP, along which the international loan market is in equilibrium. This characterization helps to identify exactly how the combination of balance-sheet effects and liability dollarization may lead to departures from the standard framework. We show, for instance, that the effect of financial imperfections is to change the slope of the BP, leaving the IS and LM unchanged. This affects comparative statics and the dynamic reaction of the economy to foreign shocks, and can give rise to results that do not appear in the standard model.

We distinguish between a situation of high indebtedness and the resulting *financial vulnerability*, so that a real depreciation raises the country risk premium, and one of *financial robustness*, in which the opposite happens. Vulnerability is likely to occur when capital market imperfections are large (in a sense to be made precise below), when total initial debt is large, and when the dollar share of that debt is also large.

This chapter makes three main points. First, devaluation may be expansionary or contractionary, depending on initial conditions. It is always expansionary in financially robust economies, as it is in standard models without balance-sheet effects. But if the economy is financially vulnerable, several subcases arise. Depending on the extend of vulnerability, devaluation may still expand both output and investment, it may expand output but cause investment to contract, or it may be contractionary for both output and investment.

Second, the precise effect of shocks depends jointly on the exchange rate regime in place *and* the extent of financial vulnerability. Under financial robustness, flexible exchange rates cushion the effects of adverse shocks, and they are the preferred policy. Under financial vulnerability, exchange rate movements can be stabilizing or destabilizing, as we saw above. The domestic effects of shocks then depend on initial conditions and parameter values, and on the extent policy allows the exchange rate to move. Under extreme financial vulnerability, limiting exchange rate movements may help limit the reaction of domestic output to shocks.

Third, for any exchange rate regime, the effects of external shocks—such as a fall in export volumes or an increase in the world real interest rate—are magnified by the presence of financial imperfections. The magnification effect is especially sharp under financial vulnerability, high original sin, and flexible exchange rates. Real depreciation and a fall in aggregate demand can exert negative feedback on each other: an initial depreciation reduces net worth sharply when dollar debts are large, pushing the risk premium up and reducing investment. This in turn may cause the relative price of domestic goods to fall (the real exchange rate depreciates even further), causing another round of investment cuts. Toward the end of the chapter, we explore the implications of this analysis for the design of exchange rate policy.

The Model

There are two periods, $t = 0,1$. Labor and capital are supplied by distinct agents called workers and entrepreneurs. Workers work and consume an aggregate of the domestic and foreign good. Entrepreneurs own capital and the firms. In order to finance investment in excess of their own net worth, entrepreneurs borrow from the world capital market. For concreteness, we focus on the effect of temporary shocks only at the start of period 0.

Domestic Production

Production of each variety of domestic goods is carried out by a continuum of firms acting as monopolistic competitors. These firms have access to a Cobb-Douglas technology given by

(1) $$Y_{jt} = AK_{jt}^{\alpha} L_{jt}^{1-\alpha}, 0 < \alpha < 1,$$

where Y_{jt} denotes output of variety j in period t, K_{jt} denotes capital input, and L_{jt} denotes labor input. Assume that workers' labor services are heterogeneous. The input L_{jt} is a CES aggregate of the services of the different workers in the economy:

(2) $$L_{jt} = \left[\int_0^1 L_{ijt}^{(\sigma-1)/\sigma} \, di \right]^{\frac{\sigma}{\sigma-1}},$$

where workers are indexed by i in the unit interval, L_{ijt} denotes the services purchased from worker i by firm j, and $\sigma > 1$ is the elasticity of substitution among different labor types. The minimum cost of a unit of L_t is given by

(3) $$W_t = \left[\int_0^1 W_{it}^{1-\sigma} \, di \right]^{\frac{1}{1-\sigma}},$$

which can be taken to be the aggregate nominal wage. The jth firm maximizes expected profits in every period. Profits are given by

$$(4) \qquad \Pi_{jt} = P_{jt}Y_{jt} - \int_0^1 W_{ijt}L_{ijt}\, di - R_t K_{jt},$$

where R_t is the return to capital, and profits are expressed in terms of the domestic currency (henceforth called peso), subject to the production function in (1) and the demand for its good,

$$(5) \qquad Y_{jt}^d = \left[\frac{P_{jt}}{P_t}\right]^{-\theta} Y_t^d,$$

where Y_t^d must be understood to include demand from domestic consumers and investors and foreign consumers. Cost minimization yields the demand for worker i's labor:

$$(6) \qquad L_{ijt} = \left(\frac{W_{it}}{W_t}\right)^{-\sigma} L_{jt},$$

where

$$(7) \qquad L_{jt} = \frac{\int_0^1 W_{ijt}L_{ijt}\, di}{W_t}.$$

Cost minimization also requires

$$(8) \qquad \frac{R_t K_t}{W_t L_t} = \frac{\alpha}{1 - \alpha}.$$

Finally, firms set prices for their differentiated product as a constant markup over marginal cost. In the symmetric monopolistic competitive equilibrium, prices are set such that

$$(9) \qquad {}_{t-1}\left\{\frac{W_t L_t}{P_t Y_t}\right\} = (1 - \alpha)\left(\frac{\theta - 1}{\theta}\right),$$

where, for any variable X_t, the notation ${}_{t-1}X_t$ denotes its expectation conditional on information available at $t - 1$.

Workers

There is a continuum of workers, whose total "number" is normalized to one. The representative worker has preferences over consumption, labor supply, and real money balances in each period t given by

$$(10) \qquad \log C_t - \left(\frac{\sigma - 1}{\sigma}\right)\frac{1}{v}L_t^v + \frac{1}{1 - \varepsilon}\left(\frac{M_t}{Q_t}\right)^{1-\varepsilon},$$

where $v > 1$, $\varepsilon > 0$, and Q is defined as below. The consumption quantity C_t is an aggregate of home and imported goods:

(11) $$C_t = k(C_t^H)^\gamma (C_t^F)^{1-\gamma},$$

where C_t^H denotes purchases of a basket of the different varieties of goods produced domestically, C_t^F purchases of the imported good, and $k = [\gamma^\gamma (1 - \gamma)^{1-\gamma}]^{-1}$ is a constant.

Assume that domestically produced goods are aggregated through the CES function

(12) $$C_t^H = \left[\int_0^1 C_{jt}^{(\theta-1)/\theta} \, dj \right]^{\frac{\theta}{\theta-1}}, \theta > 1.$$

Assume also that the imported good has a fixed price, normalized to one, in terms of a foreign currency, which we shall refer to as the dollar. Imports are freely traded and the law of one price holds, so that the peso price of imports is equal to the *nominal exchange rate* of S_t pesos per dollar.

The only asset that workers can hold is money. Then, in every period t, the ith worker's choices are constrained by

(13) $$Q_t C_{it} = P_t C_{it}^H + S_t C_{it}^F = W_{it} L_{it} + T_t - M_{it} + M_{it-1},$$

where P_t is the peso price of one unit of the basket of domestically produced goods, given by

(14) $$P_t = \left[\int_0^1 P_{jt}^{1-\theta} \, dj \right]^{\frac{1}{1-\theta}},$$

and Q_t is the minimum cost of one unit of aggregate consumption, or CPI:

(15) $$Q_t = P_t^\gamma S_t^{1-\gamma}.$$

Fiscal policy is as simple as can be: inflation tax revenues are rebated to workers through lump-sum transfers:

(16) $$M_t - M_{t-1} = T_t,$$

where $M_t = \int_0^1 M_{it} \, di$. This assumption ensures that, in the symmetric equilibrium, workers consume their nominal income:

(17) $$Q_t C_t = W_t L_t.$$

Purchasing consumption at minimum cost requires

(18) $$\left(\frac{1 - \gamma}{\gamma} \right) \frac{C_t^H}{C_t^F} = \frac{S_t}{P_t} \equiv E_t,$$

where absence of the subscript i indicates that we have imposed symmetry in equilibrium. Notice that E_t is the price of foreign goods in terms of domestic goods, or the *real exchange rate*.

Each worker optimally supplies labor to equate his marginal disutility of labor to its marginal return. Our assumptions on preferences then ensure that

$$(19) \qquad\qquad _{t-1}L_t^\nu = 1$$

in equilibrium.

Next adopt the convention that no subscript indicates an initial period variable, while a subscript 1 indicates a final period variable. Money demands in periods 0 and 1 are then given by

$$(20) \qquad\qquad \left(\frac{M}{Q}\right)^{-\varepsilon} + \beta\frac{1}{C_1}\frac{Q}{Q_1} = \frac{1}{C}$$

and

$$(21) \qquad\qquad \left(\frac{M_1}{Q_1}\right)^{-\varepsilon} = \frac{1}{C_1}.$$

Entrepreneurs

Entrepreneurs borrow from abroad in order to finance investment. Assume that entrepreneurs start with some inherited debt repayments, due at the end of the period 0. Some fraction of debt repayments is denominated in pesos, and the rest is denominated in dollars. After debt repayments, these entrepreneurs borrow from the world capital market in order to finance investment in excess of their own *net worth*. Since we do not consider shocks in the second period, we can assume without loss of generality that all new debt contracts (running from period 0 to 1) are denominated in dollars. Because of imperfections in financial markets, entrepreneurs are required to pay a risk premium over the risk-free interest rate (as in Bernanke and Gertler 1989).

Capital for next period is produced by combining home goods and imports. For simplicity, assume that capital is produced in the same fashion as consumption in equation (11). Therefore, the cost of producing one unit of capital available in period 1 is Q. The entrepreneurs' budget constraint in period 0 is therefore

$$(22) \qquad\qquad PN + SD_1 = QI,$$

where N stands for net worth, D_1 denotes the amount borrowed abroad in period 0 (to be repaid in period 1), and $I = K_1$ is investment in period 1 capital.

Net worth plays a crucial role because the interest cost of borrowing abroad is not simply the world safe rate ρ. Entrepreneurs borrow abroad paying a premium η above this risk-free interest rate. Assume that the risk premium is increasing in the ratio of the value of investment to net worth (or what is the same, in the ratio of debt to net worth), with the following functional form:

$$(23) \qquad 1 + \eta = \left(\frac{QI}{PN}\right)^{\mu} = \left(1 + \frac{ED_1}{N}\right)^{\mu}, \mu \geq 0.$$

For a derivation of this relationship from an underlying contract environment with imperfect information and costly monitoring, see Céspedes, Chang, and Velasco 2000.

Capital depreciates completely in production. In equilibrium, the expected dollar yield on capital must equal the cost of foreign borrowing,

$$(24) \qquad \frac{R_1}{Q} = (1 + \rho)(1 + \eta)\left(\frac{S_1}{S}\right).$$

Given that entrepreneurs own local firms, rental on capital is not the only income they receive. They also get the profits resulting from the monopoly power of firms. Entrepreneurs' net worth therefore is

$$(25) \qquad PN = RK + \Pi - SD^* - D = PY - WL - SD^* - D,$$

where Π is firm profits in pesos, D^* dollar debt repayment, and D peso-denominated debt repayment.

Equilibrium

Market clearing for the home goods require that domestic output be equal to demand. In period 0, the market for home goods clears when

$$(26) \qquad Y = \gamma\left(\frac{Q}{P}\right)(I + C) + E^X X.$$

Notice $E^X X$ stands for the home-good demand by the rest of the world, where $\chi > 0$.

Given that period 1 is the final period, there is no investment then. Assuming that entrepreneurs consume only foreign goods, the market-clearing condition for the second period is

$$(27) \qquad P_1 Y_1 = \gamma Q_1 C_1 + E_1^X P_1 X_1.$$

This last equation can be simplified further, since workers consume all their income each period:

$$(28) \qquad Y_1 = \tau E_1^X X_1,$$

where $\tau = [1 - \gamma(1 - \alpha)(1 - \theta^{-1})]^{-1} > 1$.

Linearization

The appendix establishes conditions under which there is a unique equilibrium when shocks are identically zero. The crucial condition is that financial imperfections, as captured by the parameter μ, cannot be too big. We will assume from here on that those conditions are satisfied.

The next step consists in obtaining log-linear approximations of the model around the no-shock equilibrium. We start by deriving the equilibrium relations in period 1. The first relation is the log-linear version of equation (17):

$$(29) \qquad q_1 + c_1 = w_1 + l_1.$$

(Lowercase letters denote log deviations from the no-shock equilibrium.) Equation (9) shows that wage income in period 1 is a fraction of the total revenue. Therefore,

$$(30) \qquad p_1 + y_1 = w_1 + l_1.$$

Combining these two equations, we obtain

$$(31) \qquad c_1 = y_1 - (q_1 - p_1) = y_1 - (1 - \gamma)e_1.$$

Assuming no export shocks in period 1, the log-linear version of the market-clearing condition for period 1 is

$$(32) \qquad y_1 = \chi e_1.$$

Putting these last two equations together, we obtain

$$c_1 = (\gamma + \chi - 1)e_1.$$

Because under no shocks labor supply is fixed at one (recall the first-order condition for labor supply), we have

$$y_1 = \alpha i.$$

Combining this with (32) we have

$$(33) \qquad \left(\frac{\alpha}{\chi}\right)i = e_1.$$

Pulling together these results, we arrive at

$$(34) \qquad c_1 = (\gamma + \chi - 1)\left(\frac{\alpha}{\chi}\right)i.$$

We can now solve the model in the initial period. The log-linear version of the resource constraint in period 0 is

$$(35) \qquad \tau y + (1 - \tau)(q + c) = \lambda(q + i) + (1 - \lambda)(\chi e + x),$$

where $\lambda = \gamma\overline{QI}/(\gamma\overline{QI} + \overline{E^xX}) < 1$ and where, due to the assumption that prices are set one period in advance, $p = 0$.[3]

Given that capital is a predetermined variable in period 0, deviations of output from its no-shock equilibrium will be matched by changes in labor only:

(36) $$y = (1 - \alpha)l.$$

Log-linearizing equation (17), we have $q + c = l$, since the nominal wage is preset. Combining these two equations, we arrive at

(37) $$q + c = \frac{y}{1 - \alpha}.$$

Substituting this last relation and $q = (1 - \gamma)e$ into (35) and reordering, we obtain the IS curve:

(38) $$y = \tau[1 - \gamma(1 - \theta^{-1})]^{-1}\{\lambda i + [\chi + \lambda(1 - \gamma - \chi)]e + (1 - \lambda)x\}.$$

For a given e, the IS schedule slopes up in (i, y) space, and its position in that space depends on the export shock x. A real devaluation (an increase in e) must increase y, given i, and the benefits of devaluation on current output naturally increase with χ.

In order to derive the effects of monetary policy, we log-linearize money demand in each period, given by equations (20) and (21). The resulting relations are

(39) $$\varepsilon(m_1 - q_1) = c_1$$

and

(40) $$\varepsilon\omega(m - q) + (1 - \omega)(c_1 + q_1 - q) = c,$$

where $\omega = 1 - \beta(\overline{QC})/(\overline{Q_1C_1})$. Note that ω is between 0 and 1 as long as the growth of nominal consumption is not too negative, which we assume from now on. The parameter ε^{-1} can be interpreted as the elasticity of money demand with respect to consumption expenditures. Using (34) and (37) to substitute out the consumptions and rearranging, we have the LM schedule:

(41) $$m = \frac{y}{\varepsilon\omega(1 - \alpha)} - (\varepsilon^{-1} - 1)(1 - \gamma)e$$
$$- (\omega^{-1} - 1)\varepsilon^{-1}(\gamma + \chi - 1)\left(\frac{\alpha}{\chi}\right)i.$$

The final block of equations to be solved is the one associated with the entrepreneurs. The log-linear version of the arbitrage relation (equation [24]) is

(42) $$(r_1 - p_1) - q = \rho + \eta + e_1 - s,$$

while the log-linear version of (8) and (30) yield $r_1 - p_1 = -(1 - \alpha)i$. Using this, the identity $q = (1 - \gamma)e$, and (33) we have

(43)
$$\left(1 - \alpha + \frac{\alpha}{\chi}\right)i = -(\rho + \eta) + \gamma e.$$

The log-linear version of the equation for the risk premium (23) is

(44)
$$\eta = \mu[(1 - \gamma)e + i - n],$$

which is obtained using the fact that $q = (1 - \gamma)e$. The log-linear version of net worth equation (25) is

(45)
$$n = \theta^{-1}[1 - (1 - \alpha)(1 - \theta^{-1})]^{-1}(1 + \psi)y - \phi\psi e,$$

where $\psi = \overline{D^T}/\overline{N} > 0, \overline{D^T} = \overline{D} + \overline{SD^*}$ is the total initial debt in units of the home good, and $\phi = \overline{SD^*}/\overline{PD^T}$ is the share of dollar-denominated debt in total (initial) debt. Note that when ψ is large, total initial debt is also large relative to net worth. If initial dollar-denominated debt is zero, then real devaluations have no effect on net worth.

Combining the last set of equations, we obtain the BP curve:

(46)
$$i = [1 - \alpha + \alpha\chi^{-1} + \mu]^{-1}$$
$$\times \{-\rho + \theta^{-1}[1 - (1 - \alpha)(1 - \theta^{-1})]^{-1}$$
$$\times \mu(1 + \psi)y + [\gamma - \mu(1 - \gamma + \phi\psi)]e\}.$$

Quite naturally, investment is decreasing in the world rate of interest. The other two terms are more novel. Investment increases with output only if capital markets are imperfect ($\mu > 0$), since higher output increases net worth and reduces the risk premium. Hence the BP curve slopes up in (i, y) space for a given real exchange rate, and the intercept depends on the shock to the world interest rate. If $\mu = 0$, the BP is horizontal.

Investment may be increasing or decreasing in the real exchange rate. Standard arbitrage forces described above push for an increasing relationship: a higher e makes borrowing abroad cheaper. But the balance-sheet effect pushes in the opposite direction: a higher e means a higher value of debt payments, and hence lower net worth and higher risk premia. It helps to give the possible cases a name. If in BP equation (46) the coefficient on e is positive, we have a *financially vulnerable economy*. If the coefficient is negative, we have a *financially robust economy*. Notice that financial vulnerability is more likely when the risk premium is very sensitive to the investment expenditure–net worth ratio (large μ); the inherited ratio of total debt to net worth is high (large ψ); the share of dollar debt in total debt is high (large ϕ); and the share of domestically produced goods in the investment and consumption aggregate is low (small γ).

Notice that if initial dollar debt is zero (so that $\phi = 0$), devaluation can only reduce investment via its effect on input costs: a real devaluation increases the cost of generating one unit of capital (in units of the home good), and therefore increases the risk premium for any given level of net worth. But if capital is produced only using home goods ($\gamma = 1$) or if capital markets are perfect ($\mu = 0$), this effect disappears.

Equilibrium under Alternative Exchange Rate Regimes

If the exchange rate floats (assuming predetermined output prices), expressions (38), (41), and (46) are three equations in three unknowns: output y, investment i, and the real exchange rate e, for a given money supply and exogenous shocks. Alternatively, if the exchange rate is fixed, e becomes policy-determined in the short run, and (38) and (46) pin down equilibrium investment and output. In turn, (41) yields the level of the money supply necessary for that particular equilibrium to obtain.[4]

Shocks, Policies, and Their Effects

In the two subsections that follow, we assume a fixed (but adjustable) exchange rate, so that we can solve the model diagrammatically in (i, y) space. We use that solution to perform comparative statics and analyze the effects of unexpected external shocks and of an unexpected devaluation on equilibrium output and investment. Later we consider the effects of shocks under flexible exchange rates.

External Shocks under Fixed Exchange Rates

Consider first the effects of a fall in current exports, depicted in figure 2.1. The shock shifts the IS up and to the left, so that for each level of investment, there is now a smaller corresponding output level. The new intersection is at point A, with lower investment and output than in the steady state. The output fall is as in the standard model with perfect capital markets and no balance-sheet effects, but the fall in investment is not. In that model, a fall in exports today does not affect the profitability of capital tomorrow, and hence it leaves investment unchanged. That is what happens in our model in the special case $\mu = 0$, so that the BP curve is horizontal. Notice that with stronger balance-sheet effects (larger μ, ϕ, and ψ), the BP becomes steeper, magnifying the adverse effects on both investment and output.

   Consider now the effects of a one-period increase in the world rate of interest. In figure 2.2 the shock shifts the BP down and to the right, so that investment is lower for each output level. The result is lower investment and output, as at point A. This is qualitatively as it would be in the standard model with perfect capital markets and a horizontal BP curve, but quantitatively there is a difference: for the same downward shift, the steeper the BP the larger the

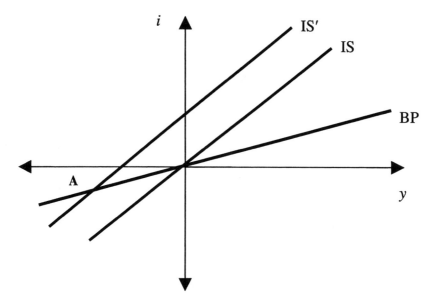

Figure 2.1 Fall in exports

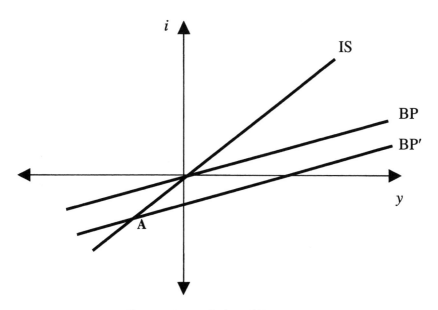

Figure 2.2 Increase in the world interest rate

reduction in investment and output. The capital market imperfections and resulting balance-sheet effects magnify the real effects of adverse interest rate shocks.[5]

Next we put some numbers on these comparative statics exercises. This calibration should not be interpreted as a "real business cycle" exercise. Our purpose is only to illustrate and add some quantitative dimension to the previous analysis. We set the structural parameters of the economy to generate three different cases. One case has no financial frictions, so the presence or absence of original sin is irrelevant. The other two do feature financial frictions and differ only in the share of debt that is denominated in dollars: with full dollarization we have a situation of *mortal sin*, while with a small share of the debt in domestic currency we have merely *venial sin*. Table 2.1 displays the assumptions regarding the main parameters of the model.

Table 2.2 presents the reaction of output and investment to a 1 percent increase in the world interest rate when the exchange rate (nominal and real) is held unchanged. (Recall that, because the exchange rate does not move on impact, the degree of original sin is irrelevant in this case.) Financial frictions amplify the shocks dramatically. The fall in output and investment are roughly four times higher under frictions plus sin.

Table 2.1. Parameter values

	No financial frictions; original sin irrelevant	Financial frictions	
		Mortal sin	Venial sin
α	0.30	0.30	0.30
χ	0.50	0.50	0.50
β	0.99	0.99	0.99
θ	2.00	2.00	2.00
γ	0.45	0.45	0.45
μ	0.00	0.20	0.20
ε	0.40	0.40	0.40
λ	0.42	0.42	0.42
ψ		10.00	10.00
ϕ		1.00	0.95

Table 2.2. Fixed exchange rates

	No financial frictions (%)	Financial frictions (%)
Output	−0.50	−2.00
Investment	−0.76	−3.05

Note: Response to a 1 percent increase in world interest rate.

Policy Shocks under Fixed (but Adjustable) Exchange Rates

What are the effects of monetary and exchange rate shocks in this model? First we answer the question analytically, and then we simulate some examples.

Start with a financially robust economy. A depreciation of the real exchange rate shifts the IS down and the BP up. This situation appears in figure 2.3. Both output and investment unambiguously go up. This is just as in the standard model: real depreciation is expansionary, and it can be used to offset the real effects of adverse shocks.[6]

Turn next to the financially vulnerable economy. Figure 2.4 illustrates the three possible situations. The IS still shifts down, but now the BP shifts down as well. The economy may settle in a point like A with higher output and investment (this is an economy that is vulnerable but not too much so); a point like B, where there is a trade-off between investment and output; and a case like C, where both output and investment decline. The last case is unambiguously contractionary devaluation, and trying to use exchange rate and monetary policy for countercyclical purposes can only make matters worse.

The intuition of why devaluation can be contractionary is simple: With imperfect capital markets, balance sheets matter; if there are enough inherited dollar liabilities, the real depreciation worsens the balance sheet and increases the

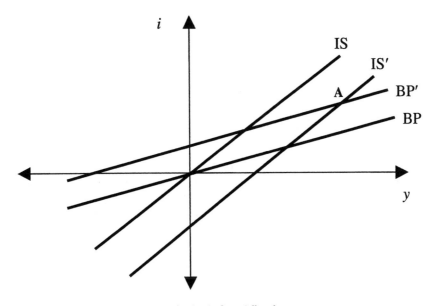

Figure 2.3 Devaluation in financially robust economy

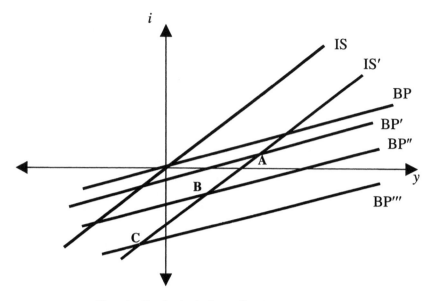

Figure 2.4 Devaluation in financially vulnerable economy

Table 2.3. Surprise devaluation

	No financial frictions (%)	Financial frictions (%)	
		Mortal sin	Venial sin
Output	1.02	0.00	0.30
Investment	0.35	−1.09	−0.77

Note: Response to a 1 percent unexpected devaluation.

risk premium; in turn, this pulls down investment and aggregate demand. If the standard demand-switching effects of devaluation are not sufficiently strong, the overall impact can be contractionary.

Again, notice that none of this could happen with perfect capital markets. In that case, the BP is horizontal and shifts up after a real devaluation. The only possible outcome is an increase in both investment and output.

Next we simulate some examples, using the same underlying parameters as in the earlier simulations but stressing the role of different degrees of original sin. Table 2.3 shows the effects on output and investment of an unexpected 1 percent devaluation.

Without financial frictions, the devaluation expands both output and investment, as in a conventional Mundell-Fleming model. When the economy does display financial frictions, the outcome depends on the extent of original sin. With venial sin, the devaluation expands output by 0.3 percent but reduces investment by nearly 0.8 percent: the presence of financial vulnerability makes the BP shift down, moving the equilibrium to a point like B in figure 2.4. With mortal sin, output is unchanged while investment falls more: almost 1.1 percent. This underscores the role of original sin in determining the real effects of exchange rate policy.

External Shocks under Flexible Exchange Rates

Turn next to the case of flexible exchange rates, which we define as a regime in which the money supply is constant and the nominal (and real) exchange rate adjusts endogenously. Now the equilibrium involves, as pointed out above, the solution to three equations in three unknowns, so a simple diagrammatic presentation is not feasible. Instead, we go directly to a simulation. Since the LM schedule now comes into play, we have to assume a value for the elasticity of money demand (ε^{-1}), which we set equal to 2.5.

Table 2.4 presents the effects of a 1 percent increase in the world interest rate under the constant money rule. A first striking result is that this rule implies little endogenous movement in the exchange rate in the robust economy (extreme case with no financial frictions at all), but much larger movements in the vulnerable economy—especially so if sin is mortal. Effects on output and investment differ accordingly.

In the economy without frictions, flexibility in the exchange rate has a stabilizing role. Comparing this outcome with that of the same shock under fixed rates (recall table 2.2), we see that the small depreciation under floating reduces the fall in output from 0.5 percent to almost zero, and dampens the investment contraction slightly.

Things are more complicated if the economy does have frictions and sin is mortal, leading to extreme vulnerability. The endogenous depreciation is large (19 percent), causing a mild recession (output falls by 0.4 percent) and a collapse of investment (it falls by 24 percent). If sin is merely venial, the depreciation is milder, output is practically constant, and the drop in investment is held down to 7.9 percent. Compared with the response to the same shock under a fixed exchange rate, we see that now the output fall is smaller, regardless of the degree of sin. But the cost of the depreciation is a much larger fall in investment,

Table 2.4. Constant-money rule

	No financial frictions (%)	Financial frictions (%)	
		Mortal sin	Venial sin
Exchange rate	0.48	19.00	6.31
Output	−0.01	−0.40	−0.13
Investment	−0.60	−24.00	−7.89

Note: Response to a 1 percent increase in the world interest rate.

with the difference in the case of mortal sin being very substantial. This suggests that investment is particularly sensitive to the share of dollar debt in total indebtedness.

With original sin, the real depreciation and the fall in investment exert negative feedback on each other, a factor that helps explain the magnitude of the equilibrium movements in both variables. An initial depreciation reduces net worth sharply when dollar debts are large, pushing the risk premium up and reducing investment. If, on the other hand, the real depreciation does not increase exports much (because the price elasticity of exports is low, as assumed in the vulnerable economy), then total demand falls for domestically produced goods. This in turn causes the relative price of domestic goods to fall (the real exchange rate depreciates even further), causing another round of investment cuts and so on, until the system finally settles on a much lower investment rate and a sharply depreciated exchange rate.

Implications for the Exchange Rate Regime

The extent to which this cycle plays itself out, of course, depends on the reaction of monetary policy. In the example above, money is constant in response to the shock. But if policymakers fear these contractionary effects of depreciation, then they might try to limit it by manipulating monetary policy, thus giving rise to fear of floating. The model presented here has stark *positive* implications for the choice of exchange rate regimes. If output and investment stabilization are paramount objectives, one should observe countries with mortal sin (Argentina? Uruguay?) trying to limit exchange rate movements, so that their observed reaction to shocks would resemble that of table 2.2. Countries with only venial sin (Chile, Brazil) would welcome the endogenous movements in the real exchange rate, in which case their observed reaction to shocks would resemble that of table 2.4, last column on the right. Venial sin allows these latter countries to enjoy stabilizing effects of exchange rates (at least as far as current output is concerned) that are not available to irredeemable sinners.

This all leaves open the question of *normative* rules to guide optimal monetary and exchange rate policy. Optimality involves a lot more than output and investment stabilization. And there may be intertemporal trade-offs that the informal discussion above ignores. In Céspedes, Chang, and Velasco (2000) we have identified conditions for floating to be welfare-maximizing in a model much like the one in this paper. There we show that floating can be optimal even with mortal sin as long as domestic and foreign goods are sufficiently substitutable in consumption and investment. Computing optimal policies for other, more complex model economies remains to be done.

Conclusions

Must original sin bring macroeconomic damnation? No, but it just might. Perhaps the most striking implication of the model presented in this chapter is that—with financial imperfections—macroeconomic outcomes depend crucially on the extent of original sin.

But while all sinful economies are equal in this respect, some are more equal than others. We have seen that other factors—the size of total debt regardless of currency denomination, the sensitivity of the risk premium to debt levels, the degree of openness of the economy, the price elasticity of demand for exports—all matter in determining how the economy will react to shocks, including unexpected movements in the real exchange rate. There may be cases in which sinful economies can use the exchange rate to offset shocks, as in the textbooks.

The model presented here simplifies perhaps a bit too much. Other links between financial imperfections and the real exchange rate may also prove crucial. Here local capitalists borrow to invest, so financial imperfections affect the demand for investment and indirectly the real exchange rate. This leaves room for monetary policy to affect aggregate demand and potentially play a stabilizing role. Alternatively, local producers could borrow abroad to pay for productive inputs. In that case, shocks that affected the risk premium (for instance, by lowering net worth) would cut domestic supply of goods directly, making it harder for aggregate demand policies to play a useful role. This is an important issue to explore in future work.[7]

Appendix

No-Shock Equilibrium

Suppose that all shocks are identically zero, and let overbars denote no-shock equilibrium values. Then, from (19)

$$\bar{L} = \bar{L}_1 = 1.$$

(Subscripts indicate future period values.) Hence, domestic production is

(47) $$\bar{Y} = A\bar{K}^\alpha, \bar{Y}_1 = A\bar{K}_1^\alpha,$$

and (28) is

(48) $$\bar{Y}_1 = \tau \bar{E}_1^\chi \bar{X}_1.$$

Next, note that if there are no shocks,

(49)
$$\overline{Q}\overline{C} = (1 - \alpha)\left(\frac{\theta - 1}{\theta}\right)\overline{P}\,\overline{Y},$$

so the goods market equilibrium condition for the domestic good becomes

(50)
$$[1 - \gamma(1 - \alpha)(1 - \theta^{-1})]\overline{Y} = \gamma\overline{E}^{1-\gamma}\overline{K}_1 + \overline{E}^X\overline{X}.$$

Since $\overline{Y}$ is given by AK^α, equation (50) is a relation between the no-shock values of $\overline{E}$ and $\overline{K}_1$. It is a schedule that slopes down in $(\overline{K}_1, \overline{E})$ space.

For a second schedule, write the interest parity condition (24) as

(51)
$$\frac{\overline{R}_1\overline{K}_1/\overline{P}_1}{\overline{Q}\overline{K}_1/\overline{P}_0} = (1 + \overline{\rho})\left(\frac{\overline{Q}\overline{K}_1}{\overline{P}N}\right)^\mu \frac{\overline{E}_1}{\overline{E}}.$$

Note now that $\overline{R}_1\overline{K}_1 = \alpha(1 - \theta^{-1})\overline{P}_1\overline{Y}_1$, and use (47), (48), and (25) to get

$$[\alpha(1 - \theta^{-1})(\tau\overline{X}_1)^{1/x}](A\overline{K}_1^\alpha)^{1-1/x}$$
$$= \frac{(1 + \overline{\rho})\overline{E}^{(1-\gamma)(1+\mu)-1}\overline{K}_1^{1+\mu}}{\{[1 - (1 - \alpha)(1 - \theta^{-1})]\overline{Y} - \overline{E}D^* - D/\overline{P}\}^\mu}.$$

This is the no-shock BP. Note that because $\overline{Y}$, D^*, and $D/\overline{P}$ are given, the preceding equation is also a relation between $\overline{E}$ and $\overline{K}_1$.

This is a complicated expression. However, note that if μ is zero, this curve must start from the origin and slope up in $(\overline{K}_1, \overline{E})$ space. Hence, if it intersects the no-shock IS, the intersection must be unique. By continuity, there is a unique no-shock equilibrium if μ is not too large.

Notes

We are grateful to Barry Eichengreen, Ricardo Hausmann, Carmen Reinhart, and seminar participants for comments, and to the National Science Foundation and the Harvard Center for International Development for generous financial support.

1. The term *original sin* was coined by Eichengreen and Hausmann (1999). Calvo (1999) and Hausmann et al. (2000) were among the first to warn about the dangers of dollarization of liabilities. See also Krugman (1999) and Calvo and Reinhart (2002).

2. An additional issue, which we do not study in detail here, is the uniqueness of equilibrium. The story in which exchange rate movements cause an economic contraction, which in turn causes capital outflows and exchange rate movements, has a strong flavor of self-fulfilling expectations. When are crises prompted by the shift to a "bad" equilibrium possible? For an analysis, see Velasco 2001; Céspedes, Chang, and Velasco 2000; Aghion, Bacchetta, and Bannerjee 2000; and Krugman 1999.

3. Note that a bar over a variable denotes its no-shock equilibrium level.

4. Recall that these are percentage deviations from the no-shock steady state, holding prices and wages constant. Without nominal stickiness, output is exogenous (pinned down by the inherited capital stock and by equilibrim labor supply $l = 0$), the IS and BP

pin down the equilibrium real exchange rate for a given output level, and the LM only determines the price level.

5. The same is true of export shocks.

6. Notice that the presence of financial imperfections has ambiguous effects on the size of the expansion. On the one hand, having $\mu > 0$ and δ_e large reduces the size of the vertical shift in the BP; on the other hand, a large μ increases the slope of the BP, which magnifies the equilibrium impact of any depreciation.

7. We are thankful to Mick Devereux for making this point.

References

Aghion, P., P. Bacchetta, and A. Banerjee. 2000. "A Simple Model of Monetary Policy and Currency Crises." *European Economic Review* 44:728–38.

Bernanke, B., and M. Gertler. 1989. "Agency Costs, Net Worth, and Business Fluctuations." *American Economic Review* 79:14–31.

Calvo, G. 1999. "Testimony on Full Dollarization." Paper presented before a Joint Hearing of the Subcommittees on Economic Policy and International Trade and Finance, U.S. Congress, April.

Calvo, G., and C. Reinhart. 2002. "Fear of Floating." *Quarterly Journal of Economics* 117: 379–408.

Céspedes, L., R. Chang, and A. Velasco. 2000. "Balance Sheets and Exchange Rate "Policy." NBER Working Paper no. 7840, National Bureau of Economic Research, Cambridge, MA, August.

———. 2002. "Dollarization of Liabilities, Net Worth Effects, and Optimal Monetary Policy." In *Preventing Crises in Emerging Markets,* ed. S. Edwards and J. Frankel. Chicago: University of Chicago Press.

Eichengreen, B., and R. Hausmann. 1999. "Exchange Rates and Financial Fragility." NBER Working Paper no. 7418, National Bureau of Economic Research, Cambridge, MA, November.

Hausmann, R., M. Gavin, C. Pages-Serra, and E. Stein. 2000. "Financial Turmoil and the Choice of Exchange Rate Regime." Working Paper no. 400, Inter-American Development Bank, Washington, DC.

Krugman, P. 1999. "Balance Sheets, the Transfer Problem, and Financial Crises." In *International Finance and Financial Crises,* ed. P. Isard, A. Razin, and A. Rose. Boston: Kluwer Academic.

Velasco, A. 2001. "The Impossible Duo? Globalization and Monetary Independence in Emerging Markets." In *Brookings Trade Forum,* ed. Susan M. Collins and Dani Rodrik, 69–99. Washington, DC: Brookings Institution Press.

A Fiscal Perspective on Currency Crises and Original Sin

Giancarlo Corsetti and Bartosz Maćkowiak

WHY DO fiscal authorities in emerging markets find it difficult to borrow in nominal terms? The literature addresses this question from different angles, but a recurrent theme is that policies guaranteeing stable prices are time inconsistent. Governments have an ex post incentive to cause inflation, any promise not to do so lacks credibility, and consequently the risk in lending in domestic currency translates into high premia.

Why is inflation fiscally beneficial? The common view is that a low inflation policy is "incredible" because a government with a fiscal problem either finds it attractive—or lacks other choices—to finance a budget deficit by "printing money." Models of policy in emerging markets often emphasize seigniorage revenues, and this is true in particular of the literature on currency crises. According to the first-generation models (after the classic work of Krugman [1979] and Flood and Garber [1984]), uncontrollable seigniorage needs are the cause of currency instability: a fiscal imbalance must be matched with seigniorage revenues. This traditional view of speculative attacks, familiar to perhaps all economists, receives renewed attention following recent currency crises in Argentina, Brazil, east Asia, Russia, and Turkey.[1]

Two developments are responsible for a recent reconsideration of fiscal benefits of inflation. The first is empirical: seigniorage revenues are moderate in several recent crisis episodes. Thus the adjustment mechanism at the center of the first-generation models is not apparent, even when crises have a striking fiscal dimension. The analysis of Burnside, Eichenbaum, and Rebelo (2001a, 2001b, 2003) is a clear illustration of the fact that seigniorage is not the only mechanism through which devaluation and inflation produce fiscal revenues, and that it may be quite irrelevant empirically.

The second development is the recent rise of a general equilibrium literature that studies the link between monetary and fiscal policy regimes and price level determinacy. This literature formalizes monetary policy in terms of interest rate rules, dichotomizing fiscal policy into Ricardian and non-Ricardian—the latter case is known as the fiscal theory of the price level (FTPL).[2] The FTPL highlights the role of maturity and degree of indexation of public debt in macro-economic dynamics. Sims (1997) observes that the FTPL and the first-generation literature are "close cousins." When one reconsiders the analysis of Krugman and Flood and Garber in an FTPL framework, the solved-forward government budget constraint by itself implies that the price level increases and the exchange rate depreciates, in such a way that the resulting wealth transfer from holders of public liabilities finances the fiscal imbalance. Unlike in the first-generation setup, one does not need to map the imbalance into a seigniorage target for the monetary authority. The analysis of how an economy adjusts to a fiscal imbalance focuses on maturity and denomination of public debt, in contrast to the emphasis on reserves and money market equilibrium in the first-generation models.

The developments outlined above have given rise to the question whether a synthesis of the FTPL and the first-generation literature can become a new framework to analyze the fiscal dimension of currency instability. Daniel (1998, 2001a) provides the first formal analysis of the link between the two literatures, interpreting a collapse of a fixed exchange rate regime as a consequence of non-Ricardian fiscal policy. Our own work (Corsetti and Maćkowiak 2000, 2003) builds a simple version of the synthetic model, developing it in several directions relative to the papers by Burnside, Eichenbaum, and Rebelo and Daniel, as well as clarifying further the link between the FTPL and the classic first-generation models.

Our aim in this paper is to provide an exposition of the synthetic model, highlighting how it enhances our understanding of the effects of denomination and maturity of public debt more generally. Our starting point is the experiment of Krugman and Flood and Garber in an economy with a fixed exchange rate and public debt (domestic- and foreign-currency, short- and long-term): we postulate an exogenous disturbance that decreases the present value of government's real primary surpluses relative to its outstanding liabilities, and analyze the dynamics of adjustment. As in the FTPL, we model fiscal policy as non-Ricardian and monetary policy as pursuing an interest rate rule. We summarize the insights from the synthetic model as follows:

1. Insufficient fiscal discipline can undermine currency stability *independently* of any need for seigniorage revenues. This paper contributes a simple illustration of this point in the context of a small open-economy model with money introduced in a standard way. We show that if the government delays devaluation in the presence of a fiscal imbalance, the present value of extra seigniorage revenues is *zero*. While the precise conclusion depends on the interest elasticity of money demand, the message is general: the role of seigniorage is akin to that of utility or technological parameters—it is *not* an essential part of the adjustment to a fiscal imbalance in an economy with public non-monetary liabilities.

2. Disturbances that cause a collapse of a fixed exchange rate can be *nominal,* and need not imply a deterioration of government's real primary surpluses. This is because nominal shocks affect the real value of debt and are thus capable per se of causing fiscal strain. For instance, a foreign deflationary shock (like an appreciation of the dollar) can jeopardize the sustainability of a currency peg independently of changes in relative goods prices or "competitiveness" problems.

3. Denomination of government debt determines the size of a currency crisis. In particular, small changes in the extent of "dollarization" of public liabilities can cause large differences in the magnitude of devaluation, in a nonlinear manner. The nonlinearity lets us understand why a government that borrows heavily in a foreign currency, like many emerging markets, is exposed to a devaluation of dramatic size. This is an important consequence of the "original sin"—the topic of this book (see also Eichengreen, Hausmann, and Panizza 2002).

4. The equilibrium relation between the devaluation rate and the long-run inflation rate is *negative,* rather than positive as predicted by the first-generation models that postulate seigniorage targets. The reason for this negative relation is that higher long-run inflation implies a larger capital loss to holders of long-term nominal debt—independent of any seigniorage revenues it may generate. This is an important result in light of the observation that currency crises of striking proportions are *not* followed by chronic inflation.

5. Maturity of nominal government debt matters for the timing of a currency crisis, with long-term liabilities making a delay possible even without seigniorage revenues. We verify that this insight from the FTPL continues to prevail in the absence of purchasing-power parity: debt maturity remains critical for understanding *when* a given fiscal shock affects the equilibrium exchange rate. In the data a real appreciation and a current account deficit often precede a speculative attack, while a real depreciation and a current account surplus coincide with a crisis. We give an example where a qualitatively identical dynamic path arises purely as part of the adjustment to a fiscal imbalance. Thus we show that the new framework is capable of accounting for the variation in the real exchange rate and the current account around crisis episodes—independent of, say, credit market imperfections or nominal stickiness.[3]

The rest of the chapter is organized as follows: The next section presents the baseline, single-good framework, then discusses shocks causing a fiscal imbalance as well as fiscal and monetary policy rules. The third section uses the framework to analyze the dynamic adjustment to the imbalance, discussing the determinants of the equilibrium exchange rate. The next section augments the baseline framework to include a traded and a nontraded good, analyzing the dynamics of the real exchange rate and the current account. We end with some concluding remarks. An appendix provides details of the model with deviations from purchasing-power parity.

The Baseline Single-Good Model

This section lays out a simplest fully specified model to study the dynamic adjustment to a one-time, unanticipated fiscal imbalance in a fixed exchange rate regime. Consider a small open economy, with a government and a representative individual who receives an endowment of a single tradable and perishable consumption good. In the single-good world economy with costless trade, the domestic price level P and the foreign (dollar) price level P^* are linked by the law of one price: $P = \varepsilon P^*$, where ε denotes the exchange rate. The economy takes exogenously the foreign real interest rate (equal to the dollar nominal rate). We assume that the interest rate is equal to a constant r such that $(1 + r)\beta = 1$, where β is the representative individual's discount factor.

The Representative Individual's Optimum Problem

The representative individual pays lump-sum taxes and holds one-period nominal bonds B paying an interest rate denoted by i_t, nominal perpetuities L selling at a price θ_t, money M that yields utility, and one-period dollar bonds B^*. We assume that M, B, and L are each strictly greater than zero, issued by the domestic government, and held only by the representative individual in the domestic economy, whereas dollar bonds can be traded internationally.[4]

The representative individual maximizes

(1)
$$\sum_{t=0}^{\infty} \beta^t \ln \left[C_t^\eta \left(\frac{M_t}{P_t} \right)^{1-\eta} \right],$$

where $0 < \eta \leq 1$, subject to

$$\frac{\theta_t L_t}{P_t} + \frac{B_t}{P_t} + \frac{M_t}{P_t} + \frac{\varepsilon_t B_t^*}{P_t} \leq \frac{(1 + \theta_t) L_{t-1}}{P_t} + \frac{(1 + i_{t-1})B_{t-1}}{P_t}$$
$$+ \frac{M_{t-1}}{P_t} + \frac{\varepsilon_t(1 + r)B_{t-1}^*}{P_t} + Y_t - \tau_t - C_t$$

in every period, as well as to

$$\lim_{t \to \infty} \left(\frac{1}{1 + r} \right)^t \left[\frac{\theta_t L_t}{P_t} + \frac{B_t}{P_t} + \frac{\varepsilon_t B_t^*}{P_t} + \left(\frac{1}{1 + i_t} \right) \frac{M_t}{P_t} \right] \geq 0,$$

where Y and C denote endowment and consumption of the single good, respectively, and τ is real lump-sum taxes (or transfers, if negative).

The first-order conditions with respect to B^* and B imply that the uncovered interest rate parity holds:

(2)
$$1 + i_t = (1 + r) \frac{\varepsilon_{t+1}}{\varepsilon_t};$$

and the first-order condition with respect to L yields an intertemporal relationship between perpetuity prices:

(3) $$\theta_t(1 + i_t) = 1 + \theta_{t+1}.$$

We solve (3) forward, arriving at a relationship between the perpetuity price and future nominal interest rates:[5]

(4) $$\theta_t = \sum_{s=0}^{\infty}\left[\prod_{k=0}^{s}\left(\frac{1}{1 + i_{t+k}}\right)\right].$$

The transversality condition of the agent's problem is

(5) $$\lim_{t\to\infty}\left(\frac{1}{1 + r}\right)^t\left[\frac{\theta_t L_t}{P_t} + \frac{B_t}{P_t} + \frac{\varepsilon_t B_t^*}{P_t} + \left(\frac{1}{1 + i_t}\right)\frac{M_t}{P_t}\right] = 0.$$

Given our earlier assumption that $(1 + r)\,\beta = 1$, the first-order condition with respect to B^* implies that the shadow value of the budget constraint is constant at λ. We then know that optimal consumption is constant and equal to η/λ. We can combine the first-order conditions with respect to B and M to obtain a money demand relation:

(6) $$\frac{M_t}{P_t} = \left(\frac{1 - \eta}{\lambda}\right)\left(\frac{1 + i_t}{i_t}\right).$$

The Government Budget Constraint

The period-by-period government budget identity is

(7) $$\frac{\theta_t L_t}{P_t} + \frac{B_t}{P_t} + \frac{M_t}{P_t} + \frac{\varepsilon_t F_t}{P_t} = \frac{(1 + \theta_t)L_{t-1}}{P_t} + \frac{(1 + i_{t-1})B_{t-1}}{P_t}$$
$$+ \frac{M_{t-1}}{P_t} + \frac{\varepsilon_t(1 + r)F_{t-1}}{P_t} - \tau_t,$$

where F denotes one-period dollar bonds issued by the domestic government.[6] Notice our assumption that the government can borrow in dollars at the world interest rate r, implying that it does not default on its dollar bonds.[7] Using the individual's first-order conditions and the following terminal condition,

(8) $$\lim_{t\to\infty}\left(\frac{1}{1 + r}\right)^t\left(\frac{\theta_t L_t}{P_t} + \frac{B_t}{P_t} + \frac{\varepsilon_t F_t}{P_t}\right) = 0,$$

we obtain a solved-forward version of the government budget constraint (7):

(9) $$\frac{(1 + \theta_t)L_{t-1} + (1 + i_{t-1})B_{t-1} + M_{t-1}}{P_t} + \frac{\varepsilon_t(1 + r)F_{t-1}}{P_t}$$
$$= \sum_{s=0}^{\infty}\left(\frac{1}{1 + r}\right)^s\left[\tau_{t+s} + \left(\frac{i_{t+s}}{1 + i_{t+s}}\right)\frac{M_{t+s}}{P_{t+s}}\right].$$

In equilibrium, the real value of public liabilities equals the present discounted value of future real primary surpluses plus interest payments avoided by maintaining real balances ("seigniorage"). In a closed-economy model, this derivation would simply make use of (5) as the terminal condition—we can see this by imagining a closed-economy model with an identical setup except that B^* (or F) would denote indexed, or "real," debt. An open-economy model like ours, however, introduces a subtle problem: it is theoretically possible that, with perfect insurance markets between countries, debt of one government can grow without a bound—corresponding to an explosive growth of assets of another government. The private sector's transversality generates a terminal condition for solved-forward budget constraints of all governments taken together, rather than for the constraint of each government separately. Like Bergin (2000), Daniel (2001b), and Sims (1999), we find it realistic to consider equilibriums that emerge when the government in an open economy faces a terminal condition in the form of (8).

Equilibrium

A competitive equilibrium in this small open-economy is a specification for a time path of the vector $\{Y, r, C, B^*, B, M, L, F, \tau, i, \theta, \varepsilon, P^*, P\}$ such that (1) when the representative individual takes the $\{Y, r, \tau, i, \theta, \varepsilon, P^*, P\}$ part of the path as given, $\{C, B^*, B, L, M\}$ solves her optimum problem; (2) the solved-forward government budget constraint (9) holds.[8]

On the Present Value of Seigniorage in Equilibrium

The classic first-generation papers focus on seigniorage as *the* adjustment mechanism to a fiscal imbalance. It is not evident that the role of seigniorage revenues is as important as that literature suggests. We mention an empirically motivated objection in the introduction. At a theoretical level, it is apparent that—in the presence of nominal public debt—seigniorage need not play *any* role in financing a fiscal imbalance. In this model for instance, with money introduced in a standard way, *the present value of seigniorage* in equilibrium, which we denote with Ω, *is independent of the path of nominal interest rates:*

$$(10) \qquad \Omega = \sum_{s=0}^{\infty} \left(\frac{1}{1+r}\right)^s \left(\frac{i_{t+s}}{1+i_{t+s}}\right) \frac{M_{t+s}}{P_{t+s}} = \left(\frac{1+r}{r}\right)\left(\frac{1-\eta}{\lambda}\right).$$

If the government delays devaluation in the presence of a fiscal imbalance, the present value of extra seigniorage revenues is zero—anticipated money growth fails to produce any fiscal gains. What matters for this conclusion is the interest elasticity of money demand: depending on its value, it is even possible for net seigniorage revenues to be negative—adding to, rather than offsetting, a fiscal imbalance.[9]

We take this result as an illustration of the fact that the role of seigniorage is akin to that of utility or technological parameters—it is *not* an essential part of the adjustment to a fiscal imbalance in an economy with nominal debt. For this reason, the rest of our analysis abstracts from money altogether, setting $\eta = 1$. In effect, we study devaluation scenarios in which no portion of an imbalance is financed by anticipated money growth, and all of it is financed by unanticipated wealth transfers from holders of nominal liabilities. With $M = 0$, we think of the price level, P, as the rate at which a newly issued, one-period nominal bond trades for the real commodity. Analogously, the nominal interest rate is the rate at which the domestic government exchanges old, one-period nominal bonds for new ones; and the perpetuity is an asset promising one unit of short-term bonds in every period from now on.

Policy Rules and Shocks Causing a Fiscal Imbalance

Suppose that the foreign price level is equal to a constant, P_α^*, and that the government fixes the exchange rate at $\bar{\varepsilon}$. For a fixed exchange rate to be sustainable, fiscal policy must be consistent with the government's solved-forward budget constraint (9) holding at $\bar{\varepsilon}$. Let $\{\bar\tau_{t+s}\}_{s=0}^{s=\infty}$ be a path of primary surpluses such that (9) holds given P_α^* and initial debt (B_{t-1}, L_{t-1}, and F_{t-1}) with the exchange rate *permanently* fixed at $\bar\varepsilon$, that is, $\varepsilon_{t+s} = \bar\varepsilon$, $s \geq 0$. By definition, then, $\{\bar\tau_{t+s}\}_{s=0}^{s=\infty}$ is a sequence such that

$$(11) \quad \sum_{s=0}^{\infty}\left(\frac{1}{1+r}\right)^s \bar\tau_{t+s} = \frac{(1+1/r)L_{t-1} + (1+r)B_{t-1}}{\bar\varepsilon P_\alpha^*} + \frac{(1+r)F_{t-1}}{P_\alpha^*}.$$

To satisfy the above condition, a sequence of τ's must eventually imply a strong feedback from debt to τ's. In response to shocks hitting the economy, policy must set a path of τ's so as to insure that primary surpluses fully back debt, given $\bar\varepsilon$. The FTPL literature refers to this fiscal policy as *passive* or *Ricardian*.

Recent contributions begin, in the spirit of Krugman, by assuming that the government fails to stick to Ricardian policy. The motivation of for example, Corsetti, Pesenti, and Roubini (1999b) and Burnside, Eichenbaum, and Rebelo (2001b), is the arrival of news about a bailout of private companies. As a complement to focusing directly on a deterioration of primary surpluses, it is appealing to motivate a fiscal imbalance as a consequence of an external shock.[10] Most economists would probably find it intuitive that a change in real international prices exogenous to a small economy, like the terms of trade or the world real interest rate, can result in fiscal slippage. What is not readily apparent, and what this model makes clear, is that a foreign *nominal* shock can also lead to a fiscal imbalance with critical consequences for a fixed exchange rate policy.

Suppose the foreign price level changes in period t to a new, permanent level P_β^*, where $P_\beta^* \leq P_\alpha^*$. Provided the inequality is strict, the shock increases on impact the real value of both nominal and dollar debt. Foreign deflation increases the quantity of the real commodity the government promises to bondholders, regardless of whether their claims are denominated in domestic or in foreign currency. Given the definition of $\{\overline{\tau}_{t+s}\}_{s=0}^{s=\infty}$, we now write the solved-forward government budget constraint (9) in period t as follows:

(12)
$$\frac{(1 + \theta_t)L_{t-1} + (1 + r)B_{t-1}}{\varepsilon_t P_\beta^*} + \frac{(1 + r)F_{t-1}}{P_\beta^*} =$$

$$\left[\sum_{s=0}^{\infty} \left(\frac{1}{1 + r} \right)^s \overline{\tau}_{t+s} \right] - \Delta,$$

where ε_t may or may not equal $\overline{\varepsilon}$ in equilibrium. In the above expression, Δ is a measure of the extent of fiscal adjustment the government undertakes in re-action to the shock, with $\Delta < 0$ corresponding to reform and $\Delta > 0$ to deteri-oration beyond the immediate effect of the shock.[11] A restriction we place on Δ is that it satisfies

$$\Delta > \left[\sum_{s=0}^{\infty} \left(\frac{1}{1 + r} \right)^s \overline{\tau}_{t+s} \right]$$

$$- \left[\frac{(1 + 1/r)L_{t-1} + (1 + r)B_{t-1}}{\overline{\varepsilon} P_\beta^*} + \frac{(1 + r) F_{t-1}}{P_\beta^*} \right].$$

Thus we, in effect, assume that the shock coincides with fiscal policy becoming *active* or *non-Ricardian*, in the terminology of the FTPL literature.

The fiscal implications of nominal shocks have not been noted by previous contributions on speculative attacks. Yet two realistic scenarios make the case $P_\beta^* < P_\alpha^*$ interesting. The first is deflation in the euro area or in the United States, or an appreciation of the dollar that decreases dollar prices of commod-ities traded in the world market. Second, we are motivated by the role of Brazil's devaluation in 1999 in the recent crisis in Argentina. A devaluation in Brazil de-creases international prices faced by Argentina. While this is an improvement in Argentina's terms of trade or a relative price change, the impact of the shock on the real value of Argentina's public debt is equivalent to that of a decrease in P^* or a purely nominal shock.[12]

While we think of the case $P_\beta^* < P_\alpha^*$ as a realistic example, our analysis al-lows for the possibility that $P_\beta^* = P_\alpha^*$ because we do not want to specialize to only one source of a fiscal imbalance. An adverse shock underlying Δ can stem from a variety of external and domestic sources. Once this disturbance occurs, the government may attempt to adjust the path of its budgets in an effort to re-verse the negative impact of the shock. What we assume is that the government cannot (or is not willing to) implement reforms such that its debt continues to be backed fully with real taxes, and equation (9) holds with the exchange rate permanently fixed at $\overline{\varepsilon}$. Thus Δ is defined as the net change in the present value of real primary surpluses *after* the government has taken all measures it deemed feasible to reverse the impact of the shock. Note that the restriction on Δ implies that $\Delta > 0$ so long as $P_\beta^* = P_\alpha^*$.

Having described fiscal policy, we complete the model by specifying an interest rate rule for monetary policy. So long as the exchange rate is fixed at $\bar{\varepsilon}$, the nominal interest rate is determined by the uncovered interest rate parity (2) evaluated at $\varepsilon_t = \bar{\varepsilon}$. In the event of a devaluation, we assume that the interest rate is set according to the reaction function

$$(13) \qquad 1 + i_{\tilde{T}+s} = \phi_0 + \phi_1 \frac{\varepsilon_{\tilde{T}+s}}{\varepsilon_{\tilde{T}+s-1}},$$

where $\tilde{T} \geq t$ is the period of devaluation, and $s \geq 0$. According to this rule, the (gross) nominal interest rate is a linear function of the (gross) depreciation rate. We assume that $\beta\phi_1 < 1$, that is, policy makes i react weakly to depreciation (or inflation)—this is an instance of *passive* monetary policy familiar from the FTPL literature.[13] To derive closed-form solutions, we specialize to a simple interest rate peg such that $i_{\tilde{T}+s} = i^P$ (that is, $\phi_1 = 0$ and $\phi_0 - 1 = i^P$), $s \geq 0$ (Corsetti and Maćkowiak [2003] examine the general rule [13]). Note that the choice of i^P determines the rate of chronic depreciation in the postdevaluation period.

Adjustment to a Fiscal Imbalance

We now use our framework to analyze the adjustment to a given fiscal imbalance, a classic topic since Krugman's work. To build intuition, we initially carry out the analysis under the assumption that the government abandons the peg in the same period in which the imbalance appears—thus causing an unanticipated jump in the exchange rate at t. We subsequently consider the case in which the parity is abandoned at some later date $\tilde{T} > t$.

Devaluation with Foreign Nominal Shocks and Shocks to Primary Surpluses

An immediate, unanticipated devaluation in period t reduces the real value of B and L, resulting in a wealth transfer, while the postdevaluation interest rate rule determines θ_t. A higher rate of chronic postdevaluation inflation reduces θ_t—by (4)—creating an additional wealth transfer. In equilibrium, the wealth transfers due to jumps in the exchange rate and the price of perpetuities finance the fiscal imbalance. Formally, once policy chooses the postcollapse nominal interest rate $i_{t+s} = i^P$, $s \geq 0$, the equilibrium condition (4) yields the perpetuity price $\theta_t = (1/i^P)$. To solve for the equilibrium devaluation rate $(\varepsilon_t/\bar{\varepsilon})$, we make use of the solved-forward government budget constraint—combining (11) with (12), we obtain the unique solution

$$(14) \quad \frac{\varepsilon_t}{\bar{\varepsilon}} = \frac{\dfrac{[1 + (1/i^P)]L_{t-1} + (1 + r)B_{t-1}}{\bar{\varepsilon}P_\beta^*}}{\dfrac{[1 + (1/r)]L_{t-1} + (1 + r)B_{t-1}}{\bar{\varepsilon}P_\alpha^*} - \dfrac{(P_\alpha^* - P_\beta^*)(1 + r)F_{t-1}}{P_\alpha^* P_\beta^*} - \Delta}$$

Equation (14) highlights several properties of the equilibrium devaluation rate $(\varepsilon_t/\bar{\varepsilon})$. First, the jump in the exchange rate is increasing in the size of the fiscal imbalance: $(\varepsilon_t/\bar{\varepsilon})$ is decreasing in P_β^* and increasing in Δ. The exchange rate change is determined both by the size of the shock and by the policy reaction to it. Second, for any given imbalance, dollar debt acts as leverage—the higher the fraction of debt denominated in dollars, the larger the devaluation rate. An economy in which the government borrows heavily in dollars, like many emerging markets, sees a larger jump in the exchange rate for a given fiscal imbalance. Third, postdevaluation interest rate policy influences $\varepsilon_t/\bar{\varepsilon}$, because the postcollapse path of interest rates determines the long-term bond price. Specifically, a higher i^P implies a larger jump in θ_t, and consequently a smaller one-time devaluation rate $(\varepsilon_t/\bar{\varepsilon})$. Thus a currency crisis followed by little long-run inflation, like that in some recent episodes, is associated with a larger initial exchange rate adjustment. In fact, setting $i^P = r$ implies that the depreciation rate in the postdevaluation steady state is zero. If no further shocks hit the economy, the dynamics involve a (relatively larger) one-time jump in the exchange rate to a new, constant level.[14]

The postdevaluation regime in the classic first-generation models exhibits chronic depreciation. Real money decreases, because a standard money market equilibrium relation makes the quantity of real money a negative function of the chronic depreciation rate. It is well known that those predictions are inconsistent with facts: some real-world postdevaluation regimes do not exhibit ongoing inflation or low money balances. Our setup makes it clear that a fiscal imbalance causes a one-time devaluation. Postdevaluation policy can set the nominal interest rate at *any* desired level, not necessarily switching to a regime of chronic depreciation. Money supply adjusts consistent with that policy, and there is no implication that real money decreases relative to the fixed exchange rate period.

It is straightforward to check that the unique solution to the solved-forward government-budget constraint satisfies the other equilibrium conditions, and therefore is the unique equilibrium exchange rate. In particular, given i^P and ε_t, the uncovered interest rate parity (2) determines the rate of depreciation $(\varepsilon_{t+1}/\varepsilon_t)$. The result, that non-Ricardian fiscal policy and passive monetary policy deliver a uniquely determinate price level and a stationary inflation rate, is familiar from the FTPL literature.[15]

Subsequent algebraic derivations are easier to follow if we assume that $P_\beta^* = P_\alpha^*$. The solution for $\varepsilon_t/\bar{\varepsilon}$ makes it clear that this assumption does not affect generality of the argument—we can simply think of Δ as a complete measure of the fiscal impact of the shock, whatever such shock may have been. So long as $P_\beta^* = P_\alpha^*$, we can normalize P^* to 1, thinking of the domestic price level as synonymous with the exchange rate. Given our earlier assumption that $(1 + r)\beta = 1$, the first-order condition with respect to B^* now implies that consumption is constant in equilibrium.

Determinants of the Rate of Devaluation: The New "Shadow Exchange Rate"

Expression (14) is the equilibrium exchange rate conditional on devaluation at time t. After Flood and Garber (1984), economists refer to equilibrium exchange rates conditional on abandoning the peg as *shadow* rates.[16] This section characterizes the shadow rate (analogous to expression [14]), if the peg is not abandoned when the fiscal imbalance materializes.

Can the government choose to delay devaluation until some period $\tilde{T} > t$? For a delay to be consistent with equilibrium, the solved-forward government budget constraint must hold with $\varepsilon_t = \bar{\varepsilon}$ exclusively by virtue of a wealth transfer from holders of nominal *long-term* debt, due to an unanticipated jump in θ_t. Thus a delay is consistent with equilibrium only if L is of sufficient size relative to the imbalance; otherwise, the exchange rate must jump immediately in equilibrium. While the model considers perpetuities for simplicity, the point is general: abstracting from seigniorage, the government can postpone devaluation only if it has a large enough stock of nominal debt of sufficient maturity. This is a condition emerging markets are less likely to satisfy than developed economies.

Assuming that this condition holds in our economy, we combine (11) and (12) with $\varepsilon_t = \bar{\varepsilon}$ to solve for the equilibrium perpetuity price in period t:

$$(15) \qquad \theta_t = \frac{1}{r} - \Delta\frac{\bar{\varepsilon}}{L_{t-1}} > 0.$$

θ_t is uniquely defined, because the jump in the bond price must guarantee that the solved-forward government budget constraint holds with $\varepsilon_t = \bar{\varepsilon}$. Letting $\tilde{T} > t$ denote the date at which the government abandons the peg, we use (2) and (3) as well as the policy rule $i_{\tilde{T}+s}^p = i^p, s \geq 0$, to obtain an intertemporal relationship between perpetuity prices in periods t and $\tilde{T}$:

$$(16) \qquad \theta_t = \frac{1}{r} + \left(\frac{1}{1+r}\right)^{\tilde{T}-t-1}\left(\frac{1 + (1/i^p)}{(1+r)(\varepsilon_{\tilde{T}}/\bar{\varepsilon})} - \frac{1}{r}\right).$$

Putting together (15) and (16), we arrive at the unique solution for the equilibrium devaluation rate $(\varepsilon_{\tilde{T}}/\bar{\varepsilon})$:[17]

$$(17) \qquad \frac{\varepsilon_{\tilde{T}}}{\bar{\varepsilon}} = \frac{(L_{t-1}/\bar{\varepsilon})}{\left(\dfrac{i^p}{1+i^p}\right)\left(\dfrac{1+r}{r}\right)\dfrac{L_{t-1}}{\bar{\varepsilon}} - \left(\dfrac{i^p}{1+i^p}\right)\Delta(1+r)^{\tilde{T}-t}}.$$

This expression together with (14) establishes properties of the shadow rate: (1) A larger imbalance Δ requires a larger jump in the bond price and a larger devaluation rate at any date. (2) A larger L acts as a cushion for the government, being associated with a smaller jump in the bond price and a smaller devaluation rate. (3) An increase in postdevaluation interest rates (or in long-run inflation) decreases the devaluation rate. (4) Delaying the collapse further into the future (i.e., an increase in $\tilde{T}$) raises the equilibrium devaluation rate.[18]

Numerical examples of the model's solution in figure 3.1 illustrate its empirically relevant, nonlinear nature. The top graph shows $\varepsilon_t/\bar{\varepsilon}$ as a function of the portion of public debt denominated in foreign currency. A relatively small change in the extent of "dollarization" can lead to large differences in the magnitude of a crisis. For example, the impact of a combination of 10 percent of foreign deflation and a fiscal imbalance of $\Delta = 0.1$ (10 percent of GDP, in present value) more than doubles when the share of dollar debt increases from 80 to 90 percent. (E.g., Levy [2002] reports for Argentina a share of dollar bonds in public debt of 87–98 percent between 1997 and 2001.) The bottom graph illustrates rapid increases in the shadow devaluation rate ($\varepsilon_{\tilde{T}}/\bar{\varepsilon}$) as the government delays devaluation (i.e., $\tilde{T} - t$ increases).[19]

The Timing of Devaluation

Our framework shares the basic feature of the first-generation models: the emergence of a fiscal imbalance implies that the currency depreciates in finite time. To see this, note that, when calculating $\varepsilon_{\tilde{T}}/\bar{\varepsilon}$, we have assumed that the fiscal imbalance Δ is no larger than the present value of the maximum wealth transfer from long-term bond holders:

$$(18) \qquad \Delta(1 + r)^{\tilde{T}-t} < \frac{L_{t-1}}{\bar{\varepsilon}}\left(\frac{1 + r}{r}\right).$$

The above formula suggests that a currency collapse must occur before the passage of time changes the sign of the above inequality, that is, before $\hat{T}$ such that

$$(19) \qquad \hat{T} = t + \frac{\log\left[\dfrac{L_{t-1}}{\bar{\varepsilon}}\left(\dfrac{1 + r}{r}\right)\right] - \log \Delta}{r}.$$

Thus conditional on L_{t-1} and Δ, there exists a finite upper bound $\hat{T}$ to the date of devaluation—note the implication that the government can borrow to defend the peg until $\hat{T}$. Following Grilli (1986), we refer to $\hat{T}$ as the time of a natural collapse of the exchange rate. In more general specifications, the natural collapse date will depend on utility and technological parameters as well as on seigniorage (perhaps most important from the viewpoint of the first-generation literature), but will remain finite. An increase in the present value of seigniorage will give the government more resources to back its debt, decreasing the shadow exchange rate much like an increase in i^p in this model (Maćkowiak 2002).[20]

While a fiscal imbalance makes devaluation inevitable, the model fails to pin down the date of the collapse—any period between t and $\hat{T}$ can be the devalu-

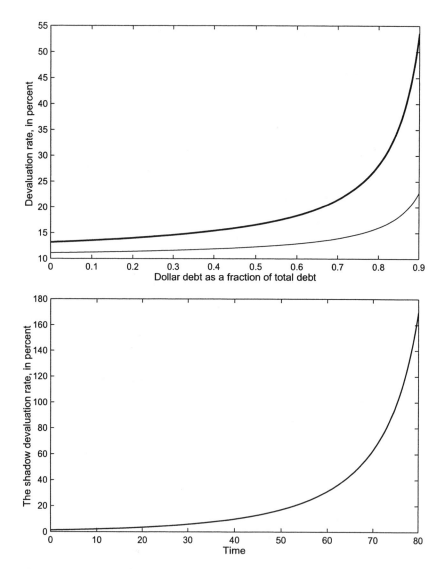

Figure 3.1 Numerical examples of the single-good model. *Top*, devaluation rate with 10 percent foreign deflation. *Thin line*, $\Delta = 0$; *thick line*, $\Delta = 0.1$. *Bottom*, delayed devaluation with $\Delta = 0.02$ and dollar debt 0.7 of total debt.

ation date. This is an important difference relative to the first-generation model, with its uniquely defined date of a speculative attack.[21]

Adjustment with Deviations from Purchasing-Power Parity

The framework laid out above assumes—like the classic first-generation literature—a single-good world economy with the law of one price, shifting the focus from reserves and the monetary base to public debt and interest rate rules. In the framework, the adjustment to a fiscal imbalance depends on maturity of debt denominated in domestic currency. But if prices deviate from purchasing-power parity, there may exist another adjustment mechanism—independent of debt maturity—via which *price level* inflation brings about a fiscal transfer consistent with a temporary *exchange rate* stability.

To address this issue, we consider a small-open economy with a traded and a nontraded good. We verify whether there is an equilibrium in which, when a fiscal imbalance appears, the price of nontradables rises in such a way that the resulting decrease in the real value of nominal public debt finances the imbalance. The government could then choose to postpone devaluation, without any long-term liabilities outstanding or without having recourse to seigniorage revenues. The adjustment mechanism would involve a real appreciation in anticipation of a speculative attack. Different from the single-good model, there would be real effects of anticipated devaluation, consisting of fluctuations in the real exchange rate and possibly the current account.

Note that, if such an equilibrium could be constructed, the augmented framework would account *qualitatively* for important empirical regularities that models with purchasing-power parity cannot match. The stylized facts are that a currency crisis is often preceded by a real appreciation and a current account deficit, and coincides with a real depreciation and a current account surplus. As we will argue below, these facts could reflect, at least in part, an adjustment to a fiscal imbalance rather than "competitiveness problems."

The Framework Augmented to Include
a Traded and a Nontraded Good

Consider the augmented framework—to save space, we do not restate expressions that are either unchanged or changed in obvious ways relative to the single-good model. In the new setup, the representative agent receives endowments of an internationally traded and a nontraded good, and maximizes

$$\sum_{t=0}^{\infty} \beta^t G_t \ln C_t,$$

where G is government spending and C is the Cobb-Douglas composite of consumption of the traded good, C_T, and the nontraded good C_N:

$$(20) \qquad C = \frac{C_T^{\gamma} C_N^{1-\gamma}}{\gamma^{\gamma}(1 - \gamma)^{1-\gamma}},$$

$0 < \gamma < 1$. The reason we introduce utility-providing G will become apparent shortly.

The period-by-period budget constraint of the individual takes the form

$$\frac{B_t}{P_t} + \frac{\varepsilon_t B_t^*}{P_t} = \frac{(1 + i_{t-1})B_{t-1}}{P_t} + \frac{(1 + r)B_{t-1}^* \varepsilon_t}{P_t}$$
$$+ \frac{P_{T,t} Y_{T,t}}{P_t} + \frac{P_{N,t} Y_{N,t}}{P_t} - \tau_t - C_t.$$

We drop the long-term bond from the menu of available assets in order to rule out the adjustment mechanism dependent on debt maturity. The price level depends on the price of the traded good, equal to εP_T^* because of the law of one price, and on the price of the nontraded good P_N:

$$P = (\varepsilon P_T^*)^{\gamma} P_N^{1-\gamma}.$$

When $(1 + r)\beta = 1$, intertemporal conditions in the agent's problem simplify to the uncovered interest rate parity (2) and to a condition relating the path of marginal utility of consumption to the paths of the exchange rate and the price level:

$$(21) \qquad \frac{G_t/C_t}{G_{t+1}/C_{t+1}} = \frac{\varepsilon_{t+1}}{\varepsilon_t} \frac{P_t}{P_{t+1}}.$$

The agent's *intra*temporal optimization is governed by the condition

$$(22) \qquad C_T \varepsilon P_T^* = \left(\frac{\gamma}{1 - \gamma}\right) C_N P_N.$$

The period-by-period government budget identity is

$$(23) \qquad \frac{B_t}{P_t} = \frac{(1 + i_{t-1})B_{t-1}}{P_t} - \tau_t + G_t,$$

where τ now denotes real lump-sum taxes (*not* the primary surplus, which equals $\tau - G$). Since we solve a local linear approximation about this model's steady state, and since we already know that the most interesting effect of dollar debt is due to a nonlinearity, we assume here that all public debt is nominal. From among a number of possibilities, we consider a simple assumption regarding the composition of government spending. Namely, G is an index of traded and nontraded goods identical to C:[22]

$$G = \frac{G_T^{\gamma} G_N^{1-\gamma}}{\gamma^{\gamma}(1 - \gamma)^{1-\gamma}}.$$

The current account identity is

$$B_t^* = (1 + r)B_{t-1}^* + P_{T,t}^*(Y_{T,t} - C_{T,t} - G_{T,t}),$$

and the equilibrium in the market for nontradables is

(24) $$Y_N - G_N = C_N.$$

It is convenient to study the dynamics of adjustment in a two-period version of this model (we denote the periods with t and $t + 1$). Consider a steady state with a constant P_T^* in which the government fixes the exchange rate permanently at $\bar{e}$, pursuing a Ricardian fiscal policy. We log-linearize the model around this steady state, using the standard notational convention according to which $\overline{X}_t$ denotes the value of the variable X in the steady state in period t, while a lower case x_t denotes the percentage deviation of X_t from $\overline{X}_t$ that is, $x_t = \log X_t - \log \overline{X}_t$.

We assume that the external shock to the log-linearized model consists of an exogenous decrease in the international price of tradables: $p_{T,t}^* < 0$ (allowing the shock to be temporary, i.e., $p_{T,t+1}^* = 0$, or persistent). Holding the exchange rate parity fixed ($e_t = 0$), the law of one price then implies a decrease in the domestic price of traded goods ($p_{T,t} < 0$), raising the real value of government debt. We suppose that fiscal policy switches to non-Ricardian coincident with the shock; that is, the path of primary surpluses fails to adjust fully to match the new, higher value of debt. Since we are interested in the dynamics of adjustment, we also suppose that policy keeps the exchange temporarily fixed, $e_t = 0$, letting the currency depreciate in period $t + 1$ ($e_{t+1} > 0$).

The appendix lists all equations of the log-linearized model. An equilibrium is a vector

$$\left(c_t, c_{t+1}, c_{T,t}, c_{T,t+1}, c_{N,t}, c_{N,t+1}, p_t, p_{t+1}, p_{N,t}, p_{N,t+1}, i_t, e_t, e_{t+1}\right)$$

that solves the equations listed in the appendix for given values of $p_{T,t}^*$ and $p_{T,t+1}^*$. The rest of this section discusses the main results and the intuition, while the details of the solution are in the appendix.

Long-Term Debt and Delayed Devaluation

Suppose we rule out changes in taxation and spending, by setting $\tau_t = \tau_{t+1} = g_t = g_{t+1} = 0$, which is equivalent to $\Delta = 0$. It is easy to show that a foreign deflationary shock ($p_{T,t}^* < 0$) implies an immediate devaluation ($e_t > 0$), like that in the single-good model, without any change in the real exchange rate. Put differently, an equilibrium with a delayed devaluation ($e_t = 0$) fails to exist, against our conjecture of an adjustment mechanism involving real appreciation at the given exchange rate parity.

Our nonexistence result is related to Uribe's analysis (2002) of the "price-consumption puzzle of currency pages." Uribe points out that, in standard optimizing models, an anticipated real appreciation must be accompanied by a declining path of consumption. In a similar fashion, a real depreciation in period $t + 1$ in our model implies a relatively high real rate of return and a decreasing path for the marginal utility of consumption. On the other hand, the adjustment mechanism we conjecture involves a current account deficit in period t followed by a surplus at the time of a delayed crisis at $t + 1$, implying a declining path for consumption. Those two implications contradict each other, if there is a monotone decreasing relationship between consumption and its marginal utility, resulting in nonexistence.

Thus the introduction of nontraded goods per se does not overturn the key result from the single-good specification—that, without long-term debt, the equilibrium involves an immediate devaluation. We interpret this finding as a confirmation that—so long as one uses an optimizing model like the one laid out thus far—debt maturity is critical for understanding *when* a given fiscal shock affects the equilibrium exchange rate.

Dynamics of the Current Account and the Real Exchange Rate

Our result above suggests that, for our model to have an equilibrium with $e_t = 0$, marginal utility of consumption at the time of an exchange rate crisis must be relatively low. In this respect, observe that, by the first-order condition (21), a declining path of consumption may be consistent with intertemporal optimality for a relatively small value of G_{t+1}/G_t. Consider then a decrease in government spending at the time of the crisis($g_{t+1} < 0$), capable of decreasing marginal utility of consumption even if consumption itself is also low. The idea is that a reduced supply of public goods (e.g., police and judicial services that guarantee private property) decreases the enjoyment of any given quantity of private goods. This modeling strategy is a way to break the monotone relationship between consumption and its marginal utility at the center of the nonexistence result in the previous subsection.

With $g_{t+1} < 0$, an equilibrium with $e_t = 0$ exists but is not unique, as the appendix discusses. To obtain a unique solution, we must introduce a feedback from predevaluation endogenous variables to postcrisis fiscal policy. The FTPL literature by now recognizes that uniqueness of equilibrium in models like ours depends on how the buildup of debt before the crisis affects the scale of fiscal reform after the abandonment of the peg (Maćkowiak 2002). The reason is that an increase in i_t drives up debt and, with insufficient postdevaluation reform, can cause a self-fulfilling increase in the equilibrium exchange rate.[23] While such self-fulfilling equilibria may be interesting per se, we prefer to rule them out by restricting fiscal reform so that the size of the decrease in G at the time of a crisis depends on the predevaluation interest rate. Specifically, we add g_{t+1} to the vector of endogenous variables, appending $g_{t+1} = \alpha_0 + \alpha_1 i_t$ (with $\alpha_1 < 0$) to the list of equations in the appendix. A feedback from devaluation expectations to the size of the fiscal retrenchment eliminates the possibility that the magnitude of the crisis be determined by self-fulfilling expectations.[24]

Numerical simulations of the unique equilibrium, in figure 3.2, suggest conclusions concerning the dynamics of the real exchange rate and the current account around the time of a currency crisis. Our model provides examples in which a foreign deflationary shock leads to abandonment of a fixed exchange rate regime, but devaluation is delayed. As the price of the nontraded good increases in the run-up to the crisis, the country experiences a real appreciation, a current account deficit, and an increase in consumption. A subsequent devaluation coincides with a real depreciation, a current account surplus, and a decrease in consumption. Thus the model matches the dynamics of the real exchange rate and the current account in the data, purely as part of the fiscal adjustment to a foreign shock—not as a result of, say, credit market imperfections or changes in output.

To an observer unaware of the fiscal implications of foreign deflation, the real appreciation in period t may suggest that the country is experiencing "competitiveness problems," and that they are responsible for the current account deficit. The same observer may feel that she is proven right by the subsequent sharp correction in the nominal and the real exchange rate, accompanied by declining prices for nontradables and a surplus in the current account.

It is remarkable that the adjustment to a fiscal imbalance is consistent with domestic price level *deflation* in period t. This is because, while the price of the nontraded good unambiguously increases, the price of tradables must fall as a consequence of foreign deflation. The latter effect on the aggregate price level is stronger in a relatively more open economy. It is also worth noting that, by causing a real depreciation at the time of the crisis, the fiscal adjustment increases the costs of servicing debt denominated in tradables. These costs are relatively lower in the run-up to the crisis.

Concluding Remarks

Maturity and currency denomination of public debt are crucial determinants of macroeconomic dynamics in an open economy. The focus of this chapter is on the dynamics of a fixed exchange rate regime in reaction to a shock that increases the real value of debt relative to government's primary surpluses, causing a fiscal imbalance. We show how monetary and fiscal policies, including maturity and denomination of debt, interact to determine the dynamic response of the economy and the magnitude of devaluation and inflation. If the government keeps the exchange rate temporarily fixed, the adjustment takes the form of a real appreciation and a current account deficit, followed by a real depreciation and a current account reversal coincident with devaluation. Our analysis suggests a broader view of (1) fiscal causes and consequences of inflation and devaluation, (2) macroeconomic effects of fiscal shocks, and (3) interactions between fiscal and monetary policies, relative to standards in the open-economy literature.

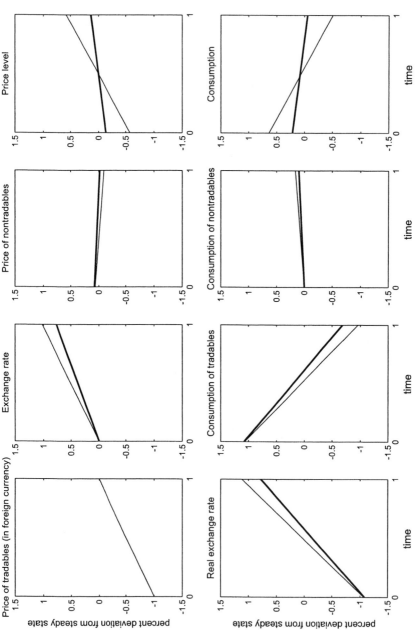

Figure 3.2 Numerical examples of the two-good model. The figure is drawn for the case where foreign deflation is temporary, $p_{T,t}^* = -0.01$ and $p_{T,t+1}^* = 0$ — conclusions from an analysis of a permanent shock are substantively the same. *Thick lines* correspond to $\gamma = 0.2$, whereas *thin lines* correspond to a relatively more open economy with $\gamma = 0.6$. The real exchange rate is defined as the price of the traded good divided by the price of the nontraded good, so that an increase in the ratio corresponds to real depreciation. Endowments of income are assumed to be constant, so that

Our framework moves away from a partial view of the adjustment to a fiscal imbalance, focused on seigniorage and therefore having little to say about the role of the "original sin" in the dynamics of currency instability. While we do not solve for currency and maturity structure of debt (they are given initial conditions in our model), our results suggest that fiscal benefits of inflation are increasing in the stock of nonindexed nominal debt. An important topic for future research is the study of time-consistent equilibria, in which the "original sin" emerges as an endogenous equilibrium feature.

Other aspects of our analysis likewise need additional research. For instance, we do not explicitly model factors that constrain fiscal reform and monetary policy after an adverse shock. Political economy and concerns about financial stability are promising areas of analysis. Finally, many devaluations coincide with both fiscal stress and sharp changes in output. Clearly, our contribution should be regarded as a building block toward future models that will simultaneously account for both aspects of actual crises.

Appendix

We list equations of the model with a traded and a nontraded good log-linearized about its steady state.

(25)
$$-c_t - p_t = g_{t+1} + e_{t+1} - c_{t+1} - p_{t+1}$$

$$e_{t+1} = i_t$$

(26)
$$c_t = \gamma c_{T,t} + (1 - \gamma)c_{N,t}$$

$$c_{t+1} = \gamma c_{T,t+1} + (1 - \gamma)c_{N,t+1}$$

$$p_t = \gamma p^*_{T,t} + (1 - \gamma)p_{N,t}$$

$$p_{t+1} = \gamma e_{t+1} + \gamma p^*_{T,t+1} + (1 - \gamma)p_{N,t+1}$$

$$g_t = \gamma g_{T,t} + (1 - \gamma)g_{N,t} = 0$$

$$g_{t+1} = \gamma g_{T,t+1} + (1 - \gamma)g_{N,t+1}$$

$$c_{T,t} + p^*_{T,t} = c_{N,t} + p_{N,t}$$

$$c_{T,t+1} + e_{t+1} + p^*_{T,t+1} = c_{N,t+1} + p_{N,t+1}$$

$$-\overline{G}_{N,t}g_{N,t} = \overline{C}_{N,t}c_{N,t}$$

$$-\overline{G}_{N,t+1}g_{N,t+1} = \overline{C}_{N,t+1}c_{N,t+1}$$

$$-\overline{R}_t\overline{P}_t(\overline{\tau}_t - \overline{G}_t)p_t = \overline{P}_{t+1}(\overline{\tau}_{t+1} - \overline{G}_{t+1})p_{t+1} - \overline{R}_t\overline{B}_t e_{t+1} - \overline{G}_{t+1}\overline{P}_{t+1}g_{t+1}$$

$$\overline{P}_{T,t}^*(\overline{Y}_{T,t} - \overline{C}_{T,t} - \overline{G}_{T,t})p_{T,t}^* - \overline{P}_{T,t}^*\overline{C}_{T,t}c_{T,t}$$
$$= -\beta\overline{P}_{T,t+1}^*(\overline{Y}_{T,t+1} - \overline{C}_{T,t+1} - \overline{G}_{T,t+1})p_{T,t+1}^*$$
$$+ \beta\overline{P}_{T,t+1}^*\overline{C}_{T,t+1}c_{T,t+1} + \beta\overline{P}_{T,t+1}^*\overline{G}_{T,t+1}g_{T,t+1}$$

We suppose that the government sets

$$g_T = \frac{1}{2\gamma}g$$

and

$$g_N = \frac{1}{2(1-\gamma)}g.$$

We consider an exogenous shock $p_{T,t}^* < 0$ and assume that policy sets $e_t = 0$ and $\tau_t = \tau_{t+1} = g_t = 0$. We assume the following values of parameters and steady-state variables: $\alpha_0 = 0, \alpha_1 = -1, \beta = 1, \overline{R}_t = 1, \overline{G}_t = \overline{G}_{t+1} = 0.3, \overline{G}_{T,t} = \overline{G}_{T,t+1} = \overline{G}_{N,t} = \overline{G}_{N,t+1}, \overline{\tau}_t = \overline{\tau}_{t+1} = 0.6, \overline{B}_{t-1} = 0.6, \overline{B}_t = 0.3, \overline{C}_{T,t} = \overline{C}_{T,t+1} = 1, \overline{C}_{N,t} = \overline{C}_{N,t+1} = 1, \overline{\varepsilon}_t = \overline{\varepsilon}_{t+1} = 1, \overline{P}_{N,t} = \overline{P}_{N,t+1} = 1, \overline{P}_{T,t+1}^* = \overline{P}_{T,t+1} = 1, \overline{Y}_{T,t} = \overline{Y}_{T,t+1} = \overline{C}_{T,t} + \overline{G}_{T,t} = \overline{C}_{T,t+1} + \overline{G}_{T,t+1}.$

We first show that, if $g_{t+1} = 0$, then there is no solution with $e_t = 0$. To see why, suppose that $e_t = 0$ in equilibrium. With the price of tradables falling together with the foreign price, that is, $P_{T,t} = p_{T,t}^* < 0$, the solved-forward government budget constraint requires that the price of the nontraded good must increase ($p_{N,t} > 0$) so as to reduce the real value of debt consistent with an unchanged path of primary surpluses. Since in equilibrium there is no change in consumption of the nontraded good, $c_{N,t} = 0$, nominal spending on this good must increase ($c_{N,t} + p_{N,t} > 0$). But spending on the traded good is proportional to spending on nontradables, so it too must increase ($c_{T,t} + p_{T,t}^* > 0$). For $c_{T,t} + p_{T,t}^*$ to be positive with $p_{T,t}^* < 0$, it must be the case that domestic agents consume more of the traded good, moving the current account toward a deficit. By (26), aggregate consumption increases ($c_t > 0$). In period $t + 1$, by contrast, aggregate consumption decreases ($c_{t+1} < 0$): the nontraded goods equilibrium still implies that $c_{N,t+1} = 0$, but the current account must move toward a surplus so that $c_{T,t+1} < 0$. This argument establishes that, if a solution with $e_t = 0$ exists, it exhibits a downward sloping path for consumption, $c_{t+1} - c_t < 0$. Elements responsible for this conclusion are valuation of public debt, intratemporal optimization, and the current account.

The crucial observation for establishing nonexistence with $e_t = 0$ is that a decreasing path for consumption is inconsistent with intertemporal optimality. The argument above implies a real depreciation in period $t + 1$ ($e_{t+1} - [p_{t+1} - p_t] > 0$), but a real depreciation is consistent with intertemporal optimization (25) only if the marginal utility of consumption follows a decreasing path. This in turn implies that $c_{t+1} - c_t > 0$, generating a contradiction.

We reconsider our experiment under the assumption that an exchange rate crisis at $t + 1$ coincides with a decrease in utility-providing government spending ($g_{t+1} < 0$). We begin by setting g_{t+1} equal to a unique value such that all equilibrium conditions hold with $e_t = 0$. This amendment implies that the marginal utility of consumption decreases in period $t + 1$, even if consumption itself follows a declining path. With $g_{t+1} < 0$, there is a unique value of $p_{N,t}$ consistent with equilibrium. However, there is a continuum of solutions for the interest rate in period t and the price level at $t + 1$. In fact, changes in i_t affect the outstanding stock of debt, and therefore can cause self-fulfilling changes in e_{t+1} and $p_{N,t+1}$. Setting $g_{t+1} = \alpha_0 + \alpha_1 i_t$ (with $\alpha_1 < 0$), we solve the model numerically, obtaining a unique solution depicted in figure 3.2.

Notes

We thank our discussant Michael Kuhmof and the conference participants for comments.

1. The models of Krugman and Flood and Garber build on Salant and Henderson (1978). The first-generation literature includes, for example, Obstfeld 1986; Buiter 1987, and Calvo 1987. Buiter, Corsetti, and Pesenti 1998; Calvo 1998; Cavallari and Corsetti 2000; Flood and Marion 1999; and Jeanne 2000 are recent discussions of the literature on currency crises. Corsetti, Pesenti, and Roubini (1999a, 1999b) adopt the first generation's setup as a starting point to interpret crises in emerging markets. In those papers, different from the Krugman model, a fiscal deficit can emerge after rather than before an exchange rate collapse.

2. Among papers on the FTPL are Benhabib, Schmitt-Grohé, and Uribe 2001; Cochrane 1999a, 1999b, 2001; Leeper 1991; Sims 1994, 1997, 1999; and Woodford 1994, 1995, 1996, 1998. Woodford 2000 is a recent review with further references, while Bergin 2000; Daniel 2001b; Dupor 2000; Canzoneri, Cumby, and Diba 1998; and Loyo 1998 are open-economy applications.

3. See, e.g., Burstein, Eichenbaum, and Rebelo 2002; Corsetti, Pesenti, and Roubini 1999a; and Milesi-Ferretti and Razin 1998 for a discussion of stylized facts concerning the real exchange rate and the current account. Schneider and Tornell (2000) derive predictions for the dynamics of the real exchange rate in a setup with a credit-market imperfection and a government-bailout guarantee. Burnside, Eichenbaum, and Rebelo (2001a) and Burstein, Eichenbaum, and Rebelo (2002) present models accounting for a large real depreciation at the time of an exchange rate crisis but not for a real appreciation prior to it.

4. The distribution of nominal claims on the government between domestic agents and foreigners matters for a welfare evaluation of a crisis, something we leave for future research.

5. In our forward solution, we restrict attention to competitive equilibria in which the following terminal condition holds:

$$\lim_{s \to \infty} \left[\prod_{k=0}^{s} \left(\frac{1}{1 + i_{t+k}} \right) \right] \theta_{t+s+1} = 0.$$

6. It is worth noting here that governments have many imperfectly indexed liabilities other than publicly traded bonds, including long-term spending commitments like pensions. For instance, in the aftermath of an exchange rate crisis, governments sometimes freeze spending in nominal terms. Even when, temporary, imperfect indexation of spending can generate large fiscal gains. A moderate change in the price level can bring about substantial wealth transfers that help resolve a fiscal crisis—in this respect, simulations on the fiscal impact of moderate inflation in Sweden by Persson, Persson, and Svensson (1998) provide an instructive example. Consistent with that study, one could interpret "nominal public debt" in our model in a broad sense, redefining τ as including only items that are fully indexed to prices.

7. It is not realistic to rule out the possibility of government default, but there is a good reason for doing so in a simple model. Outright default and the kind of implicit default on nominal government liabilities that occurs via unanticipated inflation are different phenomena. A holder of a government bond on which outright default is possible is exposed not just to to aggregate default uncertainty, but also to negotiation and legal costs as well as additional uncertainty over which creditors would bear the default cost. See Sims 1997 for a discussion.

8. Recall that we postulate (9) as an additional equilibrium condition. In a closed-economy model, an equivalent condition would be implied by (7) and private sector's optimization. Note also that in this open-economy model F, determined by government supply, need not equal B^*.

9. Lahiri and Vegh (1998) study in detail how the present value of seigniorage depends in first-generation models on the interest elasticity of money demand.

10. There is a vector-autoregressive literature documenting that a substantial fraction of macroeconomic variation in small economies originates abroad (e.g., Calvo, Leiderman, and Reinhart 1993; Canova 2003; Cushman and Zha 1997; and Maćkowiak 2001).

11. For example, one can assume that from time T_d onward, primary surpluses change by a constant d:

$$\Delta \equiv \frac{(1 + r)d}{r} \left(\frac{1}{1 + r} \right)^{T_d - t}.$$

Letting $T_d \geq t$ allows for the possibility that primary surpluses change at a future date.

12. A more realistic model, with a nominal rigidity, might predict a decrease in Argentina's output in reaction to Brazil's devaluation, and a consequent deterioration in Argentina's primary surpluses. See, e.g., Hausmann and Velasco 2002 for an analysis of the crisis in Argentina, including a discussion of the impact of Brazil's devaluation on its neighbor.

13. We also assume that $\beta\phi_0 \geq 1 - \beta\phi_1$ so that the postdevaluation (gross) chronic depreciation rate converges to a number greater than or equal to one. This assumption is inessential for substantive results of this paper, but allows us to rule out persistent deflation after devaluation.

14. We assume that i^p is chosen so that $\varepsilon_t > \bar{\varepsilon}$.

15. To determine the equilibrium level of consumption, so long as $P_\beta^* < P_\alpha^*$, we would need to make an arbitrary assumption regarding the small economy's net international asset position in dollar bonds.

16. See Cavallari and Corsetti (2000) for a generalization of the concept to first- and second-generation models.

17. An expression similar to (17) is at the center of the contributions by Daniel (1998, 2001a). (She also obtains an expression similar to [14], setting $P_\alpha^* = P_\beta^*$ and $B = 0$.) Daniel's interpretation is that monetary policy can choose (subject to equilibrium behavior of private agents) two of the three variables: the magnitude of the devaluation, its timing, and the postcollapse inflation rate.

18. Following our discussion of devaluation in period t, it should be evident that the unique solution for $\varepsilon_T/\bar\varepsilon$ satisfies the other equilibrium conditions.

19. Both numerical examples assume that public debt is 50 percent of GDP, $i_p = r = 5$ percent; the second in addition sets the share of long-term debt in total nominal debt equal to 50 percent.

20. If the government attempted to delay the devaluation past $\hat{T}$, its solved-forward budget constraint would fail to hold with $\varepsilon_t = \bar\varepsilon$, and the peg would collapse in period t. Lahiri and Vegh (2000) introduce a government bond that is assumed to have utility value—its price is therefore not determined exclusively by the uncovered interest parity. The government can borrow by issuing such bonds at increasing interest rates. Buiter (1987) directly assumes an upward-sloping supply schedule for reserves. Those considerations do not matter for the substance of our argument—they merely act to decrease $\hat{T}$ as borrowing increases.

21. Corsetti and Maćkowiak (2003) show that an interest rate rule pursued by monetary policy determines a unique timing for a devaluation in the new framework. They also explain how thinking in terms of that interest rate rule resolves paradoxes of the classical model concerning the dynamics of a speculative attack.

22. Assuming that G is entirely on nontradables gives the same qualitative results concerning equilibrium paths of the real exchange rate and the current account.

23. Our single-good model has a uniquely defined exchange rate only because, once a fiscal imbalance appears, the exchange rate depends on $\hat{T}$ but not on the stock of debt or the interest rate.

24. It is plausible that a crisis prompts some fiscal reform, and that the extent of the reform is related to the size of the crisis. Crises and reform are costly, and reform may be delayed in a heterogeneous society until a "crisis" makes it evident that costs of further fiscal inaction are sufficiently high. The political economy literature has formalized the idea that crises are beneficial for economic reforms (e.g., Drazen and Grilli 1993 and Zarazaga 1997). It is also plausible that fiscal "reform" in the context of a crisis begins with cuts in funding for law enforcement that decrease marginal utility of private consumption.

References

Benhabib, Jess, Stephanie Schmitt-Grohé, and Martin Uribe. 2001. "Monetary Policy and Multiple Equilibria." *American Economic Review* 91 (1): 167–86.

Bergin, Paul R. 2000. "Fiscal Solvency and Price Level Determination in a Monetary Union." *Journal of Monetary Economics* 45 (1): 37–53.

Buiter, Willem H. 1987. "Borrowing to Defend the Exchange Rate and the Timing and Magnitude of Speculative Attacks." *Journal of International Economics* 23:221–39.

Buiter, Willem H., Giancarlo Corsetti, and Paolo Pesenti. 1998. *Financial Markets and Européan Monetary Coordination: The Lessons from the 1992–93 ERM Crisis.* Cambridge: Cambridge University Press.

Burnside, Craig, Martin Eichenbaum, and Sergio Rebelo. 2001a. "On the Fiscal Implications of Twin Crises." Working paper, Northwestern University Evanston, IL.

———. 2001b. "Prospective Deficits and the Asian Currency Crisis." *Journal of Political Economy* 109 (6):1155–97.

———. 2003. "Government Finance in the Wake of Currency Crises." Working paper, Northwestern University, Evanston, IL.

Burstein, Ariel, Martin Eichenbaum, and Sergio Rebelo. 2002. "Why Is Inflation So Low after Large Devaluation?" Working paper, Northwestern University, Evanston, IL.

Calvo, Guillermo A. 1987. "Balance of Payments Crises in a Cash-in-Advance Economy." *Journal of Money, Credit, and Banking* 19:19–32.

———. 1998. "Varieties of Capital-Market Crises." In *The Debt Burden and Its Consequences for Monetary Policy,* ed. Guillermo A. Calvo and Mervyn King. International Economics Association Series. New York: St. Martin's Press.

Calvo, Guillermo, Leonardo Leiderman, and Carmen M. Reinhart. 1993. "Capital Inflows and Real Exchange Rate Appreciation in Latin America: The Role of External Factors." *IMF Staff Papers* 40 (1): 108–51.

Canova, Fabio. 2003. "The Transmission of U.S. Shocks to Latin America." Working paper, Universitat Pompeu Fabra, Barcelona.

Canzoneri, Matthew B., Robert E. Cumby, and Behzad T. Diba. 1998. "Fiscal Discipline and Exchange Rate Regimes." Discussion Paper 1899. Center for Economic Policy Research, London.

Cavallari, Lilia, and Giancarlo Corsetti. 2000. "Shadow Rates and Multiple Equilibria in the Theory of Currency Crises." *Journal of International Economics* 51:275–86.

Cochrane, John H. 1999a. "A Cashless View of U.S. Inflation." In *NBER Macroeconomics Annual 1998,* ed. Ben Bernanke and Julio J. Rotemberg. Cambridge: MIT Press.

———. 1999b. "Money as Stock: Price Level Determination with No Money Demand." Working paper, University of Chicago.

———. 2001. "Long-term Debt and Optimal Policy in the Fiscal Theory of the Price Level." *Econometrica* 69 (1): 69–116.

Corsetti, Giancarlo, and Bartosz Maćkowiak. 2000. "Nominal Debt and the Dynamics of Currency Crises." Economic Growth Center Discussion Paper 820, Yale University, New Haven.

———. 2003. "Fiscal Imbalance and the Dynamics of Currency Crises." Working paper, University of Rome III and Humboldt University, Berlin.

Corsetti, Giancarlo, Paolo Pesenti, and Nouriel Roubini. 1999a. "Paper Tigers? A Model of the Asian Crisis." *European Economic Review* 43:1211–36.

———. 1999b. "What Caused the Asian Currency and Financial Crisis?" *Japan and the World Economy* 3:305–73.

Cushman, David O., and Tao Zha. 1997. "Identifying Monetary Policy in a Small Open Economy under Flexible Exchange Rates." *Journal of Monetary Economics* 39: 433–48.

Daniel, Betty C. 1998. "Intertemporal Choice and Currency Crises." Working paper, State University of New York, Albany.

———. 2001a. "A Fiscal Theory of Currency Crises." *International Economic Review* 42 (4): 969–88.

———. 2001b. "The Fiscal Theory of the Price Level in an Open Economy." *Journal of Monetary Economics.* 48:293–308.

Drazen, Allan, and Vittorio Grilli. 1993. "The Benefit of Crises for Economic Reforms." *American Economic Review* 83:598–607.

Dupor, Bill. 2000. "Exchange Rates and the Fiscal Theory of the Price Level." *Journal of Monetary Economics* 45:613–30.

Eichengreen, Barry, Ricardo Hausmann, and Ugo Panizza. 2002. "Original Sin: The Pain, the Mystery, and the Road to Redemption." Working paper, University of California, Berkeley; Kennedy School of Government, Harvard University, Cambridge; and Inter-American Development Bank, Washington DC.

Flood, Robert P., and Peter M. Garber. 1984. "Collapsing Exchange Rate Regimes: Some Linear Examples." *Journal of International Economics* 17:1–13.

Flood, Robert P., and Nancy Marion. 1999. "Perspectives on the Recent Currency Crisis Literature." *International Journal of Finance and Economics* 4 (1): 1–26.

Grilli, Vittorio. 1986. "Buying and Selling Attacks on Fixed Exchange Rate Systems." *Journal of International Economics* 20:143–56.

Hausmann, Ricardo, and Andrés Velasco. 2002. "The Argentine Collapse: Hard Money's Soft Underbelly." Working paper, Kennedy School of Government, Harvard University, Cambridge.

Jeanne, Olivier. 2000. "Currency Crises: A Perspective on Recent Theoretical Developments." Special Paper in International Economics no. 20, International Finance Section, Princeton University, Princeton, NJ.

Krugman, Paul R. 1979. "A Model of Balance of Payments Crises." *Journal of Money, Credit, and Banking* 11:311–25.

Lahiri, Amartya, and Carlos A. Vegh. 1998. "The Feasibility of BOP Crises: Monetary vs. Fiscal Approach." Working paper, University of California, Los Angeles.

———. 2000. "Delaying the Inevitable: Optimal Interest Rate Policy and BOP Crises." Working paper, University of California, Los Angeles.

Leeper, Eric. 1991. "Equilibria under 'Active' and 'Passive' Monetary and Fiscal Policies." *Journal of Monetary Economics* 27:129–47.

Levy, Aviram. 2002. "Asset and Liability Dollarization in Emerging Economies: Empirical Evidence and Policy Issues." Working paper, Bank of Italy, Rome.

Loyo, Eduardo. 1998. "Going International with the Fiscal Theory of the Price Level." Working paper, Harvard University, Cambridge.

Maćkowiak, Bartosz. 2001. "External Shocks, U.S. Monetary Policy, and Macroeconomic Fluctuations in Emerging Markets." Working paper, Humboldt University, Berlin.

———. 2002. "Macroeconomic Regime Switches and Speculative Attacks." Working paper, Humboldt University, Berlin.

Milesi-Ferretti, Gian Maria, and Assaf Razin. 1998. "Current Account Reversals and Currency Crises: Empirical Regularities." Working paper 89, International Monetary Fund, Washington, DC.

Obstfeld, Maurice. 1986. "Speculative Attack and the External Constraint in a Maximizing Model of the Balance of Payments." *Canadian Journal of Economics* 19:1–22.

Persson, Mats, Torsten Persson, and Lars E. O. Svensson. 1998. "Debt, Cash Flow, and Inflation Incentives: A Swedish Example." In *The Debt Burden and Its Consequences for Monetary Policy,* ed. Guillermo A. Calvo and Mervin King. International Economics Association Series. New York: St. Martin's Press.

Salant, Stephen W., and Dale W. Henderson. 1978. "Market Anticipation of Government Policy and the Price of Gold." *Journal of Political Economy* 86:627–48.

Schneider, Martin, and Aaron Tornell. 2000. "Balance Sheet Effects, Bailout Guarantees, and Financial Crises." NBER Working Paper no. 8060, National Bureau of Economic Research, Cambridge, MA.

Sims, Christopher A. 1994. "A Simple Model for Study of the Determination of the Price Level and the Interaction of Monetary and Fiscal Policy." *Economic Theory* 4:381–99.

———. 1997. "Fiscal Foundations of Price Stability in Open Economies." Working paper, Yale University, New Haven.

———. 1999. "The Precarious Fiscal Foundations of EMU." *De Economist* 147 (4): 415–36.

Uribe, Martin. 2002. "The Price-Consumption Puzzle of Currency Pegs." *Journal of Monetary Economics.* 49:533–69.

Woodford, Michael. 1994. "Monetary Policy and Price Level Determinacy in a Cash-in-Advance Economy." *Economic Theory* 4:345–80.

———. 1995. "Price-Level Determinacy without Control of a Monetary Aggregate." *Carnegie-Rochester Conference Series on Public Policy* 43:1–46.

———. 1996. "Control of the Public Debt: A Requirement for Price Stability?" NBER Working Paper no. 5684, National Bureau of Economic Research, Cambridge, MA. Reprinted in *The Debt Burden and Its Consequences for Monetary Policy,* ed. Guillermo Calvo and Mervyn King. International Economics Association Series. New York: St. Martin's Press, 1998.

———. 1998. "Public Debt and the Price Level." Working paper, Princeton University, Princeton, NJ.

———. 2000. "Fiscal Requirements for Price Stability." Working paper, Princeton University, Princeton, NJ.

Zarazaga, Carlos. 1997. "Recurrent Hyperinflations in a Dynamic Game with Imperfect Monitoring in the Appropriation of Seigniorage." Working paper, Federal Reserve Bank of Dallas.

Original Sin, Balance-Sheet Crises, and the Roles of International Lending

Olivier Jeanne and Jeromin Zettelmeyer

A NUMBER of commentators have expressed the view that the financial crises of the 1990s were of a new kind, reflecting fragilities in the balance sheet of firms, banks, and governments rather than current account imbalances.[1] Some of them have argued that the international community should take a new approach—a balance-sheet approach—to the management of international financial crises.

One source of balance-sheet fragility that is often emphasized is foreign-currency debt. One sense in which foreign-currency debt is the "original sin" (Eichengreen and Hausmann 1999) is that it is the source of so many other problems. Foreign-currency debt constrains traditional domestic policy instruments, such as monetary or fiscal policies, in dealing with economic shocks, both homemade and foreign. Almost by default, this suggests a larger potential role for international official lending, as reflected in the heavy involvement of international financial institutions in Latin America and other areas of the world suffering from original sin. But how and why can international lending be a useful complement to domestic economic policies in these countries? More specifically, how can the role of international lending be rationalized in the context of the "balance-sheet approach" to financial crises?

This chapter answers these questions in the context of a simple framework that encompasses—in a highly stylized way—several of the models that have been proposed in the recent literature on international financial crises. As we will show, the general consensus that foreign-currency debt is problematic masks a surprising variety of opinions and models of the dangers involved. Rather than presenting one more model of the dangers of foreign-currency debt, this chapter presents a framework that is general and flexible enough to organize a discussion of the recent literature, in a way that is not dependent on modeling details. The first part of the chapter can be viewed as a brief tour of the literature for the practitioner. In the second part, we discuss some of the challenges for domestic policies that arise in this framework, and the potential roles for international crisis lending.

Our framework gives a stylized summary of two classes of models of balance-sheet crises. The first class of models combines a currency mismatch with a maturity mismatch: debt is not only in foreign currency but also short-term, typically bank deposits (Chang and Velasco 2000; Burnside, Eichenbaum, and Rebelo 2001a, 2001b, 2001c; Jeanne and Wyplosz 2001). Crises take the form of runs on short-term foreign-currency debt. The second class of models involves a currency mismatch, without maturity mismatch, in corporate balance sheets (Krugman 1999; Aghion, Bacchetta, and Banerjee 2000, 2001a, 2001b; Bacchetta 2000; Schneider and Tornell 2001). Crises involve a severe credit crunch and a fall in investment. In *both* cases, crises can be self-fulfilling, the depreciation of the exchange rate being validated by the real disruption it provokes. Both classes of models are supported by some evidence,[2] making it interesting to explore their policy implications.

We argue that the policy implications of the two classes of models are similar in some areas, but quite different in others. One policy implication that all balance-sheet approaches seem to have in common is the relative powerlessness of domestic policies—and especially monetary policy—in protecting the economy against capital account crises. Moreover, there could be an important role for international crisis lending in both classes of models, but the nature of this role is quite different. In the first class of models (models with runs), the optimal policies should be thought of by reference to banking safety nets: lending in last resort, deposit insurance, or suspension of payments. We argue that such policies do not necessarily place unrealistic demands on the volume of international crisis lending, although they raise knotty moral-hazard issues, just like domestic banking safety nets. In the context of credit-crunch models, international crisis lending may also have a useful role, but it has little to do with lending in last resort, and more with loosening credit constraints for domestic agents, including the government. A large international lender can help overcome self-fulfilling crises by lending to the government conditional on its "true" net worth, that is, its net worth in normal times, allowing it to pursue activities that mitigate the effects of the credit crunch.

There are several caveats to make. The most important one is that we look at the question from a purely ex post perspective. Original sin is taken as given. Obviously, however, the different policies we consider have an impact ex ante on the decisions to borrow in domestic or foreign currency (an endogeneity that several contributions in this volume look at). We briefly discuss this issue at the end of the chapter.

Elements of a Canonical Framework

We consider a two-period model of an open emerging economy ($t = 1, 2$). For the sake of brevity and *couleur locale*, we call the domestic and foreign currencies peso and dollar, respectively. The exchange rate S_t is defined as the time t domestic currency price of one dollar, so an increase in S means that the peso depreciates.

The objective of the model is to clarify a range of possible links between expectations about future exchange rates, S_2^e, and balance sheets—or more precisely, domestic private agents' net worth in terms of dollars, W^*. In principle, links can exist in both directions. The link from expected exchange rates to net worth follows more or less directly from the presence of unhedged foreign-currency liabilities. However, the balance-sheet problems caused by the expected depreciation could also be part of the fundamentals that market participants look at in deciding what exchange rate to expect. If that is the case, there could be multiple equilibria, one of which one could be pareto-dominated. Expectations of depreciated future exchange rates could lead to low net worth, triggering an economic crisis and depreciated exchange rates, which in turn validate the initial expectations.

To develop a framework that generates self-fulfilling crises of this kind, we must thus construct a "loop" from S_2^e to W^* and back to S_2^e. We do so in three steps. First, we describe the link from S_2^e to net worth W^*. This step is straightforward and somewhat mechanical; it follows from balance-sheet definitions and uncovered interest parity. Second, we describe two alternative links from W^* to an economic crisis state X, which is given a particular interpretation in each case. This step is not mechanical, and involves most of the economic substance of this chapter. Finally, we discuss a variety of possible ways, suggested in the literature on balance-sheet crises, in which X could affect future exchange rates. In contrast with the previous step, we do not formalize these alternative links because the (monetary and international) policy implications on which we focus in this chapter turn out to depend only on the presence of *some* link from X to a depreciated exchange rate, not on how the particular channel is modeled. Thus, it is sufficient for the purposes of this chapter to assume that a link from X to expected exchange rates exists in reduced form.

The Link from Expected Exchange Rates to Net Worth

Assume that the peso/dollar exchange rate satisfies uncovered interest rate parity (UIP):

$$S_1 = \frac{1 + i^*}{1 + i} S_2^e,$$

where S_2^e is the expected exchange rate, and i and i^* are peso and dollar riskless interest rates in period 1, respectively.[3]

Next, consider domestic private agents (firms or banks) who have debts and income streams denominated in dollars and pesos. The currency composition of income streams and debts is inherited from an earlier time, and it is exogenous to the analysis. Let D_t denote the agents' time t debt repayment in pesos, D_t^* their time t debt repayments in dollars, R_t their peso income and R_t^* their dollar income. Note that we assume that the peso value of the agents' cash flows is not affected by the exchange rate. This is not a very restrictive assumption, however, since having a peso-denominated income stream that exhibits some exchange rate pass-through could be represented as a combination of fixed peso income and dollar income (for which pass-through is unity).

We are now ready to define the agents' net worth. This is the central variable in the balance-sheet approach: all bad things, bank runs or credit crunches, happen because of insufficient or negative net worth. Using UIP and denoting by $D^* \equiv D_1^* + D_2^*/(1 + i^*)$ and $R^* \equiv R_1^* + R_2^*/(1 + i^*)$ the present-value dollar debt and dollar income of the agent, respectively, its net worth can be expressed in terms of the expected exchange rate and the interest rate,

$$(1) \qquad W^* = \frac{R_2 - D_2 + (R_1 - D_1)(1 + i)}{(1 + i^*)S_2^e} + R^* - D^*.$$

If the agent has enough pesos to repay its peso debt in each period ($R_1 \geq D_1$ and $R_2 \geq D_2$), then its net worth is decreasing with the expected exchange rate, and could become negative for high levels of S_2^e if the agent also has dollar debt (D^*). The same would be true if we looked at the peso value of the agent's net worth.

The Link from Net Worth to Crises

Why is low net worth a problem? Two answers (not necessarily mutually exclusive) are given in the literature. One view emphasizes the net worth constraint on investment that is standard in corporate finance. Firms cannot borrow more than a given fraction of their net worth; thus, net worth constrains investment. This channel is invoked in Krugman 1999; Aghion, Bacchetta, and Banerjee 2000, 2001a, 2001b; and Schneider and Tornell 2001. The alternative view emphasizes the link between net worth and banking crises (Chang and Velasco 2000; Burnside, Eichenbaum, and Rebelo 2001a, 2001c; Jeanne and Wyplosz 2001). Low net worth leads to the collapse of the banking system. We now briefly develop both views.

Banking Crises

Assume that the agent is a bank. Following Jeanne and Wyplosz (2001), we assume that the bank suffers from a combination of currency and maturity mismatches, as follows: (1) its dollar debt exceeds its dollar income both in the first period and in present-value terms, that is, $D_1^* > R_1^*$ and $D^* > R^*$; (2) while the firm has second-period income denominated in pesos, peso debt and first-period peso income equals zero ($R_1 = D_1 = D_2 = 0$). As we shall see below, assumption 1 is essential while 2 is made mainly for convenience.

Deposits are repayable on demand, and demand is served sequentially, as in Diamond and Dybvig's model of bank runs (1983). The withdrawing depositors are randomly allocated in a queue that determines the order in which they are served. The bank repays depositors by selling its claims on future pesos for dollars in the market (unlike Diamond and Dybvig 1983 and Chang and Velasco 2000, we assume that the bank's assets are perfectly liquid and can be sold at their net present value in the market). If the bank does not have enough dollars to repay all the withdrawing depositors in period 1, the depositors at the end of the queue, and those who have not joined the queue, receive nothing. In the opposite case, the assets that remain in the possession of the bank at the end of period 1 are sold in period 2 to repay the remaining depositors—those who have not withdrawn in period 1. Deposits are interest-bearing and yield the riskless international interest rate.

Under these assumptions, a fall in the bank's net worth can provoke a run. There is no run if and only if net worth is positive, that is, if and only if

$$(2) \qquad D^* \leq R^* + \frac{R_2}{(1 + i^*)S_2^e}.$$

If this solvency condition is satisfied, the bank can repay all its depositors irrespective of the date at which they withdraw, and depositors have no (strict) incentives to withdraw early. If this condition is not satisfied, then all depositors run on the bank at period 1. Some depositors will have to take a loss, and each depositor minimizes the likelihood of being one of them by withdrawing his deposits early. Note that, in contrast with the Diamond-Dybvig model, the equilibrium is unique at the level of an individual bank. Because there are no costs to early liquidation, net worth is not affected by the occurrence of a run per se. Thus, for a given balance-sheet structure, the occurrence of a run is determined only by the expected exchange rate, which is exogenous to the actions of the bank's depositors (the bank being very small).

Finally, assume that banks are heterogeneous in terms of their balance-sheet characteristics. Because we have assumed that $D^* > R^*$, each bank j has a specific cutoff exchange rate $\overline{S}_2^e(j)$ at which its net worth is zero. Assume that banks are infinitesimally small with total mass one, and that $\overline{S}_2^e(j)$ is continuously distributed with a cumulative distribution function $F(\cdot)$. For a given S_2^e, all the banks for which $\overline{S}_2^e(j) < S_2^e$, that is, whose net worth is smaller than zero, will suffer a run. Consequently, the fraction of banks on which there are runs in period 1, n, is a continuous and increasing function of the expected exchange rate,

$$(3) \qquad n = F(S_2^e) \qquad F' > 0, \qquad F(\hat{S}_2^e) = 1,$$

where $\hat{S}_2^e$ denotes the supremum of $\overline{S}_2^e(j)$, that is, the exchange rate at which the highest net worth bank becomes insolvent. An expected depreciation of the peso reduces the net worth of banks, drawing a larger number into insolvency. For $S_2^e \geq \hat{S}_2^e$, all banks are insolvent.

A Credit Crunch

Next, consider the case in which there is a currency mismatch but no maturity mismatch. Specifically, we assume that all dollar debt is long term ($D_1^* = 0$) but maintain the assumption that there is a currency mismatch with respect to the present value of dollar assets and liabilities ($D_2^*/(1 + i^*) > R^*$). This case can be interpreted as a firm that relies on some income in the nontradables sector to maintain positive net worth. For simplicity, we keep the assumption that $R_1 = D_1 = D_2 = 0$; this will be relaxed later. Dollar net worth is then

$$(4) \qquad W^* = R^* + \frac{R_2}{(1 + i^*)S_2^e} - \frac{D_2^*}{(1 + i^*)}.$$

An increase in S_2^e reduces the firm's net worth in period 1.[4] This does not provoke a default in period 1, because the firm does not have to repay or roll over debt in this period. However, it could constrain the quantity of new debt the firm can issue in period 1. In many corporate finance models, net worth is a determinant of the firm's borrowing capacity and consequently its ability to invest.

Following Aghion, Bacchetta, and Banerjee (2001b), we assume that there is a first-best level of investment, $\tilde{I}$, which the firm would like to undertake if it is not credit constrained. Whether it can actually invest $\tilde{I}$ depends on its borrowing capacity, which in turn is constrained by its net worth. Assuming a simple linear constraint and no internal funds, the firm's actual investment, in dollar terms, can be written as

$$(5) \qquad I = \begin{cases} \tilde{I} & \text{if} & \tilde{I} \leq \mu W^*(S_2^e) \\ \mu W^*(S_2^e) & \text{if} & \tilde{I} > \mu W^*(S_2^e) > 0 \\ 0 & \text{if} & \mu W^*(S_2^e) \leq 0 \end{cases}.$$

From (4) it is clear that there is a sufficiently small (i.e., appreciated) level of the second-period exchange rate so that $I = \tilde{I}$. Denote this level $\underline{S}_2^e$. Similarly, since we have assumed that $D_2^*/(1 + i^*) > R^*$. there is a sufficiently high (depreciated) level of the exchange rate such that net worth is zero, and thus $I = 0$. Denote this $\overline{S}_2^e$. We can now define an "investment gap" u that is analogous to the bank-run function (3), in the sense that it expresses the real cost of low net worth as a function of the second-period exchange rate:

$$(6) \qquad u \equiv \tilde{I} - I = \begin{cases} \tilde{I} & \text{if} & S_2^e \geq \overline{S}_2^e \\ \tilde{I} - \mu W^*(S_2^e) & \text{if} & \overline{S}_2^e > S_2^e > \underline{S}_2^e \\ 0 & \text{if} & \underline{S}_2^e \geq S_2^e \end{cases}.$$

For $\overline{S}_2^e > S_2^e > \underline{S}_2^e$, the real cost of a credit crunch is a continuous and strictly increasing function of S_2^e, since $W^*(S_2^e)$ is continuous and strictly decreasing in S_2^e. This is true for each individual firm, and it is true in the aggregate regardless of whether firms are heterogeneous. Any increase in S_2^e beyond $\overline{S}_2^e$ will cause investment to fall to zero.

The Link from Crises to Depreciated Exchange Rates

The final step is to construct a link from the bad consequences of net worth—a credit crunch, low investment, a banking crisis—to future exchange rates. Broadly classified, the literature has focused on three arguments.

1. Low investment results in a low domestic demand for home/nontradable goods or a low domestic supply of tradable goods, which forces a real depreciation. This is the channel assumed by Krugman (1999), Chang and Velasco (2000), and Schneider and Tornell (2001) in the context of purely "real" models, that is, models without money and nominal exchange rates.
2. Low investment leads to low future output. Given an assumption about future monetary policy, this implies higher prices and (with purchasing power parity) a depreciated exchange rate (Aghion, Bacchetta, and Banerjee 2000, 2001b; Bacchetta 2000; Jeanne and Wyplosz 2001).
3. The insolvency of corporations or banks leads to a debt-financed bailout (Corsetti, Pesenti, and Roubini 1999; Burnside, Eichenbaum, and Rebelo 2001a, 2001c). The increase in public debt is financed by a monetization, causing the exchange rate to depreciate.

Of these three stories, the one that is easiest to incorporate in our framework is the argument that low future output leads to depreciated exchange rates. In the context of our framework, this is convenient because it does not matter whether the output disruption comes from a credit crunch or from a banking crisis. To complete the argument, one must merely show (or assume) that the monetary authorities would want to partly accommodate the output collapse by allowing the second-period exchange rate to depreciate. One story (Jeanne and Wyplosz 2001) is that this might be optimal in order to minimize real disruptions if the authorities face a Phillips curve–type trade-off in the second period.

The debt monetization argument could also be adapted to close our stylized framework. In the context of banking crises, it provides a simple alternative rationale for why one might expect a jump in the money supply and thus a depreciation of the exchange rate. Similarly, one could assume that the government guarantees and ultimately monetizes the liabilities of insolvent corporations, as in Corsetti, Pesenti, and Roubini 1999. Finally, if the ex post problem is not bank or corporate insolvencies per se but rather low investment, one could assume that the government wishes to undertake offsetting fiscal measures that ultimately lead to higher inflation, or that low investment and low output reduce direct tax revenue and force the government to rely more on the inflation tax, driving up the exchange rate.

The real exchange rate depreciations of Krugman (1999), Chang and Velasco (2000), and Schneider and Tornell (2001) cannot be directly represented in our framework, since they require a nonmonetary, two-good model. However, they give rise to essentially the same link. In the credit-crunch story, low investment depreciates the real exchange rate in either the same period or in the future, either because investment is in home goods, or because it is critical to the future production of tradable goods. The same link applies in the banking-crisis version of the model, except that it is the collapse of the banking system that triggers the credit crunch rather than low corporate net worth directly.

In short, low corporate net worth, underinvestment, or banking crises can be linked to exchange rate depreciation in multiple ways. In the next section, we will focus on policy implications of our balance-sheet framework for which the precise nature of this link is not critical. Consequently, we confine ourselves to assuming such a link in reduced form:

$$(7) \qquad\qquad S_2 = G(x) \qquad G' > 0,$$

where x stands for either the number of runs, n (in the banking-crisis model), or the investment gap u (in the credit-crunch model).

Equilibria

Putting together the pieces derived in the last three sections, equation (7) defines the link from real economic disruptions to the second-period exchange rate, while equations (3) and (6) define the links from the expected second-period exchange rate to bank runs or underinvestment, respectively. In a rational expectations equilibrium, expected and actual exchange rates must be the same. Since (7), (3), and (6) all describe increasing functions, the models generically give rise to multiple equilibria, as shown in figure 4.1.

Except for the suggested shapes of the bank-run and credit-crunch functions (which are derived from a cumulative distribution function in the first case but not in the second), the left and right figures are very similar. In each case, there are two stable equilibria: a "good" equilibrium with low disruptions and an appreciated exchange rate (A), and a "bad" one with complete disruption and a depreciated exchange rate (C). The middle equilibrium B is not stable.

Policy Implications

What are the complications arising from the presence of balance-sheet effects? It is useful to distinguish between two classes of problems.

First, even without feedback effects, the link from the expected exchange rate to net worth complicates optimal policy responses to exogenous shocks.

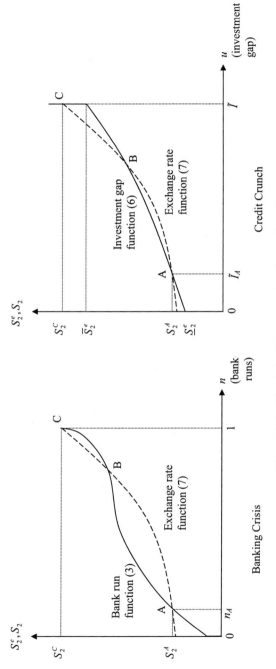

Figure 4.1 Equilibria in banking crises and credit-crunch models

Specifically, the currency mismatch in balance sheets can magnify the impact of shocks that have little to do with balance sheets originally. An exogenous deterioration in the fundamentals that makes a depreciation more likely (say, an adverse terms-of-trade shock) disrupts the real economy by decreasing the net worth of firms and banks with a currency mismatch in their balance sheets. As argued above, this can lead to bank runs and/or a collapse in investment and thus a further deterioration in the fundamentals. Whether standard policy prescriptions on how to deal with balance of payments shocks still apply is not obvious. In general, the optimal policy response—and in particular, whether monetary policy should be tightened or loosened, and whether exchange rates should be allowed to respond—will depend on the magnitude of the shock, the extent of the underlying balance-sheet vulnerability, and the remaining structure of the model (see Céspedes, Chang, and Velasco 2001, 2002, and chapter 2 in this volume and Christiano, Gust, and Roldos 2002 for two different approaches to this problem).

The presence of a feedback effect from balance sheets to exchange rates creates a further complication because of the possibility of self-fulfilling crises. In the framework outlined above, we have two stable equilibria, one of which dominates the other in output terms. Expectations of depreciated future exchange rates can lead to low net worth, low future output, and depreciated exchange rates, which validate the initial expectations. The potential task for policy is then somewhat different: rather than looking at the optimal reaction of policy to exogenous shock in the presence of a new channel through which shocks are transmitted, the question is how policy can be used to rule out the crisis equilibrium. This is the policy question on which we concentrate in the remainder of this chapter.

Exchange Rate Regimes and Dollarization

In principle, the problems described in the previous section can arise both under pegs and in floating regimes. What is important is the possibility of an adverse shift in expectations about future exchange rates, S_2^e. This could be either an expected devaluation (in a pegged regime) or just a depreciation (in a floating regime). Conditional on given balance-sheet mismatches, what matters is not the nature of the exchange rate regime per se, but the likelihood that the monetary authorities will resist a depreciation of the domestic currency. In particular, an exchange rate regime that credibly fixes S_2 removes self-fulfilling crises for all the specifications of our framework (in fig. 4.1, this would imply a completely horizontal exchange rate function [7], intersecting functions [3] and [6] in point A only). This could be an argument in favor of full dollarization: if a country permanently adopts the dollar as its currency, the currency mismatch problem disappears.

However, there are two caveats to this argument.

First, in our framework, the possibility of self-fulfilling currency crises disappears only if dollarization is viewed as sufficiently hard to reverse. If there is any chance that the economy will be "re-pesified" in an economic crisis, then dollarization is no different in principle from any other hard peg. Whether it makes a difference will depend on whether dollarization introduces costs to devaluation, from the perspective of the monetary authorities, that exceed those of other pegged regimes. In terms of figure 4.1, the question is whether the exchange rate function becomes sufficiently flat that equilibrium B disappears. Depending on what one thinks about the reversibility of dollarization, this may or may not be the case.

Second, there are versions of the balance-sheet approach to international financial crises that involve no currency at all (in particular, Krugman 1999; Chang and Velasco 2000; Schneider and Tornell 2001). In these models, the currency-mismatch problem is replaced by the assumption that the net worth of domestic firms depends on revenues from the sale of home (or nontradable) goods, and the role of the nominal exchange rate in our framework is assumed by the real exchange rate. Adverse expectational shifts no longer refer to the value of the currency, but rather to real economic variables such as the level of investment, the level of domestic demand for home goods, or the domestic supply of tradable goods. In these circumstances, multiple equilibria can arise even if the economy is fully and irreversibly dollarized, taking the argument that the exchange rate regime is irrelevant to the possibility of balance-sheet crises one step further.

Finally, it bears repeating that the view that the exchange rate regime is irrelevant is correct only as long as balance-sheet mismatches themselves are not endogenous to the currency regime. It is sometimes argued that flexible exchange rate regimes reduce currency mismatches because they encourage hedging in the corporate and banking sectors (Burnside, Eichenbaum, and Rebelo 2001b, 2001c; Goldstein 2002). If this were true, a flexible regime would be preferable because it reduces the underlying balance-sheet problem. As an empirical matter, however, the argument remains controversial,[5] and it is outside the scope of our analysis, which takes mismatches as a given.

In the remainder of this chapter, we assume that the simple solution to currency mismatches—irrevocable dollarization—is either unfeasible or undesirable for reasons outside our model. This forces us to consider the scope of economic policies in an environment that in principle allows for the possibility of adverse exchange rate expectations, taking mismatches as a given. We begin with a discussion of domestic policy and then turn to the potential roles for international lending.

Monetary Policy

Can domestic monetary policy in a floating exchange rate regime deal with the basic inefficiency introduced by the presence of foreign-currency debt, that is, eliminate the equilibrium at point C? In the two examples considered so far, the answer is clearly no. This can be seen from the fact that the peso interest rate, i, does not appear in the balance-sheet expressions (2) and (4). In the examples we have focused on so far, monetary policy is thus irrelevant: net worth is *entirely independent* of how domestic interest rates are set. This extreme result is a consequence of the assumption that $R_1 = D_1 = D_2 = 0$, which implies that net peso income in the first period $(R_1 - D_1)$ is zero. As a result, net worth in equations (2) and (4)—given international interest rates and dollar assets and liabilities—depends only on today's dollar value of *future* pesos, that is, on

$$\frac{R_2}{(1 + i^*)S_2^e} \equiv \frac{(1 + i)}{(1 + i^*)S_2^e} \cdot \frac{R_2}{(1 + i)} = \frac{1}{S_1} \cdot \frac{R_2}{(1 + i)}.$$

Raising the interest rate appreciates the exchange rate today and thus the dollar value of peso income today, but at the same time it reduces the peso value of future peso income. If the period 1 net peso cash flow is zero, the two effects cancel out, and domestic monetary policy is impotent. For an increase in interest rates to be the right policy response, the agent must have a positive net cash flow in terms of pesos in period 1, whose dollar value is increased by the appreciation (or which can be invested at the high interest rate, to put it in another way). This can be seen by going back to the net worth definition (1):

$$(8) \qquad W^* = \frac{R_2 - D_2}{(1 + i^*)S_2^e} + \frac{(R_1 - D_1)(1 + i)}{(1 + i^*)S_2^e} + R^* - D^*.$$

The first and the last two terms on the right-hand side are independent of domestic monetary policy, and the impact of domestic interest rates works entirely through first-period net income.

Does the more general balance-sheet structure underlying equation (8) still give rise to multiple equilibria, and could domestic monetary policy be used to eliminate the "bad" equilibrium? It depends. Consider first the bank-run model, which assumed that banks are heterogeneous in terms of their balance-sheet characteristics. There is obviously a trivial case where $R_1 - D_1$ is greater than zero for all banks. In this case, defending the first-period exchange rate—that is, tightening monetary policy in the face of an adverse shift in expectations—will always work: no matter how depreciated S_2^e is, there is always a sufficiently high interest rate so that positive net worth can be restored. But this is not the case when banks are heterogeneous in the sense that $R_1 - D_1$ is greater than zero for some but smaller than zero for others. Assume that in this case the central bank sets i to minimize the number of bank runs, that is, the share of banks with positive net worth, taking S_2^e as given. Denote the central bank's reaction function by $i(S_2^e)$, and by $N(S_2^e)$ the corresponding number of insolvent banks. Then, assuming that $R^* - D^* < 0$, it is easy to see that $N(S_2^e)$ is monotonically increasing in S_2^e.[6] The only difference relative to the previous section is that $N(S_2^e)$ is bounded from above by the fraction of banks for which $R_1 - D_1 < 0$, since it is always possible to maintain the solvency of the other banks through a sufficiently tough interest rate defense. Thus, if the exchange rate function (7) is steep enough (see fig. 4.1), multiple equilibria ill continue to exist. While monetary policy can minimize the impact of adverse exchange rate expectations on the banking system in the first period, it cannot prevent bank runs from occurring. Since the share of banks that suffer from runs remains a positive function of exchange rate expectations, monetary policy will not, in general, be able to rule out self-fulfilling crises.

The same logic can be applied to the credit-crunch model. Again, there is a trivial case where an interest rate defense always works: this is the case when $R_1 - D_1 > 0$ holds for all firms. If $R_1 - D_1$ is greater than zero for some firms but smaller than zero for others, then there will again be an optimal first-period monetary policy that seeks to minimize the damage from adverse exchange rate expectations. In this case, the policy would set the interest rate so as to maximize the volume of investment at any given S_2^e. Denote this maximum volume $I(S_2^e)$. Using an argument exactly analogous to the one in note 3, it can be shown that $I(S_2^e)$ is decreasing in S_2^e, that is, that the investment gap is increasing in S_2^e (again, the critical property is that for any given interest rate, net worth is falling in S_2^e). As a result, figure 4.1 still applies, and multiple equilibria will still exist in general.

The main conclusion is thus that monetary policy will be rendered ineffective, in the sense that it cannot protect the economy from adverse shifts in expectations with real costs, for a wide range of balance-sheet problems. However, this conclusion is subject to two caveats.

The first caveat refers to assuming UIP. For given exchange rate expectations S_2^e, UIP implies that interest rate policy and exchange rate policy are one and the same thing. This rules out a strategy in which the central bank seeks to prop up net worth by *both* maintaining the interest rate low *and* the exchange rate appreciated. In particular, sterilized intervention—selling dollars in the open market, while keeping interest rates constant—is ineffective.

As was mentioned earlier, there are plausible violations of UIP that would impose an even tighter constraint on monetary policy, for example, if risk premia tend to move together with exchange rate expectations and net worth. But UIP might also be violated in the sense that perfect capital mobility does not hold, either because foreign and domestic bonds are not perfect substitutes, or because of capital controls. Everything else equal, this would mitigate the impact of adverse shifts in exchange rate expectations and increase the power of monetary policy. Within certain bounds, the monetary authorities may be able to control both interest rates and exchange rates; that is, sterilized intervention might be feasible.[7] Whether this would be enough to eliminate the "bad" equilibrium in figure 4.1 is of course an open issue; it depends on the degree to which sterilized intervention is feasible.

A second channel that we have implicitly ruled out is the possibility that monetary policy could directly affect the net flows—in particular, through an effect on peso income—that make up the bank and firm balance sheets in our model. Again, dropping this assumption would weaken our conclusions but may not overturn them. Assume, for example, that some units in the economy are never constrained in their investment or spending, and that the first-period income R_1 of the banks or firms we have considered so far depends on spending by these units. Then, by lowering interest rates, the monetary authorities might be able to stimulate R_1 directly, in addition to changing the net present value of R_2 and D_2. In itself, this need not invalidate the conclusions; it just adds one additional channel that the monetary authorities have to consider when optimally setting first-period interest rates in an environment of heterogeneous agents. However, it is of course possible to conceive of a situation where this "direct revenue effect" of monetary policy is so strong that it maintains high net worth for a wide range of second-period exchange rate expectations, and eliminates the "bad" equilibrium.[8] This is just saying that the analysis presented in this chapter should be viewed as relevant to situations where balance-sheet effects are important relative to more traditional channels for monetary policy.

Fiscal Policy

To discuss fiscal policy, it is necessary to introduce the government into our framework. In the following, we limit ourselves to a simple extension in which we assume that government spending subject to an intertemporal budget constraint can in principle make up for the bad effects of bank runs and/or private underinvestment. The problem is that this constraint may become binding in a balance-sheet crisis, limiting the government's capacity to deal with the consequences of adverse exchange rate expectations just when it is needed most. Thus, economy-wide balance-sheet mismatches could place limitations on the use of fiscal policy that are similar in flavor to the ones discussed for monetary policy in the preceding section.

The simplest way to introduce the government in our framework is as an additional agent alongside firms or banks, subject to its own net worth constraint. In principle, there are two channels through which this government could break the vicious circle that leads to self-fulfilling runs: in the first period, through measures to limit the banking crisis (through bank recapitalization) or the investment gap; in the second period, by altering the feedback from these disruptions to future exchange rates. Since we have not modeled the latter except through the reduced form relationship assumed in equation (7), we focus on the former.

To maximize the potential beneficial impact from fiscal policy, we abstract from the possibility that the government itself could be subject to runs. This means assuming that government net worth, W_G^*, is described by equation (4) (the net worth constraint for firms, with no short-term dollar debt) rather than

(2) (the net worth constraint for banks). In the government context, local-currency receipts R could be interpreted as taxes, while local-currency liabilities D could be interpreted either as domestic debt or as expenditures (say, entitlements). The government may or may not have foreign-currency liabilities—the arguments that follow require a private-sector balance-sheet mismatch, but not necessarily an additional currency mismatch in the government balance sheet.

We focus on the credit-crunch story (an analogous argument could be made for the bank-run story). In principle, there are three avenues through which the government could mitigate the aggregate investment shortfall: first, by improving the net worth position of firms through either transfers or a tax cut; second, through public investment; and third, as an additional source of lending for credit-constrained private firms. The first two of these channels are about fiscal policy as it is conventionally understood, and assuming that private and public investment are perfect substitutes, they are essentially equivalent. In contrast, the third channel is somewhat different. Here the government does not actually spend funds but serves as a financial intermediary, borrowing from capital markets and lending to firms. In practice, we rarely see the government performing such functions, presumably because they require specialized monitors, such as commercial banks. We thus focus on the conventional fiscal policy channels, but briefly return to the financial intermediation story below.

Assume that the government can increase the aggregate net worth of firms either through a first-period tax cut or an increase in transfers, constrained only by its own net worth. If we assume that the government can borrow up to its net worth, this is the same as saying that the government can finance an increase in aggregate investment subject to its intertemporal budget constraint. If the government's objective is to close the economy-wide investment gap as far as possible, the aggregate gap will then be defined as in equation (6), except that investment is now constrained by *total* private- and public-sector borrowing capacity, $\max\{0, \mu W^*(S_2^e)\} + \max\{0, W_G^*(S_2^e)\}$, and the thresholds $\underline{S}_2^e$ and $\overline{S}_2^e$ are redefined as the exchange rates at which total rather than private borrowing capacity becomes equal to $\tilde{I}$ and equal to zero, respectively.

$$(6')\quad u \equiv \tilde{I} - I =$$

$$\begin{cases} \tilde{I} & \text{if} \quad S_2^e \geq \overline{S}_2^e \\ \tilde{I} - \max\{0, \mu W^*(S_2^e)\} + \max\{0, W_G^*(S_2^e)\} & \text{if} \quad \overline{S}_2^e > S_2^e > \underline{S}_2^e \\ 0 & \text{if} \quad \underline{S}_2^e \geq S_2^e \end{cases}$$

Comparing $(6')$ and (6), it is clear that the effect of the investment subsidies is to shift the investment-gap function up. The thresholds $\underline{S}_2^e$ and $\overline{S}_2^e$ must be at least as high as before, and for each exchange rate level at which the private sector is credit constrained, the investment gap must be smaller than before (strictly smaller if the government has strictly positive net worth at that exchange rate level). But is it enough to eliminate the bad equilibrium? The answer depends on the solvency of the government, as illustrated in figure 4.2.

If the upward shift in the investment-gap function relative to figure 4.1 is small (case 1), then the presence of an investment subsidy policy will lower the investment gap conditional on the good equilibrium (point A) and may remove it altogether, but it does not rule out the inferior equilibrium (point C). In this case, pooling the government borrowing capacity with that of the private sector does not add all that much. Case 2 illustrates a situation where the extra borrowing capacity makes a big difference. At the equilibrium exchange rate level corresponding to point C in case 1, the case 2 investment gap is just a little too small to validate the depreciated exchange rate level. Thus, there is a unique equilibrium at A.

A similar effect could be achieved by government *lending* to individual firms rather than fiscal policy. Since the underlying market failure is one of coordination among private creditors, the government can reduce this failure by acting as a large financial intermediary, lending to firms in the amount of the difference between their borrowing capacity conditional on the "good" equilibrium outcome, and their actual borrowing given expected exchange rates. However, as long as the government relies on funds borrowed in the capital markets, this lending policy can never be more effective in removing the "bad" equilibrium than the fiscal policy described above, since the same economy-wide borrowing constraint will apply as in equation (6'). While government intermediation could overcome the private-creditor coordination failure with respect to firms, it remains constrained by a private-creditor coordination failure with respect to its *own* borrowing.

The lesson is that the government can improve matters—be it through tax cuts, transfers, public investment, lending, or bank recapitalization—only if it is "solvent enough" even in the adverse circumstances of a balance-sheet crisis. This solvency standard is much more stringent than the conventional definition of fiscal solvency, which typically refers to positive government net worth conditional on current exchange rates. In contrast, being solvent enough to rule out a self-fulfilling balance-sheet crisis means having sufficiently high positive net worth to close the investment gap (or recapitalize banks), *even conditional on the depreciated (crisis) exchange rate.*

We have so far assumed that government net worth is given for any second-period exchange rate level. However, fiscal policy may have some control over government net worth through measures to cut expenditures or improve tax administration. To the extent that applying these measures pushes government solvency over the critical threshold where the country is no longer vulnerable to adverse shifts in expectations, fiscal adjustment could make sense as a preventive measure. Of course, if policy measures of this kind are applied at the

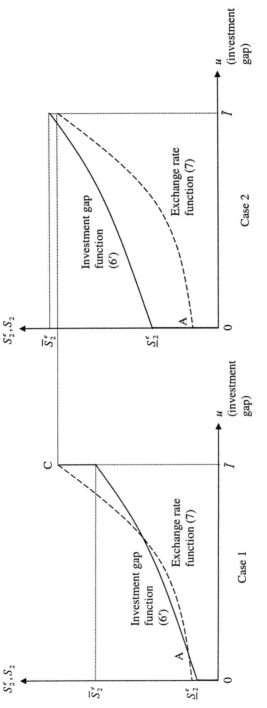

Figure 4.2 Equilibria in credit-crunch model with government

onset of a crisis, they will work only if their direct contractionary effects on output do not fully offset the expansionary benefits of the activities that they are meant to finance, namely, investment and/or bank recapitalization.

International Crisis Lending

International crisis lending is the one area in which the distinction between the credit-crunch channel and the bank-run channel of balance-sheet crises really matters. We begin by restating the Jeanne-Wyplosz (2001) argument about international lending as support of last-resort lending targeted to specific banks, and then turn to the question of how, if at all, international lending might play a role in the context of the credit-crunch model.

Throughout the section, we interpret "international crisis lending" as international *official* crisis lending. However, this is merely a reflection of the fact that in the past, large-scale lending to emerging market governments during a crisis has come mainly from official sources, namely international financial institutions and in some cases, bilateral creditors. What is essential in our framework is merely that the lender be *large*, in the sense that it acknowledges the endogeneity of exchange rates to its lending. In principle, a syndicate of banks could be a large lender in this sense. In practice, however, contingent credit lines from banks or bank syndicates have been rare, so there seem to be difficulties in placing large-scale crisis lending in the hands of the private sector (for reasons outside our framework).

Bank Runs

One feature of the "bad" equilibrium C in figure 4.1 is that both "truly insolvent" banks (those that have negative net worth even at the appreciated second-period exchange rate S_2^A associated with the "good" equilibrium) and "conditionally solvent" banks (those that would have positive net worth in "normal" circumstances, i.e., for $S_2 = S_2^A$) suffer from runs. Now suppose the domestic monetary authorities announce a policy of either lending dollars to conditionally solvent institutions that need them in the event of a run, or guarantees on the dollar deposits of these institutions.[9] If the monetary authorities have enough reserves to back these policies, both of these policies would eliminate the "bad" equilibrium by guaranteeing the continuing operation of conditionally solvent banks. "Truly insolvent" institutions would still suffer from runs and collapse, but their collapse, by definition, is consistent with the relatively appreciated exchange rate S_2^A. The bad equilibrium disappears because the banking collapses that are allowed by the authorities are too minor to validate depreciated exchange rate expectations.

More formally, let n denote the number of bank *collapses* and n_A the number of banks that collapse even in the "good" equilibrium A, that is, the "truly

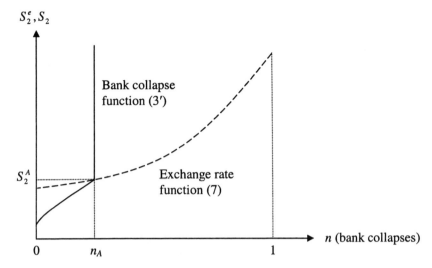

Figure 4.3 Equilibrium in banking-crisis model with last-resort lending

insolvent" banks.[10] The effect of the authorities' intervention policies is to place
an upper bound on the number of banks that can collapse:

(3′) $$n = \min\{n_A, F(S_2^e)\},$$

where $F(S_2^e)$ is defined as before, that is, as the mass of banks that become insolvent at a given expected exchange rate. Equation (3′) guarantees that the
number of banking collapses will never exceed those that occur in the "good
equilibrium," which is unique, as can be seen from figure 4.3.

To the extent that the domestic monetary authorities have insufficient reserves to cover the foreign-currency liquidity gap (i.e., $R_1^* - D_1^*$) for each of the
conditionally solvent banks, this way of ruling out the "bad" equilibrium provides a natural justification for an international lender of last resort. Thus, the
role of international lending in the bank-run model is to lend dollars to the domestic monetary authorities in sufficient amounts to enable it to implement the
domestic financial safety net described above.

Credit Crunch

Does the relatively straightforward role for international crisis lending that
arises in the bank-crisis model carry over to the credit-crunch model? The answer is clearly no. In the credit-crunch model there are no runs, and consequently there is no role for a domestic financial safety net that might require
foreign backing. The problem is not that conditionally solvent institutions go

belly up: in the credit-crunch model, such institutions make it to the second period, since they have no short-run dollar liabilities. Instead, real costs arise from
the fact that net worth constrains investment.

In this context, the potential role for international lending is quite different
from the bank-crisis case. Two possible channels seem worth considering.

Logically, the most straightforward mechanism would be one where access
to international official financing—either directly or through the intermediation of the government—substitutes for the lack of access to private credit
markets when firms are net worth constrained. As Krugman (1999, 42) observes, official "credit lines would have to do more than provide balance-of-
payments financing, or even provide lender-of-last-resort facilities to banks:
they would have to make up the credit being lost by firms, so as to allow investment to continue." To implement the "good" equilibrium in our framework, each credit-constrained firm would need to receive an official loan in the
amount of the difference between what it could borrow in the "good" equilibrium and what it can borrow in the capital market, that is, $\mu W^*(S_2^A)$ –
$\mu W^*(S_2^c)$. In this case, the "investment gap" would be capped at u_A, the level associated with the good equilibrium (see fig. 4.1), and investment-gap function
(7) from figure 4.1 would be replaced by a new function that looks exactly like
the bank collapse function (3') depicted in figure 4.3.

One difficulty with this approach is that the lender needs to know not just
whether a firm is "conditionally solvent," but its net worth both in current circumstances and in a hypothetical "normal" state. Governments are not generally equipped to collect this information, much less international lenders. Perhaps for this reason, we see comparatively little direct financial intermediation
from the government, and little direct lending from official lenders to private-
sector firms in emerging markets. While there are some exceptions, such as
lending to private corporations by the International Finance Corporation and
some of the regional development banks, these seem to be motivated by credit
constraints associated with the underdevelopment of domestic financial markets and political risk (which may be lower for official lenders), rather than the
temporary exclusion from private capital markets owing to adverse currency
expectations or capital account reversals.

An alternative channel, which may be more relevant, is to use international
lending to loosen fiscal constraints, that is, to enable the government to run a
fiscal policy that is more supportive of aggregate investment than it otherwise
could in crisis times. In the example outlined in the previous section, this would
work as follows: The international lender would announce that for any exchange
rate in excess of the "good" equilibrium level, it is prepared to extend credit to
the government in the amount that it could borrow from private markets in the
"good" (appreciated) equilibrium. The effect of this policy is to cap the overall
investment gap at $\tilde{I}$ minus the government net worth arising in the "good"

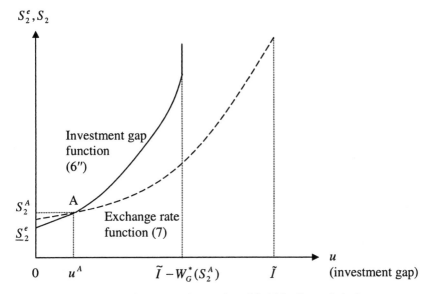

Figure 4.4 Equilibrium in credit-crunch model with lending to the budget

equilibrium, $W_G^*(S_2^A)$. Assuming that $W_G^*(S_2^A)$ and $W^*(S_2^A)$ are strictly positive, equation (6′) becomes

(6″) $u \equiv \tilde{I} - I =$

$$\begin{cases} \tilde{I} - \max\{0, \mu W^*(S_2^e)\} - W_G^*(S_2^A) & \text{if} & S_2^e \geq S_2^A \\ \tilde{I} - \mu W^*(S_2^e) - W_G^*(S_2^e) & \text{if} & S_2^A > S_2^e > \underline{S}_2^e \\ 0 & \text{if} & \underline{S}_2^e \geq S_2^e \end{cases},$$

where $\underline{S}_2^e$ is defined as before, that is, as the exchange rate level where the economy can borrow in the full amount $\tilde{I}$. Comparing (6′) and (6″), it is evident that below $S_2^e = S_2^A$ the investment gap is unchanged, that is, the same economy-wide borrowing constraint applies. In this appreciated region, no crisis lending takes place. Above $S_2^e = S_2^A$, however, international crisis lending allows a higher level of investment. Thus, the presence of the official lender has the effect of "kinking up" the investment-gap schedule at $u = u^A$. This could remove the bad equilibrium, as shown in figure 4.4. In equilibrium, net worth $W_G^*(S_2^A)$ materializes, enabling the large lender to be fully repaid.

Note, however, that unlike last-resort lending in the bank-run case, international lending to the fiscal authorities does not inevitably remove the bad equilibrium. In figure 4.4, we could have drawn the investment-gap function (6″) such that the maximum investment gap $\tilde{I} - W_G^*(S_2^A)$ is close enough to $\tilde{I}$ to give rise to a second intersection of (6″) with exchange rate function (7). The figure would then look much like case 1 in figure 4.2, and multiple equilibria would continue to exist. The critical parameter that determines whether international lending to the fiscal authorities removes the "bad" equilibrium in the credit-crunch model is $W_G^*(S_2^A)$, the net worth of the government in the "good" equilibrium.

The main conclusion from this section is that although credit crunches and banking crises play analogous roles in our framework and have similar causes—a coordination failure in capital markets, made possible by the underlying fragility of balance sheets—the implications for international crisis lending are quite different. In the bank-crisis model, the coordination failure can be removed completely using discount-window-type last-resort lending, backed by the foreign exchange reserves provided by an international agency such as the International Monetary Fund. An analogous policy in the credit-crunch case would be firm-specific crisis lending in the full amount of the investment short-fall, but there does not seem to be a plausible real-world counterpart for this type of lending. A more plausible mechanism is lending to the budget, allowing a more expansionary fiscal policy, which raises aggregate investment. In this case, however, the volume of crisis lending will be constrained by *government* net worth conditional in the "good" equilibrium, as opposed to economy-wide net worth. Depending on the solvency of the government in noncrisis times, this may or may not be enough to rule out the "bad" equilibrium.

To summarize: conditional on private balance-sheet mismatches, the presence of a crisis lender helps the government protect the economy from balance-sheet crises along two dimensions. First, a central bank that can borrow reserves internationally does not need to hold reserves itself to rule out runs on conditionally solvent banks. Second, the presence of official crisis lending reduces the standard of fiscal solvency that must be met to make a country immune to balance-sheet crises. Without a crisis lender, the government needs to be "su-persolvent," in the sense that government net worth *in the circumstances of a crisis* (i.e., conditional on depreciated exchange rates and/or high interest rates) needs to be sufficiently large to make up for the shortfall in private-sector net worth. With a crisis lender, it is sufficient if government net worth in *normal,* noncrisis times balances this shortfall.

Conclusion

This chapter has focused on a particular risk generated by currency and maturity mismatches in corporate and financial sector balance sheets: the risk of self-fulfilling financial and currency crises. Even within the confines of this focus, we find a surprising variety of models with sometimes quite different policy implications. To the practitioner, the balance-sheet approach might seem to involve a mind-boggling range of policies (from fiscal policy to lending in last resort). On this basis, one could conclude that the "balance-sheet approach" is difficult to specify, and does not result in a well-defined approach to dealing with emerging market crises.

However, as we have tried to show in a stylized framework that encompasses the main ideas from a number of models, this variety masks some common themes. We have focused on two. First, balance-sheet vulnerabilities place tight constraints on the capacity of domestic policies (monetary and fiscal) to deal with capital account crises. Second, the fact that balance-sheet crises cannot take place without a coordination failure among private creditors implies a potentially important role for large-scale crisis lending, moral-hazard concerns notwithstanding.

The main results of this chapter are elaborations of these two themes. They can be summarized in six points.

1. Conditional on the presence of private-sector balance-sheet vulnerabilities—in particular, currency mismatches—balance-sheet crises are largely independent of the exchange rate regime.
2. Private-sector balance-sheet mismatches put monetary policy in a bind. If it defends the exchange rate by raising interest rates, it will lower the present value of future domestic-currency income. If it lets the exchange rate go, it will lower the *dollar* value of both current and discounted future income. If firms or banks have dollar liabilities, there is a problem either way. In general, there will be a trade-off, so that for a given balance-sheet structure of the private sector, there is a monetary policy that minimizes the damage from an adverse shift in exchange rate expectations. But this minimal damage may still be big enough to trigger a crisis in which the currency collapses.
3. Even assuming that there are fiscal policy measures that directly limit the crisis—for example, public investment, transfers or tax cuts that support the capacity of private firms to undertake investment, or recapitalization of insolvent banks—the government may not be able to take enough of these measures because it cannot finance them (other than through monetization of debt). This is because its *own* net worth, and thus its ability to borrow, are likely to be constrained in a crisis because of high interest rates and/or depreciated exchange rate expectations.
4. The preceding argument implies that there are benefits of a fiscal adjustment prior to the crisis, if this puts the government over the threshold where it can take measures that limit crisis damage to an extent that invalidates any adverse shift in expectations. Note that the implicit solvency standard is very high, since the government must be able to finance these measures *in crisis circumstances,* that is, conditional on depreciated exchange rates.
5. International crisis lending can help in two ways that are quite different, depending on the nature of the balance-sheet crisis. In the context of bank runs, it can lend to domestic monetary authorities in the amount needed to

operate a dollar discount window, or guarantee the dollar deposits of "conditionally solvent" banks (i.e., banks that have positive net worth in "normal" times). This limits bank runs to the "truly insolvent" banks, and prevents the bad state in which even conditionally solvent banks collapse. In the context of a credit crunch, the international lender can loosen fiscal constraints, allowing the fiscal authorities to implement policies that mitigate the decline in aggregate investment. It does so by lending to the government in the amount that the government could borrow from private markets conditional on the realization of the good equilibrium, rather than conditional on actual (depreciated) exchange rate expectations.

6. While last-resort lending in a bank-run context fully removes the coordination failure that causes a self-fulfilling crisis, crisis lending to the budget may not. This is because the level of official crisis lending to the budget is constrained by the government's precrisis solvency. While the presence of a large official lender in crisis times obviates the need to hold foreign reserves in order to implement a domestic financial safety net, a sound fiscal position thus remains necessary if crisis lending to the budget is to have its desired effect.

Our analysis was limited in several important ways. First, we have looked at a special aspect of the question—the case where the crisis is self-fulfilling. Second, we took a purely ex post perspective. One must also think of how ex post policies change the financial structure ex ante. Then one has to compare the merits of stabilization policies ex post with those of regulation ex ante. Clearly a lot more research is needed before we can think of the balance-sheet approach to crises as a set of policy prescriptions—as opposed to a new way of thinking about crises.

Notes

We thank, without implication, Carlos Arteta, Barry Eichengreen, Ricardo Hausmann, Hélène Rey, Roberto Rigobon, and conference participants for helpful comments and suggestions. The views expressed in this chapter are those of the authors and do not necessarily represent those of the IMF or IMF policy.

1. See, among others, Dornbusch 1998; Krugman 1999, 2001; Pettis 2001; and recently Allen et al. 2002 and Calvo 2002.

2. On the banking-crisis channel, see Burnside, Eichenbaum, and Rebelo 2001c. On firm-level currency mismatches and investment, see Aguiar 2002 and Rodriguez 2002.

3. The role of UIP is to monotonically relate first-period interest rates to first-period exchange rates, given exchange rate expectations. As long as it preserves this link, assuming a more general form of UIP—or a specific violation of UIP—will not change the structure of our framework, and multiple equilibria remain possible. For example, the results would go through if we allowed an exogenous risk premium, and would strengthen if the risk premium depended on economy-wide net worth—as in Céspedes, Chang, and Velasco 2002, and chapter 2 in this volume—or directly on exchange rate expecta-

tions. That said, the presence of a "wedge" in the UIP relationship may also enhance the effectiveness of monetary policy in dealing with adverse shifts in exchange rate expectations, a point to which we return below.

4. Because of the currency mismatch, this is true regardless of whether net worth is expressed in dollars or in pesos. The fact that we express net worth in dollars is merely a convention.

5. Consistent with the view that flexible exchange rates reduce mismatches, Martinez and Werner (2002) find that after the 1994 currency collapse and adoption of a floating regime, Mexican corporations reduced their unhedged foreign-currency exposure. In a cross-country study, however, Arteta (2002) finds that flexible regimes are associated with a higher share of dollar deposits but not dollar credit. According to that study, exchange rate flexibility thus seems to exacerbate currency mismatches in the banking system.

6. Because the net worth of *all* banks is decreasing with S_2^e, it cannot be the case that the monetary authorities manage to reduce the number of bank runs when S_2^e increases (if they could, this would mean that interest rate policy was not optimal to begin with).

7. To give one example, consider a proportional tax t on capital inflows. Then, from the first-period perspective of (risk-neutral) foreigners, flows into the country will not occur if $(1 + i^*) > (1 + i) \cdot (1 - t)(S_1/S_2^e)$. Conversely, from the perspective of residents who want to repatriate their investment in the second period, outflows will not occur if $(1 + i) > (1 + i^*) \cdot (1 - t)(S_1/S_2^e)$. It follows that there will be no flows as long as interest rates are in the range

$$\frac{(1 + i^*)}{(1 - t)} \frac{S_2^e}{S_1} > (1 + i) > (1 + i^*) \cdot (1 - t)\frac{S_2^e}{S_1}.$$

For given expectations S_2^e, the monetary authorities can manipulate interest rates in this range while keeping the exchange rate unchanged.

8. This would be the case if the effect of loose monetary policy on R_1 is so strong that it generates a positive first-period net cash flow $R_1 - D_1$ that is sufficiently large to outweigh the negative impact of the discounted second-period cash flow. In figure 4.1, this amounts to shifting the bank-run or investment gap functions up until they no longer intersect with the exchange rate function (except on the y-axis).

9. As argued by Jeanne and Wyplosz (2001), lending or selling dollars in the open market will not work because this amounts to a sterilized intervention, which is ineffective because of UIP (see above).

10. If the central bank's strategy is to guarantee dollar deposits of conditionally solvent banks, bank collapses and bank runs coincide (any run causes a collapse). In contrast, discount-window lending prevents the collapse of banks that suffer a run, so runs and collapses are not identical. With n defined as collapses rather than runs, equation (7) holds without change, reflecting the assumption that economic activity and the second-period exchange rate are determined by the number of banks that continue to operate.

References

Aghion, Philippe, Philippe Bacchetta, and Abhijit Banerjee. 2000. "A Simple Model of Monetary Policy and Currency Crises." *European Economic Review* 44:728–38.

————. 2001a. "A Corporate Balance Sheet Approach to Currency Crises." Working Paper no. 01.05, Studienzentrum Gerzensee, November.

————. 2001b. "Currency Crises and Monetary Policy in an Economy with Credit Constraints." *European Economic Review* 45:1121–50.

Aguiar, Mark. 2002. "Investment, Devaluation, and Foreign Currency Exposure: The Case of Mexico." Manuscript, University of Chicago, Graduate School of Business, September.

Allen, Mark, Christoph B. Rosenberg, Christian Keller, Brad Setser, and Nouriel Roubini. 2002. "A Balance Sheet Approach to Financial Crisis." IMF Working Paper 02/210, International Monetary Fund, Washington, DC, December.

Arteta, Carlos. 2002. "Exchange Rate Regimes and Financial Dollarization: Does Flexibility Reduce Bank Currency Mismatches?" International Finance Discussion Papers 738, Board of Governors of the Federal Reserve System, Washington, DC, September.

Bacchetta, Philippe. 2000. "Monetary Policy with Foreign Currency Debt." Manuscript, Studienzentrum Gerzensee, February.

Burnside, Craig, Martin Eichenbaum, and Sergio Rebelo. 2001a. "Government Guarantees and Self-Fulfilling Speculative Attacks." Manuscript, Northwestern University, Evanston, IL, September.

————. 2001b. "Hedging and Financial Fragility in Fixed Exchange Rate Regimes." *European Economic Review* 45:1151–93.

————. 2001c. "Prospective Deficits and the Asian Currency Crisis." *Journal of Political Economy* 109:1155–97.

Calvo, Guillermo. 2002. "Explaining Sudden Stops, Growth Collapse, and BOP Crisis: The Case of Distortionary Output Taxes." Mundell-Fleming Lecture, presented at the International Monetary Fund Annual Research Conference, Washington, DC.

Céspedes, Luis F., Roberto Chang, and Andrés Velasco. 2001. "Balance Sheets and Exchange Rate Policy." Manuscript. Revised version of "Balance Sheets and Exchange Rates," NBER Working Paper no. 7840, National Bureau of Economic Research, Cambridge, MA, 2000.

————. 2002. "Dollarization of Liabilities, Net Worth Effects, and Optimal Monetary Policy." In *Preventing Currency Crises in Emerging Markets*, ed. Sebastian Edwards and Jeffrey A. Frankel. Chicago: University of Chicago Press.

Chang, Roberto, and Andrés Velasco. 2000. "Liquidity Crises in Emerging Markets: Theory and Policy." In *NBER Macroeconomics Annual 1999*, ed. Ben S. Bernanke and Julio Rotemberg. Cambridge, MA: MIT Press.

Christiano, Lawrence J., Christopher Gust, and Jorge Roldos. 2002. "Monetary Policy in a Financial Crisis." NBER Working Paper no. 9005, National Bureau of Economic Research, Cambridge, MA.

Corsetti, Giancarlo, Paolo Pesenti, and Nouriel Roubini. 1999. "Paper Tigers? A Model of the Asian Crisis." *European Economic Review* 43:1211–36.

Diamond, Douglas W., and Philip H. Dybvig. 1983. "Bank Runs, Deposit Insurance, and Liquidity." *Journal of Political Economy* 91:401–19.

Dornbusch, Rudi. 1998. "After Asia: New Directions for the International Financial System." Massachusetts Institute of Technology, Cambridge, MA, http://web.mit.edu/rudi/www/media/PDFs/afterasia.pdf.

Eichengreen, Barry, and Ricardo Hausmann. 1999. "Exchange Rates and Financial Fragility." NBER Working Paper no. 7418, National Bureau of Economic Research, Cambridge, MA.

Goldstein, Morris. 2002. *Managed Floating Plus*. Washington, DC: Institute for International Economics.

Jeanne, Olivier, and Charles Wyplosz. 2001. "The International Lender of Last Resort: How Large Is Large Enough?" NBER Working Paper no. 8381, National Bureau of Economic Research, Cambridge, MA.

Krugman, Paul. 1999. "Balance Sheets, the Transfer Problem, and Financial Crises." In *International Finance and Financial Crises,* ed. Peter Isard, Assaf Razin, and Andrew K. Rose. Boston: Kluwer Academic; Washington, DC: International Monetary Fund.

———. 2001. "Crises: The Next Generation." Paper presented at a conference in honor of Assaf Razin, Tel Aviv University, March.

Martinez, Lorenza, and Alejandro Werner. 2002. "The Exchange Rate Regime and the Currency Composition of Corporate Debt: The Mexican Experience." *Journal of Development Economics* 69:315–34.

Pettis, Michael. 2001. *The Volatility Machine*. Oxford: Oxford University Press.

Rodriguez, Pedro. 2002. "On the Impact of Devaluations on Investment: The Role of Currency Mismatches: Evidence from Thai Firms." Manuscript, University of Maryland, College Park, February.

Schneider, Martin, and Aaron Tornell. 2001. "Boom Bust Cycles and the Balance Sheet Effect." Manuscript. Revised version of "Balance Sheet Effects, Bailout Guarantees, and Financial Crises," NBER Working Paper no. 8060, National Bureau of Economic Research, Cambridge, MA.

How Original Sin Was Overcome

The Evolution of External Debt Denominated in Domestic Currencies in the United States and the British Dominions, 1800–2000

Michael D. Bordo, Christopher M. Meissner,
and Angela Redish

THE RECENT spate of emerging market crises in Asia has focused attention on balance-sheet problems as a key source of instability (Larain and Velasco 2001). Many emerging countries today have difficulty in borrowing domestically long-term and are unable to borrow abroad (both sovereign and corporate debt) in terms of their own currencies. Consequently they need to borrow in dollars to access foreign capital markets. As discussed in several chapters in this volume, this state of affairs is often attributed to the absence of sound and credible fiscal and monetary policy and financial underdevelopment.

In the face of a currency crisis, a depreciating domestic currency leads to insolvency as firms and governments are unable to service their dollar debts. In addition, the inability to roll over short-term debt increases the prospects for default. Eichengreen and Hausmann (1999) refer to the inability to borrow abroad in terms of domestic currency and to borrow domestically long-term as "original sin." Some solutions to the problem they posit are to attain the financial maturity and fiscal probity required to have a nation's debt denominated in domestic currency, the imposition of capital controls, dollarization, or a currency union with an advanced country. In this volume Eichengreen, Hausmann, and Panizza highlight the role of international institutions in creating new markets.

The problem of original sin also plagued many of the emerging countries in the previous age of financial globalization, the half century preceding World War I. In that era, the peripheral countries of Europe, the Americas, and elsewhere had to borrow in sterling (or franc or guilder) denominated bonds or to have gold clauses in order to access loans from London (or Paris or Amsterdam). The gold clauses protected the lender against currency risk. They also may have served as a commitment mechanism (Bordo and Flandreau 2003).

In sharp contrast to the emerging countries' experience, a select number of countries today and in the past did not have the currency mismatch problem. These countries are able to issue debt in their own currency abroad, and their domestically issued domestic-currency debt is readily traded and held on foreign markets. Selling long-term domestic debt is not impossible. This also was the case for a number of advanced countries before 1914. Eight advanced countries had their bonds listed on the London Stock Exchange in their own currencies — the United Kingdom, France, the Netherlands, Belgium, the United States, Germany, Denmark, and Switzerland (Bordo and Flandreau 2003).[1] Today the list has expanded to twenty-five countries, most of which are in the OECD, with the peripheral additions of South Africa, Hong Kong, and Singapore.

A number of questions arise from this evidence, including, What factors determine membership in the club of countries who are free from original sin? What can countries do to enter this club? Is entry permanent or transitory? Under what circumstances does entry occur — in the face of big shocks like World War I or as part of a gradual evolution? Did countries free themselves from one component of original sin (e.g., by lengthening domestic debt maturity) but not the other? Finally, does the fact that a country has little external debt in terms of its own currency necessarily make it vulnerable to crises because of a currency mismatch?

This chapter attempts to provide some answers to these questions by conducting a historical case study for a group of countries that successfully entered the club and had largely overcome the problem of original sin by the third quarter of the twentieth century. The group consists of several former colonies of Great Britain: the United States, Canada, Australia, New Zealand, and South Africa. We trace out their debt history, relating the currency to the place of issue, exploring the residency of those holding local- and foreign-currency debt, and looking at the maturity of domestic debt in the nineteenth and twentieth centuries.

We treat the United States separately from the former dominions because its experience differed considerably from the common experience of the other four countries. The U.S. government was able to issue and market small amounts of dollar bonds abroad by the beginning of the nineteenth century. For the most part, U.S. sovereign debt had implicit or explicit gold clauses until 1933. States and corporations completely borrowed in dollars only by the late nineteenth century and always did so with gold clauses until the gold standard was finally abandoned under Roosevelt. The United States never had a serious problem issuing debt long-term.

The dominions largely shifted to domestic-currency external sovereign debt after 1973; Canada was the leader, so that by the 1950s nonresidents were willing to hold the majority of their Canadian debt in local currency. Previously these dominions had borrowed in sterling and U.S. dollars. However, all these countries issued significant amounts of domestic debt in terms of their own currencies by the 1920s, and their reliance on external debt therefore was quite limited. Finally, like the United States, the dominions rarely had difficulty in issuing long-term debt.

Then we consider the factors that may explain the evolution of the United States and the dominions to a state free of original sin. We find that sound fiscal institutions, high credibility of the monetary regime, and good financial development are not sufficient to completely break free from original sin. Conversely, poor performance in these policy realms is not, for the most part, a necessary condition for original sin. The factor we emphasize for the common movements across the five countries is the role of shocks such as wars, massive economic disruption, and the emergence of global markets. The differences in evolution between the United States and the dominions we attribute to differences in size, to the traits of a key currency, which the United States possessed and the others did not, and to membership in the British Empire. The important role of major shocks suggests that the establishment of a bond market involved significant start-up costs, while the role of scale suggests that network externalities and liquidity were pivotal in the existence of overseas markets in domestic-currency debt.

We conclude with the insight that, although none of these countries really was completely free from original sin in the nineteenth century in both the senses stressed by Eichengreen and Hausmann, they really were not vulnerable to the types of risk-creating financial crises that face today's emergers. Our five countries had all developed institutions by the mid-twentieth century that greatly reduced their vulnerability.

The United States

Today the United States is home to the world's largest financial center. Debt is mainly issued at home in dollars by domestic players. Dollar assets issued by U.S. entities are readily held abroad. Nearly all other countries issue some liabilities in U.S. dollars as well. Below we document the evolution of the main aspects of original sin: ability to issue debt abroad in domestic currency, the incidence of nonresident holdings of domestic-currency debt, and the maturity of domestic debt.

The U.S. government issued foreign-currency debt in the early years after the revolution, but paid it off relatively quickly, and subsequently never issued debt in foreign currencies. However, legal-tender laws that made only gold and silver coin legal tender meant that there were implicit specie clauses in dollar-denominated debt issues, as was the case in virtually all countries adhering to the gold standard. The issue of greenbacks during the Civil War led creditors to put explicit gold clauses in their bonds, until the federal government invalidated such clauses in 1933. Thus after 1933, U.S. dollar debt was free of *any* implicit or explicit gold-indexing or fixed exchange rate clauses. Foreign willing-ness to hold these domestic-currency assets free from any fixed constraints has no doubt increased since the 1930s.

Evidence on maturities shows that private companies, like the federal and state governments, have issued debt long-term domestically since the 1780s. The United States has certainly graduated from original sin. The question is, when did it do so?

Federal Government

Until the early part of the 1790s, American finances were in a shambles. The is-sue of paper currency (the "continentals") to finance the Revolutionary War led to high inflation and extensive depreciation of the American currency. By the end of the Revolutionary War, the U.S. position in terms of debt to revenues ranked among the worst of the sovereigns in Europe—comparable to Spain, the kingdom of Poland, and lesser German states.

Dutch financing helped the country out early on. One of the first foreign loans the United States placed was backed by France and sold in Amsterdam. Thus much of the early public debt during and after the American Revolution was denominated in Dutch florins and issued in the Netherlands.

The United States increasingly relied on domestic dollar loans with gold clauses beginning in the 1780s, but Alexander Hamilton's funding plan, part of a comprehensive financial package, set the stage for the successful issuance of dollar-denominated debt. Hamilton's funding plan created approximately $65 million in domestic debt, and at the same time provided for borrowing $12 million in Dutch florins. In the event, only $8 million in Dutch bonds were issued, and they were paid off, according to schedule, between 1800 and 1810. These were the last foreign-currency-denominated bonds issued by the United States until the late twentieth century.

Foreign-currency-denominated debt outstanding had become a relic by the time of the Louisiana Purchase in 1803 (tables 5.1 and 5.2).[2] From 1803 to 1853 the fraction of public debt held abroad declined somewhat (see table 5.3). By this time whatever was held abroad was dollar denominated. This debt, which

Table 5.1. U.S. dollar debt of the federal
government held abroad

	Nominal amount held abroad (US$ millions)	Percentage of total debt
1789	4	7
June 1803	32.1	46
Dec. 1803	43.0	53

Source: Wilkins 1989, 32, 36.

Note: All dollar debt would carry an implicit gold-index clause.

Table 5.2. Nominal U.S. federal government
debt outstanding in foreign currencies

	Nominal amount of foreign-currency-denominated debt (US$ millions)	Percentage of total debt outstanding
1789	11.7	21.6
1796	11.9	14
1804	5.7	6.5
1810	0	0

Source: Wilkins 1989, 35.

Table 5.3. Amounts and percentages of U.S.
federal debt held abroad, 1789–1884

	Amount of debt held abroad (US$ millions)	Percentage of total public debt
1789	15.7	29
1803	48.7	56
1828	19.1	33
1853	27.0	46
1880	249	12
1881	150	7.5
1884	100	6.0

Source: Wilkins 1989, 54, 147.

was issued primarily domestically, promised implicitly rather than explicitly to pay in specie, as far as we can tell.[3]

In the early years of the country, there is no evidence of short maturity structures at the federal level. We have data from Elliot (1968) on new issues between 1790 and 1843. Nearly all new issues up to about 1805 were payable "at the pleasure of the United States," and no new issue had a maturity of less than eight years. During periods of turmoil, we do see maturities decline from these high levels. Some other evidence also suggests a slight relapse into sin. In 1841 and coming on the heels of international defaults by eight states, the first subsequent federal issue had a maturity of four years. This did not last long. Issues in 1842 and 1843 fell due in twenty-one and ten years, respectively.

From the Civil War to World War I

The United States suspended specie convertibility during the Civil War in January 1862 and did not resume until January 1879. "Greenbacks" or federal legal tender fiat money operated as de facto fiat currency for the entire period throughout most of the United States with the principal exception of California, where gold coin and gold-backed notes circulated.

During the Civil War, the Union increased its debt by thirty times and the

Table 5.4. Various issues of the U.S. federal government

Issue	Year	Currency	Interest payable in
4.5% funded	1876	Dollars	Coin standard of the U.S.
4% funded	1877	Dollars	Coin standard of the U.S.
Three percents	1882	Dollars	Coin standard of the U.S.
4.5% loan of 1891	1891	Dollars	Coin standard of the U.S.
4% loan	1895	Dollars	Coin
3% loan	1898	Dollars	Gold coin
2% thirty year bonds	1900	Dollars	Gold coin

Source: Stock Exchange, various years.

debt to GDP ratio reached nearly 50 percent. Most of this debt was issued at home. Wilkins (1989) suggests that only about 10 percent of the Union debt ended up being held in Europe by 1864.

Despite the increase in the debt burden, the government continued to pay nearly all of its interest payments in gold at the historical parity. But investors faced uncertainty, because the legislation stating the method of paying interest and principal on loans fluctuated (Dewey 1920). Often it was unclear whether principal and interest would be repaid in paper or specie. From 1870 until about 1900, it was uncertain if interest and principal would be paid in gold or in silver.[4]

Exceptionally, the Loan Act of 1861 made no mention of how interest and principal would be paid. This debt, about 1 percent of the overall debt, was effectively payable in the fiat currency of the time (Friedman and Schwartz 1963, 27). How much of this was held abroad is unknown.[5]

Debt authorizations between 1862 and March 1864 stated that interest and principal were to be paid "in coin." The government declared in June 1864 that interest was to be paid in coin but made no explicit statement on principal, and the issue of March 3, 1865, echoed this. Other issues had explicit gold clauses on the interest payments and left out any information on how the principal would be repaid. Later issues declared interest and principal would be repaid in the coin standard of the United States of America. This variety of wording continued to be common until the late nineteenth century.

To reassure markets, Congress approved "An Act to Strengthen the Public Credit" in March 1869. The act declared the American commitment to repay the principal of all outstanding debt in coin at a fixed rate. Again, in 1870, funding acts that authorized bond issues underscored the desire of the United States to repay all debt in legal tender coin of the country by stating that bonds were "redeemable at the pleasure of the United States . . . in coin of the standard value of the United States on said July 14th, 1870 with interest in such coin, from the day of their date. . . ."[6] Unfortunately, the inherent ambiguity of the "in coin" clause (see table 5.4) and of not explicitly stating that debt was payable *in gold* would haunt the United States until the 1890s.

Despite these ambiguities, creditors (a minority of them foreigners) accepted federal debt in the domestic currency of the United States, whatever form it took. In fact, after silverites convinced Congress to remove the gold clause from an 1895 issue, instead inserting a specie clause, these bonds were successfully sold abroad (principally London) but with a face value interest rate of 4 percent rather than the 3 percent a gold bond would have carried.

Doubt about the exchange rate regime was laid to rest in 1899 when the United States enacted a law declaring gold to be the exclusive currency of the United States. This led to the Gold Standard Act of 1900, which put the United States firmly on the gold standard. This and other propitious economic events allowed the United States to avoid further misunderstandings about how debt would be repaid and how it should be denominated. In any case, the United States did not make too many new issues on foreign markets for a period after 1899, and the amount of federal debt held in foreign hands is said to have declined quite rapidly after 1899 (Wilkins 1989). As most federal debt came to be issued and held domestically, the currency-denomination aspect of original sin became less important.[7]

The Interwar Period and the Great Depression

From the Civil War period until the abrogation of the gold clauses under Roosevelt in 1933, virtually all federal bonds carried a gold clause (Kroszner 2002). Still, debt was exclusively denominated in dollars, and after the devaluation, debt was in fact repaid in notes at the depreciated rate. To the extent that creditors could foresee such an outcome and had been willing to take this risk upon purchase, the United States had partially graduated from original sin. After this, the United States never returned to issuing significant amounts of bonds with gold clauses. We view this as the moment when the country completely and definitively broke free from original sin.[8]

World War II to the Present

After World War II, the United States continued to issue debt almost exclusively in domestic currency. Particularly in the 1970s, considerable amounts of this debt were held as official reserves by foreign governments. More recently, private-sector agents hold most of the foreign-held debt.

The most noteworthy foray into the issue of foreign-currency-denominated debt was the Roosa bonds issued in the 1960s. These bonds, denominated in the principal European currencies, were an attempt by the Treasury to stem the ongoing gold drain that dominated the Bretton Woods period. However, these bonds were issued in very limited amounts. Similar bonds were issued in the 1970s and were referred to as Carter bonds.

The federal government has also maintained the ability to borrow long-term. Average maturities on the funded debt outstanding rose from about 9.2 years in 1966 to 21.5 years (Monthly Statement of the Public Debt Outstanding). One should also note, however, that the funded debt as a proportion of the total marketable debt outstanding fell from about one-half in 1966 to one-fifth in 1985 and one-sixth in 1996.

States

State debt issues swamped federal government-debt issues in terms of total amounts outstanding by the mid-nineteenth century. The states' probity was more tainted than the federal government's. Repudiations and defaults occurred first in the 1840s, then after the Civil War in the former Confederate states and again in the 1870s. This eventually led the states to impose their own limits on borrowing. The effect was also to essentially curtail their ability to issue on foreign markets by the opening of the twentieth century (Wilkins 1989). Like the federal government, state issues carried explicit gold clauses from the Civil War until 1933.

States issued securities at home and abroad in the early nineteenth century for the purpose of building infrastructure and chartering state banks. Domestic issues, which American and British banks often eventually placed abroad, were denominated in dollars with gold clauses or fixed exchange rate clauses. At other times they were simply denominated in pounds with a fixed exchange rate clause. Early foreign issues tended to be denominated in pounds sterling or other foreign currencies (Ratchford 1941). The success of these issues led to dollar-denominated securities with gold clauses, which were issued in the United States to be transferred abroad by the 1840s. In addition it appears that most bonds were long-term—on the order of nine- to ten-year maturities or longer. The fact that not all issues were in dollars, particularly those made abroad, suggests that the U.S. states were not free from original sin prior to 1840.

After a wave of defaults in the early 1840s, states began to borrow afresh in the late 1840s. In the 1840s and 1850s, it is said that not more than about 20 percent of all state debt was held abroad. Most of this was issued domestically, and it is likely to have been dollar-denominated with fixed exchange rate clauses or gold clauses. Ratchford (1941) claims that maturities on most state bonds were thirty to forty years.

During the Civil War, northern states issued mainly domestically. Massachusetts was an exception, having nearly $2 million of sterling bounty bonds outstanding by 1866. The Union states' original bonds required repayment in specie, but Ohio, for example, stopped paying in gold by 1863. If we believe Ratchford's characterization of bonds during the antebellum period, then maturities had fallen during the war. At this time they averaged nearly twenty years.

Southern states also tended to issue bonds at home, and made only a few attempts to take loans in London. When they did so, the bonds often specified repayment in tradable goods such as cotton. Near the end of the war, most financing in the South was done through emissions of unfunded debt. Maturities on the funded debt were shorter than in the North and were about ten to twenty years.

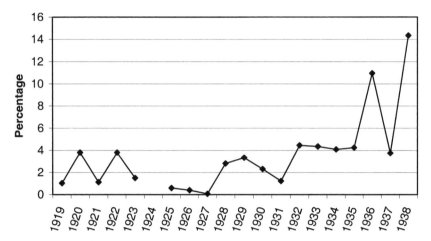

Figure 5.1   Percentage of all U.S. state borrowing falling due between 3.1 and 5 years, 1919–38. Data from Ratchford 1941, 274.

Up to 1913, new state loans abroad were rare (Wilkins 1989, 187). Uncertainty over the ability to service debt due to earlier defaults and the demand created by banking regulation in the United States meant that only two state bonds were listed in London in 1899 (Wilkins 1989). Of two loans issued by Massachusetts on London in 1896, both were gold bonds.

We have examined the *Investor's Review* from London since World War I and have not been able to find any new issues abroad of states debts. It is of course possible that foreigners came to hold debts through the course of trade or by purchasing them in New York, but we have been unable to locate any data on foreign holdings. What we do know is that nearly all varieties of American debt continued to carry specie clauses until 1933, as Kroszner (2002) suggests. After this, states are likely to have issued mainly on domestic markets. These would have to have been without gold clauses, since these were banned by law.[9]

In terms of maturities, Ratchford reports that the median time until maturity of bonds between 1919 and 1938 was fifteen to twenty years. Figure 5.1 taken from this source also shows the percentage of debt maturing between 3.1 and 5 years was always very low.[10] Interestingly, this percentage increased dramatically during the Great Depression.

Private Companies

Foreign investment in the United States has a long history. Most notable was the massive influx of British and European portfolio capital during the nineteenth century. Railroads were often the most sought-after bonds, and they took the lion's share of incoming capital, but investments went to other sectors as well.

Table 5.5. New issues of selected U.S. private companies in London, 1887–96

Issue	Amount (US$)	Year	Currency	Interest payable in
Mobile and Birmingham Railway Company 5% gold bonds	3,000,000	1887	Dollars	
Great Northern Railway of Minnesota 4% extension bonds	3,000,000	1890	Sterling	
Cleveland, Cincinnati, Chicago, St. Louis Railway Mortgage 4.5% gold bonds	4,000,000	1892	Dollars	
Illinois Central Railroad 4% gold bonds	4,000,000	1893	Dollars	
Cleveland, Cincinnati, Chicago, St. Louis Railway Mortgage 4% gold bonds	5,000,000	1893	Dollars	
Baltimore and Ohio South Western Railway Company	250,000	1893	Dollars	
Arizona Copper Company	100,000	1894	Sterling	
Chicago, Milwaukee, and St. Paul Railway Company gold bonds	2,000,000	1894	Dollars	
Baltimore and Ohio South Railroad Company 4.5% gold bonds	8,164,000	1894	Dollars	
St. Louis Merchants Bridge Terminal Railway 5% gold bonds	3,165,500	1894	Dollars	
Twin City Rapid Transit Company shares	1,500,000	1894	Dollars	
Minneapolis Western First Mortgage bonds	500,000	1895	Dollars	
Terminal Railroad Association of St. Louis 5% gold bonds	4,500,000	1895	Dollars	Gold coin of the U.S.
Cleveland and Manetta Railway Company 4.5% gold bonds	1,250,000	1895	Dollars	Gold coin of the U.S.
Alleghany Valley Railway Company 4% gold bonds	5,000,000	1895	Dollars	Gold coin of the U.S.
Pennsylvania Railroad Company 3.5% sterling bonds	1,000,000	1895	Sterling	
Alina Colony Corporation shares	116,067	1896	Sterling	
Milwaukee Electric Railway and Light Company	5,100,000	1896	Dollars	Coin of the present standard
Elmira, Cortland, and Northern Railroad Company	1,250,000	1896	Dollars	Coin of the present standard
Pacific Borax and Redwood's Chemical Works ordinary shares	310,000	1896	Sterling	
Pacific Borax and Redwood's Chemical Works preference shares	200,000	1896	Sterling	
Pacific Borax and Redwood's Chemical Works 5% debentures	100,000	1896	Sterling	

Sources: Nash, various issues, and The Investor's Review.

It is difficult to estimate how much of all outstanding debt foreigners held at any one time. Sparse data exist on the numerator and the denominator but not usually for the same years. In any case, it does not appear that any significant graduation from original sin came until the forced elimination of the gold clauses in 1933. Moreover, reliance on foreign capital markets was diminished—at least for the early years of the Bretton Woods period.

The use of foreign markets and sterling debt began in the 1850s when railroads first issued abroad. Later issues that were in dollars carried gold clauses. As late as the 1890s, American companies issued bonds on London both in sterling and in dollars, as table 5.5 shows. During and after the First World War, U.S. companies tended to issue mainly in New York, as European capital markets were perturbed and New York's prominence was rising. Nearly all long-term corporate debt outstanding in the 1930s carried gold clauses (Kroszner 2002). After 1933, companies could not issue gold-indexed debt by law in the United States. Reliance on foreign markets also remained low immediately following World War II. Hence in the corporate sector, American companies have been relatively free of original sin since at least the mid-1930s.

Summary

The United States is a special case among our countries. Since the 1850s, all players in the economy were able to issue debt denominated in U.S. dollars (with implicit or explicit gold or specie clauses) that nonresidents were willing to hold. The United States maintained specie clauses, and this largely meant hard currency repayments ex post. Because there may have been a probability that foreign creditors would be paid in paper or depreciated silver, we view this as an intermediate case. Only after 1933 did the U.S. federal government issue a significant amount of debt with no gold clause.

In the second meaning of original sin—the maturity of debt—we do see fluctuations that tend to suggest financial turmoil can put players on a shorter string. However, average maturities on funded debt and corporate paper have always been long by today's emerging-market-country standards.

The United States graduated from original sin for the most part behind the curtain of a number of large successive shocks, including the fiscal retrenchment after the Revolution, the Great Depression, World War II, and the Bretton Woods era. By the 1930s, the United States had largely purged itself of original sin. We examine the determinants of this transition more below, when explaining observed patterns.

The British Dominions

This section discusses the debt history of Canada, Australia, New Zealand, and South Africa, four settler economies that emerged from British colonies. Despite some idiosyncratic variations, the experience of these countries was remarkably similar: in the nineteenth and early twentieth century they borrowed in London in sterling, but during World War I they were cut off from the London market and developed domestic markets where they issued relatively long-term domestic-currency-denominated debt. In the interwar period, Australia and Canada issued in New York (U.S. dollar–denominated debt), but as many authors have noted, international capital flows remained small from World War I until the 1990s. Only in the last part of the twentieth century did these four economies begin to issue debt overseas in their own currency. The evidence on nonresident holdings of domestically issued debt is murky, but in Canada, a leader among these four, we find that there were significant foreign holdings of local currency debt by the 1950s.

Thus far the story sounds as though the economies indeed suffered from original sin, and did so until very recently. As we show, the story is more complex. First, at all times, the maturity of the debt outstanding—the foreign-currency/foreign-issued debt *and* the domestic-currency/domestically issued debt—was long relative to today's standards. Second, with the possible exception of the nineteenth-century experience, there were large and liquid domestic-currency debt markets.

Pre–World War I

In the prewar period, governments borrowed primarily to finance infrastructure improvements.[11] The data are most complete for Canada and show that over the period 1867 to 1914, over 90 percent of the funded debt outstanding was in the form of sterling liabilities (see fig. 5.2).[12] For the other colonies, the range was slightly lower (from 70 percent in Australia to 90 percent in New Zealand), but the bulk of borrowing was in the London market in all cases. Strikingly, there was a one-to-one correspondence between place of issue and denomination—this was sterling debt issued in London.

The loans tended to be quite long term, ten to twenty-five years, and the governments were aware of the benefits of these maturities. For example, in 1912

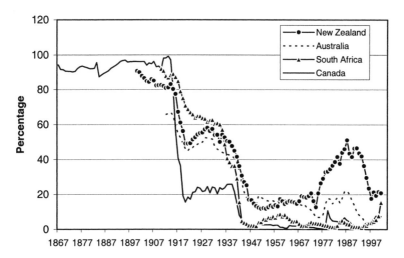

Figure 5.2 Public debt issued overseas in foreign currency as a percentage of total outstanding public debt. Data for South Africa from *Official Year-Book of the Union of South Africa and of Basutoland, the Bechuanaland Protectorate, and Swaziland,* various years; and Reserve Bank of South Africa. Data for New Zealand from *New Zealand Official Yearbook,* various years; and Reserve Bank of New Zealand. Data for Australia, 1913–39, from *Yearbook of the Commonwealth of Australia,* various years; 1950–95, from Reserve Bank of Australia. Data for Canada from Public Accounts, various years.

the Canadian minister of finance took comfort in the fact that only two issues would come due before 1930 (Field 1914, 104).

From World War I to 1939

The onset of World War I essentially closed the London capital market, and the response was similar in all four dominions. The gold convertibility of the domestic currency was suspended (and not resumed until 1925), and governments raised funds domestically, essentially creating a domestic bond market with the aid of the commercial banks. Thus in Canada, the government maintained a low-interest peg on its securities, which were largely absorbed and marketed to the public by chartered banks. Foreign issues relative to domestic issues (at least for sovereign debt) would never regain their earlier dominance. Figure 5.2 shows the decrease in the share of outstanding debt issued overseas. (The very dramatic nature of the declines reflects the quick expansion of domestically issued debt to finance the war efforts.) In Canada the Victory Loans, although issued in Canadian dollars, had explicit gold clauses.

Each country followed slightly different policies in the interwar period and had different experiences during the Depression. Canada raised funds in New York in U.S. dollars in 1917, and in the 1920s all new issues overseas were in New York in U.S. dollars (in contrast to the prewar overseas issues in London in sterling). There were new issues in the domestic markets also, but they were limited to rolling over the Victory Loans.

Canada's currency mismatch on the eve of the Depression might have left it exceptionally vulnerable. Interest on the public debt was about one-third of government expenditures (high even relative to post–World War II standards). In the early thirties, the Canadian government considered a depreciation but rejected such a policy, not because it would imply an increase in the real value of external interest payments, but rather because such policies could lead to "a flight from the Canadian dollar through fear of deflation" and the belief that depreciation "would be ruinous alike to the credit and to the future development of this country" (cited in Bordo and Redish 1990, 372).

The government's protection lay in the extended maturities of the outstanding foreign debt, which meant that the immediate liabilities of the government were not large. In March 1932, the government had C\$1.34 billion in gold bonds outstanding, but only \$34 million were due in the coming twelve months, so that the combined interest and principal due in gold was only \$93 million.[13] A significant, but not fatal, sum in relation to exports, implying that depreciation would not impose a critical burden on the public purse.

Canada dramatically reduced its currency mismatch/gold liabilities by the Conversion Loan of (March) 1931. By that loan, the government took advantage of the low interest rates of 1931 to roll over much of the outstanding Victory Loans into twenty-year bonds. In the process the gold clause was removed.

While this may have been a shrewd prelude to the depreciation of October 1931, it seems unlikely: the government was not honoring the gold clause for domestic bondholders—the majority—anyway.[14] Throughout the period, the link between denomination of the debt and the place of issue remained close. There were no foreign issues of Canadian dollar–denominated debt. Yet there was some intermediation similar to the case of the United States in the nineteenth century. In 1948, a Dominion Bureau of Statistics survey (1949) of the balance of payments stated that an "appreciable total" of Canadian dollar–denominated securities were held outside Canada, "even before the recent war." These would have been bonds issued in Canada, and most likely bought by U.S. insurance companies. Unfortunately the context does not help define "appreciable"!

Australia too developed its own debt market during World War I, and continued to issue domestically in the interwar period. One advantage of issuing at home in the late 1920s and early 1930s was the lower face-value interest rate on debt. The average face-value rate in London and New York was about 4.86 percent, while debt issued locally had an average face-value interest rate of 3.8 percent (*Official Year Book of the Commonwealth of Australia* 1934, 405). Despite moving toward domestic sources, officials in Australia noted the benefit in lower interest payments when sterling was devalued in September 1931 (*Official Year Book of the Commonwealth of Australia* 1939), and argued in August 1931 that further local depreciation would have aggravated the government deficit due to the increase in the interest charges on external debt. External debt therefore was not in domestic currency. On the other hand, both the international and the domestic debt continued to be relatively long-term. Table 5.6 shows that the average maturities ranged from about ten years for the internally issued debt to roughly twenty years for the externally issued debt.

New Zealand cut the link to gold in 1929, much earlier than most countries during the Great Depression. The dependency on exports of primary goods was

Table 5.6. Maturity structure (in years) for states in Australia and the Commonwealth, 1932 and 1939

Year	Debt payable by states in			Debt payable by Commonwealth and states in		
	London	New York	Australia	London	New York	Australia
1932	19.02	22.23	10	19.5	22.6	11.8
1939	19.38	16.28	9.19	11.45	10.03	8.99

Sources: Official Year Book of the Commonwealth of Australia, 1933 and 1939.

Notes: Debt is payable in the currency of the market where it is payable. 1932 includes A£79 million of debt payable in London on an annual basis. For column 6 the figures exclude A£11 million debt redeemable at an indefinite date or at the treasurer's discretion.

associated with a sudden onset of the crisis in this year. Nearly half of New Zealand's debt was issued in London at this time, and nearly all of this was held abroad and payable in sterling in London.[15]

Some tabulations available also suggest that the average maturity until payment on New Zealand debt was slightly longer on debt issued in London (13.2 years) than on debt issued at home (12.5 years). The average face value of interest charges on debt in 1939 was again higher in London at 4.25 percent versus 3.44 on internal debt (*New Zealand Official Yearbook* 1939–40).

The growth rate of the South African public debt during World War I was considerably less than that of the other British Dominions discussed here, and most likely as a result of that, the shift to domestic bond issues relative to foreign issues was least marked in that country. Nevertheless, the share of sterling debt in South Africa fell from 90 percent in 1910 to 70 percent in 1920 and to 60 percent by 1930. The experience of South Africa during the Depression was also somewhat anomalous, because of the increasing real value of their gold resources and hence the ability to service external debt.

World War II and Bretton Woods

Throughout this period, the correspondence between currency of issue and place of issue remained strong, and as in World War I, government debt grew dramatically and was funded domestically, leading to a further erosion in the share of the debt funded overseas.

The Canadian government continued to issue domestic debt in Canadian dollars, while New York issues were payable (at least optionally) in U.S. dollars, and London issues were payable in sterling. But even more than before the war, there is evidence of Americans buying Canadian dollar–denominated debt issued in Canada. By the end of 1946, it is estimated that about $600 million of such debt was held in the United States, significantly more than the $178 million of U.S. dollar–denominated Canadian debt outstanding, but a negligible proportion of the $16.6 billion in Canadian dollar–denominated Canadian debt outstanding.

Data on purchases and holding of Canadian debt by nonresidents start to become available after World War II, and we can trace the development of foreign holdings of Canadian debt by currency with some precision. The Canadian government did not issue very much debt during the Bretton Woods period, but figure 5.3 shows that *of the amount purchased by nonresidents* an average of 17 percent was denominated in Canadian dollars. There are no records of foreign issues of Canadian dollar–denominated bonds, so that this represents bonds bought—most probably by Americans—in Canada. Again insurance companies were highly represented among buyers.

To fund chronic public imbalances, Australia issued debt in many different foreign markets between 1950 and 1972, and, as in Canada, the currency of de-

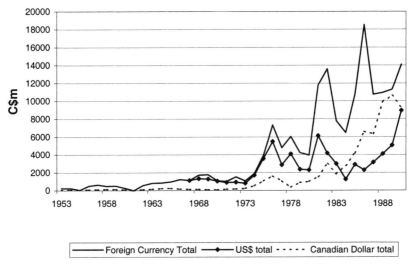

Figure 5.3 Nonresident purchases of new issues by currency of denomination, Canada, 1953–90. Data from Statistics Canada.

nomination typically coincided with the place of issue. Debt was issued in sterling, U.S. dollars, and to a lesser degree Swiss francs, Canadian dollars, German marks, Dutch guilders, and Japanese yen. The government attempted to use the depth of foreign markets in order to ensure that adequate funding was available. It does not appear that any significant amount of debt sold overseas was denominated in Australian dollars during this period. Evidence on average maturity lengths for domestic-currency-denominated, domestically issued debt shows that the average maturity, which had fallen from 8.99 years in 1939 to 6.25 years in 1955, rose secularly to 10.3 years in 1972.

In New Zealand, the amount of government debt increased sevenfold during World War II, but the level of sterling/London indebtedness did not change, explaining the dramatic decline in the amount of outstanding debt issued overseas. The story in South Africa is similar, with a tenfold increase in domestically issued, domestic-currency debt, and a contraction in the sterling/London debt.[16]

Post–Bretton Woods

This period has seen radical innovations in the debt markets, so that by the end of the period, the use of derivatives had detached the currency of a liability from both its place of issue and its initial currency of issue. A key step in this evolution was the development of the Eurobond market. This market first developed in 1963 following the introduction of the U.S. interest equalization tax—

designed to stem capital (and hence gold) outflows—which raised the cost of foreign borrowing in the United States. Similar markets later developed for currencies other than the dollar.[17]

In November 1974, the Bank of Canada amended the perennial title of table 29, "Net new securities issues payable in foreign currency," by adding in parentheses "includes Canadian dollar issues placed in overseas markets" (Bank of Canada 1974, s67). This seems like an appropriate signal of Canada's baptism: figure 5.3 shows that beginning in 1974 there was a gradual increase in the amount of Canadian dollar–denominated new issues purchased by nonresidents. In the 1980s, nonresident purchases of new issues both in foreign currency other than the U.S. dollar and in Canadian dollars rose sharply. Portfolios saw the same transformation as the new issue market. "In 1980, only 18 percent of Canadian bonds held by nonresidents were payable in Canadian dollars, while 71 percent were payable in U.S. dollars. By 1993, Canadian dollar bonds represented 43 percent of Canadian bonds held by nonresidents, while the share of U.S. dollar bonds had fallen to 44 percent" (Bank of Canada 1994, 47).[18]

A similar picture is painted by estimates from the Economic Council of Canada (1990, 72). They find that the amount of Canadian bonds denominated in Canadian currency placed outside Canada and the United States rose from $5 million in the period 1963–70 (0.5 percent of all Canadian issues placed outside Canada and the United States), to $4 billion (30 percent) in the period 1971–80, and to $16 billion (25 percent) from 1981 to 1987.

In Australia, the 1980s was a period of debt consolidation and heightened concern with the debt. Australia's total foreign debt to GDP ratio was over 40 percent in the mid-1980s (Argy 1995). During these years, the debt-management strategy changed radically in an attempt to reduce the real burden. Exchange rates were allowed to float, so volatility and average servicing costs could not be taken for granted. In addition, the Australian market became deep enough to supply more funds for government borrowing needs. The government has not issued any debt abroad since 1987. At that point in time, foreign-currency-denominated debt equaled about 30 percent of the total outstanding debt. By the early 1990s, the gross debt to GDP ratio had declined to 16 percent and the amount of foreign denominated debt outstanding was falling rapidly. By 1997, foreign-currency-denominated debt was a mere 1 percent of total debt.[19]

New Zealand's gross public debt to GDP ratio has fallen since the early 1990s from almost 50 percent to 32 percent. New Zealand is still exposed to foreign-currency liabilities. The ratio of external debt to internal debt is about 25 percent as of 2001. This is a large decline from the beginning of the 1990s, when the proportions were almost equal. In 1993, roughly half of the external debt was issued in U.S. dollars, while the rest was issued in other key currencies.

On the other hand, there is also some evidence that nonresidents are willing to hold "internal debt" or bonds denominated in New Zealand dollars. Fig-

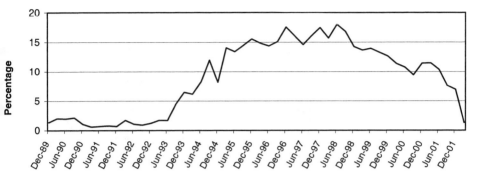

Figure 5.4 Percentage of internal New Zealand dollar debt held by foreigners, 1989–2001. Data from Reserve Bank of New Zealand.

ure 5.4 shows that foreign holdings of New Zealand dollar-denominated debt peaked around 1997 at 16 percent of the total internal debt. This is most likely a lower bound on holding, however, as not all foreign bondholders could be identified accurately in the registers.

In South Africa, the public external debt stayed low as a percentage of total public debt after 1970 although there is a slight rise in recent years (fig. 5.2). Corroborating this secular rise in domestic credibility or financial capacity, we see in figure 5.5 that maturity lengths on domestically issued debt lengthened. This may in fact be a continuation of trends that emerged in the 1930s. It appears that credibility has its roots in the 1930s (as we have seen, the maturity length increased slightly from 10.7 to 12.6 years for domestic debt between 1928 and 1937).[20] Figure 5.6 shows that a significant percentage of South Africa's *total* gross debt payable to nonresidents (i.e., public and private) has been denominated in rands since at least 1994. Since the 1960s, South Africa has issued external debt in a number of different currencies.

Summary

The evolution of government borrowing in the British Dominions is easy to summarize. Prior to 1913, borrowing was almost entirely long-term bonds issued in pounds sterling in the London market. During the war, domestic savings were tapped by the issue of domestic debt, which was denominated in domestic currency, though often this carried a gold clause. The interwar period saw much of the domestic war debt rolled over and, at least in Canada, without a gold clause. Canada and Australia borrowed in the New York market, in U.S. dollars. World War II again led to expanded domestic debt as a percentage of the total, and during the postwar/Bretton Woods period there was little access to foreign capital markets. The breakdown of Bretton Woods and growth in

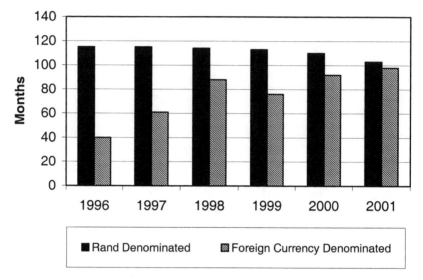

Figure 5.5 Average maturity of marketable national government debt in South Africa, 1996–2001. Data from South African Reserve Bank, *Quarterly Bulletin*, various years.

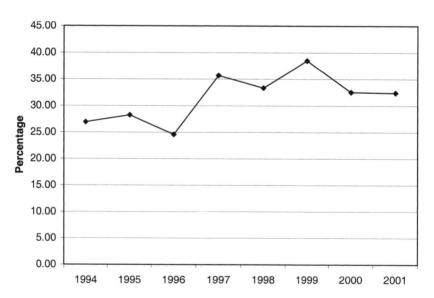

Figure 5.6 Debt denominated in rands as a percentage of all debt payable to foreigners, 1994–2001. Data from South African Reserve Bank, *Quarterly Bulletin*, various years.

government borrowing in the 1970s led to an expansion of external debt, and all the dominions began issuing a significant amount of domestic-currency debt overseas.

Some Explanations for the Patterns Observed

Below we review the salient patterns observed in our case studies of debt history of the Anglo countries. We then pose some explanations for the common patterns observed for the five countries and for some special features of the United States.

The Patterns in Evolution Away from Original Sin

Across all five of our countries, we see little evidence in the historical record of original sin in the sense of an inability to borrow at long-term maturities whether domestically or abroad. There are a few episodes when maturities shortened, especially during the Great Depression, but these rarely affected the average maturity length.

For original sin in the sense of the inability to issue domestic-currency-denominated debt abroad, none of the countries were completely free of it until the third decade of the twentieth century. The United States was the leader; it weaned itself from foreign currency (guilder) sovereign debt very early in the nineteenth century, and dollar debt was listed and issued on foreign markets with implicit or later explicit specie or gold clauses until the Great Depression. State and corporate debt followed a similar pattern of evolution from sterling to dollar debt with gold clauses later in the nineteenth century.

The dominions borrowed externally in sterling exclusively until World War I, but developed domestic debt markets after this. After the war, there was a decline in reliance on external debt. It was only after the breakdown of the Bretton Woods system and the advent of derivatives that these countries began issuing external debt in their own currencies. In the secondary markets, it appears that local-currency debt (sans gold clauses) has been held abroad since the 1950s in Canada, and although our evidence is somewhat incomplete, it appears that similar patterns emerged in the other countries by the 1970s.

Explanations

While the data are not structured in a way that facilitates statistical techniques, we have sufficient information to make some informed conjectures on some of the leading hypotheses posed in this volume as well as on other determinants. We initially consider four factors that might explain the *common* pattern of evolution away from original sin across the five countries: sound and credible fiscal institutions, credible monetary regimes, financial development, and major shocks. We then discuss two factors that made the U.S. experience different from that of the dominions: size and the effect on how much of a "vehicle" the currency was, and the differing extent of dependence and independence from Europe.

Sound and Credible Fiscal Institutions

Corsetti and Maćkowiak (chapter 3 in this volume) suggest that weak public finances could lead governments to address imbalances with an inflation tax. Fearing this, agents avoid long-term, noninstitutional domestic-currency debt and hold only foreign-currency debt. This was not the case in our five countries, all of which had developed relatively sound fiscal institutions by the nineteenth century, compared to today's emergers.

Hamilton, the secretary of the treasury from 1789 to 1795, put together in 1790 one of the most successful financial programs in history. The package included four elements: funding the national debt, creation of a sinking fund, securing sufficient tax revenue, and creation of a national bank, the First Bank of the United States (Perkins 1994; Bordo and Vegh 2002). His program was based on the idea that domestic bond prices were a measure of the creditworthiness of a nation, and he attempted to increase that price through timely domestic interest payments, consolidation of all federal and state debt, and "small-scale redemptions." This improved the chances of garnering further domestic confidence and attracting more foreign loans at favorable terms. In addition, a sinking fund was also established to "manipulate" the price of bonds in the open market and to enhance credibility. Finally, the whole package was secured by instituting a national tariff of 10 percent on import values as well as excise taxes to provide sufficient tax revenues to continuously service the debt. These policies succeeded in raising domestic bond prices, enlarging the domestic bond market and ultimately reinforcing the credibility of the foundling republic.

The Funding Act of 1790 and Hamilton's ability put American credit on a trajectory to gain a strong international reputation. This act, along with the Napoleonic Wars, paved the way for a European interest in domestically issued American securities with implicit specie clauses. The wars made investments in the fledgling country look relatively more secure, and the Funding Act was a provision "to fulfill the engagements of the U.S. in respect to foreign debt."

Hamilton's plan was based on British precedent—the creation of a long-term bond market and permanent servicing with indirect taxes—set in the early eighteenth century. Similar institutions were adopted by Canada (Bordo and Redish 2001) and the other British Dominions in the nineteenth century.

The principal exception to the story of fiscal probity was the U.S. states in the 1840s. Their defaults shut them out of foreign markets for an extended period (Wilkins 1989). These events did not help the progression to be free of original sin.

The federal government in the United States developed a sound fiscal base with Alexander Hamilton's stabilization package. Overall, this plan allowed for a very limited graduation from original sin, as we have argued above. Subsequent reliance on explicit gold clauses suggests, however, that it takes more than sound finances to completely break free.

Credible Monetary Regimes

Jeanne (chapter 7 in this volume) suggests that agents favor foreign-currency-denominated debt when domestic monetary policy is not credible. Bad monetary policy increases the ex ante interest rate on domestic-currency-denominated issues. Likewise it might be argued that if policy were credible, then these costs should disappear, releasing countries from original sin.

The history of all five countries suggests that lack of credibility in the monetary regime was not a necessary condition for original sin and that credible monetary regimes were not sufficient to be totally free of it. For the most part, all of these countries had credible regimes over the long run. All the countries were part of the specie standard that prevailed until World War I. All credibly followed the rule of the maintenance of convertibility as paramount. The rule followed was contingent in the sense that credibility could be temporarily suspended in the event of a wartime emergency, which indeed was the case during and after the U.S. Civil War and for the dominions during World War I (Bordo and Kydland 1995).

The U.S. case was most interesting because the specie standard followed de jure until 1900 was bimetallic, leaving open the possibility of silver risk and hence the need for gold clauses. The United States remained on the gold standard until 1933, when Roosevelt abrogated the gold clauses. After World War II, the dollar (officially convertible into gold) became the key currency of the world, and U.S. dollar debt was widely held abroad. This has continued with the demise of Bretton Woods and the advent of a fiat money regime. Although the United States followed unorthodox monetary policy in the Great Depression and in the great inflation of the 1970s, neither the dollar nor dollar debt was ever shunned.

Canada was on the gold standard from its origins as a British colony, with the Canadian dollar fully convertible into gold until 1914. Australia, New Zealand, and South Africa were fully "sterlingized" prior to the turn of the twentieth century and then turned to gold-standard adherence with domestic currencies. These countries credibly adhered to the gold standard and followed the contingent rule during World War I. In the Bretton Woods years, all the dominions except Canada followed the adjustable peg. Canada floated from 1950 to 1962 but followed a more stable monetary policy than the United States, which suggests it may have continued to follow the contingent rule (Bordo

2001). In the immediate post–Bretton Woods period, all the dominions had inflationary experiences similar to the other advanced countries and since the mid-1990s have learned to follow a fiat nominal anchor with low inflation.

Financial Development

Authors such as Chamon and Hausmann (chapter 8 in this volume) have emphasized that the inability to write complex agreements that maintain the value of domestic-currency-denominated debt in the case of depreciation diminishes the size of the domestic-currency debt market. Also Caballero and Krishnamurthy (2001) argue that financial underdevelopment can lead to excessive hard-currency debt.

All five of our countries had significant financial development by the end of the nineteenth century. All of the countries had extensive banking systems and high ratios of M2 to GDP (Bordo and Flandreau 2003). The dominions had nationwide branch banking, which encouraged financial stability. In the dominions, the banks were the dominant financial intermediary, supplemented by insurance companies and investment dealers (Davis and Gallman 2000).

The United States had unit banks prone to runs and panics. In the United States in part because of the restrictions on branching and interstate banking, which hobbled the size of bank assets, other financial markets and institutions such as commercial paper, stock markets, and investment banks evolved to fill the gap.

None of the countries had central banks before 1910. With the establishment of the Federal Reserve in 1914 and central banks in the dominions by the end of the 1930s, this absence was corrected. In the United States, the lack of a lender of last resort was only partially made up by alternative private arrangements (clearing-house loan certificates) and treasury actions. Banking crises were frequent. In the dominions, large commercial banks served as the governments' fiscal agents and with the Department of Finance (e.g., in Canada) served as lenders of last resort. Banking crises were a rare event, with the principal exception of Australia in 1893.

Financial underdevelopment was unlikely to be a reason for original sin in these countries. It took a major financial innovation—the development of derivatives in the 1970s—for the dominions to issue external debt in their own currencies. It took terrible economic woes to end hard-currency debt in the United States.

Shocks

The record for all five of our countries demonstrates that the major changes in patterns of evolution away from original sin occurred after wars and other significant shocks. The evidence suggests that these disturbances forced the creation of markets for the local-currency debt. For example, World War I made it very costly (or impossible) for the dominions to borrow in the London market. This may have made it more rational for economies to bear the high start-up costs of creating a domestic debt market. After those costs were borne, the domestic markets continued to flourish even after normal conditions prevailed in the traditional markets. These facts highlight how path dependence can help explain how nations break free from original sin.

In the U.S. case, foreign holdings of dollar-denominated debt (with implicit versus explicit gold clauses) rose rapidly after the Revolution and Hamilton's revamping of the fiscal system between 1790 and 1803. The Great Depression ended the gold standard and the gold clauses. The same was true to an extent in Canada.

Similarly, in the dominions, World War I was the key event that led to the rise of domestic-currency internal debt relative to external sterling debt and for Canada initially, the substitution of U.S. dollar external debt in place of sterling. It is after World War II that we first see evidence of nonresidents holding internally issued Canadian dollar debt. Finally, the breakdown of the Bretton Woods system with the advent of nominal floating and the end of capital controls set the stage for the development of the derivatives that led to the creation of international bonds in the Dominion currencies.

U.S. Exceptionalism and the Role of History

We posit that the United States was different from the other Anglo countries in its ability to abstain from loans denominated in foreign currencies and to have its securities listed in dollars in foreign markets. Two factors are responsible.

Key Currencies and Size

The United States was different from the others because of its economic size and political importance. Moreover, although it was less dependent on international trade than the others, its volume of trade and the network of international transactions was also an order of magnitude greater. Such factors have long been identified as the hallmarks of vehicle currencies, which are used to invoice trade and financial contracts. Indeed, Wilkins (1989) reports that in the nineteenth century, domestically issued U.S. debt often ended up abroad because agents viewed the assets as useful in international transactions.

From the very beginning, the United States explicitly tried to avoid sovereign debt in foreign currencies, as evident in the following quote from Alexander Hamilton:

> The Payment of interest and installments of principal of our foreign debt in the countries where it was contracted is found by experience to be attended with difficulty, embarrassment, some loss, and a degree of casualty which occasionally puts in jeopardy the national credit. Loans for reimbursement must be made beforehand, as the market suits, and necessarily involve double interest for a greater

or less time. The procuring of bills to be remitted for payment of interest cannot be depended upon in coincidence with the periods of payment, which, co-operating with distance, renders inconvenient anticipations necessary. . . . If, therefore, the place of these could, with consent of the creditors upon an equitable indemnification to them for the transfer, be changed to the United States, the operation would be, in various lights, beneficial . . . [proposal to convert all foreign debt to domestic debt.]

It could not be necessary to observe, except for the sake of dispelling jealousy or apprehension on the part of the creditors, *that while the plan is experiment, and afterward, with regard to all who do not embrace it,* everything is to proceed as heretofore, and as the contracts respecting the debt require. (United States Bureau of the Census, 7:334, emphasis in original)

It is unlikely a small country could have created a debt market from scratch as Hamilton did. The Funding Act converted and consolidated nearly all outstanding debt to domestic debt. Moreover, as the country developed in the nineteenth century and financial markets expanded and deepened, the states and corporations were able to fund much of their requirements in the domestic markets, obviating the need for foreign debt regardless of the currency of denomination.

The U.S. dollar did not fully emerge as a key currency until after World War I, but by the end of the nineteenth century, it was on a par with European currencies other than those of the core countries (Lindert 1969). Finally, the thick market externalities associated with the medium of exchange may have factored into the denomination of assets as is the case with the medium of exchange.

The British Empire

All of the areas we analyze were once British colonies, and for the countries besides the United States nearly all had special relationships with the British until very recently. Colonial status and special relationships entailed sundry institutional connections that might have made it simply more convenient to issue debt in sterling. Three of these countries (Australia, New Zealand, and South Africa) used sterling until the twentieth century, and it was legal tender in Canada. Even if there was a financial crisis, colonial status could avoid the negative repercussions of balance-sheet effects. Debtors and creditors could reschedule debt more easily. If worst came to the worst, government intervention could make debtors repay by rights guaranteed in the colonial stock acts; denomination in sterling facilitated accounting and eliminated day-to-day risk for British creditors.

Borrowing in London for the dominions also had a significant financial advantage over domestic borrowing, as borrowing costs were lower there. This is precisely the opposite of Hamilton's observation about the expenses of issuing debt abroad that we mentioned above. Still, we realize that this explains the denomination of the debt instruments only insofar as place of issue equaled the currency of denomination in the nineteenth century.

Commonwealth ties may have been significant in other ways. Under the Colonial Stock Acts, colonial public debt was often admissible to be held by trusts in the United Kingdom (see Ferguson 2002). Also, the proceeds of debt issues were often spent on capital goods to be imported from Britain, and loans were (indirectly) repaid with exports sold in Britain; thus the costs of currency mismatch were reduced.

Take as an example Australia, which had accumulated one of the highest debt per capita ratios in the world at over £100 by the interwar period. During the 1930s, policymaking was contentious, and exchange rate policy was on the minds of policymakers because of the possibility of increased interest payments if Australia were to stop shadowing the pound. The Liberal premier of New South Wales proposed suspending payments on external debt. Nevertheless, a more orthodox conversion process carried the day. After 1932, Australia engaged in a number of loan conversions in London, rewriting the contracts for over one-quarter of all external debt. Exchange savings were large (*Official Year Book of the Commonwealth of Australia* 1933–34). These conversions stipulated payment in pounds sterling while external debt issued in the 1920s was originally to be paid in a fixed amount of gold. Conversions between 1932 and 1934 list savings in terms of exchange of 25 percent, corresponding to the depreciation of sterling from pre-Depression parity.

In New Zealand during the interwar period, because of the increase in debt charges, the country was forced to devise various means of easing the burden. The newly created central bank, the Reserve Bank of New Zealand, founded in 1933, enacted various plans, including the total conversion of nearly all of the domestic debt outstanding. In 1934, a conversion of externally issued debt was undertaken as well. Most important, under the Hoover plan for debt forgiveness, Great Britain refrained from demanding repayment of £24 million in war debts after 1931.

In sum, our survey suggests that few of the factors cited in the recent literature on original sin in today's emerging markets were pivotal for the experience of the Anglo countries studied here. These countries had sound fiscal institutions, adhered to credible monetary regimes, and were financially developed over a century ago. The key factor in their progression from original sin in the sense of issuing external debt in terms of their own currencies or generating local-currency debt that was held by nonresidents was a response to shocks—wars, the Depression, and the collapse of Bretton Woods.

The United States evolved at a much more rapid pace than the others in part because of its size. This allowed it to generate a market for domestic debt and made it less costly to hold the debt despite the lack of an explicit gold clause.

Finally, we attribute some of the delay in the dominions to special features of the British Empire making foreign-currency debt less costly for the borrowers.

Conclusion

In conclusion, we raise and answer some questions suggested by our study of the debt history of the five former British colonies. First, was there original sin in the five countries? The answer is no, in the sense that all countries studied issued long-term domestic debt from the earliest years of their experience. The answer is yes, in the sense that until well into the twentieth century, their external debt was denominated in foreign currencies (the dominions) or had gold clauses (the United States). For the United States, the key feature is the ambiguity in the gold clauses, suggesting a somewhat more advanced trajectory.

Second, how did they get free from original sin? The answer seems to be that it took big external shocks to eliminate the vestiges of original sin. For the United States, the Revolutionary War set the stage for Hamilton's fiscal miracle, and the Great Depression ended gold clauses. For the dominions, World War I ended dependence on sterling debt, and the demise of Bretton Woods provided the derivatives that made it possible to issue foreign bonds in currencies with thin markets.

Third, does original sin come and go? Our long-run view suggests that this is a possibility, but any change is strictly marginal. Gold clauses became more explicit in the late-nineteenth-century United States, following uncertainty about the currency. Maturities on new issues declined during the Great Depression. In the dominions, similar evidence for changes in holdings and maturities is evident. Still, the evidence indicates only large shocks not associated with these factors can make large changes.

Finally, did the presence of original sin in the Anglo countries matter back then as much as it does for today's emergers? The answer we posit is no. The five countries had sounder fiscal and monetary institutions than today's emergers. Their financial policies were more credible (with the exception of the interwar period), and they were less exposed to the balance-sheet risks of maturity mismatches because their debt was mostly long-term, and to currency mismatches because the amounts involved were relatively small.

This different experience is reflected in the incidence and severity of financial crises in the five countries over the past century, compared to the emergers today. Of the four dominions surveyed, the only country to have a serious crisis on the scale of the recent Asian crises was Australia, which had a banking crisis in 1893 (Bordo and Eichengreen 1999; Delargy and Goodhart 1999).[21] The United States, of course, had several serious banking crises between 1880 and 1914 and one twin crisis (1893). It also had the banking panics of the 1930s. The dominions also had a number of currency crises in both the interwar and

Bretton Woods periods, but all of these reflected overvaluation and the inherent flaws of the gold-exchange standard and the adjustable peg regimes. None of these crises, however, were associated with the balance-sheet effects associated with recent emerging market crises that induced debt crises and defaults. This record suggests that, while original sin may have been present in our five countries, it didn't really matter.

Notes

For helpful comments on earlier drafts we thank Pierre Duguay, Barry Eichengreen, Chuck Freedman, Ricardo Hausmann, Jorge Braga de Macedo, Peter Rousseau, Alan Taylor, and participants at the preconference at the Kennedy School of Government and the conference at the Inter-American Development Bank. For valuable research assistance we thank Antonio David, Sonal Dhingra, and Nicholas Vrousalis. For financial support we thank the National Science Foundation and the U.K. Economics and Social Science Research Council.

1. Although, according to Flandreau and Sussman (chapter 6 in this volume), two of these (France and Denmark) had gold clauses on their debt during certain periods. They also include Austria, Italy, Russia, and Spain in a group that had some amount of bonds listed in their own currencies on London and Paris. The United States, as we discuss below, usually had some form of coin and gold clause.

2. Debt issued abroad for this transaction was denominated in dollars, but lenders had the option of repayment at the rate of £1 sterling for US$4.44 or one French franc for each US$0.40 issued.

3. A note from Levi Woodbury in 1840, reproduced in Elliot 1968, 969, suggests that the Treasury had always paid "in specie or its equivalent" prior to the 1830s. In fact, Hamilton's Funding Act was predicated on the appropriation of funds collected from tariffs and land sales, both of which would have been in specie. Still, a joint resolution of Congress in 1816 apparently relaxed the legal constraint and allowed for notes of specie paying banks to be accepted for payment at the Treasury and hence may have been used to pay some interest payments.

4. Silver had been secularly depreciating against gold since 1873.

5. By 1880 the outstanding U.S. federal debt included $1.17 billion in registered bonds and $537 million in coupon bonds (Bayley 1880). All were in U.S. dollars with the above stipulations. A congressional investigation concluded (by looking at the domicile of the registered bonds and asking the large New York banks where the coupons they were surrendering came from) that about $250 million—or 14 percent—was held by foreigners.

6. Curiously, the original proposal was to sell debt abroad that would be payable in sterling, francs, and thalers. Congress rejected this idea immediately, leaving the United States to denominate its debt in dollars while paying at a fixed rate in terms of gold (see Wilkins 1989, 681 n. 154).

7. The United States went to the London Stock Exchange for four issues of debt in 1880 and two in 1900, but made fifteen and eleven issues in New York during the respective years (Davis and Cull 1994, 67).

8. The maturity structure of the debt reveals no lack of confidence; maturities were on the order of five to forty years prior to 1913. Maturities on new issues of bonds did fall quite precipitously about 1931 with the deepening of the Great Depression, but they apparently recovered by around 1935. Data from the *Financial Chronicle* lists all new issues for each of the four years between 1932 and 1935, and suggests that the average maturity was 2.56, 4.9, 5.8, and 12.3 in each successive year after 1932. Still, the weighted average of all outstanding debt between 1932 and 1935 was, respectively, 12.2, 11.5, 11.8, and 15.3 years.

9. However, we have seen no evidence on the level of foreign holdings of these bonds during this period.

10. Ratchford's figures imply that either no debt was outstanding with maturities of less than 3.1 years or he has simply disregarded this bunch of debt. The former is more likely the correct interpretation.

11. We discuss here sovereign debt, because we lack data on local government and private-sector debts.

12. Canadian data for the period 1867–1900 are from the Public Accounts, 1950/1, which lists debts owing in London and New York, with the implication that the debt is denominated in the place of issue. For the period 1900–2001, the data on unmatured federal debt are from Statistics Canada's CANSIM database, CANSIM II series V151538; for unmatured debt in foreign currency they are series V151547.

13. The C$1.34 billion includes $790 million in gold bonds in Canada, and the $93 million includes $36.67 million in interest due on those bonds. It is extremely unlikely that the government would have paid Canadians in gold. On occasions when gold had been demanded, the government responded that because gold could not be exported, it was only worth its face value, and that a suit for damages would be rejected. The Ontario government asked Ottawa for help in halting the practice of Canadians sending their "gold" coupons to U.S. banks to receive interest there in the gold they would not be paid in Canada! See Bordo and Redish 1990.

14. In addition, the records show virtually no debate over the gold clause; the deputy minister of finance asked once for a list of loans with exact wording "in regard to the question of payment in gold," but the list is not in the records and there is no further mention of it.

15. By 1939 one figure suggests that for £17 million of debt outstanding issued in London (a part of the external debt), about £1.1 million was held by New Zealand institutions. Another reference in the *New Zealand Official Yearbook* of 1939 suggests that of £5.2 million of interest payments on debt issued in London, about 2 percent was payable in New Zealand to domestic holders of sterling-denominated debt.

16. Further work should investigate not only issues but residency of creditors.

17. Eurobonds are generally bearer bonds, tax free, underwritten by an international syndicate of banks, and sold mainly in countries other than that of the currency of denomination (Davis 1992).

18. Bond issues, with the exception of federal government issues, were often placed in the Eurobond market (Bank of Canada 1994, 43).

19. However, the government has used swaps and other instruments to *increase* its exposure to the U.S. dollar as part of its diversification efforts (Johnson 1997). It appears that some amount of U.S. dollar exposure provides a hedge for other debt outstanding.

20. This excludes a large amount of debt without a definite redemption date.
21. New Zealand had a milder crisis in 1893 (Butlin 1961). South Africa also had a banking crisis in 1889–90 (Schuman 1938).

References

Argy, Victor. 1995. "Monetary and Exchange Rate Policies, 1973–1991: The Australian and New Zealand Experience." In *Capital Controls, Exchange Rates, and Monetary Policy in the World Economy,* ed. Sebastian Edwards. Cambridge: Cambridge University Press.
Bank of Canada. 1974. *Bank of Canada Review,* November, s67.
———. 1994. "Canada's International Net Indebtedness." *Bank of Canada Review* (summer): 37–50.
Bayley, R. A. 1880. *National Loans of the United States from July 4, 1776, to June 30, 1880.*
Bordo, Michael D. 2001. "Alternating Exchange Rate Regimes: The Canadian Experience, 1820–2000." In *Revisiting the Case for Flexible Exchange Rates.* Ottawa: Bank of Canada.
Bordo, Michael D., and Barry Eichengreen. 1999. "Is Our Current International Economic Environment Unusually Crisis Prone?" In *Capital Flows and the International Financial System,* ed. David Gruen and Luke Gower. Sydney: Reserve Bank of Australia.
Bordo, Michael D., and Marc Flandreau. 2003. "Core, Periphery, Exchange Rate Regimes, and Globalization." In *Globalization in Historical Perspective,* ed. Michael D. Bordo, Alan Taylor, and Jeffrey Williamson. Chicago: University of Chicago Press.
Bordo, Michael D., and Finn E. Kydland. 1995. "The Gold Standard as a Rule: An Essay in Explorations." *Explorations in Economic History* 32:428–64.
Bordo, Michael D., and Angela Redish. 1990. "Credible Commitment and Exchange Rate Stability: Canada's Interwar Experience." *Canadian Journal of Economics* 23:357–80.
———. 2001. "The Legacy of French and English Monetary Institutions for Canada." In *Transferring Wealth and Power from the Old World to the New World: Monetary and Fiscal Institutions in the Seventeenth through the Nineteenth Century,* ed. Michael D. Bordo and Roberto Cortes-Conde. New York: Cambridge University Press.
Bordo, Michael D., and Carlos A. Vegh. 2002. "What If Alexander Hamilton Had Been Argentinean? A Comparison of Argentina and the United States." *Journal of Monetary Economics* 49:459–94.
Butlin, S. J. 1961. *Australia and New Zealand Bank: The Bank of Australia and the Union Bank of Australia Limited, 1828–1951.* London: Longmans.
Caballero, Ricardo, and Arvind Krishnamurthy. 2001. "Excessive Dollar Debt: Financial Development and Underinsurance." Manuscript, Northwestern University, September.
Davis, E. P. 1992. "Euromarkets." In *The New Palgrave Dictionary of Money and Finance,* ed. Peter Newman, Murray Milgate, and John Eatwell, 783–85. London: Macmillan.
Davis, Lance, and Robert Gallman. 2000. *Waves, Tides, and Sandcastles: The Impact of Foreign Capital Flows on Evolving Financial Markets in the New World, 1865–1914.* Cambridge: Cambridge University Press.

Delargy, P. J. R., and Charles Goodhart. 1999. "Financial Crises: Plus ça change, plus c'est la meme chose." LSE Financial Market Group Special Paper no. 108, London School of Economics, London.

Dewey, Davis Rich. 1920. *Financial History of the United States.* New York: Longmans, Green and Co.

Dominion Bureau of Statistics. 1949. *The Canadian Balance of International Payments, 1926 to 1948.* Ottawa: E. Cloutier.

Economic Council of Canada. 1990. *Globalization and Canada's Financial Markets.* Ottawa: Minister of Supply and Services.

Eichengreen, Barry, and Ricardo Hausmann. 1999. "Exchange Rates and Financial Fragility." In *New Challenges for Monetary Policy,* 329–68. Kansas City, MO: Federal Reserve Bank of Kansas City.

Elliot, Jonathan. 1968. *The Funding System of the United States and of Great Britain.* New York: Augustus M. Kelley.

Ferguson, Niall. 2002. "Globalization and Gunboats: The Costs and Benefits of the British Empire Revisited." Manuscript, Oxford University.

Field, Frederick. 1914. *Capital Investment in Canada.* 3rd ed. Montreal: Monetary Times of Canada.

Friedman, Milton, and Anna J. Schwartz. 1963. *A Monetary History of the United States, 1867–1960.* Princeton, NJ: Princeton University Press.

The Investor's Review. Various issues. London: Longmans.

Johnson, Andrew. 1997. "Australian Government Foreign Debt Management." Presentation at the World Bank Sovereign Foreign Debt Management Forum, Washington, DC. Australian Treasury, http://www.treasury.gov.au/documents/202/PDF/Article04.pdf.

Kroszner, Randall S. 2002. "Is It Better to Forgive Than to Receive? Repudiation of the Gold-Indexation Clause in Long-Term Debt during the Great Depression." Manuscript, University of Chicago.

Larain, Felipe, and Andrés Velasco. 2001. "Exchange Rate Policy in Emerging Market Economies: The Case for Floating." *Essays in International Finance,* no. 224, Princeton, NJ, December.

Lindert, Peter. 1969. *Key Currencies and Gold, 1900–1913.* Princeton Studies in International Finance, no. 24. Princeton, NJ: Princeton University Press.

Monthly Statement of the Public Debt Outstanding. Bureau of the Public Debt. http://www.publicdebt.treas.gov/opd/opdhisms2.htm.

Nash, Robert Lucas. Various issues. *Fenn's Compendium of the English and Foreign Funds, Debt, and Revenue of All Nations, Together with Statistics Relating to National Resources and Liabilities, Imports, Exports, Population, Area, Railway Guarantees, Municipal Finance and Indebtedness, Banks of All Nations and all Descriptions of Government, Provincial and Corporate Securities held and dealt in by Investors at Home and Abroad.* London.

New Zealand Official Yearbook. Various years. Wellington: Register-General's Office.

Official Year Book of the Commonwealth of Australia. Various years. Melbourne: Census and Statistics Bureau.

Perkins, Edwin J. 1994. *American Public Finance and Financial Services, 1700–1815.* Columbus: Ohio State University Press.

Ratchford, B. U. 1941. *American State Debts.* Durham, NC: Duke University Press.

Schuman, Christian Gustav Waldemar. 1938. *Structural Changes and Business Cycles in South Africa, 1806–1936.* London: P. S. King.

Stock Exchange (London). Various years. *The Stock Exchange Official Intelligence.* London: Spottiswoode, Ballantyne and Co.

United States Bureau of the Census. 1884. *Tenth Census.* Washington, DC: Government Printing Office.

Wilkins, Myra. 1989. *The History of Foreign Investment in the United States to 1914.* Cambridge, MA: Harvard University Press.

Old Sins

Exchange Clauses and European Foreign Lending in the Nineteenth Century

Marc Flandreau and Nathan Sussman

The Origins of Original Sin

RECENT EMERGING-MARKET crises have shown that the combination of foreign-currency-denominated debts and exchange crises can be explosive: exchange crises lead to financial crises through the increased burden of external liabilities. As a result, countries that have debts denominated in foreign currencies tend to exhibit some reluctance in using exchange rate as an adjustment device to its full possible extent, displaying what has become known as a "fear of floating." Foreign-currency-denominated debts are not randomly distributed throughout the world. They predominate in the liabilities of less-developed nations of Asia and Latin America, which tend to be precisely those with the highest risk to run into a serious exchange rate crisis. The so-called original sin hypothesis describes this phenomenon and its implications: some countries just do not issue debt denominated in their own currency, and as a result, the array of exchange rate strategies available to them is typically smaller than that available to the Western world.

One popular explanation for original sin emphasizes expectations. Some countries do not have a sufficient record to borrow in their own currency. The market would then ration them, or would dictate terms that would deter them from borrowing in their own currency. From a policy point of view, the response to these problems would be to establish credibility by creating institutions: an independent central bank, the rule of law, and protection of property rights would be what is needed to establish a record that would in turn enable to borrow in one's own currency.

This chapter challenges this popular, "expectations driven" interpretation of original sin. Since these institutions are typically exogenous in the short run and endogenous in the longer run, we use history to guide us in our search for an appropriate interpretation. Moreover, there is a striking parallel between the crises of the 1990s and those of the 1890s. As a matter of fact, the 1890s crises in Argentina, Brazil, and Portugal all began with an exchange crisis that triggered a default or near default through the governments' liability exposure to exchange depreciation. Like today, a number of emerging nations had borrowed in gold or set a fixed exchange rate for the coupon, which led to defaults. Bordo and Flandreau (2003) argue that this situation, just like today, led to a measure of "fear of floating" especially among emerging markets and was a factor explaining the spread of the gold standard as a fixed exchange rate system.

In providing a historical perspective on the emergence of original sin problems, we discuss what were the historical determinants of the ability of a country to borrow internationally, long-term, and in its own currency in the nineteenth century. We focus on southern and eastern European countries, as well as Latin America. In order to address these questions, we had to construct, from original sources, a database on foreign bonds and exchange rate clauses. We surveyed both London and Paris to make sure that the phenomena we discuss were not specific to one single market. We also surveyed foreign lending before the classic 1880–1914 period to make sure this was not purely a "gold standard" phenomenon. The facts we establish thus cover a wide array in both time and space. The empirical challenge of classifying exchange rate clauses was not trivial either. We know fairly little about these exchange rate clauses, which seem at first a highly technical and possibly secondary topic. Thus one needs to document the record of exchange rate clauses in the past, providing a careful discussion that will enable identification of who used them, when, and how.

The evidence we collected points to two related facts concerning the emergence of original sin. The first distinguishes between primary-market issue of foreign bonds and secondary-market trading in foreign bonds. Using this distinction, we document that, starting in the nineteenth century, owing largely to the Rothschild banking company that mandated them, exchange rate clauses were related to initial public offerings, IPOs, of foreign bonds in the major financial centers. Almost all IPOs, which were issued exclusively in London or Paris, *regardless of country of origin* were denominated in pounds or francs. *Thus these exchange rate clauses were not a result of credibility concerns.* The second fact is that some countries' bonds, denominated in their domestic currencies, were traded or held in foreign markets. This rules out simple explanations that emphasize lack of sophistication among investors, nominal illusion, and so on.

What may explain these two phenomena? Our hypothesis is that currency liquidity is the underlying cause of our findings. Owing largely to trade finance, some currencies emerged as vehicle currencies commanding international liquidity. As a corollary, states that had internationally accepted currencies could also circulate their debt instruments in secondary markets: having a liquid money market enabled them to issue the debt in their country in the first place. Agents were willing to hold foreign debt instruments issued by states that had leading currencies, because they knew that they could always cash the coupons or the bonds and convert the proceeds into their domestic currency, at a low cost, though not necessarily at a fixed rate. On the other hand, governments whose currencies did not enjoy a vehicle-currency status faced steep premia if they sought to borrow in their own currency, and this led them to rely on fixed exchange rate clauses. Once they had issued in the financial center's own currency, their bonds would have been able to trade almost everywhere, since all other centers quoted that center's currency and were willing to hold assets denominated in that currency. Even those governments that enjoyed a vehicle-currency status could, at times, borrow in foreign financial centers, presumably because they expected to face lower rates than they would have had to pay at home. We infer that when they attempted to tap foreign centers, their own-currency-denominated money markets would have charged them a higher rate. Alternatively, these governments wanted to reap the benefits of liability diversification. Therefore, borrowing at a liquid financial center where the local-currency money market was cheaper, in that center's currency, makes perfect sense.

In sum, the ability to circulate, internationally, bonds denominated in your own currency was related to the status of your currency in terms of international liquidity. Going for an IPO in a foreign financial center in your own currency was going to cost more than borrowing in that center's currency, and all the more so if you had a "junior" currency. The result was, and we think still is, that countries with less-developed money markets displayed an exclusive reliance on foreign exchange clauses, while countries with "senior" currencies went farther toward achieving liability diversification. To support this alternative interpretation of original sin, we are able to show that there exists a near perfect correlation between the existence of a foreign exchange market and a secondary foreign debt market denominated in domestic currencies. Some countries, enjoying a substantial foreign circulation for their domestic bonds, were not countries of particularly sound macroeconomic or political record. "Problem nations" such as Russia, Spain, and Austria-Hungary could circulate their domestic debts abroad, thanks to their well-developed and well-connected financial systems. By contrast, currency clauses prospered when the country's currency was very rarely (if at all) used abroad, as in the case of reputable countries such as Denmark, Sweden, and Norway. Finally, countries with international currencies (such as France and Germany) also occasionally tapped foreign markets.

Our interpretation places international money markets at the center of the stage. Since the existence of foreign exchange markets was deeply rooted in trade history, sometimes going back to medieval times, it appears that our explanation of original sin, in contrast with the credibility argument, focuses on history. Thus while institutions and reforms help agents form expectations about future behavior, path dependency has played a much more significant role in selecting the countries that were to suffer from original sin. Only a major change in countries' ranking in the world trade order (which might have been the outcome of institutional change, for better or for worse) can change these outcomes.

The remainder of this chapter is organized as follows. First, we discuss the prehistory of original sin and focus on London early issues 1825–50, offering our explanation for why IPOs had to be in foreign exchange. Next we take a look at London and Paris in 1883, using *Fenn's Compendium* (thirteenth edition, 1883) for London and more heavily relying on Courtois's *Manuel des Fonds Publics* (eighth edition, Nash 1883) for Paris to document the variety of borrowing practices, and show who circulated debt in domestic currency and who did so in foreign currency. We look at Russia, a large and fairly typical borrower from the European periphery with substantial issues (with and without specie clauses) in Paris, London, and other financial centers. These sections point to a number of hypotheses regarding the determinants of currency clauses in international borrowing, which are at odds with credibility, commitment, and institutional reform hypotheses for original sin. Finally, we tie the pieces together, and offer our conclusions.

The Prehistory of Foreign Exchange Clauses

By the late nineteenth century, gold clauses, or clauses that fixed the coupon in terms of some gold-related unit, had become pervasive. They were a standard feature of the financial packages to which borrowing governments were subjected when they sought to tap the international capital market. We reproduce in figures 6.1 and 6.2 a "typical" bearer's bond issued in 1913 by the Chinese government. As can be seen, the coupon was stated in sterling, francs, marks, rubles, and yen—all gold or gold-exchange currencies at that time.

This highly polarized system emerged from a much more varied setting whose origins can be found in the eighteenth century. Finance, by its very nature, has always tended to internationalize. The first financial markets that emerged, such as Amsterdam and later London, quickly became international markets. European investors compared the various centers when making a decision to invest, and borrowers looked at alternative sources of finance. Not a single country, not even England, could be said to have been an exception to that rule: it is commonly argued that until the Napoleonic Wars, England was a net borrower of capital, largely from Amsterdam (Bordo and White 1991; Brezis 1995; Neal 2000; Oppers 1993). This import of capital could take two forms. Either British securities initially issued in London found their way to Amsterdam, or the British government went directly there to raise funds (Riley 1980).

With Amsterdam's occupation by the French, London emerged as the world's leading financial market of the nineteenth century. Capital flew there, and Continental securities ended up in London, encouraging their listing and trading in

Figure 6.1 Bearer's bond, issued by the Chinese government in 1913

the London Stock Exchange. A typical list of these bonds included those of Austria, France, the Netherlands, Naples, Portugal, Russia, and Spain. Just like British bonds in Amsterdam, these bonds had been issued in their country of origin and were traded in London as a secondary market. European investors thus looked at the various markets as a whole and could shift their balances from one place to the other. The London *Times* of the early 1800s supplied its readers with frequent reports on the quotations of foreign bonds in their respective

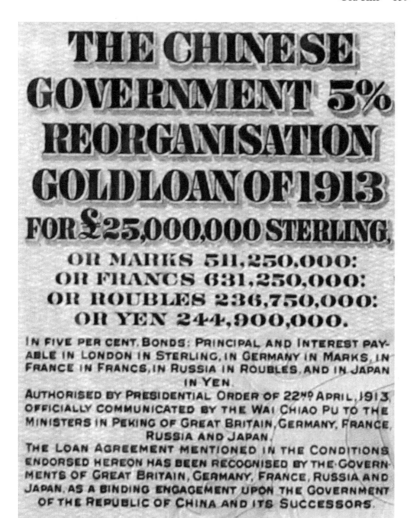

Figure 6.2 Detail, Chinese bearer's bond, 1913

home stock markets and in other financial centers. Conversely, in a fashion that replicated what had happened for Amsterdam, a number of governments began issuing directly in London, and in that case they denominated their issues in the local currency. The London House of Rothschild is generally credited for having introduced sterling bonds to the British capital market (Ferguson 1998, 124–25). With their five branches in Europe (Frankfurt, London, Paris, Vienna, and Naples), the Rothschilds were in a unique position to act as intermediaries

Table 6.1. Foreign bonds traded in London, May 21, 1821

	Coupon	IPO	Currency	Exchange rate clause	Yield at issue
Austria	5%		Silver	Silver	6.6%
Colombia	6%	IPO	Sterling	Sterling	7%
Denmark	5%	IPO	Sterling and marks banco	Sterling/marks banco	5.9%
France	5%		Francs	25.2 F to 25 s	5.7%
Naples	5%	IPO	Ducats	No	7.3%
Prussia	5%	IPO	Sterling	Sterling	5.8%
Russia	6%	IPO	Ruble	11.5 d per 1 ruble	7.3%
Russia	5%	IPO	Silver ruble	Silver	6.5%
Spain	5%		Dollars	No	8%
Spain	5%	IPO	Sterling	Sterling	8%

for these operations and, especially, in facilitating the cashing of coupons in local currencies (Ferguson 1998, 6). The benchmark issue was the Prussian 5%
loan of 1817, and it was followed by other similar contracts. In some cases, the
currency clause could be introduced later as a further facility for investors who
had already become accustomed to given securities. For instance, on October 9,
1821, the London *Times* reported that holders of Spanish bonds, traded as secondary debt in the London Stock Exchange, complained that they could not cash
their coupons in London.[1] Rothschild agreed to act as an agent to the Spanish
crown, and soon thereafter, Spanish debt was issued in sterling, too. The result
of these individual experiences was a mix of sterling clauses or double denominations, illustrated in table 6.1. In some cases (Russia and France), the coupon
was stated in terms of a foreign currency (fixed exchange rate clause); sometimes (Austria, Naples, and Russia) it was stated in terms of the metallic parity
of the domestic currency (specie clause).[2] The specie clause generally came with
a fixed exchange rate clause, but there could be fixed exchange rate clauses without specie clauses.

The 1820s, following Britain's return to gold, saw a large increase in London
foreign lending. Most of the European powers borrowed there to reconstruct
their economies and public finances. Latin American colonies and newly independent countries also rushed to raise capital. For the first time in European financial history, there was a deluge of new issues in one financial center, comprising a large variety of grades of borrowers—from mighty European powers
to the emerging markets of Latin America. Sterling clauses became a routine
feature of new London issues, and were significantly applied to all Latin American securities issued in those years.

Just as Britain had followed the practices of Amsterdam, the financial markets of the Continent that expanded after 1830, such as Paris or Brussels, followed the British example. As these markets became important providers of in-

ternational capital (Cameron 1961), an increasing number of foreign securities began to be traded, while outright introduction on these markets typically displayed currency clauses as an entry badge. Similar arrangements became widespread, since most European markets tended to be international. One outcome of this development was the considerable variety of fixed exchange rate clauses. Owing to the variety in underlying monetary regimes that prevailed until 1873 on the Continent, we find among the gold or gold-related clauses (when countries borrowed in London), bimetallic clauses (when countries borrowed in Paris) and silver clauses (when countries borrowed in Amsterdam). A measure of correspondence existed between the monetary standard of the borrowing country and that of the lending market. Countries such as (silver-standard) Austria were often found to have gone to (silver-based) Amsterdam or Hamburg. Similarly, one of us argued elsewhere (Flandreau 2000) that one force that drove the making of the Latin Union in 1865 was the desire by France's satellites to attract French capital. Italy, for instance, and earlier Belgium, tapped the Paris market (again through the agency of Rothschild frères) and was induced to include franc clauses: this currency then became a natural basis when these nations considered adopting a new monetary regime, as part of their newly acquired independence.

In other cases borrowers tried to take advantage of several foreign markets at once. If these markets had different monetary standards, issuers then set their coupon in terms of both gold and silver units. Table 6.1 reports one London-traded Danish bond whose coupons were reported as cashable in both gold sterling and silver mark banco of Hamburg. These "bimetallic" clauses meant an implicit fixed exchange rate between the two metals. This fixed rate could differ from the actual gold-silver exchange rate, creating scope for arbitrage opportunities in the cashing of coupons. However, as long as French bimetallism ruled the exchange rate between gold and silver countries (Flandreau 1996, 2002, 2004), the near complete stability of the gold-silver exchange rate limited this opportunity.[3]

The transition of the main capital-exporting countries to the gold standard in the 1870s dramatically simplified matters. Silver clauses were generally suspended. In the case of silver fixed exchange rate clauses, this occurred as a natural result of the countries in whose currencies these clauses had been stated shifting to the gold standard (this was the case of Dutch florins or mark banco clauses): former silver clauses were now gold clauses. In the case of silver specie clauses (which related the coupon to the currency's silver parity), the suspension of silver coinage meant that at some point paper became better than silver, as was the case in Russia and Austria-Hungary. From that point on, new clauses became typically gold (specie clause) or gold-related (fixed exchange rate clauses). A side effect of the emergence of the gold standard was thus a dramatic simplification in the variety of coupon clauses that could be found on the market, with all clauses being gold or gold-related on the eve of World War I, as argued at the opening of this section.

In order to begin our inquiry into the sources of exchange rate clauses, it might be useful to start from the explanations we find in contemporary sources. At a very broad level, the intuition was that they "improved the market's willingness to lend." This interpretation is put forward by Ferguson (1998) when he argues that, as underwriters of the Prussian and subsequent sterling-denominated bonds, the Rothschilds must have assumed that they could sell them more easily if they were denominated in pounds. When we dig slightly deeper to get a better grasp of the rationale behind the alleged improved marketability, we find reference to two main interpretations. The first focuses on nominal income illusion. McCulloch's *Dictionary* (1837) allocates numerous pages to explanations and tables assisting in the calculation of annuities' values (also present values). Computations are made in the understanding that his readership holds only sterling coupons, as no mention is made of foreign-currency-denominated coupons. Lévy (1901) would latter claim that French investors were reluctant to "put in their portfolio any bond whose nominal income would not be stable." Thus the coupon clauses would have to be understood as (possibly irrational) conditions imposed on borrowers by powerful groups of lenders.[4] The second interpretation focuses on risk aversion and information asymmetries. According to various contemporary authorities such as Lévy (1901), French investors were "cautious" and "badly informed when it comes to exchange rates." Similarly, de Block (1889) motivates the exchange rate clauses in Russian bonds as a necessary incentive, given the country's lack of "credibility."

One may advance some arguments against the explanations based on nominal income illusion. The period between the end of the French wars and the stabilization of the pound in 1821 was characterized by violent fluctuations between sterling and Continental currencies. However, we know that this did not prevent British investors from buying Continental securities. Similarly, the collapse of silver currencies and the suspension of silver specie clauses left investors in France and the Netherlands with large amounts of Austrian securities whose dividends, formerly paid in silver, were now paid in paper. Yet there is evidence (Courtois 1883) that these paper bonds remained much in vogue with the French public. This implies a probably greater sophistication than contemporary statements imply. Nevertheless, the existence of sophisticated bondholders does not rule out the existence of less sophisticated ones. Wanting to tap a larger pool of investors (which would have reduced the borrowing rate) may have prompted underwriters to adopt sterling clauses.

In a discussion of the excess risk aversion or asymmetric information argument, the Latin American lending boom in London in the 1820s provides interesting insights. As shown in table 6.2 (adapted from Dawson 1990), the

Table 6.2. Latin American loans (all in sterling)
raised in London, 1820s

Country	Year	Coupon	Yield at issue
Brazil	1824	5%	6.6%
	1825	5%	5.9%
	1829	5%	9.2%
Buenos Aires	1824	6%	7%
Chili	1822	6%	8.6%
Colombia	1822	6%	7.1%
	1824	6%	6.8%
Guatemala	1825	6%	9.5%
Mexico	1824	5%	8.6%
	1825	6%	6.9%
Peru	1822	6%	6.8%
	1824	6%	7.3%
	1825	6%	7.7%

Source: Dawson 1990.

many uncertainties relating to the issues by countries and colonies that had no credit history to speak of did not result in borrowing rates much higher than those accorded to established European powers. In the lending bubble of the 1820s, Latin American countries followed suit and issued bonds in sterling in London. Thus exchange rate clauses did not emerge in order to enhance credibility or signal commitment or macroeconomic stability. The bond mania of the 1820s and its swift collapse show that this was not the case at all.[5] The amount of Latin American loans floated in the London market was almost 22 million sterling, slightly higher than the 20 million sterling floated at the same time by European borrowers.[6] If credit risk or information asymmetry had been an issue, the boom would have never occurred in the first place.[7] That it occurred anyway suggests that currency clauses must have had other motivations than serving as seals of creditworthiness.

At this stage, our brief survey of the history of fixed exchange rate clauses shows that these clauses do not seem to have been a mandatory step for a given security to become "international." Rather, they seem to have been tightly associated with a very specific kind of operation: namely, new foreign issues. In the next section, we go deeper into this issue and establish our iron rule of fixed exchange rate clauses: fixed exchange rate clauses were always a companion of foreign IPOs.

A London and Paris Snapshot: Primary Markets, Secondary Markets, and Specie Clauses

Having examined the early history of foreign exchange clauses, we move on toward the last quarter of the nineteenth century, when we conveniently have two sources from two centers of international lending, London and Paris. These sources allow us to study in more detail the portfolios of international investors at a given time and to gauge the secondary markets for these assets. Examining the secondary markets, therefore, complements our view of the primary market discussed above. This snapshot from 1883 allows us to establish that there was nothing new under the lending sun and that the trends started in the 1820s prevailed throughout the nineteenth century.

For Paris we use the eighth edition of Courtois's *Manuel des Fonds Publics* (1883), an investors' handbook, which is a convenient source for exchange rate clauses.[8] First, unlike other French sources, such as the annual *Manuel des Agents de Change,* Courtois's book is extremely specific and careful when it comes to currency denominations. His *Manuel,* meant to inform investors, at a given date, on the entire array of investment opportunities, goes beyond the official market (or "Parquet") in Paris or the provinces (such as Lyon or Bordeaux) to list other relevant stocks. These include the securities listed in the parallel markets in France (known as the Coulisse) as well as foreign markets. Indeed, for wealthy Europeans, the relevant market was not their local one but a network of financial centers where they could, with the agency of investment banks and, increasingly, commercial banks, purchase foreign securities. A casual list of these foreign markets is provided by Courtois: it comprises "London, Berlin, Brussels, Hamburg, Frankfurt, Madrid, Rome, Florence, Saint-Petersburg etc."[9] The inclusion of such places as Madrid, Rome, and St. Petersburg is intriguing, and we shall return to it later. For London we use a similar source, *Fenn's Compendium* (Nash 1883), which lists all the foreign public debts of nations that circulated in London.

Using these sources, we proceeded country by country, and compiled the information relevant for the bonds listed. This included the unit in which the coupon was paid, the market(s) where the bond was initially issued (primary issues), and the market(s) where it was mostly traded (secondary markets). We then grouped these countries according to the exchange rate clause into three groups: I, only with exchange rate clauses; II, those with both domestic currency and exchange rate clauses; and III, countries who issued bonds with no exchange rate clauses. The results are presented in table 6.3. Perhaps unsurprisingly, the evidence suggests that groups II and III are much smaller than group I. More interestingly, this table suggests that the breakdown worked along geographical, rather than institutional, lines: those countries in groups II and III, for which at least some domestic-currency issues were found, are typically European nations, regardless of their "institutional" or macroeconomic performance. Moreover, they even include countries that would not a priori qualify for the top league. Countries like Austria and Russia, for instance, had a number of well-known problems in the mid-1880s—the least one being a floating exchange rate. By contrast, well-behaved countries such as the Scandinavian group, for all their gold convertibility, parliamentary system, division of power,

Table 6.3. Countries and exchange rate clauses, 1883

Group I: only exchange rate clauses	Group II: mixed	Group III: only domestic currency
Europe Denmark, Finland, Greece, Hungary, Norway, Poland, Romania, Sweden	*Europe* Austria, Italy, Portugal, Russia, Spain, [France]	*Europe* Germany, [Belgium], Great Britain, Netherlands, [Switzerland]
Latin America Argentina, Bolivia, Brazil, Chile, Colombia, Costa Rica, Dominican Republic, Ecuador, Guatemala, Haiti, Honduras, Mexico, Paraguay, Peru, Uruguay, Venezuela		
Africa and Middle East Egypt, Liberia, Transvaal, Tunisia, Turkey		
English speaking and dominions Australia, Canada, India, New Zealand, United States, other British colonies		
Asia China, Japan		

Notes: Cases that have some ambiguity are in brackets. Belgium and Switzerland, as part of the Latin Union, have a French franc–based franc. France is included in the mixed list because the 5% indemnity loan issued in 1871 included a fixed exchange rate clause for payments made in London. Note, however, that the sterling clause of the French indemnity loan is not reported by Courtois.

thrift, and Protestant ethic, were with the troubled regimes of Latin America in the first group and in the gallant company of the United States, whose bonds that "mattered" for English and French investors had all gold or sterling clauses.[10]

A more careful examination suggests a finer characterization of the evidence. When we break the bonds' data according to the place of initial issue, an interesting feature emerges. Tables 6.4 and 6.5 list the bonds according to place of issue. Looking first at countries that issued in their domestic markets (table 6.4), we find that these are predominantly members of groups II and III: Dutch bonds denominated in florins were primarily issued in Amsterdam. German bonds, issued in German financial centers, were mark (earlier thaler) denominated. The same would hold for Belgian, Swiss, British, and other bonds. For these issuers, the "main" market was typically the national financial market. In practice (as illustrated by their presence in Courtois's list of "relevant stocks"), these bonds found their way (officially through their inclusion in the "cote officielle" or through some other way) to the French market and London market (or to some other market that was important to French investors). In other words, domestic-currency bonds usually had a large and active secondary market in other leading financial centers.

The reverse picture holds for the countries of group I: foreign-currency-denominated instruments of these countries were issued in the foreign centers whose currency had been used as unit of denomination. Tables 6.5 and 6.6 list

Table 6.4. International securities issued in own market (selection)

Designation	Year	Amount (millions)	Coupon	Currency	Place of issue	Main secondary market	Other secondary market	Underwriter
				Germany				
German Empire								
Bearer's bonds	1877	251	4%	Marks	Berlin	Berlin	Paris	
Prussia								
4.5% consols	1869	523	4.5%	Thalers/marks	Berlin	Berlin	Paris	
4% consol ides	1877–78	1159	4%	Marks	Berlin	Berlin	London, Paris	
Baden								
4% 1867	1867	24	4%	Thalers/marks	Berlin	Berlin	Paris	
4% 1875	1875	30	4%	Marks	Berlin	Berlin	Paris	
4% 1878	1878	92	4%	Marks	Berlin	Berlin	Paris	
Bavaria								
4% 1875	1875	15	4%	Marks	Berlin	Berlin	Paris	
4% 1879	1879	38	4%	Marks	Berlin	Berlin	Paris	
4% 1866	1866	48	4%	Marks	Berlin	Berlin	Paris	
Oldenburg								
4% consols	1873	14	4%	Marks	Oldenburg	Oldenburg	Paris	
Saxe								
3% 1876	1876	342	3%	Marks	Berlin	Berlin	Paris	
Württemberg								
4% 1881	1881	168	4%	Marks	Frankfurt	Frankfurt	Paris	

2.5% perpetual	n.a.[a]	n.a.	2.5%	Dutch guilders	Amsterdam	Amsterdam	London, Paris	
3% perpetual	n.a.[a]	n.a.	3.0%	Dutch guilders	Amsterdam	Amsterdam	London, Paris	
4% perpetual	n.a.[a]	n.a.	4.0%	Dutch guilders	Amsterdam	Amsterdam	London, Paris	
4% 1878	1878	43	4.0%	Dutch guilders	Amsterdam/Paris	Amsterdam	Paris, London	Paribas
Belgium								
2.5% rentes			2.5%	Belgian francs	Brussels, Paris	Brussels	Paris	Rothschild frères, Sté Générale
3% rentes			3.0%	Belgian francs	Brussels, Paris	Brussels	Paris	Rothschild frères, Sté Générale
4% rentes (1st series)			4.0%	Belgian francs	Brussels, Paris	Brussels	Paris	Rothschild frères, Sté Générale
4% rentes (2nd series)			4.0%	Belgian francs	Brussels, Paris	Brussels	Paris	Rothschild frères, Sté Générale

[a]The perpetual rentes were issued at various dates by the government on the domestic market according to financial needs.

Table 6.5. International securities issued in foreign markets (selection)

Latin America

Designation	Date	Amount (millions)	Coupon	Currency	Place of issue	Main secondary market	Other secondary market	Underwriter/coupon
Federal government						Argentina		
6% 1866–68	1866–68	3	6%	Sterling	London	London	Paris, Amsterdam	Baring, Hope
6% 1871	1871	6	6%	Sterling	London	London	Paris	Murrieta
6% hard dollar	1872	23	6%	Gold peso	London, Buenos Aires	London,		Stern[a]
6% chemins de fer	1880	£2.45	6%	Sterling, francs	London, Paris	London, Paris		Murrieta, Comptoir d'Escompte Paribas
Province of Buenos Aires								
6% 1824	1824	1	6%	Sterling	London	London		Baring
6% 1870	1870	1	6%	Sterling	London	London		Murrieta
6% 1873	1873	2	6%	Sterling	London	London		Baring
6% province de Buenos Aires	1882	2	6%	Sterling	London	London		Baring
Province of Santa Fe								
7% 1874	1874	0	7%	Sterling	London	London		Murrieta
Province of Entre Rios								
7% 1872	1872	0	7%	Sterling	London	London		Murrieta
						Bolivia		
6% 1872	1872	2	6%	Sterling	London	London		Lumb, Wanklyn & Co.
						Brazil		
4.5% 1852	1852	1	4.5%	Sterling	London	London		N.M. Rothschild
4.5% 1858	1852	2	4.5%	Sterling	London	London		N.M. Rothschild
4.5% 1860	1860	1	4.5%	Sterling	London	London		N.M. Rothschild
4.5% 1863	1863	4	4.5%	Sterling	London	London		N.M. Rothschild
5% 1865	1865	7	4.5%	Sterling	London	London		N.M. Rothschild
5% 1871	1871	3	5.0%	Sterling	London	London		N.M. Rothschild
5% 1875	1875	5	5.0%	Sterling	London	London	Paris	N.M. Rothschild, Rothschild frères
4.5% Gold "1975"	1879	52	4.5%	Gold milreis	Brazil	London		N.M. Rothschild

Loan	Year	No.	Rate	Currency	Market		Banker
3% 1842	1842	1	3%	Sterling	London		Baring
4.5% 1858	1858	2	4.5%	Sterling	London		Baring
7% 1866	1866	1	7%	Sterling	London		Morgan
6% 1867	1867	2	6%	Sterling	London		Morgan
5% 1870	1870	1	5%	Sterling	London		Morgan
5% 1873	1873	2	5%	Sterling	London		Oriental Bank Corp.
5% 1875	1875	2	5%	Sterling	London		Oriental Bank Corp.
						Colombia	
4.75% 1873	1873	2	4.8%	Sterling	London	London	London and County Banking Co.
						Paraguay	
8% 1871	1871	1	8%	Sterling	London	London	Robinson, Fleming & Co.
8% 1872	1872	2	8%	Sterling	London	London	Robinson, Fleming & Co.
						Peru	
6% loan 1869	1870	£12	6%	Sterling, francs	Paris, London	Paris, London	Sté Générale/Henry Shröder
5% loan 1869	1872	£37	5%	Sterling, francs	Paris, London	Paris, London	Sté Générale/Henry Shröder
						Venezuela	
4% 1881	1881	3	4%	Sterling	London	London	CFBH[b]
						Asia	
						China	
China 8% 1874-75	1874–76	1	8%	Sterling	London	London	Hong Kong and Shanghai Banking Corp.
China 1877	1877	2	8%	Sterling	London	London	Hong Kong and Shanghai Banking Corp.
						Japan	
9% 1870	1870	1	9%	Sterling	London	London	Shröder, Oriental Bank Corp.
7% 1873	1873	2	7%	Sterling	London	London	

(continued)

Table 6.5. (continued)

Designation	Date	Amount (millions)	Coupon	Currency	Place of issue	Main secondary market	Other secondary market	Underwriter/coupon
Europe								
Greece								
5% 1878	1878	1	5%	Sterling	London	London		Ionian Bank
5% 1880	1881	120	5%	Francs, sterling	Paris, London	Paris, London	Greece	Comptoir d'Escompte Baring, National Bank of Greece, Banque de Constantinople, Crédit Industriel de Grèce
Portugal								
3% "exterior"	1852–80	60	3%	Sterling	Paris, London	Paris, London		Crédit Lyonnais, Portuguese Financial Commission
3% "interior"	n.a.	n.a.	3%	Francs, sterling	Paris, London, Lisbon	Paris, London, Lisbon		n.a.
5% 1876	1876	8	5%	Francs, sterling, florins P.B.	Paris, London, Amsterdam, Lisbon			Sté de Dépôts en Comptes Courants; Lippman, Rosenthal and Co.; Portuguese Financial Commission; Portuguese Treasury
5% 1879	1879	38	5%	Francs, sterling, florins P.B.	Paris, London, Amsterdam, Lisbon			Marcuard; Comptoir d'Escompte; Lippman, Rosenthal and Co.; Portuguese Financial Commission; Portuguese Treasury
5% 1881	1881	103	5%	Francs, sterling, florins P.B.	Paris, London, Amsterdam, Lisbon			Portuguese Treasury Marcuard et Comptoir d'Escompte; Lippman, Rosenthal and Co.; Portuguese Financial Commission; Portuguese Treasury

Denmark

4% 1850–61	1850–61	0.4	4%	Sterling	London	London		Hambro
4% 1862	1862	0.66	4%	Sterling	London	London		Hambro

Norway

4.5% 1874	1874	23	4.5%	Marks	Berlin, Hamburg, Copenhagen	Berlin, Hamburg, Copenhagen		Warschauer Norddeutsche Bank, Privat-Banken i Kjobenhavn
4.5% 1876	1876	1	4.5%	Sterling	London	London	Paris	Hambro
4.5% 1878	1878	2	4.5%	Sterling (marks)	London, Berlin	London, Berlin	Paris	Hambro, Nordeutsche Bank
4% 1880	1880	1	4.0%	Sterling (francs, marks)	London, Paris, Hamburg	London, Paris, Hamburg		Hambro, Comptoir d'Escompte, Norddeutsche Bank

Sweden

4% 1852	1852	0	4.0%	Sterling	London	London		Dent, Palmer and Cy
5% 1868	1868	1	5.0%	Sterling	London, Stockholm	London, Stockholm		Raphael & Sons
4.5% 1875	1875	27	4.5%	Marks	London (Berlin?)	London (Berlin?)		Erlanger
4.5% 1876	1876	2	4.5%	Sterling	London, Stockholm	London, Stockholm		Hambro
4% 1878	1878	2	4.0%	Sterling (francs)	London, Paris	London, Paris		Hambro, Sté de Dépôte en Compte Courants
4% 1880	1880	4	4.0%	Sterling (krone, marks, francs)	London, Stockholm, Paris, Hamburg, Frankfurt	London, Stockholm, Paris, Hamburg, Frankfurt		Hambro, Paribas, Norddeutsche Bank, Bethmann, Erlanger, Ricksguldkontoret, Scandinavska Credit Actieboilaget

(continued)

Table 6.5. (continued)

Designation	Date	Amount (millions)	Coupon	Currency	Place of issue	Main secondary market	Other secondary market	Underwriter/coupon
					North America			
					Canada			
6%	Varied	4	6%	Sterling	London	London		Baring; Glyn, Mills, Currie & Co.
5% consol	1860	6	5%	Sterling	London	London		Baring; Glyn, Mills, Currie & Co.
4% 1868	1868	6	4%	Sterling	London	London	Paris	Baring; Glyn, Mills, Currie & Co.
4% 1874	1874	12	4%	Sterling	London	London	Paris	Baring; Glyn, Mills, Currie & Co.
					United States (only federal and Massachusetts)			
Federal government								
6% 1881			6%	Gold dollars	??		Paris	
5% 1881			5%	Gold dollars	??		Paris	
4.5% 1891c			4.5%	Gold dollars	London	London		
Massachusetts								
5% 1866	1868	0.83	5%	Sterling	London	London		Baring
5% 1868	1868	0.61	5%	Sterling	London	London		Baring
5% 1870	1870	0.62	5%	Sterling	London	London		Baring
5% 1871	1871	0.62	5%	Sterling	London	London		Baring
5% 1871	1871	0.30	5%	Sterling	London	London		Baring
5% 1873	1873	0.12	5%	Sterling	London	London		Baring
5% 1875	1875	0.31	5%	Sterling	London	London		Baring
5% 1875	1875	0.27	5%	Sterling	London	London		Baring

aCoupon paid in Buenos Aires.
bDefaulted. Coupon paid through arrangements with the Council for Foreign Bondholders.
cDebt denominated according to year of likely redemption.

Table 6.6. Foreign bonds traded in London, *Fenn's Compendium*, 1883

Country	Yield	Currency	Exchange rate clause
Austria	5%	Paper	No
Austria	5%	Silver	Silver/florins
Austria	4%	Gold	Gold
Belgium	2.5%, 3%, 4%	Francs	25 francs = 1 sterling
Brazil	4.5%, 5%	Sterling	Sterling
France	3.5%	Francs	25 francs = 1 sterling
France	4.5%	Francs	No
Germany	4%	Marks	
Hungary	5%	Silver	10 florins = 1 sterling
Hungary	6%	Gold	10 florins = 1 sterling
Italy	5%	Lire	25 francs = 1 sterling
Mexico	6%	Dollars	No
Mexico	6%	Sterling	Sterling
Netherlands	2.5%, 4%	Florins	Silver
Portugal	3%	Sterling	Sterling
Russia	5%	Sterling	Sterling
Russia	5%	Silver rubles	Silver
Russia	5%	Paper rubles	No
Russia	5%	Silver ruble	Sterling, francs, florins
Russia	5%	Silver ruble	125 rubles = 20 sterling
Spain	5% conversion	Sterling	Sterling
Spain	3%	Pesetas	No
Sweden	4%	Sterling	Sterling
United States	3%, 4%, 4.5%	Dollars	No
U.S. Massachusetts	5%	Sterling	Sterling
U.S. Virginia	5%	Sterling	Sterling
U.S. Virginia	6%	Dollars	No

the countries who issued bonds denominated in foreign currencies. As can be seen, there is virtually a perfect correlation between the currency denomination and the market, or markets, where the IPO took place. Thus most Argentinean, Brazilian, and Chilean bonds were initially introduced to the market by London houses, or houses with a London branch, and were sterling denominated. Similarly, those issues that took place in several foreign markets at once had their coupon payable at a fixed exchange rate in all their "primary" markets. The long list of examples include the Greek 5% 1880 loan issued both in Paris and London; the Norwegian 4.5% 1878 issued in London and Berlin but whose coupon could be cashed in Paris as well; and the Peruvian 6% of 1869 issued in Paris and London. These had, respectively, their coupon paid in sterling and francs (Greece); sterling, francs, and marks (Norway); and francs and sterling (Peru).

This correlation of currency in the market where public debts were issued and denomination of the issue stands as the rule, which also extends to cases of issues that were issued mainly abroad but also had a small domestic issue component. In such cases, the loan was typically denominated in the specie counterpart of the domestic currency. Examples of this kind of arrangement are provided by the Argentinean "hard dollar" gold peso loan of 1872, the Brazilian gold milreis loan of 1879, the Italian gold lira rentes of the 1850s and 1860s, the Swedish 4% loan of 1880, and so on. This finding echoes the views in Flandreau (2000), according to which the financial market played an important role in spreading the use of certain monetary standards (French and English) and thus causing the emergence of currency areas, such as the franc-based Latin Union or the sterling gold standard. In effect, it seems that, for some countries, getting access to a given foreign capital market while retaining a share of the issue at home meant a de facto tying of its currency to that of the foreign market it had targeted.

It is important to emphasize that we did not find any exceptions to these rules. Moreover, our finding may shed light on some apparent puzzles: for instance, France ended up in group II because of the sterling clause that was included in the indemnity loan of 1871. As the story goes, the French government decided to include the clause in agreement with Rothschilds, in order to insure the success of the operation (Say 1874; Kindleberger 1993). Given the enormous size of the issue, officials had sought to tap directly both Paris *and* London, rather than issue in Paris and let London investors use their intermediaries to purchase French securities in their "home" market. The result was a franc issue with a fixed sterling exchange rate: thus, once again, the currencies of the IPO had been used.

That currency clauses had much to do with IPOs can also be illustrated by looking at the group II category. There we find a number of countries (such as Italy, Russia, and Austria) that are typically thought of as belonging to the European "periphery." For these countries (of which several floated), we find evidence of important holdings in the London and Paris markets. The case of Austrian "silber rentes" is interesting. Initially issued with a silver clause in both Vienna and Paris (at a time when the French currency was bimetallic and thus silver related), they certainly illustrate the IPO effect. Once silver depreciated and its coinage was suspended in Austria, the rentes were tantamount to a paper bond. Yet it appears that they retained a large foreign market (Courtois mentions that they were much in vogue in Paris): clear evidence that having a paper currency and paper bonds did not ban countries from foreign capital markets. The cases of Italian and Russian paper bonds (the Italian 1849 and 1850 bonds and the Russian 1864–66 and 1877–79 interior 5% paper bonds) illustrate a similar mechanism: while these bonds had originally been issued in domestic markets (thus explaining their denomination in lira or paper rubles), they found their way to Paris (and London) as a secondary market and were actively traded there. Thus again, while on the one hand the currency of denomination is the currency of the IPO, nothing seems to have prevented—at least for a subgroup of European countries—the development of an offshore market in domestic-denominated debt. Moreover, as the case of Russian bonds issued in 1890 (found in the *Annuaire officiel de la Compagnie des agents de change de Paris*) shows, some peripheral countries could undertake foreign issues without gold clauses—provided that domestic institutions were prepared to assume a leading role in the process.[11]

A Russian Case Study

Russia provides a very interesting case study of the evolution and functioning of the foreign bond market in London and Paris. Russian bonds were traded in London since the end of the Napoleonic Wars and composed one of the largest foreign bond holdings in London throughout the nineteenth century. In 1875 Russian bonds represented 6.5 percent of total foreign bonds in the London market, and in 1905 that figure doubled to 11.7 percent.[12] By any measure, Russia was at the time a relatively "backward" country: although it was a European military power, it lagged behind other European powers in terms of economic growth, as well as commercial growth, and maritime development. Its political regime was the most autocratic in Europe, and of a quasi feudal nature until the 1860s, when serfdom was finally abolished. In terms of institutional development, and especially in view of the variables listed in the introduction, Russia would rank very low on a contemporary European scale. Its currency, nominally bimetallic, was most of the time inconvertible, with paper rubles and copper petty currency (copecs) dominating in daily transactions. Thus in almost every respect Russia then, like Russia now, was an "emerging" market that should have suffered from original sin.

As alluded to above, however, this was hardly the case. Russia issued bonds in various currencies and financial centers: from St. Petersburg to London, Paris, Amsterdam, Hamburg, Berlin, and Warsaw—in sterling, francs, florins, marks, and rubles, in gold, silver, and paper. Its bonds had exchange rate clauses, metallic clauses, and no clauses at all. Table 6.7 lists the Russian bonds found in London and Paris, a list that, while impressive, is probably not exhaustive.

The heterogeneity exhibited in table 6.7 may suffice to refute any simpleminded hypothesis of original sin; a few additional facts may make our case stronger. One original sin hypothesis suggests a "lemons" story, whereby no domestic debt is issued because the creditors know that the government will renege on it. Table 6.7 shows this was not the case for Russia. The second hypothesis suggests that the domestic market for debts is small compared to the foreign one. Table 6.8 shows the ratio of domestic to foreign bond issues for Russia for selected years. The table shows that the domestic debt proportion was actually significant, suggesting that credibility at home was not the issue. Rather than a credibility story, we can suggest a liquidity story—that given available domestic savings, Russia could borrow on better terms abroad.

Three additional anecdotes from Russian borrowing add an interesting

Table 6.7. Russian bonds in London and Paris

Year	Yield	Currency	Place of issue	Coupons
1821	6%	Rubles	St. Petersburg	11.5d per ruble
1821	5%	Silver rubles	St. Petersburg	Silver
1822	5%	Silver	St. Petersburg	3s 1d per ruble in London; current rate in St. Petersburg
1822	5%	Sterling	London	Sterling
1824	5%	Silver rubles	Amsterdam	No
1827	6%	Paper rubles	St. Petersburg	No
1827	6%	Silver rubles	St. Petersburg	Payable in paper at the current price of silver
1827	6%	Gold rubles	St. Petersburg	Payable in paper at the current price of gold
1827	6%	Florins	Amsterdam	Florins
1831	4.32%	Paper rubles	St. Petersburg	No
1840	4%	Silver rubles	St. Petersburg, Amsterdam, Warsaw	Silver
1841	4%	Silver rubles	Amsterdam	Silver
1844	4%	Silver rubles	St. Petersburg	Payable in paper at the current price of silver
1847	4%	Silver rubles	St. Petersburg	Payable in paper at the current price of silver
1849	4.5%	Sterling	London, Paris	Sterling
1855	5%	Silver rubles	Berlin, Hamburg, Amsterdam?	Silver
1857	4.5%	Silver rubles	London, Paris, Amsterdam	Sterling, francs, and florins; none after 1867
1859	3%	Sterling	London, Berlin	Sterling, thalers (6.75 = 1 sterling) and marks (20.25 = 1 sterling)
1859	5%	Paper rubles	St. Petersburg	No
1860	4.5%	Sterling, florins	London, Amsterdam	Sterling, florins
1861	5%	Paper rubles	St. Petersburg	No
1862	5%	Sterling, francs, rubles	London, Paris	Sterling, francs, florins
1864	5%	Sterling, florins	London, Amsterdam	Sterling, florins
1864	5%	Paper rubles	St. Petersburg, Berlin	No
1866	5%	Paper rubles	St. Petersburg, Berlin	No
1866	5%	Sterling, florins	London, Amsterdam	Sterling, florins
1867	4%	Sterling, francs, florins	London, Paris, Amsterdam	Sterling, francs, florins
1869	4%	Sterling, francs, florins	London, Paris, Amsterdam	Sterling, francs, florins
1869	5%	Paper rubles	St. Petersburg	No
1870	5%	Sterling, francs, rubles	London, Paris, St. Petersburg	Sterling, francs, rubles
1871	5%	Sterling, francs, rubles	London, Paris, St. Petersburg	Sterling, francs, rubles
1872	5%	Sterling, francs, rubles	London, Paris, St. Petersburg	Sterling, francs, rubles
1873	5%	Sterling, francs, rubles	London, Paris, St. Petersburg	Sterling, francs, rubles
1875	4.5%	Sterling	London, Paris	Sterling
1876	5%	Paper rubles	St. Petersburg	No
1877	5%	Sterling, francs, florins, marks	London, Paris, Amsterdam, Berlin	Sterling, francs, florins, marks
1877	5%	Paper rubles	St. Petersburg	No

(*continued*)

Table 6.7. (continued)

Year	Yield	Currency	Place of issue	Coupons
1878	5%	Paper rubles	St. Petersburg	No
1879	5%	Paper rubles	St. Petersburg	No
1880	4%	Metallic rubles	St. Petersburg	Gold, current rate
1880	4.5%	Gold rubles	Paris, St. Petersburg	Gold
1881	5%	Paper rubles	St. Petersburg	No
1881	4.5%	Silver rubles	St. Petersburg, Warsaw	Silver
1887	5%	Marks	Berlin	Marks
1889	5%	Paper rubles	St. Petersburg	No
1889	3%	Gold rubles	St. Petersburg	Gold
1889	4%	Gold rubles	St. Petersburg	Sterling, francs, marks, florins, current rubles
1891	3%	Gold rubles	?	Gold
1893	4%	Silver bonds	St. Petersburg	Silver
1894	4%	Sterling	London	Sterling
1894	4%	Gold rubles	?	Gold
1894	4%	Rubles	?	1 sterling = 9.45 rubles

Table 6.8. Ratio of Russian debt held at home
(millions of silver rubles)

	1827	1841	1866
Home	263	115	207
Foreign	389	103 [a]	441
Total	652	218	648
Ratio of home debt	40%	55%	32%

Source: Times (London).

[a] Excluding Dutch loans (77 million florins).

flavor to our story. In 1841 the Russian Commission of Amortisement reported: "But by deducting the sum of 476,526 Roubles 22 13/14 Copecs of silver, on which the Treasury had made a profit on the exchange, a means adopted as the basis for foreign payments, the committee received in fact 18,822,317 Roubles 72 1/14 Copecs" (Times [London], July 24, 1841).

The Russian Treasury gained some 2.5 percent profit on the exchanges: while a fixed exchange rate clause provided a floor for the investor, if the ruble appreciated (rare, but not an impossible event), the issuer had a nice gain at the investor's expense. This anecdote suggests that some borrowers had risk aversion and money illusion when it came to fixed exchange clauses.

A second story relates to a Russian loan of 50 million silver rubles from 1855, in the midst of the Crimean War. The London Times (September 14, 1854) reports: "In June 1854, an attempt was made to raise a loan of 50,000,000 silver Roubles in Russia itself, but the experiment was not so successful that it is likely to be repeated. As matters now stand, it is evident that Russia has no chance of raising money in foreign countries and her internal resources are so little developed that she cannot hope to obtain much at home."

Lo and behold, a year later we find the following report:

> The statement that the house of Mendelssohn which is amongst the first banking establishments in Berlin, has been allowed by the Prussian government to open subscriptions in that capital for the attempted Russian loan of 50,000,000 of Roubles . . . has been received with surprise amounting almost to disbelief. The readiness of Prussia to assist in every way the prolongation of the war. . . . [I]t is alleged that one third of it will be offered in Berlin, one third in Hamburg and the other in Amsterdam. As far as the last city is concerned, after the intimation already put forth by the Dutch government, it may be presumed that the operation can only be a covert one . . . although the lowness of the price seems to be intended as a compensation [of] more than 10 percent. (*Times* [London], December 14, 1855)

The story told above shows that, because of a lack of internal resources and a political situation that was obviously hostile to Russian loans in London, Russia had to find other foreign markets. With Prussia and the Netherlands as possible options, it had found itself including a silver clause (the currency of these markets) and was thus able to borrow at the cost of a fifty-basis-point increase in long-term interest rates. Echoing the findings of Sussman and Yafeh (2000) for Japan, institutions played a secondary role in lending risk premia during wars and political instability.

Finally, the story of the 1857 imperial railway bond can shed light on the IPO reason behind exchange rate clauses. The 4.5% 1857 imperial railway bond was converted in 1899 into a 4% bond. Attached to these bonds we found the following statement: for silver ruble bonds in London, Paris, and Amsterdam, the "company abandoning to these 3 places the right given by art 26 of the statutes of altering the rate of exchange after the 10th year." [13] The bonds could have been converted at the old exchange rate (1857) or the current exchange rate "payable in Russia at sight rate of the Rouble on London."

This finding suggests that exchange rate clauses were sometimes temporary; after the first ten years, redemption by drawing used to start. Therefore, the exchange rate clause mattered usually for the first years since issue, a finding that lends support to our IPO story. Apparently, bondholders found this arrangement a disadvantage, and we can only speculate that, at their demand, the Russian government decided to forgo its right to alter the exchange rate clause after ten years. Furthermore, during the frequent conversions and redemptions, the exchange rate question became an issue even in bonds with fixed exchange rate clauses.

To conclude, the experience of Russian borrowing during the nineteenth century does not seem to support the main original sin hypotheses. Rather, it conveys a more traditional story of foreign borrowing affected by political and military difficulties and the lack of sufficient resources at home. The exchange rate clauses seem to be related therefore to an IPO story—borrowing abroad, via the main international underwriters, had these clauses attached to it. More important, secondary Russian debt, issued in St. Petersburg in paper rubles, found its way to London and Paris even though it had no exchange rate clause attached to it. Finally, wars and internal instability affected borrowing premia more than exchange rate clauses.

Tying the Strings: IPOs, Secondary Markets, and Liquidity

Our examination of the history of the British and French capital markets of the nineteenth century and the Russian case study leads us to conclude that there was little correlation between exchange rate clauses and macroeconomic stability or institutional reforms that foster commitment of governments toward bondholders. Some European countries that would not have passed the criteria of reputable policies were able to issue in their own currency—a prime example is Russia (others include Spain, Portugal, and Austria). For other much more reputable countries (most notably the Scandinavian), we could not find evidence of anything, in foreign markets, other than sterling debts. Some reputable countries such as France and the United States had to occasionally include gold clauses when they attempted to sell their debt abroad. Which patterns might account for this phenomenon? Obviously, there cannot be a simple linear relation between domestic institutions and policies and ability or willingness to issue domestic debts abroad.

First, the most important distinction to make is between primary debt issues, for which we draw the analogy of IPOs, and secondary-market listings and transactions for which we draw the analogy of cross-listing. Our evidence shows that the international bond markets started out with countries issuing debt in their own currency, in their own stock markets. That debt was then either held or subscribed to by foreign residents and bankers, or found its way, as the outcome of international capital settlements, to foreign financial centers. The bonds were in turn cross-listed with the home financial center, as local investors realized that they could take advantage of mutually profitable exchanges. Once this point was reached, it also became possible to directly issue abroad domestic debts, and this is where foreign exchange clauses came into the picture. As English, French, Dutch, and German bankers competed against each other for the right to offer subscriptions of foreign debt, the Rothschilds (who dominated European finance with the aid of a Europe-wide branch system that covered five financial centers simultaneously) came out with a formula that proved tremendously successful, and was adopted not only by the disreputable countries of Latin America but also by a number of leading powers: they suggested including foreign exchange clauses when new issues were floated. Thus foreign exchange clauses appear to have little to do with reputation, but a lot to do with the market mechanism. We call this the IPO puzzle: that the foreign issues of reputable countries displayed fixed exchange rate clauses is all the more puzzling when we realize that these countries' domestic-currency-denominated securities, which had no fixed exchange rate clauses, had found their way into the portfolios of residents of the precise market that appeared to "request" a fixed exchange rate clause when the IPO occurred.

The theoretical solution to the IPO paradox that we put forward here emphasizes the role of liquidity, at both the domestic level and the international level. It also rests on a distinction between necessary and sufficient conditions for convenient trading, in given financial centers of given foreign securities. For a given security to reach cross-listing status, it must, by definition, have been primarily issued in a domestic stock exchange or money market. In order for the security to circulate abroad, it also had to provide for a low-cost means of cashing the coupons. Otherwise, dealing in foreign securities remains too costly, and holding them will always be dominated by holdings of other local instruments. This means that investors must have access to a foreign exchange market in order to convert the coupon into domestic currency. This also means that various transaction costs must be reduced through financial progress: a considerable improvement of international finance after the 1820s was, from that respect, the standardization of procedures to cash the coupon where bonds were held or traded, either through the intervention of international bankers or through the creation of offshore government agencies.[14] From this perspective, fixed exchange rate clauses with their accompanying financial technology dramatically simplified the process: the experience of Latin American countries borrowing in the 1820s suggests that issuing in sterling enabled countries (quite apart from matters of solvency and commitment) to get access to London resources. Thus while having a money market or a stock exchange was a *necessary* condition for a country to issue debt in its own currency at home, issuing in a foreign currency was a *sufficient* condition for raising capital in the corresponding country (for the right price).

This would imply that countries that had minor currencies (in that they were traded in a limited number of foreign centers) or that suffered from poor or underdeveloped local money markets could typically not achieve cross-listing, since they did not even meet the necessary conditions for their domestic securities to internationalize. These countries had no choice other than to issue directly in foreign markets and include foreign exchange clauses, since not including foreign exchange clauses would mean that foreign investors would suffer big losses when cashing their coupons. For those countries with major currencies and money markets, the formal issue of new securities was in general unnecessary, since all that was needed was to issue domestically and then provide the financial technology that would ensure the smooth purchasing of the bonds and later efficient cashing of the coupon. At the same time, these countries could in some cases find their own money markets illiquid, or insufficiently liquid given the amounts they wanted to borrow. In this case, they had no choice other than to formally tap foreign markets, and thus purchase the liquidity services that issuing in a foreign currency could secure.

To support our interpretation, we provide evidence on the international status of a large number of currencies in the late nineteenth century, and seek to relate it to the predictions of the model we put forward in the previous discussion. It has long been known that some currencies are more equal than others. The debate about original sin may be seen as a remake of an old controversy. In a classic paper, Peter Lindert (1969) identified that on the eve of World War I there were a limited list of "key currencies" that were held as reserves by official monetary institutions. These currencies included most prominently, and probably quite unsurprisingly, the pound, franc, and mark. Foreign exchange was held in the form of private bills bearing typically at least two to three signatures, generally issued in the normal course of trade finance and then endorsed by bankers as they circulated. The bills were then payable in some given financial center where they would eventually be cashed. Before being cashed, however, they had an international circulation, as these bills were held by merchant banks who used them as a tool of choice to transfer funds from one market to the other. Bills, rather than gold or silver, were thus the main instrument for international settlement. In effect, when Germany collected the indemnity on France, it insisted on being paid not in gold or silver, but in a mixture of British, Dutch, and German bills. In sharp contrast, McCulloch (1837) reports in his entry for Rio de Janeiro that "there are no commercial or discount banks in any part of Brazil."

The similarity between the restricted number of countries that could issue bonds denominated in their own currency and the number of "key currencies" led us to decide that the question should be explored more carefully. Specifically, our intuition was that a precondition for the existence of a (secondary) offshore market for domestic-currency-denominated debt was the availability of exchange facilities that would enable investors to price and possibly cover their foreign exchange exposure. The key nonmanageable risk that one faces when holding foreign bonds denominated in a foreign currency comes from the possible inability to trade the long-term bond for short-term assets in that currency.

If this story is true, there should be a close link between the availability of bills of exchange markets on the one hand, and the clauses attached to long-term contracts on the other. And as a matter of fact, we know that there were *no* markets for bills of exchange denominated in some currencies. Table 6.9 shows the list of currencies quoted in London and Paris around the mid-nineteenth century. As can be seen, the lists of financial centers, quoted in Paris and London, overlap to a very large extent. But they are also striking in that they seem to incorporate a strong regional bias with a vast predominance of European

Table 6.9. Exchange centers quoted in Paris and London

Paris, 1850	London, 1844
Amsterdam, London, Hamburg, (Berlin), (Augsburg), Frankfurt, Madrid, Cadiz, (Bilbao), Lisbon, Oporto, Genoa, Leghorn, Naples, (Venice), Milan, Palermo, Messina, Antwerp, (Basel), Vienna, Trieste, St. Petersburg	Amsterdam, Rotterdam, Paris/France, Hamburg, Frankfurt, Berlin, Madrid, Bilboa, Cadiz, Barcelona, Oporto, Lisbon, Genoa, Venice, Leghorn, Naples, Palermo, Messina, Antwerp, Vienna, Trieste, St. Petersburg, Rio de Janeiro

Sources: For Paris, *Cours authentiques;* London, *Economist.*

Notes: Places in parentheses had no activity. Bold type indicates markets quoted in both Paris and London.

centers. Rio de Janeiro, the London exception, would in effect disappear from the foreign exchange list in the 1850s. The inclusion of given currencies in the list does not seem to have been caused by reputation: those hardly trustworthy countries, such as Russia, Spain, Portugal, and possibly Italy, appear in both the Paris and the London lists. By contrast, some trustworthy currencies, such as the Scandinavian, are not in the list. We find that this evidence is consistent with that reported earlier in this chapter.

In order to go beyond this impression, we began collecting information on which foreign exchange centers were quoted in a large list of countries, comprising European and American (United States, Brazil) nations. This enabled us to construct an index of the main financial markets of the time, ranking countries according to their occurrence in other countries' lists of financial centers (fig. 6.3).

Several features are important. It appears that the three-tier system described in our discussion of exchange rate clauses is noticeable here as well. Besides the restricted group of leading currencies that were traded almost everywhere (those of the United Kingdom, Belgium, France, Germany, and the Netherlands), we find a group of intermediary nations that, interestingly, overlap with group II, identified above: Austria-Hungary, Russia, Italy, Spain, and Portugal. We also find a large list of nations (not reported here) that were quoted nowhere. These include the Latin American and Asian countries, but also a number of British colonies that were all unable to issue in their own currency.

The conclusion we draw from figure 6.3 is that—at least for the nineteenth century—the possibility of developing a foreign market for domestic debt is not related to institutional factors, as the original sin story would predict. Rather, it has to do with the functioning of underlying money markets. This conclusion follows naturally from our assertion, backed by our findings, that currency clauses in the nineteenth century were an IPO phenomenon rather than a strict requirement of investors. It now seems obvious that countries that were able to develop a secondary market for their domestic-currency-denominated public liabilities in foreign centers were precisely those with intense foreign exchange relations with the rest of the world.

At the heart of the original sin issue lies the question whether it is *necessary* for some countries to issue with fixed exchange rate clauses, and whether this necessity could be related to inappropriate macropolicies or institutions, which appropriate reform could fix. Our findings stand as a challenge to this notion. We do not find that countries' commitment and macroeconomic stability were important factors. The latter played a role in pricing the securities, not in their listing on the stock exchange and their existence in portfolios. In contrast, we found that, in the nineteenth century, the existence of a liquid domestic market and a liquid foreign market for foreign exchange was a *necessary* condition for achieving cross-listing status. Conversely, the absence of such market institutions was a *sufficient* condition for forcing domestic authorities to include foreign exchange clauses when floating loans in the international bond market. As for countries that had well-developed market institutions, accessing the more liquid market to obtain a lower borrowing rate went hand in hand with borrowing in that center's more liquid currency. And this is what determined their borrowing policies at any given point in time.

Concluding Remarks

Our foray into the nineteenth century's international bond market, the precursor of the modern global financial market, suggests that original sin has little explanatory power. Instead, we document that exchange rate clauses of all sorts were essentially an IPO story—when countries attempted to float debt primarily in a foreign financial center, they had to do it in that center's currency or include exchange rate clauses. In doing so, they tapped the resources of a more liquid market that could supply them with their borrowing needs at a lower cost than their home market would have. Floating a debt in a major currency, in a major financial center such as London, also enabled the issuer to tap resources of the entire Europe-wide network of financial markets that were willing to trade sterling-denominated assets. However, this did not preclude the listing and trade in domestic-currency-denominated debt that was primarily issued at the home country. While we investigated only government bonds in this chapter, the same rationale should also apply to private companies' bonds.

Foreign investors did trade and hold domestic-currency-denominated bonds, without exchange rate clauses, of some countries that would fail the institutional or political maturity credibility test, but not of all countries. We hypothesized and were able to show that this was made possible because of underlying foreign exchange markets with bills of exchange. The existence of these markets, however, was independent of institutional or credibility issues. They

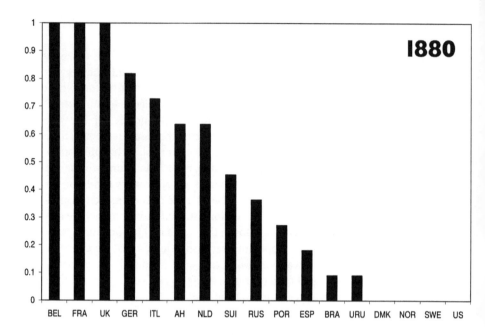

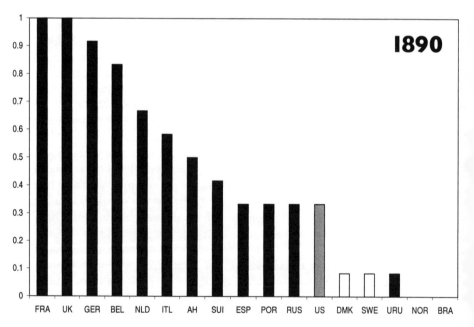

Figure 6.3 Proportion of countries where a currency is quoted

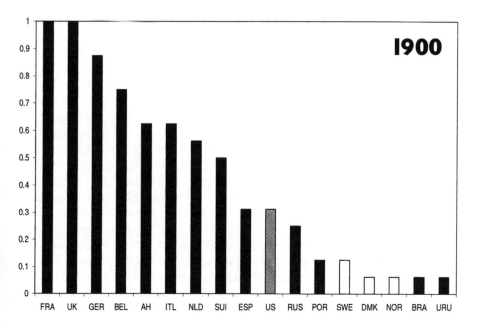

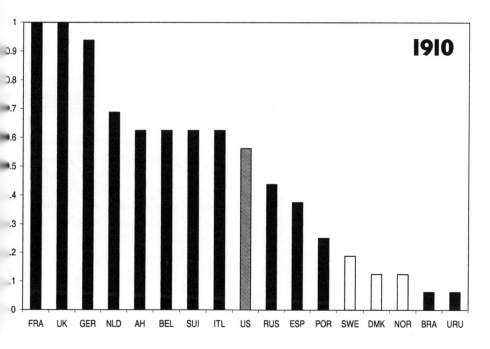

owed their existence to the network of trade relations that emerged in the early modern era—an era when issues of original sin had little impact. Thus the strong trade relationship between Britain and Portugal (immortalized by Ricardo's famous comparative-advantage example), which fostered the bills-of-exchange market and allowed Portuguese bonds, denominated in reis, to be held in London, was certainly not owing to Portugal's sound public finances or modern property-right-enhancing institutions. Institutions were perhaps a good predictor for future economic development, but afforded no immediate substantial change in the home money market liquidity. Liquidity was achieved by transforming the national currency into a key currency. The status of key currency was path-dependent on historical trade and trade finance relations and in some cases political and military finance. Entering and exiting from the exclusive club of vehicle currencies was a very protracted historical process. For the twentieth century, the rise of the United States and Japan is a positive example; the Russian and Eastern Bloc adoption of communism is an example to the contrary. Path dependence and persistence could also matter a lot, as illustrated by the experience of Amsterdam and Brussels, by the late nineteenth century no longer predominant commercial powers, but still retaining their status of vehicle currency. The evidence for the United States in figure 6.3 shows its rise from a junior status (right-hand side of a) to a more senior status (middle category) in 1910. If we were to continue these graphs for after World War I, one would probably see the U.S. dollar displacing the mark and franc (but probably not sterling) in many markets. This rise is closely associated with the rising role of the United States in the world economy and finance.

Our story suggests that the European experience of the nineteenth century is a clear indication that financial development and political development need not go hand in hand. Having said that, it remains that countries that issued debt in foreign currency were exposed to a default induced by an exchange rate crisis, and thus understandingly displayed a fear of floating. However, the policy implication we draw from this analysis is that sound macropolicy and protection of property rights would be insufficient in alleviating that problem. Only emerging as a large economy with large trade flows, as Japan (yen) did after the Second World War, may solve the problem. Put differently, had a country such as Bhutan successfully adopted modern institutions and adhered to the Maastricht Treaty parameters for years, would any investor be willing to hold ngultrum-denominated bonds?

Notes

1. Most of the debt issued abroad necessitated cashing the coupons abroad, too. One important development of the nineteenth century was the coupon-cashing services provided for bondholders of foreign debt. For some issuers, however, there remained no

designated coupon-cashing agency in London. According to the *Investors Monthly Manual* of 1885, this was the case for all Austrian and some French, Dutch, Portuguese, and Spanish bonds.

2. Monetary unions such as the Latin Union that combined the adoption of a common denomination with that of a common standard introduced the possibility of hybrid products.

3. There were also cases when the exchange rate clause was conditional upon the place where the coupon was cashed or the nationality of those who cashed it, as was the case for Spain after 1821.

4. As described by a number of historians (Lévy-Leboyer 1964; Cameron 1961), during the early nineteenth century there emerged a large class of individual bondholders—as distinct from bond traders and underwriters—to whom the bond issues were sold. These got organized in England in bondholders associations in the 1840s, and these associations came with a number of requirements. Fixed exchange rate clauses would thus be similar to these other conditions described by McCulloch (1837), according to which countries issued bonds with dividends paid biannually, typically January and July and March and September (or April to October) to allow bondholders quarterly income flow.

5. Dawson (1990) reports on a bond issue of a fictitious country by the name of Poyais!

6. Of course, Latin American issues were equal to the entire stock, whereas for European countries they were only marginal loans.

7. Moreover, it could be emphasized that Latin American countries had no "fear of floating" and issued in sterling without worrying about their ability to pay in sterling. To their expense, neither did investors show any concern over this issue. Most of the Latin American debt ended in default or arrears.

8. Courtois happened to be the first chief economist of Crédit Lyonnais research department (see Flandreau 2003).

9. "Principaux fonds cotés à Londres, Berlin, Bruxelles, Hambourg, Francfort, Madrid, Rome, Florence, Saint Petersbourg, etc." (Courtois 1883, vi).

10. Interestingly, Courtois (1883) goes a long way to explain that because of the act of July 14, 1870 and the suspension of silver coinage of 1873, the dollar coupon has to be understood as being gold payable, barring a return to bimetallism—"an unlikely event according to American men of finance": "Nous disons en or: pour être plus exact, il faudrait dire en or ou en argent. En effet l'engagement pris par la loi du 14 juillet 1870 dit 'en monnaie métallique ayant cours légal à ce moment' (à celui de la promulgation de la loi). Or l'argent cessa d'avoir cours légal en 1873. Tant que la faculté libératoire ne lui sera pas rendue, ce sera l'or seul qui pourra rembourser les trois emprunts. . . . Mais si l'argent rentrait dans ses anciens droits, rien ne dit que le trésor fédéral ne rembourserait pas en monnaie d'argent de préférence à la monnaie d'or. Ce serait son droit au moins. Cependant, l'opinion, en Amérique, chez les hommes de finances, est qu'il n'usera pas de ce droit dans cette hypothèse" (97).

11. The 1890 issue involved three issues, the first—the second tranche of a 4% "gold" loan with coupon payable in franc—was worth 300 million francs. The second—the third tranche of the same loan—was worth 370 million francs. The third—a 4.5% loan—was actually a paper ruble loan whose IPO was taking place in Paris. It was worth 75 million paper rubles or about 300 million francs of the time. Upon more careful scru-

tiny, however, it appeared that the bulk of the issue had taken place in St. Petersburg with a Russian bank as main underwriter.

12. Based on the *Investors Monthly Manual,* which probably understates Russian bonds known to be held in London that did not appear in its listing.

13. In the Russian bonds collection at the School of Russian and Slavonic Studies, University of London, series RUI.

14. This coupon-cashing procedure introduced an important element of geography to the story. It seems that being close to the financial center made it easier for foreign debts to get cross-listing, since the cost of cashing coupons was reduced. Thus for a British investor, cashing Dutch coupons in Amsterdam via mail or courier was less costly than cashing a coupon in New York.

References

Bordo, Michael D., and Marc Flandreau. 2003. "Core, Periphery, Exchange Rate Regimes, and Globalization." In *Globalization in Historical Perspective,* ed. Michael D. Bordo, Alan Taylor, and Geoffrey Williamson. Chicago: University of Chicago Press.

Bordo, Michael D., and Eugene N. White. 1991. "A Tale of Two Currencies: British and French Finance during the Napoleonic Wars." *Journal of Economic History* 51 (2): 303–16.

Brezis, Elise S. 1995. "Foreign Capital Flows in the Century of Britain's Industrial Revolution: New Estimates, Controlled Conjectures." *Economic History Review* 48 (1): 46–67.

Cameron, Rondo. 1961. *France and the Economic Development of Europe, 1800–1914: Conquests of Peace and Seeds of War.* Princeton, NJ: Princeton University Press.

Courtois, Alphonse. 1883. *Manuel des Fonds Publics et des sociétés par actions.* 8th ed. Paris: Garnier Frères.

Dawson, Frank Griffith. 1990. *The First Latin American Debt Crisis: The City of London and the 1822–1825 Loan Bubble.* New Haven, CT: Yale University Press.

de Block, M. 1889. *Les finances de la Russie.* Paris: Dupont.

Ferguson, Niall. 1998. *The House of Rothschild: Money's Prophets, 1798–1848.* New York: Viking.

Flandreau, Marc. 1996. "The French Crime of 1873: An Essay on the Emergence of the Gold Standard." *Journal of Economic History* 56:862–97.

———. 2000. "The Economics and Politics of Monetary Unions: A Reassessment of the Latin Monetary Union, 1865–1871." *Financial History Review* 7:25–43.

———. 2002. "Water Seeks a Level: Modeling Bimetallic Exchange Rates and the Bimetallic Band." *Journal of Money, Credit, and Banking* 34:491–519.

———. 2003. "Caveat Emptor: Coping with Sovereign Risk without the Multilaterals, 1870–1914." In *The International Financial System in the Twentieth Century,* ed. Marc Flandreau, Harold James, and Carl-Ludwig Holtfrerich. Cambridge: Cambridge University Press.

———. 2004. *The Glitter of Gold: France, Bimetallism, and the Emergence of the International Gold Standard, 1848–1873.* Oxford: Oxford University Press.

Kindleberger, C. P. 1993. *A Financial History of Western Europe.* New York: Oxford University Press.

Lévy, Raphael-Georges. 1901. Le role des valeurs mobilières dans le commerce international et dans les reglements financiers internationaux. In *Congres International des caleurs mobilières*. Paris: Dupont.

Lévy-Leboyer, Maurice. 1964. *Les banques européennes et l'industrialisation internationale dans la première moitié du XIXème siècle*. Paris: Presses Universitaires de France.

Lindert, Peter. 1969. *Key Currencies and Gold, 1900–1913*. Princeton Studies in International Finance, no. 24. Princeton, NJ: Princeton University Press.

McCulloch, John Ramsey. 1837. *Dictionary, Practical, Theoretical and Historical, of Commerce and Commercial Navigation*. London: Longman.

Nash, Robert Lucas. 1883. *Fenn's Compendium of the English and Foreign Funds, Debts and Revenues of all Nations*. 13th ed. London: Effingham Wilson.

Neal, Larry. 2000. "How It All Began: The Monetary and Financial Architecture of Europe during the First Global Capital Markets, 1648–1815." *Financial History Review* 7 (2): 117–40.

Oppers, Stefan E. 1993. "The Interest Rate Effect of Dutch Money in Eighteenth-Century Britain." *Journal of Economic History* 53 (1): 25–43.

Riley, J. 1980. *International Government Finance and the Amsterdam Capital Market, 1740–1815*. Cambridge: Cambridge University Press.

Say, Léon. 1874. *Rapport fait au nom de la commission du budget de 1875, sur le paiement de l'indemnité de guerre et sur les operations de change qui en ont été la consequence*. Versailles: Imprimerie de l'Assemblée Nationale.

Sussman, Nathan, and Yishay Yafeh. 2000. "Institutions, Reforms, and Country Risk: Lessons from Japanese Government Debt in the Meiji Era." *Journal of Economic History* 60 (2): 442–67.

Why Do Emerging Economies Borrow in Foreign Currency?

Olivier Jeanne

IN AN INFLUENTIAL PAPER, Barry Eichengreen and Ricardo Hausmann have put forward the idea that one important reason that less-developed countries are more vulnerable to international financial crises than developed countries is the currency composition of their debts. Namely, for less-developed countries "the domestic currency cannot be used to borrow abroad or to borrow long term, even domestically" (Eichengreen and Hausmann 1999, 3). Instead, many emerging-market countries borrow in foreign currency, a situation that Eichengreen and Hausmann describe as the "original sin" of international finance.[1]

This chapter addresses the following question: Why is it that emerging-market borrowers find it more difficult or less desirable to issue long-term debt denominated in domestic currency? To put it succinctly, the hypothesis proposed in this chapter is that "original sin" is the result of the lack of credibility in domestic monetary policy.[2] Unpredictable monetary policy makes borrowers unsure about the future *real* value of their domestic-currency debts, and may induce them to dollarize their liabilities. This is so even though foreign-currency debt is itself dangerous, especially in the event of a large depreciation. I illustrate this point with a model of a fixed currency peg in which increasing the probability of devaluation induces domestic firms to borrow in foreign currency. Somewhat paradoxically, an increase in the devaluation risk may lead domestic borrowers to take *less* insurance against this risk.

The argument that foreign-currency debt results from a lack of monetary credibility may not sound very new. In fact, it is a classic argument in the literature on sovereign debt, which has emphasized how foreign-currency debt provides discipline for monetary policymakers tempted by the evil of discretion (Calvo 1996; Bohn 1990). The argument developed in this chapter is quite different, however. It relies on optimal hedging at the level of individual borrowers rather than incentives at the level of the government. Furthermore, it is more general in the sense that it can be applied to both sovereign and private debt.

This generality is useful since some of the recent crises, especially in Southeast Asia, involved primarily private, not sovereign, debt.

Although the purpose of this chapter is primarily theoretical, I present some evidence that is suggestive of a link between monetary credibility and the currency composition of debt. As Hausmann and Panizza (2002) show, this link disappears if one looks at debt issued in the main international financial centers, which is almost completely in foreign currency for developing countries, irrespective of their monetary policy.[3] Thus, on empirical grounds, lack of monetary credibility seems more convincing as an explanation for the currency composition of *domestic* debt than it is for *international* debt. As I shall argue later, the explanation for the currency composition of international debt has probably more to do with financial practices in the center of the international financial system than with monetary policy in its periphery. It is important to emphasize this distinction, as some chapters in this volume look exclusively at international debt (e.g., Flandreau and Sussman, chapter 6).

The chapter is structured as follows. First, I discuss the relationship of this chapter to the existing literature. I then present the assumptions of a simple partial equilibrium model of the currency composition of a firm's debt, and analyze the entrepreneur's problem. I show how monetary policy can provide insurance to domestic borrowers, who take advantage of it by borrowing in domestic currency. The next part of the chapter studies how the currency composition of debt depends on the firm's international exposure, followed by an illustration of how a lack of monetary credibility can generate liability dollarization. Then I show how the basic argument can be transposed to sovereign debt and present some stylized facts. The last part discusses some policy implications, and I conclude with thoughts on possible further developments of the ideas presented in this chapter.

Literature

An important branch of literature focuses on the currency composition of *sovereign* debt. The main theme in that literature is that foreign-currency debt may be a solution to the time consistency problem in monetary policy. The temptation to inflate is lower for a government that cannot inflate away its debt because it is in foreign currency (see, e.g., Calvo 1996; Bohn 1990).

This argument works well for sovereign debt, but as noted by Calvo (2001), it is difficult to transpose to private debt. The problem is that private borrowers, whose individual debt is typically very small relative to the economy, do not internalize the impact of their liabilities on domestic policy. These borrowers are unwilling to bear the private risks of foreign-currency debt in order to produce the public good of a better policy. As a result, transposing the discipline argument to private debt implies that there is *too little* foreign-currency debt in the private sector (Tirole 2002).

A number of recent papers endogenize the currency composition of private debt, but look at channels that are not primarily related to monetary policy. These papers have developed instead the following themes:

- Foreign-currency debt arises because of the moral hazard created by bailout guarantees: McKinnon and Pill 1998; Burnside, Eichenbaum, and Rebelo 2001; Schneider and Tornell 2001.
- Foreign-currency debt arises because of a lack of domestic financial development: Caballero and Krishnamurthy 2003.
- Foreign-currency debt arises because of commitment or signaling problems at the level of domestic firms: Jeanne 2000; Aguiar 2000; Chamon 2001; Broda and Levy Yeyati 2003.

The first two arguments invoke failures in other areas than monetary policy.[4] These failures can play a role in principle—and some of them may have played a significant role in Southeast Asia.[5] However, the mere fact that we are talking about currencies should make monetary policy a prime suspect. It makes sense to explore how far we can go simply with monetary policy.

More closely related to this chapter are the contributions of Ize and Levy Yeyati (1998) and Ize and Parrado (2002). These authors look at how domestic monetary policy influences the currency composition of domestic portfolios. They show that suboptimal monetary policy (which, as in this chapter, could refer to a policy that is procyclical or lacks credibility) increases the demand for foreign-currency assets. In the general equilibrium model of Ize and Parrado (2002), this portfolio effect induces liability dollarization, because domestic firms are risk-neutral, and ready to accommodate the demand of households for foreign-currency assets.

By contrast with these papers, I focus here on the determinants of liability dollarization on the side of borrowers. In my model, the currency composition of portfolios is indeterminate because all agents are risk-neutral and uncovered interest parity applies. Dollarization is driven instead by borrowers' attempts to reduce their probability of default. This demand-side approach tends to reinforce the results obtained in the portfolio approach: in particular, my model has positive and normative implications similar to those in Ize and Parrado 2002.

Finally, this chapter is also related to the corporate finance literature on optimal hedging. Smith and Stulz (1985) and Froot, Scharfstein, and Stein (1993) present models in which a firm hedges so as to reduce the expected cost of default. Albuquerque (2001) looks at the optimal currency-hedging strategies in a similar context. These papers typically assume the existence of derivative instruments (in particular, currency options) that allow firms to engage in non-linear hedging strategies. Here the analysis is restricted to the more simple linear hedging strategies that are achieved by varying the currency composition of debt—consistent with the scarcity of currency-hedging instruments observed in emerging-market countries (Cowan 2003). The role played by market incompleteness in my results is discussed in the concluding section of this chapter.

The Currency Composition of Corporate Debt: A Simple Framework

I adopt a deliberately partial equilibrium approach, by looking at the choice of the currency composition of its debt by a small firm that takes domestic monetary policy as given. The analysis is based on the classical model of debt with costly state verification (Townsend 1979; Gale and Hellwig 1985) that is extended to incorporate a choice between domestic-currency debt and foreign-currency debt.[6]

The model has two periods $t = 0, 1$. The domestic and foreign currencies are called peso and dollar respectively, and the exchange rate at time 1 (the price of one dollar in terms of pesos) is denoted by S.

I focus on one entrepreneur in an emerging-market economy. The entrepreneur is endowed with a project that requires the sacrifice of I^* dollars in period 0 and yields a stochastic return in period 1. The return of the project can be expressed in terms of dollars, R^*, or in terms of pesos, $R = SR^*$. Both are stochastic viewed from period 0.

The domestic entrepreneur has no funds in period 0, and must borrow from (domestic or foreign) investors. Debt contracts are written in nominal terms, and can be denominated in dollars or pesos. In period 0, the entrepreneur promises to repay D pesos and D^* dollars in period 1. D and D^* are nonnegative. If the entrepreneur cannot repay the debt, the creditors pay a "verification cost" of C^* dollars and collect the project's payoff. The entrepreneur receives nothing in the event of default. The risk-free dollar interest rate is normalized to zero. There is perfect competition on the side of lenders, who reap no rent from lending to the entrepreneur.

For simplicity, I assume that the entrepreneur and investors are risk-neutral, and maximize their net incomes expressed in terms of dollars. This assumption abstracts from potentially interesting determinants of the currency composition of debt, but considerably simplifies the analysis. The final utilities of the entrepreneur and its creditors are respectively given by

$$U = \max\left(0, \frac{R - D}{S} - D^* \right)$$

$$V = \min\left(\frac{R}{S}, \frac{D}{S} + D^* \right) - \delta C^*$$

where δ is a dummy variable that is equal to one if the entrepreneur defaults, and to zero otherwise.

The entrepreneur chooses his debt structure taking the stochastic distribution of R and S as given. At time 0 the entrepreneur maximizes his expected dollar income subject to the participation constraint of the lenders,

$$(P) \begin{cases} \max_{D,D*} E(U) \\ E(V) \geq I* \end{cases}.$$

Ex post (in period 1) the state of the economy $x \in X$ is revealed. Each state is characterized by an exchange rate $S(x)$ and a return $R(x)$. State x occurs with probability $\pi(x)$. I look at how the equilibrium currency composition of debt depends on the structure of states, that is, the mapping

$$X, \pi(\cdot), S(\cdot), R(\cdot) \Rightarrow (D, D*).$$

The Entrepreneur's Problem

In equilibrium, the participation constraint of lenders binds, so that the entrepreneur's utility is equal to the total payoff of the project (net of the default cost) minus the cost of the investment.

$$E(U) = E(U + V) - I* = E(R*) - E(\delta)C* - I*$$

$E(R*)$ and $I*$ being given, the entrepreneur chooses the currency composition of his debt so as to minimize the probability of a default $E(\delta)$, subject to the participation constraint of lenders. Although the default cost is paid by the creditors ex post, it is borne by the entrepreneur ex ante. The entrepreneur's problem can be rewritten

$$(P') \begin{cases} \min_{D,D*} E(\delta) \equiv \Pr(R* < D* + D/S) \\ E(V) \geq I* \end{cases}.$$

PROPOSITION 1. *The entrepreneur chooses the currency composition of his debt so as to minimize the probability of default conditional on the lenders' participation constraint.*

Note the contrast with moral-hazard theories of foreign-currency debt. In those theories, entrepreneurs borrow in foreign currency to undertake excessive risk—for example, in the hope of a bailout (Burnside, Eichenbaum, and Rebelo 2001) or because of the limited liability constraint (Chamon 2001). Here the entrepreneur attempts to *minimize* the risk of default; that is, the currency composition of debt is the result of an optimal hedging strategy. The entrepreneur does not benefit from increasing the default probability, because the determinants of this probability are observed at the time of borrowing and fully priced in the debt contract.

The entrepreneur reduces the probability of default to zero, if possible. He can do so if the maximum expected repayment that can be pledged to creditors conditional on a default-free debt structure (such that the firm does not default in any state $x \in X$) is larger than I^*. If not, the entrepreneur cannot finance his project with a default-free debt structure and must accept the risk of a default in some states.

Let us denote by $\hat{V}$ the maximum expected repayment that the entrepreneur can pledge to creditors conditional on a zero probability of default. $\hat{V}$ is the solution to the following problem:

$$\begin{cases} \max D^* + DE(1/S) \\ \forall\, x \in X,\, D + D^*S(x) \le R(x) \end{cases}$$

The constraints in this problem are represented graphically in figure 7.1, with the exchange rate S on the x axis and the peso payoff R on the y axis. Each point corresponds to a state $x \in X$. A default-free debt structure (D, D^*) is such that the line $R = D + D^*S$ is below all the points.

It is easy to see that if the points corresponding to the states are not all on the same line,[7] then at least one point will have to be some distance above the line $R = D + D^*S$ in a default-free debt structure (e.g., point A or B in fig. 7.1). In the corresponding state, the firm repays strictly less than the return of the project. As a result, $\hat{V}$ is in general strictly lower than the expected payoff $E(R/S)$.

The interesting case is when $\hat{V} < I^* < E(R/S)$. Then the project is profitable but cannot be financed without taking the risk of a default. The entrepreneur must increase V by accepting to default in some states. He will do so if the project remains profitable in spite of the default risk. For the entrepreneur, choosing the currency composition of debt is equivalent to choosing the states in which he defaults.

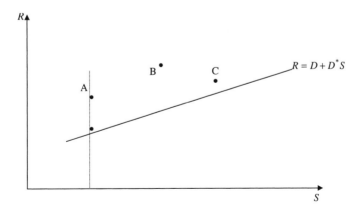

Figure 7.1 A default-free debt structure

Monetary Policy as a Source of Insurance

Intuitively, the extent to which the entrepreneur can insure himself against the risk of default depends on the macroeconomic environment, and in particular on the correlation between the exchange rate and the return of the project. The following result states a condition under which the entrepreneur can hedge perfectly against the risk of default by borrowing in domestic currency:

> PROPOSITION 2. *If* min $R \geq I^*/E(1/S)$, *the entrepreneur reduces his default probability to zero by borrowing in domestic currency.*

The intuition and the proof are straightforward. Conditional on no default, the entrepreneur can finance the investment by issuing a quantity of domestic-currency debt equal to $D = I^*/E(1/S)$. Conversely, if the minimum realization of R is larger than $I^*/E(1/S)$, the entrepreneur can always repay D, and the default probability is zero. In other words, an entrepreneur who expects to receive a minimum quantity of pesos takes no risk by committing himself to repay a lower quantity of pesos.

The condition stated in proposition 2 can be interpreted as a condition on the macroeconomic policy environment in which the entrepreneur operates. In a general equilibrium macroeconomic model, R and S would be determined by exogenous shocks and monetary and fiscal policies. The condition in proposition 2 is more likely to be fulfilled if countercyclical monetary and fiscal policies limit the downside realizations of the firm's peso income. Conditional on such policies, the entrepreneur insures himself against default by borrowing in domestic currency.

Proposition 2 gives a condition under which the entrepreneur borrows in domestic currency. The hypothesis developed in this chapter is that this condition is less likely to be satisfied in less-developed countries than in more-developed ones, so that firms tend to borrow more in foreign currency in the former than in the latter. Of course, foreign-currency debt may expose borrowers to risks. But conditional on the macroeconomic environment, foreign-currency debt may be less risky at the margin than domestic-currency debt. This insight is very general and can be developed in different contexts.

A Capital Asset Pricing Model

I now show that conditional on a new assumption on the distribution of R and S, the entrepreneur's problem can be simplified in a way that gives a simple closed-form expression for the currency composition of debt. This expression is interesting for its own sake and because it brings out the link between a firm's international exposure and the currency composition of its debt. The new assumption is that $1/S$ and R/S are normally distributed and that the probability of default is strictly positive but smaller than ½.

Let me define the project's net return as the payoff net of debt, expressed in terms of dollars.

$$r \equiv \frac{R - D}{S} - D^*.$$

Then the entrepreneur can find the optimal currency composition of his debt by solving the following mean-variance problem:

$$(P'') \begin{cases} \min \text{Var}(r) \\ E(r) = \text{constant} \end{cases},$$

that is, by minimizing the variance in the net return conditional on its mean.

The reason is the following. If (D, D^*) were not a solution to the mean-variance problem (P''), then it would be possible to simultaneously decrease the probability of default and increase the utility of lenders, implying that (D, D^*) would not be a solution to problem (P') either. To see this, assume that the variance of r can be decreased while keeping $E(r)$ constant. Then the tail probability of a default is also decreased (see fig. 7.2).[8] The utility of lenders also increases for two reasons: the verification cost is paid less often, and the average residual value of the project conditional on a default is higher. More formally, the expected payoff of lenders can be written

$$V = D^* + DE\left(\frac{1}{S}\right) + \int_{-\infty}^{0} (r - C^*)f(r)dr$$

$$= E\left(\frac{R}{S}\right) - E(r) + \int_{-\infty}^{0} (r - C^*)f(r)dr,$$

where $f(\cdot)$ is the probability density function of r (which is normal by assumption). The first equality says that the value of debt is equal to the expected repayment conditional on no default, plus a negative term reflecting the lower repayment and the payment of the verification cost conditional on a default. The second equality is then derived by substituting out D and D^* using the definition of r. The last expression increases if one reduces the variance in r while keeping $E(r)$ constant (see fig. 7.2).

Then noting that $\text{Var}(r) = \text{Var}(R/S) + D^2\text{Var}(1/S) - 2D\text{Cov}(R/S, 1/S)$ and maximizing this expression over D, it follows that the optimal level of domestic-currency debt is given by the following proposition.

PROPOSITION 3. *Assume R/S and 1/S are normally distributed and the probability of default is strictly positive but less than ½. Then the optimal level of domestic-currency debt is given by*

$$D = \frac{\text{Cov}(R/S, 1/S)}{\text{Var}(1/S)}.$$

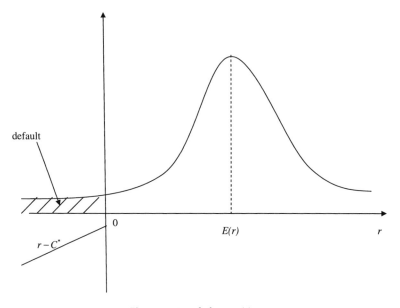

Figure 7.2 Proof of proposition 3

This expression is reminiscent of the capital asset pricing model. This is not surprising, because problem (P'') is a mean-variance portfolio optimization problem. The entrepreneur's problem is to minimize the probability of a negative net return conditional on the value of his debt, which (with normal distributions) is achieved by minimizing the variance in the net return conditional on its mean.[9]

The covariance term in the expression above depends on the correlation between the firm's receipts and the exchange rate. To illustrate, let me assume that part of the firm's nominal income is given in pesos while the other part is in dollars:

$$R = a + bS,$$

where a and b are stochastic, uncorrelated with $1/S$.

Coefficients a and b could be interpreted as reflecting the international exposure of the firm. For example, a firm that extracts and sells a tradable good for which the law of one price applies (say oil) has a equal to zero and b equal to the dollar price of its net output. On the other hand, a firm active in the nontradable sector should have a higher a and a lower b.

Applying proposition 3 then gives

$$D = E(a).$$

The firm's peso debt is equal to the expected value of its peso-denominated receipts. Thus, firms that are internationally less exposed (with higher a and lower b) tend to have more debt denominated in domestic currency. This is consistent with popular conceptions of optimal currency hedging, and with the available evidence on firms' hedging behavior.[10] The following section presents another specification of the model where optimal hedging takes a more surprising form.

Monetary Policy as a Source of Risk

This section presents the main point of this chapter: lack of monetary credibility can induce domestic firms to borrow in foreign currency, even though this makes them vulnerable to large depreciations of the domestic currency.

I illustrate this general point with an example. For the sake of relevance and simplicity, I consider the case of a fixed currency peg. However, the logic of the argument carries over to floating exchange rate regimes, as I shall argue at the end of this section. The case of a fixed currency peg is important because the emerging-market countries that had a crisis in the 1990s also had a fixed currency peg. Furthermore, currency pegs have been faulted for generating excessive levels of foreign-currency debt, by generating a "false sense of security" (Corden 2002) or because of implicit guarantees on foreign-currency debt (Burnside, Eichenbaum, and Rebelo 2001; Martinez and Werner 2001). I present here a different channel, based on the lack of credibility of the currency peg.

The capital asset pricing model formula derived in the previous section relied on assumptions on the conditional distribution of the exchange rate that are not satisfied by an imperfectly credible fixed currency peg. Thus, I return to the general specification of the model that was presented earlier. For simplicity, I consider an example with three states—the minimum number of states for the hedging problem to be nontrivial. The structure of states is described in table 7.1.

At time 0, the domestic authorities announce that they will maintain a fixed exchange rate peg S_0. They fulfill this promise with probability $1 - \mu$. With probability μ they do not, and there is a devaluation. The devaluation can be small ($S = S_1 > S_0$) or large ($S = S_2 > S_1$). The conditional probabilities of a small and a large devaluation are, respectively, p_1 and $p_2 = 1 - p_1$. The question

Table 7.1. A fixed but adjustable currency peg

State	Exchange rate	Nominal return	Probability
0: fixed peg	S_0	R_0	$1 - \mu$
1: small devaluation	S_1	R_1	μp_1
2: large devaluation	S_2	R_2	μp_2

I look at is how the currency composition of debt changes as the credibility of the fixed peg decreases (μ increases).

I assume that a depreciation is associated with an increase in the peso value of the firm's revenue but a decrease in its dollar value. This could be the case, for example, because the entrepreneur is active in a nontradable industry with a low exchange rate pass-through. This case is interesting to consider because liability dollarization is more challenging to explain in the nontradable sector, where the currency mismatch is the most damaging in the event of a devaluation.

$$R_0 < R_1 < R_2, \frac{R_0}{S_0} > \frac{R_1}{S_1} > \frac{R_2}{S_2}$$

Finally I make the following concavity assumption:

$$\frac{R_2 - R_1}{S_2 - S_1} < \frac{R_1 - R_0}{S_1 - S_0}.$$

The peso income of the firm increases less than proportionately with the size of the nominal devaluation. This assumption is essentially technical: it simplifies the analysis by making the problem concave (in a sense defined more precisely in the appendix). The analysis is not difficult to extend to the (convex) case where the direction of the inequality in the expression above is reversed.[11] However, it is important that the inequality be strict—otherwise, the problem becomes linear and perfect insurance is possible.

The equilibrium currency composition of debt is characterized as follows:

PROPOSITION 4. *The minimum share of foreign-currency debt in total debt is increasing with the devaluation probability μ. There are two thresholds in the devaluation probability, $\underline{\mu}$ and $\overline{\mu}$, such that (1) if the devaluation probability is smaller than $\underline{\mu}$, the entrepreneur issues no or little foreign-currency debt and defaults with probability zero; (2) if the devaluation probability is between $\underline{\mu}$ and $\overline{\mu}$, the level of foreign-currency debt is high enough to trigger a default conditional on a large devaluation; (3) if the devaluation probability is larger than $\overline{\mu}$, the entrepreneur cannot finance his project.*

The intuition runs as follows (the formal proof is given in the appendix). If the fixed peg is perfectly credible ($\mu = 0$), the firm receives R_0 with certainty, and there is no exchange rate risk. The firm can borrow in domestic currency and never defaults, provided that the project is profitable ($R_0/S_0 > I^*$). The foreign and domestic currencies are perfectly substitutable, and as a result the minimum share of the foreign currency in total debt is zero.

As the probability of a devaluation increases, so does the peso nominal interest rate. Given risk neutrality and free capital mobility, uncovered interest parity implies that the risk-free peso interest rate is given by

$$1 + i = \frac{E(S)}{S_0},$$

where the exchange rate is assumed to be equal to the fixed peg level S_0 in period 0.

Dollar debt is dangerous for the standard reason—it may bankrupt the firm if there is a large devaluation. However, domestic-currency debt is also dangerous because it implies a high ex post real repayment in the *no-devaluation* state. There is a level of the peso interest rate above which the entrepreneur can no longer avoid default in all states. The firm is caught in a dilemma between issuing "too much" foreign-currency debt—and defaulting conditional on a large devaluation—and issuing "too much" domestic-currency debt—and defaulting conditional on the maintenance of the fixed peg. The entrepreneur chooses to default in the state that is less likely, which is the large devaluation state if the devaluation probability is small enough. This is achieved by issuing foreign-currency debt.

Hence in equilibrium the firm issues "too much" foreign-currency debt when the credibility of the fixed peg falls below a threshold. The level of foreign-currency debt is excessive in the sense that it bankrupts the firm conditional on a large devaluation. While ex post this might look like a failure to hedge appropriately, the firm's behavior is in fact optimal ex ante, given the high interest rate on peso debt. It might seem counterintuitive that the firm stops hedging against the risk of a large devaluation precisely when this risk increases. However, this reflects optimal hedging, given that the hedging possibilities shrink at the same time as the risk increases.

Figure 7.3 provides a numerical illustration of proposition 3.[12] As the devaluation probability increases, so does the spread on peso debt. When the peso

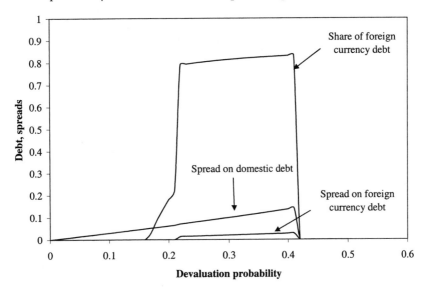

Figure 7.3 Devaluation risk and foreign-currency debt

spread exceeds some threshold, the firm stops hedging against the risk of a large devaluation and borrows almost completely in foreign currency.[13] A spread appears in the interest rate at which the firm can borrow dollars because of the risk of default. The spread remains higher on peso debt, however, the difference being due to the risk of depreciation. Finally, if the devaluation probability is too high, the firm cannot borrow at all because the net value of its project becomes negative.

Practitioners often entertain the view that foreign-currency debt arises "simply" because the interest rate is so much higher on domestic-currency debt. This argument is often dismissed by economists as a case of nominal illusion—the practitioner failing to see the difference between nominal and real interest rates. As this model shows, the practitioner's view makes perfect sense once it is interpreted as relating to the uncertainty in the ex post real interest rate, and there are bankruptcy costs. The variability in the *ex post* real interest rate explains why domestic-currency debt is dangerous—potentially more so than foreign-currency debt.

To conclude this section, let me note that the argument is not specific to fixed currency pegs. A floating exchange rate regime that lacks credibility could induce liability dollarization through the same channel as with a fixed peg. Let us assume that state 0, instead of being a fixed peg, is a managed floating exchange rate regime in which the monetary authorities let the exchange rate adjust to shocks within some range. That is, state 0 can be decomposed in a "cloud" of n substates $O_1, \ldots, O_n$. The managed float is imperfectly credible in the sense that there is a risk of a very large depreciation (a free fall of the currency). Then if the peso interest rate increases because a large depreciation is perceived as more likely, domestic borrowers will dollarize their debts for the same reason as in the fixed peg case. Imperfectly credible floating exchange rates might not be very different, in this respect, from imperfectly credible fixed pegs.[14]

Sovereign Debt

The model has been applied so far to the currency composition of corporate debt. It would be nice to extend the analysis to sovereign debt, since monetary credibility would then offer a unified explanation for the dollarization of private and public liabilities. This section presents a variant of the model that makes it applicable to sovereign debt.

Let us consider a country that needs foreign capital to exploit a natural resource. The country must invest I^* dollars in period 0 to produce a quantity of tradable good worth $R^* > I^*$ dollars in period 1. The domestic government finances the investment by selling sovereign debt to foreign investors. As in the private debt model, the government promises to repay D pesos and D^* dollars in period 1. It actually repays if the output of tradable good is sufficiently high

$(R^* > D^* + D/S)$; otherwise the country defaults on its sovereign debt, and foreign creditors collect $R^* - C^*$, where C^* represents the cost of a sovereign default.

The difference with the case of a firm is that monetary policy is no longer exogenous: the government determines the exchange rate S. For simplicity, let me assume that the exchange rate is set in period 0 by an incumbent policymaker who may or not stay in power in period 1. The incumbent policymaker commits to a fixed exchange rate peg $S = 1$, conditional on his staying in power in period 1. Hence, if the policymaker is certain to stay in power, foreign-currency debt and domestic-currency debt are perfect substitutes and the minimum level of foreign-currency debt is zero.

Assume, however, that with an exogenous probability μ, the incumbent policymaker is replaced by an opportunist policymaker who engineers hyperinflation so as to reduce the value of domestic-currency debt to zero (effectively expropriating the foreign holders of domestic-currency debt). For simplicity, hyperinflation is modeled as setting S to infinity, or equivalently $1/S$ to zero. The incumbent policymaker chooses the currency composition of sovereign debt given μ so as to minimize the probability of default.

For simplicity, let me further assume that R^* is known in period 0.[15] Because R^* is deterministic, the incumbent policymaker can set the default probability to zero. A default-free sovereign debt structure must satisfy

$$\begin{cases} I^* = D^* + (1 - \mu)D \\ D^* + D \leq R^* \end{cases}.$$

The first equation is the zero-profit condition for lenders, and the second equation ensures that maintaining the fixed peg does not trigger a default. Substituting D out gives

$$D^* \geq R^* - \frac{R^* - I^*}{\mu}.$$

The minimum level of foreign-currency debt increases with μ, from zero if $\mu \leq 1 - I^*/R^*$ to I^* for $\mu = 1$. The intuition is similar to the case of a firm. Domestic-currency debt is dangerous if the fixed peg is maintained. As the credibility of the fixed peg decreases and the interest rate on peso debt increases, domestic-currency borrowing must be reduced to avoid a default if the fixed peg is maintained.

There are several ways the model could be made more realistic as a model of sovereign debt, of course. The main purpose of the model in this section, however, is not realism. Rather, it is to show how the basic argument can be extended from private to sovereign debt with minimal changes to the model.

A Look at the Data

This section takes a look at the data in light of the model. At this point it is important to distinguish between domestic and international original sins, that is, between debt issued domestically and debt issued abroad. This distinction does not arise very naturally in my model, in which the jurisdiction under which debt is issued and the residency of investors are both irrelevant for the equilibrium currency composition of debt. But it cannot be avoided in assessing the relevance of the model for the real world.

As documented by Hausmann and Panizza (2002), debt issued *abroad* by emerging-market economies is overwhelmingly in foreign currency, and the small cross-country variations that exist do not seem to result from differences in countries' policies. By contrast, the extent of domestic debt dollarization differs a lot across countries. This is illustrated in figure 7.4, showing the share of dollar debt in total liabilities of publicly traded firms in five Latin American countries.[16]

The contrast between domestic and international original sin is somewhat puzzling. Why is it that some borrowers can issue domestic-currency debt domestically, but not under a foreign jurisdiction? One might conjecture that international original sin has more to do with the way the international financial

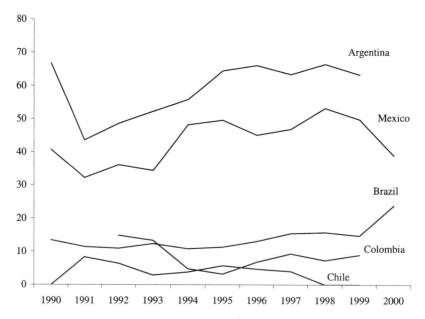

Figure 7.4 Percentage of dollar debt in total liabilities for a sample of publicly traded firms. Data from Bleakley and Cowan 2002, based on Bloomberg/Economatica.

system works at its center than with countries at the periphery. That is, international original sin seems more about the way finance is done in New York, London, or Tokyo than about the way monetary policy is done in Chile or Malaysia.[17]

This said, one should not focus exclusively on the international segment of the debt market. The magnitude of the problems posed by the incompleteness of this particular market depends a lot on the alternative sources of credit. Countries in which borrowers can issue domestic-currency debt in domestic markets are likely to suffer much less from international original sin.

Thus, it seems important to include domestic debt in the empirical analysis. My aim here is to show that once domestic debt is included, a rough look at the data is rather encouraging for the monetary hypothesis. This evidence is meant as suggestive, and much further research would be needed to actually test this hypothesis against alternatives.

One difficulty in measuring domestic original sin is the lack of a consistent cross-country data set on domestic debts in emerging-market countries. I draw here on two data sources: the J. P. Morgan *Guide to Local Markets* compiled by Hausmann and Panizza (2002, table 3), and the Bank for International Settlements data set used by Burger and Warnock (2003).[18] The Hausmann-Panizza data set covers domestic sovereign debt for twenty-four emerging-market countries. The Burger-Warnock data set has a wider coverage in terms of debts and countries, since it includes domestic and foreign as well as private and public debt for fifty countries (including OECD countries). The advantage of the Hausmann-Panizza data set is that it provides more detailed information on the structure of debt.[19] Both data sets give the amounts of debt outstanding at the end of 2001.

The model predicts that, other things equal, countries with unpredictable monetary policies should have less domestic-currency debt both in absolute terms and as a share of total debt. Thus, I define two indexes for the development of the domestic-currency debt market: dev1 is the size of this market as a fraction of GDP, and dev2 is its share in total debt. In the Hausmann-Panizza data set, dev1 is defined as the ratio of long-term fixed-rate domestic government bonds denominated in domestic currency to GDP, and dev2 is the ratio of the same numerator to total outstanding domestic government bonds. The ratios are defined in the same way for the Burger-Warnock data set, except that the universe of debt is larger—it includes debt issued abroad and debt issued by the private sector.

I look at the cross-country correlation between these indexes and monetary instability, proxied by the volatility of inflation. To the extent that the volatility of inflation makes the ex post real interest rate more difficult to predict, it provides an appropriate measure of the determinant of liability dollarization in the model. Figure 7.5 presents plots of dev1 and dev2 against the five-year conditional volatility of the inflation rate over the period 1965–2002. In all cases the

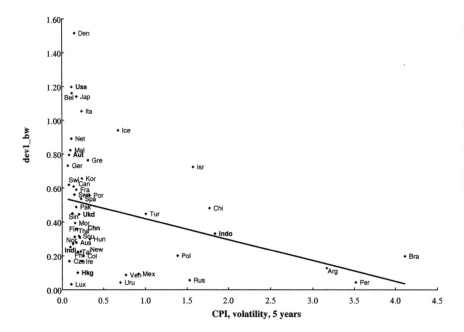

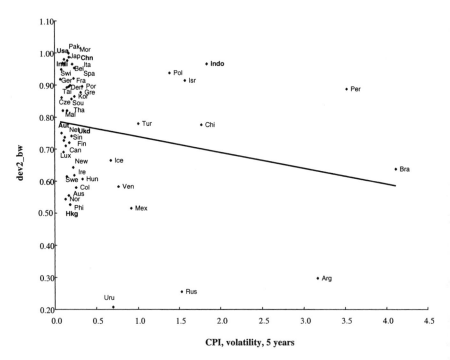

Figure 7.5 Inflation volatility and domestic-currency debt

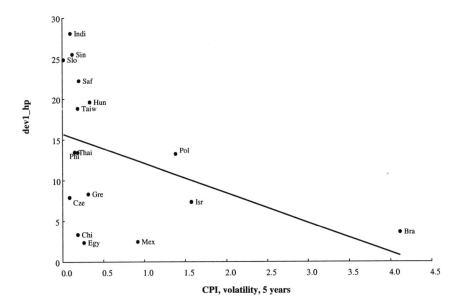

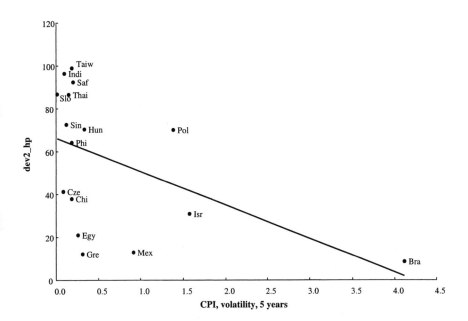

Table 7.2. Domestic-currency debt and monetary credibility

	dev1–bw (1)	dev2–bw (2)	dev1–hp (3)	dev2–hp (4)
Volatility—CPI	−0.123**	−0.050	−0.036**	−0.156**
	(2.34)	(1.62)	(1.77)	(7.23)
Constant	0.542	0.788	0.157	0.663
Observations	50	50	16	16

Note: Absolute value of t statistics in parentheses. dev1 is the ratio of domestic-currency debt to GDP, and dev2 is the ratio of domestic currency debt to total debt. Columns (1) and (2) use the Burger-Warnock data set; columns (3) and (4) use the Hausmann-Panizza data set.
*Significant at 10%. **Significant at 5%.

relationship is negative, as predicted by the model. Simple ordinary least squares regressions suggest that this relationship is statistically significant in three out of four cases (see table 7.2).[20] The relationship is also economically significant: according to the results in the first column of table 7.2, lowering inflation volatility from the Brazilian to the Swedish level increases the domestic-currency debt market from virtually zero to more than 50 percent of GDP. These results are broadly consistent with those of Hausmann and Panizza (2002), Burger and Warnock (2003), and Ize and Levy Yeyati (1998), who run similar regressions. Claessens, Klingebiel, and Schmukler (2003) also find that higher inflation is associated with lower development of the domestic bond market and a lower share of foreign-currency bonds.

There are, of course, a number of reasons that these regression results should not necessarily be interpreted as causality from inflation volatility to liability dollarization. The causality could run the other way, for example, because of the disciplining effect of foreign-currency debt. The relationship could also be driven by common factors.[21] These caveats notwithstanding, a preliminary look at the data seems sufficiently encouraging for the monetary hypothesis to justify more rigorous testing in future research.

Policy Implications

A key policy question is how emerging-market countries can graduate from original sin. I have presented a model in which original sin comes from the lack of monetary credibility. The policy implication, then, is straightforward: it is to establish a credible monetary regime. Improving monetary credibility should allow emerging-market countries to issue more long-term domestic-currency debt domestically, and thus reduce their reliance on foreign-currency debt issued abroad.

That emerging economies should enhance the credibility of their monetary regime is certainly not a new policy recommendation. However, this chapter highlights a new benefit of credibility. Monetary credibility induces domestic firms to borrow in domestic currency ex ante, which enhances the leverage of monetary policy ex post. Conversely, the lack of credibility induces liability dollarization, which reduces the benefit of monetary autonomy. The impact of monetary policy on liability dollarization reinforces the standard arguments in favor of monetary credibility.

Some have advocated a *regulatory approach* to the problems posed by foreign-currency debt, such as taxing, or forbidding international bank lending in foreign currency (see, e.g., Krueger 2000; Goldstein 2002). It is easy to see that this approach does not work in my model: for example, taxing foreign-currency debt unambiguously decreases the welfare of entrepreneurs, because the currency composition of debt is efficient ex ante conditional on monetary policy. For the regulatory approach to work, it needs some kind of externality, and the model has none. Of course, one can think of various negative externalities potentially associated with foreign-currency debt.[22] If the core of the problem is the lack of monetary credibility, however, the regulatory approach is unlikely to be at the core of the solution. The solution is to establish a credible monetary framework.

There are important questions related to transition policies. A large literature focuses on the institutional reforms that may enhance monetary credibility. While these measures are certainly desirable in the class of models I have presented, monetary credibility is not established overnight in the real world, but as the outcome of a time-consuming process of building up reputation and institutions. One question, then, is what are the optimal transition policies with regard to original sin? I shall come back to this question at the end of the chapter.

Concluding Thoughts and Directions for Further Research
Monetary Policy and Debt Structure

I have looked so far at the choice between domestic-currency and foreign-currency debt. There are other alternatives, however, such as indexed debt, or short-term debt (which provides a form of indexation). Indeed, we observe a lot of variety in the structure of domestic debt in emerging-market economies. The large differences between Argentina, Brazil, and Chile shown in figure 7.4, for example, reflect in part the importance of short-term domestic-currency debt in Brazil and of inflation-indexed debt in Chile. The approach adopted in this chapter, then, could be extended by looking at the impact of monetary factors on domestic liability structures more broadly defined.

Nonlinear Hedging

The hedging strategies were limited in my model to the choice of the currency composition of debt. The hedging possibilities could be extended by allowing firms to use derivative instruments.[23] For example, one can check that in the three-state example above, an option to sell pesos at a strike price between S_1 and S_2 allows the entrepreneur to hedge perfectly.

When the number of states increases, however, so must the number of options to achieve perfect insurance. To the extent that options are costly, it should remain true that, other things equal, less monetary credibility leads to less insurance and more financial fragility. It would be interesting to see how the results in this chapter can be generalized to the case where foreign exchange derivative markets are available.

General Equilibrium

The partial equilibrium model presented here could be used as a building block in a more general equilibrium approach to endogenizing liability dollarization. First, the joint distribution of firms' receipts and the exchange rate could be endogenized in a general equilibrium model with money. It would be interesting, in such a model, to quantify and compare the extent of liability dollarization in the tradable and nontradable sectors. It would also be possible to quantify the welfare loss that a noncredible monetary policy can inflict through the channels emphasized in this chapter.[24]

In a multigood model, foreign and domestic investors will not assess portfolio returns with the same price indexes, so that the question of the allocation of domestic and foreign-currency debt in domestic and portfolio is no longer trivial. It would be interesting to study the extent to which such taste differences can explain a "home bias" in the currency composition of portfolios. This could constitute a first step toward explaining the differences between domestic and international original sin.

The two extensions above could be pursued taking monetary policy as exogenous. Another area for further research is to better understand the reverse causality, from liability dollarization to monetary policy. This question has been studied in several papers on the disciplining role of private foreign-currency debt (e.g., Chamon and Hausmann, chapter 8 in this volume; Tirole 2002; Gale and Vives 2002).

Another Interpretation of Original Sin

Eichengreen and Hausmann (1999) use the term "original sin" to convey the idea that emerging-market economies are condemned to foreign-currency debt because of the way international finance works, not because of faulty domestic policies. I have argued that, while this may be true for debt issued abroad, one may not need to look much further than domestic monetary policy to find an explanation for domestic original sin.

This does not mean, however, that redemption from domestic original sin is quick and easy. Establishing monetary credibility is a time-consuming process, and this process may be made more difficult by liability dollarization. One difficulty is that the government's behavior when liabilities are dollarized might give little information on how it would behave if liabilities were in domestic currency—and the temptation to inflate were greater.[25] This might create a "credibility barrier" between less-developed and developed countries. For countries with low credibility, full dollarization might be a better option than attempting to overcome the barrier. Thus, even domestic original sin could be determined in the long run by history and initial conditions.

Appendix

Preliminaries

It is useful to distinguish two classes of problems (P), the concave and convex ones. But in order to do so, I must first define the lower envelope of states in the space (S, R). Let me remove from X all the states x such that there is another state $x' \neq x$ with the same exchange rate but a strictly lower return ($S[x] = S[x']$ but $R[x'] < R[x]$). (That is, I remove points like A in fig. 7.1.) This leaves me with a subset of states $X' \subset X$. Then let me define the locus (C) as the curve joining all the points in X'. This curve is piece-wise linear if there is a finite number of states in X', but could be smooth if X' includes a continuum of states.

I say problem (P) is globally concave if curve (C) is globally concave, and globally convex if (C) is globally convex (fig. 7A.1 illustrates the concave case). In general, it could be that problem (P) is neither globally convex nor globally

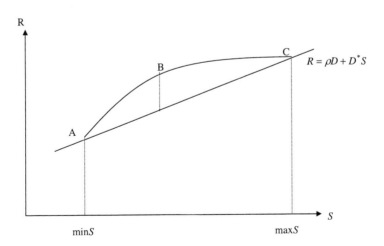

Figure 7A.1 The concave case

concave because (C) is convex in some parts and concave in others. However, problems that are globally convex or concave have nice properties (the concave variety more so).

In particular, the maximum pledgeable income of the entrepreneur $\hat{V}$ is quite easy to compute when problem (P) is concave. The corresponding debt structure is such that the no-default constraint $D + D*S(x) \leq R(x)$ is binding for the two extreme states corresponding to the lowest and highest levels of the exchange rate in X' (points A and C in fig. 7A.1). If the no-default constraint is satisfied for these two states, then it is strictly satisfied for all other states by concavity of (C).

If the firm's debt structure is not default-free, then the states in which the firm defaults also depend on the nature of problem (P). If this problem is concave, the firm will default in extreme states, with the highest or lowest exchange rates. By contrast, if (P) is convex, the firm will default in intermediate states.

Proof of Proposition 4

The model given in "Monetary Policy as a Source of Risk" above is a concave problem with three states. It can be represented as in figure 7A.2. The default-free debt structure $(D, D*)$ that maximizes the firm's pledgeable income is such that the line $R = D + D*S$ goes through points 0 and 2. The firm's pledgeable income is

$$\hat{V} = E\left(\frac{R}{S}\right) - \mu p_1 \eta,$$

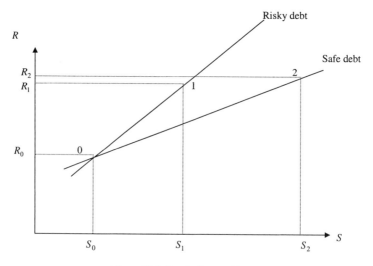

Figure 7A.2 Proof of proposition 4

where η is the gap between the dollar income of the firm and its dollar repayment in state 1. If one writes S_1 as a weighted average of S_0 and S_2 with weights $1 - \lambda$ and λ respectively, this gap is equal to

$$\eta = \frac{R_1 - (1 - \lambda)R_0 - \lambda R_2}{S_1}.$$

Because the problem is concave, if $\hat{V} < I^*$ the entrepreneur must choose between defaulting in state 0 (no devaluation) and defaulting in state 2 (large devaluation). As long as the probability of a devaluation μ is lower than $1/(1 + p_2)$, the entrepreneur chooses to default in the large devaluation state. Conditional on this, the debt structure (D, D^*) that maximizes the firm's pledgeable income is achieved when the line $R = D + D^*S$ goes through points 0 and 1. The expected repayment is then given by the project's expected return, net of the cost of default in state 3:

$$\hat{V} = E\left(\frac{R}{S}\right) - \mu p_2 C^*.$$

The firm's maximum pledgeable income is larger under a risky debt structure if the expected default cost is not too large. That is, $\hat{V} > \tilde{V}$ if and only if

$$p_2 C^* < p_1 \eta,$$

a condition that I assume to be satisfied. Then the proof of proposition 4 easily follows. The thresholds $\underline{\mu}$ and $\overline{\mu}$ are the values of μ for which $\hat{V}$ and $\tilde{V}$ are equal to I^* respectively. Let us denote by $\gamma \equiv \mu(R_0/S_0 - p_1 R_1/S_1 - p_2 R_2/S_2)$ the decrease in the project's dollar return resulting from a devaluation, and by $\beta \equiv R_0/S_0 - I^*$ the net benefit of the project conditional on no devaluation. Then it follows from $E(R/S) = I^* + \beta - \mu\gamma$ that the probability thresholds $\underline{\mu}$ and $\overline{\mu}$ are given by

$$\underline{\mu} = \frac{\beta}{\gamma + p_1 \eta}, \qquad \overline{\mu} = \frac{\beta}{\gamma + p_2 C}.$$

Notes

1. A number of recent papers look at the various problems caused by foreign-currency debt and currency mismatches in balance sheets; see Aghion, Bacchetta, and Banerjee 2001; Burnside, Eichenbaum, and Rebelo 2001; or Jeanne and Zettelmeyer 2002.

2. Or the lack of credibility of fiscal policy, to the extent that monetary policy is fiscally determined.

3. Hausmann and Panizza (2002) distinguish between *domestic* and *international* original sin. The former refers to debt issued domestically while the latter relates to debt issued under a foreign jurisdiction (e.g., bonds issued in New York, London, or Tokyo).

The distinction is in terms of the jurisdiction of issuance, not the residency of the debt-holders. In Hausmann and Panizza's terminology, this chapter looks for an explanation of domestic, not international, original sin.

4. These other policy areas could be related to monetary policy, however. For example, a sound monetary framework could be a necessary condition for financial development. Indeed, the model presented in this chapter suggests that monetary credibility is necessary to the development of a long-term domestic-currency debt market.

5. The evidence is not very encouraging for Latin America. Barajas and Morales' study (2003) of the determinants of dollarization in the banking sectors of fourteen Latin American countries finds that, contrary to Caballero and Krishnamurthy's prediction (2003), financial development (measured by the ratio of private-sector credit to GDP) is *positively* correlated with dollarization, while deposit insurance coverage (a measure of moral hazard) has ambiguous effects.

6. The model of debt with costly state verification has been used in the macroeconomic literature on monetary policy, for example, by Bernanke, Gertler, and Gilchrist (1998). Other models of costly default could be considered, such as Diamond's model (1984) of debt with a nonpecuniary punishment for default, or models where default involves the early termination or restructuring of projects (Bolton and Scharfstein 1990; Dewatripont and Tirole 1994).

7. Which is possible only if there are three states or more.

8. This is where the assumption that the default probability be strictly positive but smaller than $\frac{1}{2}$ is necessary. If the default probability were zero, there would be no strict benefit to reducing the variance in r. If it were larger than $\frac{1}{2}$, the tail probability event would no longer be the default but the absence of default: reducing the variance of r would increase the default probability.

9. Indeed, this is the way Roy (1952) arrived at the capital asset pricing model at the same time as Markowitz (1952); see Bernstein 1993.

10. Aguiar (2002), Gelos (2003), and Martinez and Werner (2001) find a strong correlation between foreign-currency debt and the share of sales exported of Mexican firms. Cowan (2003) finds the same pattern for a larger sample of Latin American countries.

11. The only difference is that the entrepreneur defaults in state 1 (small devaluation) instead of state 2 (large devaluation).

12. Figure 7.3 was constructed using the following parameter values: $(S_0, S_1, S_2) = (1, 1.3, 5)$, $(R_0, R_1, R_2) = (1.05, 1.3, 2)$, $(p_1, p_2) = (0.9, 0.1)$, and $C = 0.1$.

13. The shift involves a discontinuous upward jump in foreign-currency debt because of the discontinuous increase in the default probability.

14. Arteta's empirical study (2001) suggests that floating regimes exacerbate, rather than ameliorate, currency mismatches in domestic financial intermediation.

15. That R^* is constant implies that the country can perfectly hedge against a default, and that domestic-currency debt cannot strictly dominate foreign-currency debt. As for a firm, the analysis can be extended to a stochastic R^*, but the optimal currency composition is then more complicated to derive.

16. I thank Kevin Cowan and Hoyt Bleakley for sharing these data with me.

17. Incidentally, the question is not only why countries do not issue domestic-currency debt in London or New York, but also why they do not issue other forms of debt, like commodity-indexed or GDP-indexed bonds (Caballero 2002; Borensztein

and Mauro 2002). Borensztein and Mauro give an interesting discussion of possible barriers to financial innovation in the international debt market.

18. I thank Frank Warnock and John Burger for sharing these data with me.

19. The Hausmann-Panizza data provide four categories of domestic-currency debt: long-term fixed-rate, short-term fixed-rate, short-term or long-term indexed to the interest rate, and long-term indexed to prices. Long-term fixed-rate debt is the best empirical counterpart for domestic-currency debt in my model.

20. The small number of observations in the Hausmann-Panizza data makes it difficult to take the significance test seriously, however.

21. For example, Burger and Warnock (2003) find that the impact of monetary variables on liability dollarization is attenuated when a measure for the rule of law is added to the regressors.

22. An important source of externality could be financial contagion.

23. See Albuquerque 2001 for a comparison of forwards and options in hedging exchange risk in the presence of bankruptcy costs.

24. Mendoza (2001) calibrates the welfare cost of lack of policy credibility in an open-economy model with financial frictions, and finds it to be significant.

25. This idea is formalized in independent work by Cowan and Do (2003).

References

Aghion, Philippe, Philippe Bacchetta, and Abhijit Banerjee. 2001. "Currency Crises and Monetary Policy in an Economy with Credit Constraints." *European Economic Review* 45 (7): 1121–50.

Aguiar, Mark. 2000. "Foreign Currency Debt in Emerging Markets." Manuscript, University of Chicago, Graduate School of Business.

———. 2002. "Investment, Devaluation, and Foreign Currency Exposure: The Case of Mexico." Manuscript, University of Chicago, Graduate School of Business.

Albuquerque, Rui. 2001. "Optimal Currency Hedging." Manuscript, University of Rochester.

Arteta, Carlos. 2001. "Exchange Rate Regimes and Financial Dollarization: Does Flexibility Reduce Bank Currency Mismatches?" Manuscript, University of California, Berkeley.

Barajas, Adolfo, and R. Armando Morales. 2003. "Dollarization of Liabilities: Beyond the Usual Suspects." IMF Working Paper 03/11, International Monetary Fund, Washington, DC.

Bernanke, Ben, Mark Gertler, and Simon Gilchrist. 1998. "The Financial Accelerator in a Quantitative Business Cycle Framework." NBER Working Paper no. 6455, National Bureau of Economic Research, Cambridge, MA.

Bernstein, Peter L. 1993. *Capital Ideas.* New York: Free Press.

Bleakley, Hoyt, and Kewin Cowan. 2002. "Corporate Dollar Debt and Devaluations: Much Ado about Nothing?" Manuscript, Massachusetts Institute of Technology, Cambridge, MA.

Bohn, Henning. 1990. "A Positive Theory of Foreign Currency Debt." *Journal of International Economics* 29:273–92.

Bolton, Patrick, and David Scharfstein. 1990. "A Theory of Predation Based on Agency Problems in Financial Contracting." *American Economic Review* 80:93–106.

Borensztein, Eduardo, and Paolo Mauro. 2002. "Reviving the Case for GDP-Indexed Bonds." Policy Discussion Paper no. 02/10, International Monetary Fund, Washington, DC.

Broda, Christian, and Eduardo Levy Yeyati. 2003. "Endogenous Deposit Dollarization." Federal Reserve Bank of New York Staff Reports, no. 160.

Burger, John D., and Frank E. Warnock. 2003. "Diversification, Original Sin, and International Bond Portfolios." International Finance Discussion Paper no. 755, Board of Governors of the Federal Reserve System, Washington, DC.

Burnside, Craig, Martin Eichenbaum, and Sergio Rebelo. 2001. "Hedging and Financial Fragility in Fixed Exchange Rate Regimes." *European Economic Review* 45: 1151–93.

Caballero, Ricardo. 2002. "Coping with Chile's External Vulnerability: A Financial Problem." Manuscript, Massachusetts Intstitute of Technology, Department of Economics, Cambridge, MA.

Caballero, Ricardo, and Arvind Krishnamurthy. 2003. "Excessive Dollar Debt: Financial Development and Underinsurance." *Journal of Finance* 58 (2): 867–93.

Calvo, Guillermo. 1996. *Money, Exchange Rates, and Output.* Cambridge, MA: MIT Press.

———. 2001. "Capital Markets and the Exchange Rate." *Journal of Money, Credit, and Banking* 33 (2): 312–34.

Chamon, Marcos. 2001. "Why Don't We Observe Foreign Lending to Developing Countries in Their Currency (Either Nominal or Indexed to Inflation)?" Manuscript, Harvard University, Department of Economics, Cambridge, MA.

Claessens, Stijn, Daniela Klingebiel, and Sergio Schmukler. 2003. "Government Bonds in Domestic and Foreign Currency: The Role of Macroeconomic and Institutional Factors." Manuscript, World Bank, Washington, DC.

Corden, Max. 2002. *Too Sensational: On the Choice of Exchange Rate Regimes.* Cambridge, MA: MIT Press.

Cowan, Kevin. 2003. "Firm Level Determinants of Dollar Debt?" Manuscript, Inter-American Development Bank, Washington, DC.

Cowan, Kevin, and Quy-Toan Do. 2003. "Financial Dollarization and Central Bank Credibility." Manuscript, Inter-American Development Bank, Washington, DC.

Dewatripont, Mathias, and Jean Tirole. 1994. "A Theory of Debt and Equity: Diversity of Securities and Manager-Shareholder Congruence." *Quarterly Journal of Economics* 109 (4): 1027–54.

Diamond, Douglas. 1984. "Financial Intermediation and Delegated Monitoring." *Review of Economic Studies* 51 (3): 393–414.

Eichengreen, Barry, and Ricardo Hausmann. 1999. "Exchange Rates and Financial Fragility." In *New Challenges for Monetary Policy,* 329–68, Kansas City, MO: Federal Reserve Bank of Kansas City.

Froot, Kenneth A., David S. Scharfstein, and Jeremy C. Stein. 1993. "Risk Management: Coordinating Corporate Investment and Financing Policies." *Journal of Finance* 48 (5): 1629–58.

Gale, Douglas, and Martin Hellwig. 1985. "Incentive Compatible Debt Contracts: The One-Period Problem." *Review of Economic Studies* 52 (4): 647–63.

Gale, Douglas, and Xavier Vives. 2002. "Dollarization, Bailouts, and the Stability of the Banking System." *Quarterly Journal of Economics* 117 (2): 467–502.

Gelos, Gaston. 2003. "Foreign Currency Debt in Emerging Markets: Firm-Level Evidence from Mexico." *Economic Letters* 78:323–27.

Goldstein, Morris. 2002. *Managed Floating Plus.* Policy Analyses in International Economics 66. Washington, DC: Institute for International Economics.

Hausmann, Ricardo, and Ugo Panizza. 2002. "The Mystery of Original Sin: the Case of the Missing Apple." Paper prepared for the conference "Currency and Maturity Matchmaking: Redeeming Debt from Original Sin," Inter-American Development Bank, Washington, DC.

Ize, Alain, and Eduardo Levy Yeyati. 1998. "Dollarization of Financial Intermediation: Causes and Policy Implications." Working Paper 98/28, International Monetary Fund, Washington, DC.

Ize, Alain, and Eric Parrado. 2002. "Dollarization, Monetary Policy, and the Pass-Through." Working Paper 02/188, International Monetary Fund, Washington, DC.

Jeanne, Olivier. 2000. "Foreign Currency Debt and the Global Financial Architecture." *European Economic Review* 44:719–27.

Krueger, Anne O. 2000. "Conflicting Demands on the International Monetary Fund." *American Economic Review* 90 (2): 38–42.

Markowitz, Harry. 1952. "Portfolio Selection." *Journal of Finance* 7:77–91.

Martinez, Lorenza, and Alejandro Werner. 2001. "The Exchange Rate Regime and the Currency Composition of Corporate Debt: The Mexican Experience." Manuscript, Bank of Mexico, Mexico City.

McKinnon, Ronald, and Huw Pill. 1998. "International Overborrowing: A Decomposition of Credit and Currency Risks." *World Development* 7:1267–82.

Mendoza, Enrique G. 2001. "The Benefits of Dollarization When Stabilization Policy Lacks Credibility and Financial Markets Are Imperfect." *Journal of Money, Credit, and Banking* 33 (2): 440–74.

Roy, A. D. 1952. "Safety First and the Holding of Assets." *Econometrica* 20 (3): 431–49.

Schneider, Martin, and Aaron Tornell. 2001. "Balance Sheet Effects, Bailout Guarantees, and Financial Crises." Manuscript, University of California, Los Angeles, Department of Economics.

Smith, Clifford, and René Stulz. 1985. "The Determinants of Firms' Hedging Policies." *Journal of Financial and Quantitative Analysis* 20 (4): 391–405.

Tirole, Jean. 2002. "Inefficient Foreign Borrowing: A Dual-and-Common-Agency Perspective." Manuscript, Toulouse.

Townsend, Robert. 1979. "Optimal Contracts and Competitive Markets with Costly State Verification." *Journal of Economic Theory* 21:265–93.

Zettelmeyer, Jeromin, and Olivier Jeanne. 2002. "'Original Sin,' Balance Sheet Crises, and the Roles of International Lending." Working Paper no. 02/234, International Monetary Fund, Washington, DC.

Why Do Countries Borrow the Way They Borrow?

Marcos Chamon and Ricardo Hausmann

WHY DO companies and households in many emerging markets borrow in foreign currency? After all, the recent spate of crises in which dollar debts have interacted with drastic real depreciations to create massive bankruptcies and economic havoc suggests that it is an important source of financial fragility. The preceding chapters have established the ubiquity of foreign-currency denomination in international lending—referred to as "original sin"—and have studied their unpleasant macroconsequences. In this chapter, just as in the previous one, a potential causal mechanism is proposed. A significant part of the literature on the causes of original sin has focused on moral-hazard interpretations. If companies expect to be bailed out by governments, they will not fully internalize the risks they bear (Dooley 2000; Burnside, Eichenbaum, and Rebelo 2001; Schneider and Tornell 2004). In this view, countries do not borrow in local currency because they find it too expensive, given the alternative of borrowing in foreign currency and being bailed out in case of a large depreciation. But the telltale signs of moral hazard in terms of the pattern of lending have not found much empirical support (Eichengreen and Hausmann 1999; Fernández-Arias and Hausmann 2000; Kamin 2002; Ortiz 2002). A more recent literature has proposed other models. Caballero and Krishnamurthy (2003) present a model where excessive dollar debt is the result of domestic financial constraints that lead firms to undervalue the social benefit of borrowing in local currency. Jeanne in chapter 7 of this volume argues that liability dollarization can be a safe play when low monetary credibility keeps interest rates in domestic currency high. Chamon (2001) and Aghion, Bacchetta, and Banerjee (2001) present a model where the correlation of devaluation risk and default risk makes domestic-currency lending unattractive. In their setup, it is possible for a firm to expropriate the claim that domestic-currency creditors have on the residual value of the bankrupt company by increasing their borrowing in foreign currency, given that in the context of a bankruptcy, the claims of domestic-currency creditors will be automatically written down by the concomitant depreciation. In anticipation of this, investors refrain from lending in domestic currency.

Broda and Levy Yeyati (2003) independently present this interplay between currency and credit risk in the context of dollarization of bank deposits. Tirole (2003) proposes a dual-and-common agency approach to the problem, where a foreign investor's return depends not only on the behavior of a private borrower but also on that of the borrower's government, with whom he does not contract. Since the government does not value the welfare of foreign investors, it can negatively affect their return through nominal or real exchange rate manipulation. As a result, local-currency debt markets can actually reduce welfare.

In this chapter we explore the interplay between an individual borrower's choices for liability denomination through their effect on the optimal monetary response of the central bank, given those choices. We start from the assumption that the debt in domestic currency cannot be contracted at long maturities and at fixed rates. As a result, the terms in which it is rolled over or repriced will depend on changes in the domestic interest rate. In chapter 1, Eichengreen, Hausmann, and Panizza show that, for a sample of twenty-two emerging markets, all of the countries that can borrow abroad in local currency can also borrow long term at fixed rates in local currency in the domestic market. The converse, however, is not true; there are countries that can borrow domestically long term but cannot denominate their external debt in local currency. Our assumption would help explain why absence of a domestic long-term market may preclude the ability to borrow in local currency, but would not explain why original sin persists even in the presence of long-term domestic markets.

In the model presented, there is a shock to the expected future exchange rate. Since agents are forward looking, that shock affects the present interest and exchange rates. The central bank uses monetary policy to determine how the absorption of that shock is divided between changes in the interest rate and in the exchange rate. If most liabilities are dollarized and the central bank cares about preventing bankruptcy, it will stabilize the exchange rate at the expense of larger movements in the interest rate. Alternatively, if most liabilities are denominated in pesos, the central bank will stabilize the interest rate at the expense of larger movements in the exchange rate. This can generate multiplicity of equilibria in the liability composition, since if an atomistic agent expects all other agents to denominate their debt in dollars (pesos), he or she will expect the monetary policy to be tailored for that particular liability denomination and as a result may find it optimal to borrow in dollars (pesos) as well. It is worth noting that the policymaker in our model does not attempt to expropriate foreign investors to the benefit of domestic residents as in Tirole (2003). Instead, it is only trying to make dollar debt safer, given that those contracts have already been written.

The interaction of liability denomination and monetary policy has received recent attention. Calvo and Reinhart (2002) and Hausmann, Panizza, and Stein (2001) show that emerging markets that formally float their currency tend to limit the movement of the exchange rate vis-à-vis the interest rate and to accumulate significantly larger stocks of international reserves. Hausmann et al. show that this behavior is strongly correlated with measures of the ability of a country to borrow internationally in its own currency. Hence, the title of their paper "Why Do Countries Float the Way They Float?" receives implicitly the answer "because they borrow the way they borrow." There is also a recent literature relating the structure of liabilities to the choice of monetary policy. Aghion, Bacchetta, and Banerjee (2001) show how balance-sheet effects can make devaluations contractionary and optimal monetary policy apparently procyclical. Céspedes, Chang, and Velasco in chapter 2 of this volume present a model where the effectiveness of monetary policy, although still positive, is significantly compromised in its ability to dampen cyclical fluctuations by the presence of original sin. These works focus on how original sin can affect the optimal monetary policy. There is also a literature that studies how monetary policy can affect the currency composition of corporate debt (e.g., Jeanne 2000; Tirole 2003). In this chapter, we focus on how the choice of an individual entrepreneur's liability composition can be affected by the choice of the other entrepreneurs through the effect of their choice on the resulting monetary policy.

The Basic Environment

Consider a small open economy subject to shocks to its expected future exchange rate. These shocks are assumed to be out of the control of the economy's policymaker (e.g., terms-of-trade shocks) and are not modeled explicitly. We assume the resulting exchange rate expectations are distributed according to a random variable z_t.

The focus of the model is on a small segment of the nontradable sector, which consists of atomistic entrepreneurs. Those entrepreneurs have access to a production function that requires an initial investment of one unit of the local currency (henceforth pesos) and whose output is worth A pesos. Two types of debt are considered. The first, which we refer to as dollar debt, is denominated in the foreign currency. The second type, which we refer to as peso contracts, is denominated in the home local currency. We assume one cannot write peso contracts in terms of a fixed domestic interest rate. Instead, peso debt contracts must pay the ex post domestic interest rate for the period the loan was made. This assumption aims at capturing the fact that in practice the maturities of local-currency contracts are much smaller than those of foreign-currency ones in emerging markets, and that by borrowing through short-term local-currency debt the borrowers are vulnerable to shocks to the interest rate at which that debt is rolled over.

The debt contracts must be written at the beginning of time t when the exchange rate is given by e_t^0. The expectation at time t for the exchange rate in period $t + 1$ is given by the random variable z_t, whose realization occurs at the beginning of period t, but only after the debt contracts have been written. The higher z_t, the larger the expected depreciation (which can be interpreted as the result of an adverse shock). Thus, the expected exchange rate in period $t + 1$ at the beginning of period t is given by $E_t^0[e_{t+1}] = E[z_t]$ and is updated to $E_t[e_{t+1}] = z_t$ following the realization of that uncertainty.

The monetary authority decides how to accommodate the shock $z_t - E[z_t]$ between changes in the interest rate and in the exchange rate. We assume an uncovered interest parity condition must be satisfied:

(1)
$$1 + i_t = (1 + i^*)\frac{z_t}{e_t},$$

where i_t is the domestic risk-free rate, i^* the constant world interest rate, and e_t the value of the exchange rate following the realization of that shock. The value of e_t^0 is given by arbitrage between peso and dollar instruments at the beginning of time t:

$$E_t^0[1 + i_t] = (1 + i^*)\frac{E_t^0[e_t]}{e_t^0}.$$

We assume that entrepreneurs are risk-neutral, but face a nonpecuniary cost associated with defaults (in addition to the loss of their output). As a result, when deciding whether to borrow in pesos or dollars, they seek to minimize the probability of a default occurring.[1] An entrepreneur that has borrowed through peso debt, paying a risk premium r_{peso}, defaults if

$$A < (1 + i_t)(1 + r_{\text{peso}}),$$

while an entrepreneur that borrowed through dollar debt paying a risk premium $r_\$$ defaults if

$$A < (1 + i^*)(1 + r_\$)e_t/e_t^0.$$

In principle an entrepreneur could mix the two denominations, but we show that this is not optimal in this model.

The timing of events is summarized below.

1. Debt contracts are written.
2. The shock to the expectation of the next period exchange rate is realized.
3. Given that shock and the currency composition of the debt contracts, the monetary authority sets i_t and e_t.

The monetary authority (henceforth the central bank) takes that cost of default into account when choosing i_t and e_t. It also seeks to minimize the gap between the economy's output and an ideal target and to minimize the inflation rate. Output and inflation are a function of the interest rate and of the exchange rate, given by the equations below where a sans-serif font indicates that a variable is expressed in log terms:

(2) $$\mathsf{Y_t} = \overline{\mathsf{Y}} + \alpha \mathsf{e_t} - \beta \mathsf{i_t}$$

and

(3) $$\pi_t = \overline{\pi} + \gamma \mathsf{e_t} - \delta \mathsf{i_t},$$

where $\mathsf{Y_t}$ is the log of the output, π_t is the inflation rate, $\overline{\mathsf{Y}}$ and $\overline{\pi}$ are constants, and α, β, γ, and λ are positive constants. Since the entrepreneurial sector that borrows from abroad is assumed to be small, the effect of its liability composition on these parameters is ignored. The central bank's inflation versus output trade-off is given by the loss function

(4) $$\ell = (\tilde{\mathsf{Y}} - \mathsf{Y_t})^2 + \chi \pi_t^2,$$

where $\tilde{\mathsf{Y}}$ is the log of the ideal output target and χ is a constant. In addition to that trade-off between output and inflation, the central bank's welfare function is also affected by the share of entrepreneurs that would default given its choice for i_t and e_t. The central bank's loss function taking this effect in consideration is given by

(5) $$L = \ell + s(i_t, e_t)C,$$

where $s(i_t, e_t)$ is the share of bankrupt entrepreneurs given the monetary policy, and C is the cost of that default to the central bank's welfare. That cost differs from the private one incurred by the entrepreneurs depending on the extent to which the central bank internalizes their welfare and on the externalities that their bankruptcy can impose on the rest of the economy. Even though that entrepreneurial sector is assumed to be small (so as not to affect aggregate output and inflation), it seems plausible to assume that its bankruptcy can still impose nonnegligible costs on the economy as a whole. These assumptions are made for expositional purposes. If the bankruptcy of those entrepreneurs were to adversely affect output (in addition to the exogenous bankruptcy costs assumed), the central bank would be even more willing to accommodate the shock in a way that prevents their bankruptcy. That would increase the strategic complementarities among the entrepreneurs' choices for liability composition, strengthening the multiple equilibria result presented in this chapter. While the assumptions made do not change the qualitative features of the model, their relaxation would introduce discontinuities on the central bank's loss function, substantially complicating the analysis.

   An equilibrium for this economy is defined as a situation where each entrepreneur's choice of liability composition is optimal given his or her beliefs for the choice of the other entrepreneurs and resulting expectations for the central bank's policy, and the central bank's choice for e_t and i_t is optimal given the realization of z_t and the liability composition of the entrepreneurs.

It is useful to initially consider the case where the central bank does not take into account bankruptcy considerations when setting its monetary policy (i.e., $C = 0$). The central bank's loss function becomes $L = \ell$. Minimizing (4) subject to (1) yields the following policy rules:

$$(6) \qquad\qquad e_t = \phi + \varsigma z_t$$

and

$$(7) \qquad\qquad i_t = i^* - \phi + (1 - \varsigma)z_t,$$

where

$$(8) \qquad \phi = \frac{(\alpha + \beta)(\tilde{Y} - \bar{Y} - \beta i^*) - \chi(\gamma + \delta)(\bar{\pi} - \delta i^*)}{(\alpha + \beta)^2 + \chi(\gamma + \delta)^2},$$

$$\varsigma = \frac{(\alpha + \beta)\beta + \chi(\gamma + \delta)\delta}{(\alpha + \beta)^2 + \chi(\gamma + \delta)^2},$$

and $0 < \varsigma < 1$. Thus, the central bank accommodates the shock in a way that both the elasticities of i_t and e_t with respect to z_t are positive but smaller than one and together they add to unity.

Consider the case where parameters are such that $\varsigma = \frac{1}{2}$ (i.e., the central bank distributes the shock to z_t between i_t and e_t with the same elasticity). We solve the recursive equilibrium and show that if everyone else borrows in dollars, an atomistic entrepreneur is better off borrowing in dollars as well, because the monetary authority will stabilize the exchange rate at the expense of higher volatility in the interest rate. The opposite is true if everyone were to borrow in pesos.

Suppose that in the first stage of the game all entrepreneurs choose to borrow in dollars. The monetary authority knows that in order to prevent a default from occurring, it must set e_t below a critical e_t^c level given by

$$(9) \qquad\qquad e_t^c = \frac{Ae_t^0}{(1 + i^*)(1 + r_\$)}.$$

There are three regions of interest for the problem solved by the monetary authority in stage 3.

Region 1: The condition $e_t \leq e_t^c$ is not binding. In this region, the realization of z_t is such that the monetary authority does not need to worry about defaults occurring. As a result, it sets e_t and i_t according to (6) and (7):

$$(10) \qquad\qquad e_t = \phi + \frac{1}{2}z_t,$$

$$(11) \qquad\qquad i_t = i^* - \phi + \frac{1}{2}z_t,$$

and both e_t and i_t increase on the square root of z_t.

Region 2: The realization of z_t is such that the central bank chooses to set $e_t = e_t^c$ in order to avoid defaults and accommodates the remaining part of the shock through i_t. In this region the central bank sets

$$e_t = e_t^c$$

and

$$i_t = i^* + z_t - e_t^c.$$

Note that instead of increasing on the square root of z_t, i_t is linear on z_t in this range.

Region 3: The realization of z_t is so large that the central bank gives up accommodating the change in e_t and lets the entrepreneurs go bankrupt. The central bank decides to "throw in the towel" if the interest rate hike necessary to keep the exchange rate at e_t^c is so high that the loss function is actually larger than the one where it lets them go bankrupt and accommodates the shock between the two instruments. The central bank's loss function given a realization of z_t when ignoring bankruptcy issues can be defined as a function of e_t. The difference between the value of that function obtained by setting $e_t = e_t^c$ as opposed to the level $\phi + \frac{1}{2}z_t$ it would choose in the absence of bankruptcy considerations is obtained by taking a Taylor-series expansion.[2]

$$\ell(e_t^c) - \ell\left(\phi + \frac{1}{2}z_t\right) = \ell'\left(\phi + \frac{1}{2}z_t\right)\left(e_t^c - \left(\phi + \frac{1}{2}z_t\right)\right)$$
$$+ \frac{\ell''(\phi + \frac{1}{2}z_t)}{2}\left(e_t^c - \left(\phi + \frac{1}{2}z_t\right)\right)^2$$
$$= \frac{\ell''(\phi + \frac{1}{2}z_t)}{2}\left(e_t^c - \left(\phi + \frac{1}{2}z_t\right)\right)^2$$

The above expression is increasing on the difference between e_t^c and $(\phi + \frac{1}{2}z_t)$. Thus, for large enough z_t, that loss will dominate the one associated with the cost C of letting the entrepreneurs go bankrupt. Once that level is reached, the central bank's response is given by (10) and (11). Note that there is a discontinuity around that critical value of z_t with a discrete increase in e_t and a discrete decline in i_t. (See fig. 8.1.)

So far, we have shown that given dollarization of liabilities, the central bank will "float with a lifejacket," letting the exchange rate float over some range but aggressively intervening if a certain threshold is reached. But for a high enough realization of z_t, it will give up on that intervention and let it float again. It remains to show that given that the central bank will act this way, agents would indeed prefer to borrow in dollars.

Since the entrepreneurs are risk-neutral, when choosing the composition of their liabilities they only care about which of them decreases the likelihood of a default.

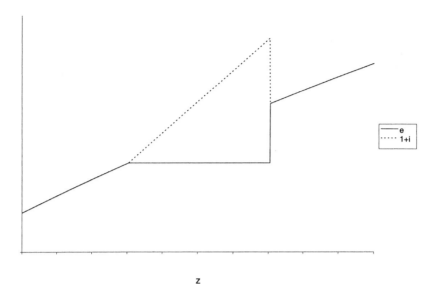

Figure 8.1 Exchange rate and interest rate if $\varsigma = \frac{1}{2}$ and liabilities are denominated in dollars

Let $z_\$^c$ and z_{peso}^c denote the critical values of the realization of the z_t above for which an entrepreneur would default given dollar and peso liabilities, respectively.

Since from arbitrage both types of liabilities must yield the same expected return to the lenders, we have

$$\int_{\underline{z}}^{z_\$^c} (1 + i^*)(1 + r_\$)\frac{e_t}{e_t^0}\Pr(z)\,dz = \int_{\underline{z}}^{z_{peso}^c} (1 + r_{peso})(1 + i_t)\Pr(z)\,dz,$$

where both e_t and i_t are increasing functions of z, and the risk premia $r_\$$ and r_{peso} are decreasing on $z_\$^c$ and z_{peso}^c. Arbitrage between risk-free short-term peso and dollar instruments implies

(12) $$\int_{\underline{z}}^{\bar{z}} (1 + i^*)\frac{e_t}{e_t^0}\Pr(z)\,dz = \int_{\underline{z}}^{\bar{z}} (1 + i_t)\Pr(z)\,dz.$$

The solution of the central bank's problem implies that there exists z_A and z_B such that $z_A > z_\$^c > z_B$ and

(13) $$e_t(z_A) - e_t(z_B) \leq \frac{1}{2}(z_A - z_B) \leq i_t(z_A) - i_t(z_B),$$

with strict inequalities for some z_B.

PROPOSITION 1. $z_\$^c > z_{\text{peso}}^c$

PROOF. Suppose $z_\$^c \leq z_{\text{peso}}^c$.

Equation (12) can be rewritten as

$$\frac{(1 + i^*)}{e_t^0}\left(\int_{\underline{z}}^{z_{\text{peso}}^c} e_t \Pr(z)\,dz + \int_{z_{\text{peso}}^c}^{\bar{z}} e_t \Pr(z)\,dz \right) = \int_{\underline{z}}^{z_{\text{peso}}^c} (i + i_t)\Pr(z)\,dz$$

$$+ \int_{z_{\text{peso}}^c}^{\bar{z}} (1 + i_t)\Pr(z)\,dz.$$

The equation above and inequality (13) imply

$$\frac{(1 + i^*)}{e_t^0} \int_{\underline{z}}^{z_{\text{peso}}^c} e_t \Pr(z)\,dz < \int_{\underline{z}}^{z_{\text{peso}}^c} (i + i_t)\Pr(z)\,dz,$$

which implies

$$\frac{(1 + i^*)}{e_t^0} \int_{\underline{z}}^{z'} (1 + r_{\text{peso}})\Pr(z)\,dz < \int_{\underline{z}}^{z_{\text{peso}}^c} (1 + r_{\text{peso}})(i + i_t)\Pr(z)\,dz$$

for some $z' > z_{\text{peso}}^c$. That implies $r_\$ < r_{\text{peso}}$, which in turn implies $z_\$^c > z_{\text{peso}}^c$, a contradiction. ■

Thus, if all other entrepreneurs borrow in dollars, the resulting monetary policy is such that dollar debt is safer. Note that since e_t and i_t are perfectly correlated in the range where dollar debt holders would default, there are no benefits from mixing the two debt denominations (unless the borrowers could short the peso instrument, which we do not allow in our analysis).

The problem presented is completely symmetric between e_t and i_t. As a result, if all liabilities were in short-term pesos the resulting monetary policy would be such that short-term peso instruments would be safer.[3] Therefore, if an atomistic agent expects all others to borrow through dollar (peso) debt, he or she will choose to borrow through dollar (peso) debt as well, and multiplicity of equilibria in the debt composition occurs.

Preference toward Exchange Rate or Interest Rate Adjustment

The previous section focused on the case where the elasticities of the exchange rate and the interest rate with respect to z_t were the same. But if parameters are such that the resulting optimal monetary policy exhibits a strong preference toward exchange rate or interest rate stability, the problem changes quite significantly. While for some range of parameters there is still multiplicity of equilibria, welfare is higher in the equilibrium where firms choose to borrow in the instrument whose return the central bank is trying to stabilize. Hence, if the central bank is more concerned with exchange rate stability, social welfare is higher if entrepreneurs borrow in dollars. Some ability to coordinate would allow them to choose the better equilibrium. This ability may be provided either by a few large borrowers or by the fiscal authority. If the government were to denominate its debt so as to minimize the risk of debt service to the fiscal accounts, it would choose dollar debts, and firms would just follow suit. Moreover, once a large enough asymmetry is introduced, there is a unique equilibrium for the debt composition.

Recall equation (8), which defines the elasticity ς of the exchange rate with respect to z_t according to the parameters that determine the effects of the exchange rate and of the interest rate in the output and inflation of that economy (in the region where the central bank ignores bankruptcy considerations). If ς is small, most of the shock will tend to be accommodated through changes in the interest rates. That elasticity is small when the expansionary effect of exchange rates on output is low (α is small), the exchange rate pass-through to inflation is high (γ is large), and interest rates have little impact on aggregate demand and inflation (β and δ are small). These assumptions seem particularly relevant to emerging markets. Because of that, we focus on the case where ς is small. But just as in the previous section, the actual realizations of e_t and i_t are influenced by the composition of debt liabilities.

Figure 8.2 illustrates the case where ς is small and liabilities are denominated in dollars. The range of z_t in which a default occurs is smaller than in the basic scenario of the previous section, because the central bank is now more willing to stabilize e_t at the expense of i_t. But if liabilities are denominated in pesos, the central bank's greater willingness to stabilize the exchange rate will conflict with its willingness to prevent bankruptcy. That case is illustrated in figure 8.3. For some range of z_t, the central bank will refrain from raising i_t beyond a certain threshold in order not to bankrupt the entrepreneurs, accommodating the rest of the shock through the exchange rate. In that range, i_t is held constant while e_t increases linearly in z_t. But just as in the analysis of the previous section, this deviation from the central bank's ideal rule for accommodating the shock becomes too costly for a large enough realization of z_t. Beyond that critical point, the central bank gives up trying to save the entrepreneurs and is again willing to stabilize the exchange rate at the expense of larger movements in the interest rate. Therefore the set of values of z_t for which a default under dollar debt occurs can be disjoint because e_t is not monotonic in z_t. For example, if an entrepreneur borrows in dollars, she may be bankrupt for a given realization z_A if that realization lies in the region where the central bank lets the exchange rate depreciate more in order to keep interest rates low. But she may be solvent for realizations $z_B > z_A$ if z_B is in the range where the central bank would have given up trying to save the peso borrowers *and* $e(z_B) > e(z_A)$. Whether the resulting distributions of e_t and i_t can sustain an equilibrium where the debt is denominated in pesos depends on parameter values. If the costs of default are low (or if they are high but the central bank does not internalize them much) or if the

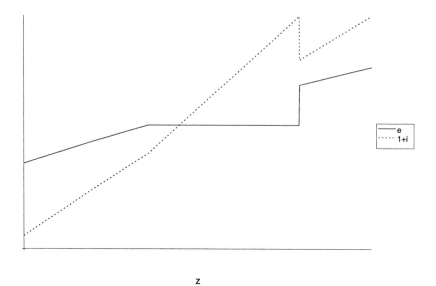

z

Figure 8.2 Exchange rate and interest rate if ç is small and liabilities are denominated in dollars

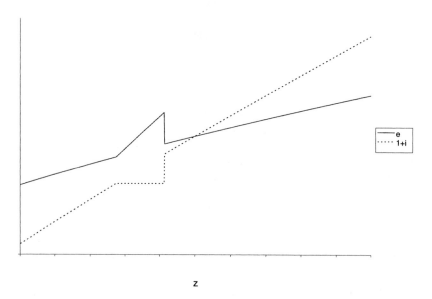

z

Figure 8.3 Exchange rate and interest rate if ç is small and liabilities are denominated in pesos

central bank is much more concerned about e_t than about i_t, then one would prefer to borrow in dollars even if everyone else were to borrow in pesos. As a result, there would only be a single equilibrium where all debt is denominated in dollars. But again, if parameters are such that multiplicity of equilibria still occur, welfare is higher in the equilibrium where the debt is denominated in the instrument whose movements the central bank would rather stabilize. It seems reasonable to assume that if large players are involved (such as the government), the economy will eventually manage to coordinate on the preferred of the two equilibria.

Discussion

The model presented in this chapter argues that the interplay between individual borrowers' choices for liability composition and the optimal monetary policy can lead to an outcome where liability dollarization is widespread. That result was obtained under a policymaker that is fairly benign toward foreign investors in the sense that it is not attempting to expropriate them to the benefit of domestic borrowers. Instead, all that policymaker is trying to do is to make dollar debt safer given that those contracts have already been written.

While the model presented predicts only corner solutions, a richer model with different types of shocks is likely to generate equilibria with internal solutions for the share of dollarized liabilities (with that share depending on how the monetary policy responds to different shocks). The preferences of the central bank toward exchange rate or interest rate adjustments can play a very significant role in terms of focusing the market on a type of borrowing and of monetary policy. In this sense, countries that exhibit original sin are countries where the central bank cares more about exchange rate movements than about interest rate movements. This is often the case in emerging markets, which can be explained by a number of reasons. In those countries, the exchange rate pass-through into prices tends to be higher than in developed ones, and the evidence for devaluations being expansionary is at best mixed. Moreover, a low level of financial development weakens the link between interest rates and aggregate demand, and as a result domestic interest rates have a lower impact on inflation and employment. All these elements will bias the choice toward more stable exchange rates at the expense of higher volatility in interest rates. Finally, emerging markets have more imperfect and incomplete financial markets, so the costs of bankruptcy are likely to be larger. As a result, that bias toward exchange rate stability is amplified, with the monetary authority being more willing to use interest rates aggressively in order to stabilize the exchange rate in the presence of dollarized liabilities. In fact, the volatility of interest rates tends to be much higher in emerging markets than in developed economies.[4]

Why do countries borrow the way they borrow? Why do some countries borrow in pesos while others borrow in dollars? This model suggests that the countries most likely to suffer from original sin would be countries where volatility and bankruptcy costs are high while the small size of the country's financial system and the high inflation pass-through increase the central bank's preference for exchange rate stability.

Finally, while the model has focused on the borrower's choice for liability denomination, some of the insights can shed light on the related problem of denomination of savings. If households are risk averse and their income is not correlated with the shock to the expected future exchange rate, then they would rather just save in whatever instrument makes the value of their savings more stable. For example, if the debt composition is such that the central bank stabilizes the exchange rate at the expense of the interest rate and the parameters are such that the resulting distribution of peso savings is riskier than that of dollar ones, the households would rather save in dollars. If, however, the realization of the shock to the expected future exchange rate is correlated with household income (e.g., if it reflects productivity shocks that affect the marginal product of labor and as a result the household's labor income), then matters become more complicated. On the one hand, households dislike uncertainty on the return to their savings. On the other hand, they want that return to covary negatively with their labor income. As a result, they will be willing to hold some peso-denominated instruments, since those instruments do better than dollar-denominated ones over some range of "bad" realizations of the shock.[5] The share of their savings held in peso instruments will depend on the distribution of returns and on how that shock to the expected future exchange rate covaries with their income. If countries fix and devalue in crises (which are associated with deep recessions), then holding dollars has zero consumption risk except when it has a high positive return in bad times. By contrast, if a country floats with a lot of volatility but no one-directional jumps, then the risk is high and the covariance may be less important.

Notes

The authors are grateful to Roberto Chang, Kevin Cowan, Federico Sturzenegger, and seminar participants at LACEA 2002 and the IADB Currency and Maturity Matchmaking Conference for helpful comments. Any errors are ours. This paper was written while Marcos Chamon was a graduate student at Harvard University. The views expressed in this paper are the authors' only and do not necessarily reflect the views or policies of the International Monetary Fund.

1. Since entrepreneurs are risk-neutral, an inefficiency must be introduced in the default states in order for their liability composition to matter. Instead of a nonpecuniary cost, we could have assumed that the output seized by a creditor is worth less than it would have been under the control of the entrepreneur. But that would introduce discontinuities on the creditor's payoff. Thus, the assumption of a nonpecuniary nature for the cost of default simplifies the problem.

2. Note that, since $\ell(e_t)$ is quadratic, $\ell^{(n)}(e_t) = 0$ for $n > 2$.

3. In theory there could be a third equilibrium where half the liabilities are denominated in dollars and half in pesos. The central bank would not be able to help both groups of creditors and would randomize which group to help. But that equilibrium is not robust to small perturbations, because if one agent were to switch from peso to dollar debt, every agent would prefer to borrow only through dollars and vice versa.

4. Hausmann (2003) estimates the volatility of changes in twelve-month real interest rates in a sample of Latin American countries in the period 1994–99. Using a sample that excludes observations when inflation exceeded 40 percent, the average volatility was 10.5 percent, while the corresponding figure for the United States was only 0.9 percent.

5. The central bank will give up trying to stabilize the exchange rate for very bad realizations of the shock, and dollar savings would provide higher returns than peso savings in those states. But for intermediate levels of a bad shock, the exchange rate is stabilized at the expense of an interest rate hike, and peso savings will have a larger return than dollar ones.

References

Aghion, P., P. Bacchetta, and A. Banerjee. 2001. "A Balance-Sheet Approach to Currency Crises." Working Paper no. 01.05, Studienzentrum Gerzensee, November.

Broda, C., and E. Levy Yeyati. 2003. "Endogenous Deposit Dollarization." Federal Reserve Bank of New York Staff Reports, no. 160.

Burnside, C., M. Eichenbaum, and S. Rebelo. 2001. "Prospective Deficits and the Asian Currency Crises." *Journal of Political Economy* 109:1155–97.

Caballero, R., and A. Krishnamurthy. 2003. "Excessive Dollar Debt: Financial Development and Underinsurance." *Journal of Finance* 58:867–94.

Calvo, G., and C. Reinhart. 2002. "Fear of Floating." *Quarterly Journal of Economics* 113 (3): 379–408.

Céspedes, L., R. Chang, and A. Velasco. 2000. "Balance Sheets and Exchange Rate Policy." NBER Working Paper no. 7840, National Bureau of Economic Research, Cambridge, MA.

Chamon, M. 2001. "Why Can't Developing Countries Borrow from Abroad in Their Currency?" Manuscript, Harvard University.

Dooley, M. 2000. "A Model of Crises in Emerging Markets." *Economic Journal* 110 (460): 256–72.

Eichengreen, B., and R. Hausmann. 1999. "Exchange Rates and Financial Fragility." NBER Working Paper no. 7418, National Bureau of Economic Research, Cambridge, MA.

Fernández-Arias, E., and R. Hausmann. 2000. "What's Wrong with International Financial Markets?" IADB Working Paper no. 429, Inter-American Development Bank, Washington, DC, August.

Hausmann, R. 2004. "Good Credit Ratios, Bad Credit Ratings: The Role of Debt Denomination." In *Rules-Based Fiscal Policy in Emerging Markets: Background, Analysis, and Prospects*, ed. G. Kopits and G. Perry. Macmillan.

Hausmann, R., U. Panizza, and E. Stein. 2001. "Why Do Countries Float the Way They Float?" *Journal of Development Economics* 66:387–414.

Jeanne, O. 2000. "Foreign Currency Debt and the Global Financial Architecture." *European Economic Review* 44:719–27.

———. 2003. "Why Do Emerging Markets Borrow in Foreign Currency?" IMF Working Paper no. 03/177, Washington, DC.

Kamin, S. 2002. "Identifying the Role of Moral Hazard in International Financial Markets." International Finance Discussion Papers no. 736. Federal Reserve Board, Washington, DC, September.

Ortiz, G. 2002. "Recent Emerging Market Crises: What Have We Learned?" Per Jacobson Lecture, International Monetary Fund, Washington, DC, July.

Schneider, M., and A. Tornell. 2004. "Balance Seet Effects, Bailout Guarantees, and Financial Crises." *Review of Economic Studies.* Forthcoming.

Tirole, J. 2003. "Inefficient Foreign Borrowing: A Dual-and Common-Agency Perspective." *American Economic Review* 93 (5): 1678–1702.

The Mystery of Original Sin

Barry Eichengreen, Ricardo Hausmann,
and Ugo Panizza

PREVIOUS CHAPTERS have shown that inability to borrow abroad in the domestic currency ("original sin") is an important factor in the macroeconomic and financial instability of emerging markets. Indeed, it can be argued that this source of financial fragility is a defining characteristic that differentiates emerging markets from their advanced-economy counterparts. Closing the capital account (which forgoes the benefits of foreign finance), accumulating massive amounts of international reserves (the yield on which is generally substantially below the opportunity cost of funds), and/or increasing the country's reliance on short-term domestic debt at volatile interest rates (creating maturity mismatches) are three possible ways of preventing original sin from resulting in dangerous currency mismatches, but each of these solutions has significant costs. Helping emerging markets to acquire the capacity to borrow abroad in their own currencies should thus be a priority for officials striving to make the world a safer financial place and at the same time seeking to quicken the pace, sustainability, and resilience of growth.

Defining and implementing appropriate solutions requires first that we identify the distortion that gives rise to the problem. The economist's instinctual reaction is that the inability to borrow abroad in one's own currency reflects the weakness of policies and institutions. The bulk of the literature has thus focused on the shortcomings of borrowing countries, in particular on the underdevelopment of their market-supporting and policymaking institutions. A number of other chapters in this book focus on these usual suspects—on the instability and imperfect credibility of monetary and fiscal policies, for example.

Yet evidence for the presumption that the incidence of original sin reflects the instability of policies and the weakness of market-supporting institutions is based more on presumption and anecdote than on fact. To our knowledge there exists no systematic empirical study for a cross section of countries attempting to test the empirical power of different explanations for original sin.

We seek to provide that analysis here, using the indicators of original sin defined and developed in chapter 1. We present evidence on the explanatory power of a series of alternative explanations. Our surprising finding is that the conventional hypotheses have remarkably little explanatory power for the phenomenon at hand. In other words, the standard policy and institutional variables shed remarkably little light on why so many emerging markets find it so difficult to borrow abroad in their own currencies, and they offer little in the way of an explanation for why a small number of emerging markets have been able to escape this plight.[1]

These results prompted us to explore the possibility that the problem of original sin has at least as much to do with the structure and operation of the international financial system as with the weakness of policies and institutions. As we show, country size is a robust factor accounting for the incidence of original sin, suggesting that economies of scale or network externalities may be at work in explaining the structure of international finance. Moreover, emerging markets that have achieved redemption from original sin have overcome the obstacles posed by the structure of the international system only with the help of foreign entities—multinational corporations and international financial institutions—that have found it attractive, for their own reasons, to issue debt in the currencies of these countries. This observation leads us in the next chapter to offer a proposal for an international solution to the problem.

Original Sin and the Level of Economic Development

In table 9.1 we explore the relationship between original sin and the level of economic development as measured by the log of per capita GDP. We control for country size and for the groupings across which the incidence of the phenomenon clearly differs.[2] Three relevant dimensions of size are the log of total GDP, the log of total domestic credit (valued in U.S. dollars), and the log of total trade. Table 9.1 uses the first principal component of the three measures, which we denote SIZE. All equations are estimated using weighted Tobit.

A first striking finding is that the coefficient on per capita GDP is not significant at conventional confidence levels. We ran several sensitivity checks to establish the robustness of this result. For example, we dropped the financial centers, which left the result unaffected (table 9.1, column [2]). We could only get a significant effect by dropping the entire vector of country group dummies (column [3]), but this effect is not robust to changing the estimation technique to ordinary least squares. Moreover, even this result is of limited significance in that it suggests that GDP per capita cannot explain the within-group difference in original sin.

In contrast to GDP per capita, the other variable included in these equations, country size, is strongly correlated with original sin even when we control for country groups. In other words, the ability to borrow abroad in one's own currency seems to be heavily concentrated among large countries. (We have more to say about this below.)

Table 9.1. Original sin and economic development

	OSIN3 (1)	OSIN3 (2)	OSIN3 (3)
LGDP_PC	−0.141	−0.128	−0.170
	(1.59)	(1.43)	(2.99)***
SIZE	−0.310	−0.310	−0.415
	(3.37)***	(3.33)***	(4.51)***
FIN_CENTER	−0.680		
	(1.99)*		
EUROLAND	−0.126	−0.152	
	(0.62)	(0.74)	
OTH_DEVELOPED	0.007	−0.021	
	(0.03)	(0.10)	
Constant	2.522	2.414	2.833
	(3.39)***	(3.24)***	(5.46)***
Observations	75	71	75

Notes: OSIN3 equals one minus the ratio of total international debt in a country's currency to total international debt issued by that country. Whenever the variable would take on a negative value, it is set to zero. t statistics in parentheses (Tobit estimates).
*Significant at 10%. ***Significant at 1%.

The fact that original sin is not strongly correlated with economic development has disturbing implications. If original sin is not robustly correlated with the level of development, at least within the class of developing countries, then country characteristics that are correlated with the level of development are also unlikely to explain the variance in original sin. Still, in order to give these country characteristics their due, we examine a number of them in turn.

Monetary Credibility

An obvious hypothesis is that original sin is a symptom of inadequate policy credibility, which tends to be a problem in developing countries. This is the approach taken by Olivier Jeanne in chapter 7, where he finds that if the central bank is expected with low probability to engineer a high burst of inflation and depreciation, interest rates in pesos will be high. Borrowers will prefer to denominate their obligations in dollars and go bankrupt in the event of the inflationary crisis, rather than borrowing in pesos and going bankrupt because of high interest rates, if the crisis is avoided. Moreover, as argued by Tirole (2002), foreigners will take account of the fact that the government has less of an incentive to protect their property rights and may choose to inflate away their claims if they denominate them in a unit that they can manipulate. They will lend only in foreign currency, which is protected against inflation risk, or at short maturities, so that interest rates can be adjusted quickly to any acceleration of inflation.

In this view, original sin is not a problem in itself; it is merely a symptom of deeper dysfunctions. It is a miner's canary, signaling the presence of weak policies and institutions. Redemption can therefore be achieved by pursuing institutional changes that strengthen the authorities' anti-inflationary credibility. Specifically, the political and economic independence of the central bank should be reinforced. Budgetary policy should be centralized and made more transparent and accountable, rendering inflationary finance superfluous. Political support for policies of price stability should be cultivated. The country should accumulate a track record and develop a reputation for maintaining price stability. In this view, the standard advice given by the International Monetary Fund and World Bank regarding macroeconomic policies and institutional reforms is both necessary and sufficient for redemption from original sin.

But if inadequate anti-inflationary credibility is the cause of original sin, then it should be possible to achieve redemption simply by issuing inflation-indexed debt (Chamon 2001).[3] Yet we do not see very many countries able to issue internationally inflation-indexed debt in their own currencies. In addition, while only governments have the capacity to inflate away debts denominated in their own currency, corporations in many emerging markets also find themselves unable to borrow abroad in that currency, despite the fact that this moral hazard, to the extent that it even exists, is indirect.[4]

We explore the cross-country correlation between original sin and monetary credibility in table 9.2. As a metric of monetary credibility, we take different measures of inflation for the 1980–98 period. We regress these measures on OSIN3, once again using Tobit, after controlling for country groupings and size. In column (1) we use the average value of the log of inflation and find a positive but statistically insignificant relationship. In column (2), we substitute for average inflation the log of maximum inflation over the period and again find no significant relationship with original sin. To test potential nonlinearities in the relationship between inflation and original sin, in column (3) we use both the average log of inflation and its square. In this case, none of the coefficients on inflation are significant. Column (4) uses the principal component of average inflation and maximum inflation and again finds no significant correlation with original sin. The results are also the same when we drop financial centers (column [5]). Only if we drop the country group dummies does inflation become statistically significant (column [6]). But this relationship seems to be driven by a few high-inflation countries (fig. 9.1). Thus, while inadequate anti-inflationary credibility may help explain the inability of a few chronic high-inflation sufferers to borrow abroad in their own currency, it cannot explain the extremely widespread nature of the phenomenon.

It could be argued that the estimated coefficient on inflation is attenuated by endogeneity. If the debt is in dollars, then the benefits from inflation are low. This would imply that original sin causes low inflation, in which case reverse causation lowers the value of the estimated coefficient. To deal with this problem we

Table 9.2. Original sin and monetary credibility

	OSIN3 (1)	OSIN3 (2)	OSIN3 (3)	Dropping financial centers			OLS same sample as (8)	Instrumental variables
				OSIN3 (4)	OSIN3 (5)	OSIN3 (6)	OSIN3 (7)	OSIN3 (8)
AV_INF	0.306 (1.19)		0.436 (0.69)					
AV_INF2			−0.116 (0.23)					
MAX_INF		0.067 (0.95)						
INF				0.085 (1.09)	0.083 (1.07)	0.175 (2.08)**	0.022 (0.35)	0.314 (1.13)
SIZE	−0.318 (3.57)***	−0.318 (3.54)***	−0.316 (3.52)***	−0.318 (3.55)***	−0.318 (3.50)***	−0.503 (5.75)***	−0.323 (4.27)***	−0.319 (4.30)***
FIN_CENTER	−0.866 (2.88)***	−0.897 (2.99)***	−0.857 (2.83)***	−0.881 (2.93)***			−0.603 (2.77)***	−0.550 (2.52)***
EUROLAND	−0.304 (2.12)**	−0.329 (2.31)**	−0.296 (1.99)*	−0.315 (2.21)**	−0.318 (2.21)**		−0.360 (2.80)***	−0.312 (2.39)**
OTH_DEVELOPED	−0.199 (1.47)	−0.224 (1.67)*	−0.192 (1.37)	−0.211 (1.56)	−0.213 (1.57)		−0.207 (2.15)**	−0.155 (1.52)
Constant	1.277 (10.87)***	1.310 (11.60)***	1.259 (8.83)***	1.346 (13.56)***	1.347 (13.46)***	1.358 (13.41)***	1.321 (14.07)***	1.233 (10.29)***
Observations	74	74	74	74	70	74	33	33

Notes: t statistics in parentheses (Tobit estimates). The instrument for column (8) is Cukierman's index of Central Bank Independence.

*Significant at 10%. **Significant at 5%. ***Significant at 1%.

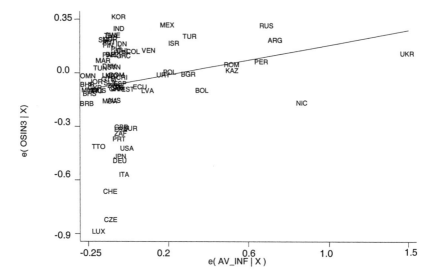

Figure 9.1   Original sin and inflation

run an instrumental variable regression, using as our instrument the Cukierman (1995) index of central bank independence. Equation (7) runs the same equation as (1) but for the sample for which we have the Cukierman index. Equation (8) runs the instrumental variables regression on this sample (we use Tobit in the second stage). The estimated coefficient is now higher but still not significantly different from zero. While this suggests that endogeneity could be contributing to the weak relationship, even the instrumental variables estimates do not provide any strong evidence for the fact that original sin is significantly correlated with past inflation.[5]

Fiscal Solvency and Original Sin

Other theories attribute the inability to borrow abroad in one's own currency to the chronic weakness of fiscal policy. A government that has weak fiscal accounts, this argument runs, will have an incentive to debase the currency in order to erode the real value of its obligations (Lucas and Stokey 1983; Calvo and Guidotti 1990). The solution is to index the debt to some real price or to issue short-term debt so as to increase the cost of eroding the debt with inflation.

We explore the relationship between original sin and alternative fiscal variables in table 9.3. Equations (1), (2), and (3) consider the debt-to-GDP ratio, the average deficit, and the debt-to-revenue ratio, while equation (4) uses the principal component of these three measures. While in a few cases we observe a negative relationship between measures of original sin and fiscal fundamentals,

Table 9.3. Original sin and fiscal sustainability

	OSIN3 (1)	OSIN3 (2)	OSIN3 (3)	OSIN3 (4)	Instrumental variables estimates	
					OSIN3 (5)	OSIN3 (6)
DE_GDP2	−0.073 (0.50)					
DEFICIT		1.777 (0.92)				
DE_RE2			0.014 (0.24)			
FISC				−0.025 (0.30)	−0.024 (0.28)	−0.061 (0.22)
SIZE	−0.350 (3.71)***	−0.327 (3.52)***	−0.354 (3.51)***	−0.342 (3.42)***	−0.345 (3.40)***	−0.124 (2.17)**
FIN_CENTER	−0.825 (2.72)***	−0.926 (3.09)***	−0.816 (2.57)**	−0.839 (2.66)**		−0.736 (4.12)***
EUROLAND	−0.344 (2.61)**	−0.361 (2.66)***	−0.327 (2.22)**	−0.348 (2.48)**	−0.348 (2.46)**	−0.149 (1.21)
OTH_DEVELOPED	−0.275 (2.18)**	−0.215 (1.54)	−0.245 (1.73)*	−0.272 (2.01)**	−0.272 (1.99)*	−0.117 (0.67)
Constant	1.426 (11.99)***	1.311 (11.46)***	1.370 (10.06)***	1.382 (12.04)***	1.385 (11.93)***	0.996 (34.99)***
Observations	64	74	57	57	54	54

Notes: t statistics in parentheses (Tobit estimates). The instrument for column (6) is OLD.

*Significant at 10%. **Significant at 5%. ***Significant at 1%.

that relationship is never even close to being statistically significant at conventional confidence levels. In some cases not even the negative correlation obtains; note, for example, that countries with *more* original sin have less public indebtedness.

Again, there may be reason to worry about reverse causality. As documented in chapter 2, original sin lowers credit ratings—for any given level of debt—by making debt service more uncertain. This limits the ability to place debt securities and may cause an attenuation bias in our estimates. Hence, we may be finding a negative result that is in fact expressing the impact of original sin on the ability of governments to accumulate debt, not the impact of public indebtedness on original sin.

To address this possible source of reverse causality, we again employ an instrumental variable approach, where we use the proportion of the population over age sixty-five as an instrument for the fiscal fundamental. The results are presented in equation (6). Again, the key findings are unaffected.

Thus, we find little traction for fiscal interpretations of the causes of original sin. Within the class of emerging markets, there is little association of original sin with obvious fiscal fundamentals such as the level or persistence of public debts and deficits. Indeed, one can point to any number of emerging markets that have successfully maintained low inflation, avoided large budget deficits, and followed international guidelines for the efficient design of their monetary and fiscal institutions—Chile is a case in point for Latin America, while Korea is a good example for Asia—but are nonetheless chronically unable to borrow abroad in their own currencies.

The Strength of Institutions

It is sometimes argued that investors are reluctant to lend to governments and corporations where the institutions designed to enforce their claims are weak or unreliable and there is significant risk of debt repudiation. Chamon (2001) and Aghion, Bacchetta, and Banerjee (2001) develop models in which, when a company defaults, its assets are distributed among the creditors in proportion to their nominal claims on it. If depreciation and default risk are correlated, then domestic-currency lenders will likely see a double decline in the value of their claims when a default occurs: they will receive a portion of the residual value of the company which will be diminished by the concomitant depreciation. If all lending takes place simultaneously, domestic-currency lenders will charge for this effect. If lending takes place sequentially, however, firms will have an incentive to increase the proportion of foreign-currency lending in order to transfer part of the residual value of the defaulted company from old domestic-currency lenders to new foreign-currency investors. In anticipation of this, the domestic-currency market will disappear. This mechanism can be overcome if bankruptcy courts can enforce complicated contracts that, for example, distinguish between creditors of different seniority. But if these contracts are infeasible, then domestic-currency lending may be affected.

To analyze the importance of institutions, we study the relationship between original sin and a measure of rule of law (RULEOFLAW), drawn from Kaufmann et al. (1999) that should proxy for the quality of contract enforcement. Table 9.4 shows that the relationship between institutional quality and original sin is neither statistically nor economically significant. These negative findings are not entirely surprising, given the fact that these indexes of institutional quality are strongly correlated with the level of development found in table 9.1 to have only a weak relationship with original sin.

This result is clearly controversial, given the presumption in much of the recent literature of the importance of institutions for economic and financial development (see, e.g., Rodrik 2001; La Porta et al. 1997). Again, we therefore subjected the finding to a variety of sensitivity tests. For example, using instead the La Porta et al. (1997) index of creditor rights yields similar results, although the sample size is more limited in this case. To address the possibility of endogeneity bias, we used Acemoglu, Johnson, and Robinson's data (2001) on settler mortality as an instrument for the Kaufmann et al. measure of institutions; this did nothing to alter the result (column [4]).[6] Alternatively, building on the literature linking geography and climate to economic development, we used latitude as an instrument (column [6]); again, there was no evidence of a connection between institutions and original sin at anything approaching conventional confidence levels.[7]

The one change that made a difference was when we dropped the vector of dummy variables for country groups (financial centers, Euroland countries, other advanced economies).[8] In this case, institutions appear to matter both when settler mortality is used as an instrument and when no instrumental variables are used (columns [7] and [8]).[9] This is not surprising, since the advanced-industrial countries have both stronger institutions and a greater capacity to borrow abroad in their own currencies than their emerging-market counterparts. But within these groups (which is what we are analyzing when we include the dummies for groups of countries), variations in the strength of institutions have no discernible impact on the extent and incidence of original sin. Compared to Colombia, Canada has both stronger institutions on the Kaufmann et al. measure and a greater capacity to issue debt in its own currency to foreigners. But this does not mean that Colombia, by strengthening its institutions, can acquire the capacity to place local-currency debt with foreigners anytime soon or that, by building stronger institutions than some of its other Latin American counterparts, it will be able to sell foreign investors more local-currency debt.

Table 9.4. Original sin and institutions

	OSIN3 (1)	OSIN3 (2)	OSIN3 (3)	Instrumental variables		Instrumental variables	Instrumental variables	
				OSIN3 (4)	OSIN3 (5)	OSIN3 (6)	OSIN3 (7)	OSIN3 (8)
RULEOFLAW	-0.050	-0.053	-0.002	-0.249	-0.050	1.58	-0.182	-0.332
	(0.46)	(0.49)	(0.06)	(0.86)	(0.46)	(0.50)	(2.33)**	(2.40)**
SIZE	-0.323	-0.322	-0.040	-0.223	-0.323	-0.318	-0.480	-0.241
	(3.53)***	(3.48)***	(091)	(1.46)	(3.53)***	(3.54)***	(5.32)***	(1.50)
FIN_CENTER	-0.883				-0.883	-1.179		
	(2.65)**				(2.65)**	(2.16)**		
EUROLAND	-0.326	-0.325			-0.326	-0.553		
	(1.81)*	(1.79)*			(1.80)*	(1.50)		
OTH_DEVELOPED	-0.203	-0.201			-0.203	-0.501		
	(1.03)	(1.01)			(1.03)	(1.05)		
DEVELOPING			0.450	0.034				
			(4.00)***	(0.07)				
Constant	1.388	1.390	0.518	1.224	1.388	1.260	1.486	1.349
	(13.2)***	(13.1)***	(4.59)***	(2.29)**	(13.2)***	(8.00)***	(12.3)***	(8.14)***
Observations	75	71	29	29	75	75	75	29

Notes: t statistics in parentheses (Tobit estimates). In columns (4) and (8) the instrument is settler mortality. In column (6) the instrument is latitude.
*Significant at 10%. **Significant at 5%. ***Significant at 1%.

Trade Links

It can be objected that what matter are not institutions, which can always be changed at some cost, but the fundamental incentives for respecting one's contractual obligations. In terms of respecting the claims of foreigners, it can be argued that countries that trade heavily with their creditors have an incentive to meet their contractual obligations because failing to do so will provoke commercial retaliation or at minimum interrupt the supply of trade credits. This was the insight of the early Eaton and Gersovitz (1981) model of sovereign lending in the presence of potential repudiation, where lending could be supported only in the presence of potential trade sanctions with output costs. Exponents of this view point to Argentina in the 1930s, which was one of the few Latin American countries to stay current on its debts, something that is commonly explained by its exceptional dependence on the British export market and the threat of tariff retaliation (Diaz-Alejandro 1984). More recently, Rose (2002) has shown that borrowing countries that default on their debts in practice suffer a significant reduction in trade with their creditors. Rose and Spiegel (2002) show further that borrowers with economically consequential trade links to their creditors are significantly more likely to service their debts.

This story linking the threat of trade sanctions to the credibility of financial policies is appealing to the extent that it suggests that current account liberalization provides an automatic solution to the problems posed by capital account opening. However, table 9.5 finds no correlation between the incidence of original sin and the standard measure of trade openness (exports as a share of GDP). The result is unchanged if we drop financial centers and is robust to additional sensitivity tests.[10]

Table 9.5. Original sin and trade openness

	OSIN3 (1)	OSIN3 (2)
OPEN	−0.174	−0.183
	(1.28)	(1.36)
SIZE	−0.359	−0.360
	(3.74)***	(3.73)***
FIN_CENTER	−0.937	
	(3.23)***	
EUROLAND	−0.360	−0.360
	(2.71)***	(2.71)***
OTH_DEVELOPED	−0.269	−0.270
	(2.15)**	(2.15)**
Constant	1.515	1.523
	(9.60)***	(9.64)***
Observations	75	71

Note: t statistics in parentheses (Tobit estimates).
**Significant at 5%. ***Significant at 1%.

On reflection, this result is not entirely surprising. Trade may explain the absence of opportunistic defaults and the existence of debt markets, but it is hard to see why it should affect the denomination of those debts, per se. Trade sanctions can be imposed whether debt is denominated in the domestic currency or foreign currency. And if the presence or absence of the potential for such sanctions is what determines ability to borrow, then we should also see punishments meted out to countries that denominate their debt in their own currencies but then depreciate the exchange rate, thereby eroding the value of creditors' claims. But, in practice, we do not observe countries that issue in their own currency being punished when the exchange rate weakens. In the last thirty years, we have seen large trend or cyclical depreciations in many of the countries that suffer least from original sin: Australia, Canada, New Zealand, the United Kingdom, and South Africa, to name five. In practice, these depreciations have not triggered either trade or credit sanctions.

Political Economy Explanations

It can be argued that what is required to induce governments to respect the value of the local currency (and of financial liabilities denominated therein) is a domestic constituency of local-currency debt holders prepared to penalize a government that debases the currency. If the median voter holds sovereign bonds, a government will suffer political sanctions if it defaults opportunistically or inflates away the value of the principal. By contrast, if foreigners are the main holders of public and private debts (the argument continues), then there is likely to be a larger domestic political constituency in favor of weakening the value of their claims. Foreign creditors, no fools they, will be reluctant to lend in local currency unless protected by a large constituency of local savers. This is the logic behind Tirole (2002): lending in the currency of the borrower is deterred by a form of sovereign risk arising from the fact that the government cannot commit to protect the rights of foreigners whose welfare it does not value. Redemption can therefore be achieved by developing domestic financial markets.

Our crude measure of these influences is the size of the domestic financial system, proxied alternatively by domestic credit normalized by GDP (DC_GDP), the ratio between foreign liabilities (measured as the sum of bank claims and securities from the two Bank for International Settlements databases described above) and domestic credit (FOR_DOM), and an index built using the principal component of the previous two variables (SIZE_FIN). The theory predicts that original sin should exhibit a negative correlation with DC_GDP, a positive correlation with FOR_DOM, and a negative correlation with SIZE_FIN.[11]

Table 9.6 shows that the relationship between size of the financial system and

Table 9.6. Original sin and size of the financial system

	OSIN3 (1)	OSIN3 (2)	OSIN3 (3)	OSIN3 (4)	OSIN3 (5)	OSIN3 (6)	OSIN3 (7)
DC_GDP	-0.332				-0.311		
	(1.49)				(1.53)		
FOR_DOM		-7.289				7.224	
		(2.15)**				(0.86)	
SIZE_FIN			0.261	0.354			-0.918
			(0.53)	(0.70)			(1.62)
SIZE	-0.290	-0.360	-0.326	-0.332	-0.320	-0.323	-0.306
	(3.22)***	(4.02)***	(3.43)***	(3.42)***	(3.82)***	(3.72)***	(3.61)***
FIN_CENTER	-0.753	-0.843	-0.997		-0.663	-0.895	-0.698
	(2.40)**	(3.02)***	(3.25)***		(2.33)**	(3.23)***	(2.52)**
EUROLAND	-0.226	-0.301	-0.410	-0.421	-0.142	-0.299	-0.156
	(1.37)	(2.34)**	(2.86)***	(2.92)***	(0.94)	(2.42)**	(1.09)
OTH_DEVELOPED	-0.224	-0.223	-0.278	-0.280	-0.187	-0.254	-0.200
	(1.75)*	(1.86)*	(2.18)**	(2.19)**	(1.62)	(2.16)**	(1.76)*
Constant	1.521	1.431	1.377	1.383	1.501	1.291	1.312
	(10.13)***	(13.76)***	(13.44)***	(13.33)***	(10.94)***	(11.15)***	(14.44)***
Observations	74	73	72	68	73	72	71

Note: t statistics in parentheses (Tobit estimates).

*Significant at 10%. **Significant at 5%. ***Significant at 1%.

original sin is not statistically significant in the case of DC_GDP and that it is statistically significant but *with the wrong sign* in the case of FOR_DOM. This is in part due to the fact that Luxembourg is an outlier in this sample. If we drop it (equation [6]), the coefficient of FOR_DOM becomes positive but not statistically significant.

Even if there existed a relationship between original sin and the domestic financial system, there would still be the question of what governments can do to promote the development of a large constituency of domestic bondholders.[12] Conceivably, they could create a constituency of investors in long-term domestic-currency-denominated debt at one fell swoop by using force majeure to change the currency denomination of existing claims or eliminating from existing contracts provisions indexing principal and interest to the exchange rate. Something along these lines occurred in the United States in 1933, it is argued, when Franklin Delano Roosevelt disregarded the gold clauses in U.S. government and corporate bonds in 1933 on devaluing the dollar, and his decision was upheld by the Supreme Court. Doing so did not demoralize the bond markets because the economy's improved growth prospects (with their positive implications for the debt-servicing capacity of borrowers) more than outweighed the effects of the dilution of investor rights (Kroszner 1999).

Whether a similar forced conversion would in fact reassure investors in emerging markets today is another question.[13] The problem with this argument is that it implies the traditional trade-off between the positive effects associated with a more sustainable debt achieved through force majeure and the negative reputational effects related to tampering with the sanctity of contracts. Investors may react negatively if the second effect dominates and become even more reluctant to absorb new debt issues on the margin. The policy would then be counterproductive from the point of view of "redemption," that is, of being able to have sustained market access in local currency going forward.[14]

Another approach, less likely to alarm investors but also less capable of delivering immediate results, would be to require banks, pension funds, and the social security system to hold long-term, domestic-currency-denominated, fixed-rate debt. The government could require the banks to hold domestic-currency-denominated bonds as reserves. It could privatize the social security system and require pension funds to hold a specified share of the retirement portfolios in such bonds. But to the extent that the government has the strength to promulgate such regulations—in effect, to twist the arms of these individuals and institutions—the individuals and institutions in question will presumably lack the leverage to throw a government engaging in opportunistic debt management policies out of office. Hence other investors may lack assurance that there exists an effective class of domestic stakeholders to constrain opportunistic policy.

Not everyone will be convinced by this critique; they will argue that emerging markets should emulate the policies of financial repression used by Western European governments after World War II (see, e.g., Wyplosz 2001). There, strict capital controls and tight restrictions on the currency composition of newly issued debt securities succeeded in forcing residents to hold long-term domestic-currency-denominated bonds by offering them few alternative funding or investment opportunities, accelerating the creation of a domestic investor constituency. But even in postwar Europe, a quarter of a century and more was required before those controls could be removed and foreign investors could be enticed into absorbing significant volumes of domestic issues. Financial repression is no quick fix, in other words. And, again, this approach—encouraging the development of some markets by suppressing the operation of others—may be regarded by investors as disturbingly contradictory and inconsistent.

Evidence from emerging markets suggests that these considerations may in fact be at work and that capital controls may help the development of long-term fixed-rate domestic markets in local currency but prevent the international acceptance of local-currency debt obligations. Recall from chapter 2 that we were able to identify virtually no country that can borrow abroad in local currency but that has no long-term fixed-rate domestic markets, suggesting that domestic-market development is a necessary condition for redemption from original sin. However, that analysis also suggested that it is not a sufficient condition: we found a number of countries that suffer from international original sin while having "achieved redemption" on the domestic front. Hausmann and Panizza (2003) explore different potential explanations to distinguish between these three groups of countries. Their most striking result relates to the role of capital controls. The seven countries that have been able to develop their domestic market but still lack the capacity to borrow abroad in their own currency have levels of capital control that are much higher than the countries in the two other quadrants (the difference is always statistically significant at the 10 percent confidence level). This evidence is suggestive of the idea that capital controls facilitate the development of domestic markets, explaining why capital controls are higher in the countries located in the fourth quadrant vis-à-vis the countries located in the second quadrant. While in place, however, they hinder the capacity to use that currency in international borrowing, explaining thus the difference between the countries in the third quadrant and the countries in the fourth quadrant.

This pattern is clearly reminiscent of the European experience mentioned above. It is also suggestive of the importance given by Bordo, Meissner, and Redish in chapter 5 to the world wars in their impact on the development of domestic markets in the British Dominions.

As a policy prescription, this approach is likely to be especially problematic in low-income countries where there is only a limited pool of domestic savings and domestic market liquidity is limited. Limiting foreign participation could be particularly onerous. Moreover, the smaller the market, the less likely are foreign investors to willingly hold debt securities denominated in the currency in question. (In fact, precisely the same logic applies to residents.) This observation is key: it points to where to look for the causes—and the solution—to original sin.

Putting Things Together

To this point we have tested various theories of original sin one by one and found a strong correlation only between original sin and country size, along with a somewhat weaker correlation between original sin and past inflation and original sin and the level of development. We now jointly test the different theories simultaneously, running a set of multivariate regressions that include the entire vector of explanatory variables.

Table 9.7 reports a set of regressions both with and without controls for country groups and financial centers. The results are basically unchanged: once again the only robust determinant of original sin is country size. In one regres-

Table 9.7. The determinants of original sin

	OSIN3 (1)	OSIN3 (2)	OSIN3 (3)
LGDP_PC	−0.286	−0.333	−0.314
	(1.96)*	(2.70)***	(2.09)**
FISC	0.082	−0.078	−0.098
	(0.70)	(0.76)	(0.96)
SIZE	−0.342	−0.404	−0.347
	(2.79)***	(3.82)***	(3.37)***
SIZE_FIN	0.084	0.338	0.650
	(0.20)	(0.61)	(1.07)
RULEOFLAW	0.312	0.268	0.245
	(1.69)*	(1.55)	(1.43)
INF	0.112	0.109	0.129
	(1.10)	(1.08)	(1.11)
OPEN	−0.093	−0.131	−0.102
	(0.52)	(0.62)	(0.43)
FIN_CENTER	−0.683		
	(1.85)*		
EUROLAND	−0.143		−0.034
	(0.56)		(0.14)
OTH_DEVELOPED	0.009		0.035
	(0.03)		(0.13)
Constant	3.674	4.170	3.941
	(3.15)***	(4.06)***	(3.31)***
Observations	56	56	53

Note: t statistics in parentheses (Tobit estimates).
*Significant at 10%. **Significant at 5%. ***Significant at 1%.

sion, the Kaufmann et al. measure of institutions (RULEOFLAW) is marginally significant at the 10 percent level, but this result is not robust to dropping the dummy variables for financial centers and other country groups. In some specifications, the level of development also appears statistically significant, but this result is not robust to changes in measures of original sin or estimation techniques. As shown in the appendix, GDP per capita is not significantly correlated with OSIN1 and OSIN2. Moreover, the correlation between GDP per capita and OSIN3 is not robust to using weighted ordinary least squares with robust t statistics instead of weighted Tobit. Of the variables considered, only country size appears to be truly robust.

International Causes

What accounts for the concentration of the world's portfolio in few currencies and for the fact that it is mainly large countries that seem to be able to issue foreign debt in their own currencies? Obviously, each additional currency adds opportunities for diversification, but with decreasing marginal benefits. At the same time, however, each currency also adds costs and risks. In a world with transaction costs, the optimal portfolio will have a finite number of currencies. The fact that few currencies survive is indicative that with each additional currency, the benefits of diversification fall faster than the costs.[15]

Imagine the following situation. There are two countries: one has N trees while the other has one tree. All trees are identical in their expected income and its variance; the large country just has more of them. Shocks to each tree are uncorrelated. Assume that the exchange rate moves with the realization of relative output. If there were no transaction costs of investing abroad, then it would be optimal to hold a globally diversified portfolio: the large country would invest $1/(N + 1)$ of its wealth in the small country, while the latter would invest $N/(N + 1)$ in the large country. Now introduce costs to international transactions. If all countries were of size 1, then the presence of transaction costs would not affect the composition of the world portfolio. But if country size differs, then the benefits of international diversification will be greater for the small country than for the large one. There will be less appetite in the large country to hold the currency of the small country, while there will still be a large appetite for the small country to hold the assets of the large one. This is to say, large countries offer significant diversification possibilities, while small countries do not. If the transaction costs associated with international diversification are the same for investors in both countries, then the world will choose to invest in a few large currencies. Notice that this is through no fault of the small country, but a consequence of the existence of cross-border costs and asymmetries in size and diversification.

An implication of this view is that even if we identify characteristics that have allowed a few small countries to issue debt in their own currencies—such as

South Africa, New Zealand, and Poland—it would be a fallacy of composition to assume that, if other small countries acquired those same characteristics, they would all make it into the world portfolio. Each successful country may limit the chances of the others, given the declining marginal benefits of diversification.

A further implication of this approach is that country size matters for original sin. Large countries have an advantage in shedding original sin because the large size of their economies and currency issue makes their currency attractive as a component of the world portfolio. In contrast, the currencies of small countries add few diversification benefits relative to the additional costs they imply.

We explore this hypothesis further in table 9.8. There we use three entirely different measures of size: the log of total GDP, the log of total domestic credit (valued in U.S. dollars), and the log of total trade, in addition to again constructing the first principal component (SIZE, as in previous tables). We also control for country groupings. Equation (1) presents the regression with just the country groups dummy. In equations (2) to (4), we use alternatively our three different measures of size. Equation (5) uses the principal component of the three measures, as in the previous tables. In equations (6) and (7), we test for robustness with respect to dropping the financial centers and not controlling for country groupings.

The results show that all measures of size are robustly related to original sin. The relationship between original sin and size is also economically important: the effects of SIZE in table 9.7 account for more than half of the difference in original sin between developed and developing countries.[16]

SIZE can explain why large countries like the United States and Japan do not suffer from original sin. But what about Switzerland and, for that matter, the United Kingdom? Note that the financial-center dummy in the equations in table 9.8 remains large and significant even after controlling for country size. This is another way of saying that the United Kingdom and Switzerland are immune from the problem. But if becoming a financial center is evidently another way of shedding original sin, this is much easier said than done. Countries that either are or were major commercial powers (e.g., the United States and Japan today, Britain in the past) clearly have a leg up; the developing countries are not major commercial powers, by definition. In addition, some countries have been able to gain the status of financial centers as a quirk of history or geography (e.g., Switzerland, a mountainous country at the center of Europe which was hard to take over and small enough to retain its neutrality, became a convenient destination for foreign deposits). Network externalities giving rise to historical path dependence have worked to lock in their currencies' international status: once the Swiss franc was held in some international portfolios and used in some international transactions, it became advantageous for additional in-

Table 9.8. Original sin and country size

	OSIN3 (1)	OSIN3 (2)	OSIN3 (3)	OSIN3 (4)	OSIN3 (5)	OSIN3 (6)	OSIN3 (7)
LGDP		-0.113 (3.32)***					
LTRADE			-0.138 (3.67)***				
LCREDIT				-0.128 (3.67)***			
SIZE					-0.320 (3.52)***	-0.320 (3.47)***	-0.562 (6.16)***
FIN_CENTER	-1.522 (5.39)***	-1.013 (3.53)***	-1.021 (3.69)***	-0.833 (2.72)***	-0.954 (3.19)***		
EUROLAND	-0.671 (5.56)***	-0.418 (3.48)***	-0.402 (3.32)***	-0.298 (2.12)**	-0.383 (2.86)***	-0.385 (2.85)***	
OTH_DEVELOPED	-0.508 (4.17)***	-0.331 (2.86)***	-0.340 (2.96)***	-0.229 (1.79)*	-0.274 (2.15)**	-0.275 (2.15)**	
Constant	1.279 (15.95)***	1.662 (10.07)***	2.042 (8.34)***	1.619 (10.87)***	1.375 (13.77)***	1.376 (13.66)***	1.387 (13.14)***
Observations	90	80	88	75	75	71	75

Note: t statistics in parentheses (Tobit estimates).

*Significant at 10%. **Significant at 5%. ***Significant at 1%.

vestors and traders to do likewise. And because Britain was the world's leading industrial, trading, and lending nation once upon a time, sterling acquired its position as a prominent currency for the denomination of international claims, a luxury that the country enjoys to this day, albeit to a lesser and declining extent. These observations are related to the literature on the determinants of key currency status (Kiyotaki, Matsuyama, and Matsui 1992), which explains the dominance of a small number of currencies in international markets as a function of network externalities and transaction costs. This literature does not say that additional countries cannot gain admission to this exclusive club, but it suggests that they face an uphill battle.

All this suggests that the global portfolio is concentrated in a very few currencies for reasons largely beyond the control of the excluded countries.

Lessons from Outliers

An interesting fact about the international issuance of bonds in exotic currencies is that it is done mostly by nonresidents. Table 9.9 presents data on the proportion of local-currency debt issued by foreigners in the non-major-currency countries that have original-sin OSIN3 ratings below 80 percent. As the table shows, over 80 percent of the cross-border debt issued in the currencies of a number of these countries—Poland, New Zealand, South Africa, and the Czech Republic—was issued by foreigners (see fig. 9.2). The proportion exceeds half of total issuance in the cases of Canada and Denmark.

Why would nonresidents issue debt denominated in exotic currencies? Consider the following case. The Inter-American Development Bank (IDB) has issued debt in New Zealand dollars, in Greek drachmas, and in Russian rubles, although none of these countries is a member of the IDB and their well-being is not a goal of the institution. The reason is that the investment banks underwriting the IDB issue are able to swap the debt-service obligation back into U.S. dollars in such a way that the net cost of borrowing for the IDB, inclusive of the swap, is less than or equal to the opportunity cost of borrowing directly in U.S. dollars.

The investment bank is able to offer this swap because there are scarce opportunities to hedge the currency mismatch; hence investors there are willing to pay a premium for the privilege. Borrowers with foreign-currency liabilities are willing to pay for the swap to entice otherwise indifferent foreigners to issue internationally in local currency.

Why the market favors this structure is an interesting question. One possibility is that the markets value the ability to separate currency and credit risk. While the local-currency debt issued by emerging-market residents has both currency and credit risk and the dollar debt issued by emerging-market residents has only credit risk, the debt issued by an international financial institution has only currency risk (and a small, uncorrelated, and well-priced credit risk). Markets may prefer to separate these risks in order to facilitate the pricing of risk and thus facilitate the development of market liquidity. In addition, if there is a positive correlation between default and devaluation risk, as is likely in potential sufferers of original sin, an instrument that has both sources of risk

Table 9.9. Proportion of debt issued by foreigners and measures of original sin, average 1999–2001

Country	% foreign	% SIN33
Czech Republic	100.0	0.0
South Africa	97.6	9.5
New Zealand	82.0	4.5
Poland	81.7	0.0
Hong Kong, China	59.7	29.4
Denmark	57.1	71.1
Canada	51.2	75.5
Singapore	35.4	69.5
Australia	31.5	69.8
Taiwan	0.0	54.0

Note: Table includes all non-major-currency countries with measures of OSIN3 less than or equal to 0.8.

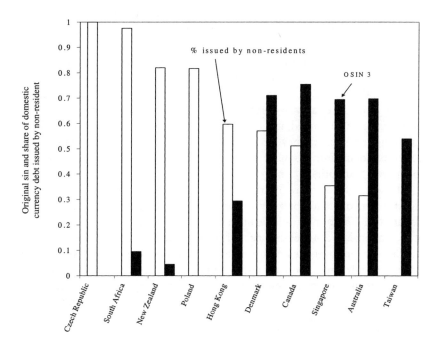

Figure 9.2 Original sin in exotic currencies

may be inefficient in the sense that it will have each source of risk plus twice the covariance between them. Under these conditions, the market may prefer to have those two risks in separate instruments in order to get rid of the covariance term. The international financial institutions (IFIs) are particularly well placed to issue bonds that have the currency risk without the country's credit risk.

In fact, the IFIs have played a very significant role in international bond issuance in exotic currencies (see table 9.10). The IFIs issued almost half of all internationally placed bonds in exotic currencies in the period 1992–98. This includes countries like the Czech Republic, Portugal, Spain, and South Africa. In the more recent period, the relative participation of IFIs in these currencies has declined as the market has found its footing, but it has increased in other newer entrants such as Estonia, Taiwan, and Trinidad and Tobago.

Conclusion

In attempting to understand the causes of original sin, this chapter started with a lineup of the usual suspects. Most of these suspicious characters turn out to have convincing alibis. There is little support for the view that the inability of emerging markets to borrow abroad in their own currencies reflects the instability and imperfect credibility of monetary and fiscal policies. There is little evidence that it reflects the weakness of their market-supporting institutions, the manipulability of their institutions of contract enforcement, or an unfavorable constellation of political economy forces.

In a sense this is not surprising. The quality of monetary and fiscal policies and the development of market-supporting institutions vary enormously across countries. Contrast Chile with Venezuela, for example, or Korea with Indonesia. But while the quality of institutions and policies varies enormously, original sin is very widespread; it is all but universal in the developing world. Even emerging markets that have made major investments in strengthening their policies and institutions have made relatively little headway in redeeming themselves from original sin.

The widespread nature of original sin leads us to search for a source in the structure and operation of the international financial system. To be clear, we are not arguing that country policies are irrelevant. Strong policies and institutions at the national level are clearly necessary to escape the problem. But they may not be sufficient over the horizon relevant for practical policy decisions. Even countries with strong policies and institutions apparently find it difficult to infiltrate their currencies into international investment portfolios. It is not hard to see why: both theory and evidence suggest that international portfolio diversification eventually encounters diminishing returns. And even in the era of modern information technology, there will be significant costs to managing a portfolio of many exotic currencies that are obligations of small economies,

Table 9.10. Bonds in exotic currencies

	Total debt (US$ billions)	Share of instruments with fixed interest rate (%)	Top three issuers (%)			Type of issuer (%) Govt.	Fin. inst.	Private corp.
Czech Republic								
1992–98	0.93	100.0	Int. org. 40.0	Germany 21.0	U.S. 10.0	8.0	52.0	0.0
1999–2001	1.11	80.0	Germany 24.0	Int. org. 22.0	Neth. 15.0	3.0	71.0	4.0
Estonia								
1999–2001	0.30	100.0	Int. org. 99.0	Finland 1.0		0.0	1.0	0.0
Hong Kong								
1992–98	21.41	64.3	Hong Kong 40.0	Int. org. 38.0	Australia 8.0	3.0	43.0	16.0
1999–2001	43.93	82.0	Int. org. 29.0	Hong Kong 27.0	Australia 17.0	8.0	59.0	4.0
Poland								
1992–98	0.54	56.0	Int. org. 43.0	Poland 28.0	U.S. 12.0	12.0	14.0	31.0
1999–2001	1.79	92.0	Int. org. 34.0	Germany 26.0	Ireland 7.0	1.0	63.0	2.0
Portugal								
1992–98	10.00	39.0	Int. org. 40.0	U.K. 12.0	U.S. 11.0	9.0	43.0	8.0
Singapore								
1992–98	2.30	15.0	Singapore 52.0	Hong Kong 45.0	U.K. 3.0	0.0	45.0	55.0
1999–2001	12.74	99.8	U.S. 26.0	Singapore 15.0	Int. org. 11.0	20.0	61.0	8.0

(continued)

Table 9.10. (continued)

	Total debt (US$ billions)	Share of instruments with fixed interest rate (%)	Top three issuers (%)	Type of issuer (%)		
				Govt.	Fin. inst.	Private corp.
Slovak Republic						
1992–98	0.46	100.0	Int. org. 65.0 / Germany 20.0 / Neth. 15.0	0.0	35.0	0.0
1999–2001	2.58	76.0	Int. org. 44.0 / Germany 20.0 / Austria 12.0	0.0	44.0	0.0
South Africa						
1992–98	2.99	97.0	Int. org 56.0 / Germany 18.0 / Neth. 11.0	7.0	29.0	8.0
1999–2001	6.17	99.0	Int. org. 48.0 / Germany 13.0 / S. Africa 13.0	3.0	33.0	16.0
Spain						
1992–98	36.48	87.0	Int. org. 59.0 / Spain 9.0 / Germany 7.0	11.0	27.0	3.0
Taiwan						
1992–98	3.04	0.0	Int. org. 0.0 / Taiwan 100.0	0.0	0.0	100.0
1999–2001	7.06	94.0	98.0 / Taiwan 2.0	0.0	0.0	2.0
Thailand						
1992–98	7.87	77.5	Hong Kong 34.0 / Thailand 29.0 / S. Korea 14.0	5.0	55.0	39.0
1999–2001	12.15	5.0	Thailand 95.0 / U.S. 4.0 / Australia 0.8	0.0	85.0	15.0
Trinidad and Tobago						
1992–98	0.40	100.0	Int. org. 100.0	0.0	0.0	0.0
1999–2001	1.06	100.0	100.0	0.0	0.0	0.0

Source: Author's calculations based on unpublished data from the Bank for International Settlements.

each with its own distinctive politics and circumstances. This suggests that developing countries and their currencies, which are latecomers to the international financial game, face an uphill battle when attempting to add their currencies to the international portfolio. They do not enjoy first-mover advantages—to the contrary. In turn, this suggests that the problem of original sin can more readily be addressed by an international initiative that heightens the attractions of these currencies for international investors. We propose one such initiative in the next chapter.

Appendix

Table 9A.1. Original sin and the level of economic development

	OSIN3 (1)	OSIN3 (2)	OSIN3 (3)	OSIN1 (4)	OSIN2 (5)
LGDP_PC	−0.141	−0.128	−0.170	−0.031	0.000
	(1.59)	(1.43)	(2.99)***	(0.95)	(0.03)
SIZE	−0.310	−0.310	−0.415	−0.199	−0.024
	(3.37)***	(3.33)***	(4.51)***	(4.48)***	(1.43)
FIN_CENTER	−0.680			−0.254	−0.592
	(1.99)*			(2.15)**	(9.69)***
EUROLAND	−0.126	−0.152		−0.067	−0.267
	(0.62)	(0.74)		(0.86)	(6.36)***
OTH_DEVELOPED	0.007	−0.021		−0.074	−0.112
	(0.03)	(0.10)		(0.90)	(2.30)**
Constant	2.522	2.414	2.833	1.498	0.991
	(3.39)***	(3.24)***	(5.46)***	(5.42)***	(10.20)***
Observations	75	71	75	75	75

Note: t statistics in parentheses (Tobit estimates).
*Significant at 10%. **Significant at 5%. ***Significant at 1%.

Table 9A.2. Original sin and monetary credibility

| | OSIN3 (1) | OSIN3 (2) | OSIN3 (3) | OSIN3 (4) | OSIN1 (5) | OSIN2 (6) | Dropping financial centers | | OLS same sample as (8) | Instrumental variables |
							OSIN3 (7)	OSIN3 (8)	OSIN3 (9)	OSIN3 (10)
AV_INF	0.306		0.436							
	(1.19)		(0.69)							
AV_INF2			−0.116							
			(0.23)							
MAX_INF		0.067								
		(0.95)								
INF				0.085	0.009	0.005	0.083	0.175	0.022	0.314
				(1.09)	(0.31)	(0.43)	(1.07)	(2.08)**	(0.35)	(1.13)
SIZE	−0.318	−0.318	−0.316	−0.318	−0.201	−0.024	−0.318	−0.503	−0.323	−0.319
	(3.57)***	(3.54)***	(3.52)***	(3.55)***	(4.51)***	(1.44)	(3.50)***	(5.75)***	(4.27)***	(4.30)***
FIN_CENTER	−0.866	−0.897	−0.857	−0.881	−0.310	−0.587			−0.603	−0.550
	(2.88)***	(2.99)***	(2.83)***	(2.93)***	(3.03)***	(10.38)***			(2.77)***	(2.52)***
EUROLAND	−0.304	−0.329	−0.296	−0.315	−0.116	−0.263	−0.318		−0.360	−0.312
	(2.12)**	(2.31)**	(1.99)*	(2.21)**	(2.03)**	(7.30)***	(2.21)**		(2.80)***	(2.39)**
OTH_DEVELOPED	−0.199	−0.224	−0.192	−0.211	−0.128	−0.107	−0.213		−0.207	−0.155
	(1.47)	(1.67)*	(1.37)	(1.56)	(2.17)**	(2.57)**	(1.57)		(2.15)**	(1.52)
Constant	1.277	1.310	1.259	1.346	1.241	0.992	1.347	1.358	1.321	1.233
	(10.87)***	(11.60)***	(8.83)***	(13.56)***	(25.50)***	(78.09)***	(13.46)***	(13.41)***	(14.07)***	(10.29)***
Observations	74	74	74	74	74	74	70	74	33	33

Notes: Robust t statistics in parentheses (Tobit estimates). The instrument for column (10) is Cukierman's (1993) index of Central Bank Independence.
*Significant at 10%. **Significant at 5%. ***Significant at 1%.

Table 9A.3. Original sin and fiscal sustainability

	OSIN3 (1)	OSIN3 (2)	OSIN3 (3)	OSIN3 (4)	OSIN3 (5)	OSIN1 (6)	OSIN2 (7)	Instrumental variables estimations OSIN3 (8)
DE_GDP2	−0.073 (0.50)							−0.061 (0.22)
DEFICIT		1.777 (0.92)						
DE_RE2			0.014 (0.24)					
FISC				−0.025 (0.30)	−0.024 (0.28)	−0.015 (0.43)	0.003 (0.14)	
SIZE	−0.350 (3.71)***	−0.327 (3.52)***	−0.354 (3.51)***	−0.342 (3.42)***	−0.345 (3.40)***	−0.188 (3.82)***	−0.037 (1.73)*	−0.124 (2.17)**
FIN_CENTER	−0.825 (2.72)***	−0.926 (3.09)***	−0.816 (2.57)**	−0.839 (2.66)**		−0.411 (3.55)***	−0.537 (8.18)***	−0.736 (4.12)***
EUROLAND	−0.344 (2.61)**	−0.361 (2.66)***	−0.327 (2.22)**	−0.348 (2.48)**	−0.348 (2.46)**	−0.138 (2.34)**	−0.224 (5.68)***	−0.149 (1.21)
OTH_DEVELOPED	−0.275 (2.18)**	−0.215 (1.54)	−0.245 (1.73)*	−0.272 (2.01)**	−0.272 (1.99)*	−0.150 (2.44)**	−0.100 (2.24)**	−0.117 (0.67)
Constant	1.426 (11.99)***	1.311 (11.46)***	1.370 (10.06)***	1.382 (12.04)***	1.385 (11.93)***	1.237 (23.07)***	0.997 (63.29)***	0.996 (34.99)***
Observations	64	74	57	57	54	57	57	57

Notes: t statistics in parentheses (Tobit estimates). The instrument for column (8) is OLD.

*Significant at 10%. **Significant at 5%. ***Significant at 1%.

Table 9A.4. Original sin and institutions

	OSIN3 (1)	OSIN3 (2)	OSIN1 (3)	OSIN2 (4)
RULEOFLAW	−0.050	−0.053	−0.039	−0.003
	(0.46)	(0.49)	(0.90)	(0.19)
SIZE	−0.323	−0.322	−0.206	−0.024
	(3.53)***	(3.48)***	(4.53)***	(1.44)
FIN_CENTER	−0.883		−0.261	−0.586
	(2.65)**		(2.23)**	(9.72)***
EUROLAND	−0.326	−0.325	−0.078	−0.263
	(1.81)*	(1.79)*	(1.09)	(6.71)***
OTH_DEVELOPED	−0.203	−0.201	−0.077	−0.106
	(1.03)	(1.01)	(0.94)	(2.22)**
Constant	1.388	1.390	1.257	0.994
	(13.17)***	(13.08)***	(24.35)***	(80.77)***
Observations	75	71	75	75

Note: t statistics in parentheses (Tobit estimates).
*Significant at 10%. **Significant at 5%. ***Significant at 1%.

Table 9A.5. Original sin and trade openness

	OSIN3 (1)	OSIN1 (2)	OSIN2 (3)	OSIN3 (4)	OSIN3 (5)
OPEN	−0.174	−0.088	−0.020	−0.183	−0.233
	(1.28)	(1.34)	(0.97)	(1.36)	(1.42)
SIZE	−0.359	−0.220	−0.032	−0.360	−0.600
	(3.74)***	(4.70)***	(1.73)*	(3.73)***	(6.23)***
FIN_CENTER	−0.937	−0.313	−0.586		
	(3.23)***	(3.27)***	(10.58)***		
EUROLAND	−0.360	−0.109	−0.261	−0.360	
	(2.71)***	(2.11)**	(7.41)***	(2.71)***	
OTH_DEVELOPED	−0.269	−0.126	−0.109	−0.270	
	(2.15)**	(2.39)**	(2.69)***	(2.15)**	
Constant	1.515	1.311	1.012	1.523	1.573
	(9.60)***	(18.17)***	(45.62)***	(9.64)***	(8.75)***
Observations	75	75	75	71	75

Note: t statistics in parentheses (Tobit estimates).
*Significant at 10%. **Significant at 5%. ***Significant at 1%.

Table 9A.6. Original sin and size of the financial system

	OSIN3 (1)	OSIN3 (2)	OSIN3 (3)	OSIN3 (4)	OSIN1 (5)	OSIN2 (6)
DC_GDP	−0.332 (1.49)					
FOR_DOM		−7.289 (2.15)**				
SIZE_FIN			0.261 (0.53)	0.354 (0.70)	0.237 (1.39)	−0.004 (0.06)
SIZE	−0.290 (3.22)***	−0.360 (4.02)***	−0.326 (3.43)***	−0.332 (3.42)***	−0.213 (4.69)***	−0.025 (1.36)
FIN_CENTER	−0.753 (2.40)**	−0.843 (3.02)***	−0.997 (3.25)***		−0.347 (3.57)***	−0.590 (10.12)***
EUROLAND	−0.226 (1.37)	−0.301 (2.34)**	−0.410 (2.86)***	−0.421 (2.92)***	−0.144 (2.77)***	−0.266 (7.35)***
OTH_DEVELOPED	−0.224 (1.75)*	−0.223 (1.86)*	−0.278 (2.18)**	−0.280 (2.19)**	−0.136 (2.65)**	−0.110 (2.65)**
Constant	1.521 (10.13)***	1.431 (13.76)***	1.377 (13.44)***	1.383 (13.33)***	1.250 (26.07)***	0.994 (72.76)***
Observations	74	73	72	68	72	72

Note: t statistics in parentheses.
*Significant at 10%. **Significant at 5%. ***Significant at 1%.

Table 9A.7. The determinants of original sin

	OSIN3 (1)	OSIN3_NOI (2)	OSIN3 (3)	OSIN3 (4)	OSIN3 (5)	OSIN1 (6)	OSIN2 (7)
GDP_PC	−0.286 (1.96)*	−0.230 (1.98)*	−0.333 (2.70)***	−0.314 (2.09)**	−0.286 (1.96)*	−0.083 (1.53)	0.011 (0.48)
DISC	0.082 (0.70)	−0.136 (1.73)*	−0.078 (0.76)	−0.098 (0.96)	0.082 (0.70)	−0.073 (1.79)*	0.006 (0.27)
SIZE	−0.342 (2.79)***	−0.323 (4.06)***	−0.404 (3.82)***	−0.347 (3.37)***	−0.342 (2.79)***	−0.193 (3.88)***	−0.050 (2.03)**
SIZE_FIN	0.084 (0.20)	0.314 (0.71)	0.338 (0.61)	0.650 (1.07)	0.084 (0.20)	0.436 (1.98)*	−0.015 (0.17)
RULEOFLAW	0.312 (1.69)*	0.134 (1.01)	0.268 (1.55)	0.245 (1.43)	0.312 (1.69)*	−0.030 (0.46)	0.006 (0.17)
INF	0.112 (1.10)	0.067 (0.73)	0.109 (1.08)	0.129 (1.11)	0.112 (1.10)	0.046 (1.00)	0.002 (0.13)
OPEN	−0.093 (0.52)	−0.071 (0.39)	−0.131 (0.62)	−0.102 (0.43)	−0.093 (0.52)	0.055 (0.57)	−0.051 (1.33)
FIN_CENTER	−0.683 (1.85)*	−0.600 (2.04)**			−0.683 (1.85)*	−0.249 (1.74)*	−0.561 (7.22)***
EUROLAND	−0.143 (0.56)	−0.050 (0.25)		−0.034 (0.14)	−0.143 (0.56)	0.011 (0.11)	−0.241 (4.53)***
OTH_DEVELOPED	0.009 (0.03)	−0.048 (0.22)		0.035 (0.13)	0.009 (0.03)	0.039 (0.35)	−0.130 (2.11)**
Constant	3.674 (3.15)***	3.265 (3.57)***	4.170 (4.06)***	3.941 (3.31)***	3.674 (3.15)***	1.892 (4.47)***	0.948 (5.41)***
Observations	56	56	56	53	56	56	56

Note: t statistics in parentheses (Tobit estimates).
*Significant at 10%. **Significant at 5%. ***Significant at 1%.

Table 9A.8. Original sin and country size

	OSIN3 (1)	OSIN3 (2)	OSIN3 (3)	OSIN3 (4)	OSIN3 (5)	OSIN3 (6)	OSIN3 (7)	OSIN1 (8)	OSIN2 (9)
LGDP	-0.113 (3.32)***								
LTRADE		-0.138 (3.67)***							
LCREDIT			-0.128 (3.67)***						
SIZE				-0.320 (3.52)***	-0.320 (3.47)***	-0.562 (6.16)***	-0.278 (2.12)**	-0.304 (7.31)***	-0.030 (1.95)*
FIN_CENTER	-1.013 (3.53)***	-1.021 (3.69)***	-0.833 (2.72)***	-0.954 (3.19)***					
EUROLAND	-0.418 (3.48)***	-0.402 (3.32)***	-0.298 (2.12)**	-0.383 (2.86)***	-0.385 (2.85)***			-0.047 (0.95)	-0.262 (8.19)***
OTH_DEVELOPED	-0.331 (2.86)***	-0.340 (2.96)***	-0.229 (1.79)*	-0.274 (2.15)**	-0.275 (2.15)**			-0.065 (1.20)	-0.107 (2.87)***
Constant	1.662 (10.07)***	2.042 (8.34)***	1.619 (10.87)***	1.375 (13.77)***	1.376 (13.66)***	1.387 (13.14)***	1.312 (10.95)***	1.299 (23.55)***	0.994 (89.71)***
Observations	80	88	75	75	71	75	54	75	71

Note: t statistics in parentheses (Tobit estimates).

*Significant at 10%. **Significant at 5%. ***Significant at 1%.

Notes

We are grateful to Alejandro Riaño for excellent research assistance.

1. Some readers will find the absence of a smoking gun counterintuitive; this is why we refer to the "mystery" of original sin. We therefore provide an extensive sensitivity analysis establishing the robustness of our results in the appendix to this chapter.

2. That there are large differences in the extent of original sin between the financial centers, other advanced economies, and developing countries came through clearly in chapter 2. Not controlling for these country fixed effects would therefore bias an analysis of its determinants.

3. Tirole (2002) argues that governments could still attempt to influence the real exchange rate. The ability of the government to influence this relative price in a sustained manner is questionable, however, and the political case for doing it is less compelling.

4. To explain this, Chamon (2002) and Aghion, Bacchetta, and Banerjee (2000) argue that the existence of a positive correlation between default risk and devaluation risk means that the claim of dollar lenders on the residual value of a firm goes up relative to those that lend in domestic or CPI-indexed debt. Under these conditions, peso lenders will fear the contingent expropriation implied by future additional dollar borrowing by firms.

5. It should also be noted that we use the 1980–98 period to give inflation the maximum chance to explain original sin. Had we presented the same equations using only the inflation in the 1990s, we would have found even weaker results.

6. Column (3) runs a noninstrumented regression using the same sample of column (4). Because of the small sample size, rather than controlling for country groups we just include a dummy that takes value 1 in developing countries.

7. Column (5) runs a noninstrumented regression using the same sample of column (6).

8. Recall that developing countries is the omitted alternative.

9. In contrast, when latitude is used as an instrument, there is still no statistically significant effect (results not reported).

10. The results are also robust to dropping two outliers (Singapore and Suriname).

11. Since DC_GDP and FOR_DOM are supposed to have opposite effects on original sin, SIZE_FIN was constructed with the negative of FOR_DOM.

12. There is also the problem that our measure of the size of the financial system does not capture the size of the domestic-currency market. Countries may have a large, but dollarized, domestic financial system. The section on international causes focuses on this issue and on attempts to estimate what determines domestic original sin.

13. To some extent the Argentine forced *pesification* of dollar claims bears some similarity to the U.S. 1933 experiment. It involved allowing the currency to depreciate while limiting the wealth effects associated with the dollar-linked (instead of gold-linked) assets.

14. Why this contradiction was not more demoralizing in 1933 is an interesting issue that would reward further study.

15. This is especially true if the additional currency exposes the investor to concentrated risks. Note that in making this argument we are paralleling the literature on portfolio diversification with transaction costs, in which it is shown that optimizing inves-

tors, faced with transaction costs, will include only a limited number of securities in their portfolios, balancing the diversification benefits of adding an additional currency, which decline on the margin, against the transaction costs of purchasing additional securities, which may not.

16. We find that size is also significant in a subsample of developing countries.

References

Acemoglu, Daron, Simon Johnson, and James Robinson. 2001. "The Colonial Origins of Economic Development: An Empirical Investigation." *American Economic Review* 91:1361–1401.

Aghion, Philippe, Philippe Bacchetta, and Abhijit Banerjee. 2000. "Currency Crises and Monetary Policy in an Economy with Credit Constraints." Manuscript, University College, London.

Calvo, Guillermo, and Pablo Guidotti. 1990. "Indexation and the Maturity of Government Bonds: An Exploratory Model." In *Public Debt Management: Theory and History,* ed. Rudiger Dornbusch and Mario Draghi, 52–82. Cambridge: Cambridge University Press.

Chamon, Marcos. 2001. "Why Can't Developing Countries Borrow from Abroad in Their Currency?" Manuscript, Harvard University.

Cukierman, Alex. 1995. *Central Bank Strategy, Credibility, and Independence.* Cambridge, MA: MIT Press.

Diaz-Alejandro, Carlos. 1984. "Stories of the 1930s for the 1980s." In *Financial Policies and the World Capital Market,* ed. Pedro Aspe Armella, Rudiger Dornbusch, and Maurice Obstfeld, 5–40. Chicago: University of Chicago Press.

Eaton, Jonathan, and Mark Gersovitz. 1981. "Debt with Potential Repudiation: Theoretical and Empirical Analysis." *Review of Economic Studies* 48:289–309.

Hausmann, Ricardo, and Ugo Panizza. 2003. "On the Determinants of Original Sin: An Empirical Investigation." *Journal of International Money and Finance* 22:957–90.

Jeanne, Olivier. 2002. "Monetary Policy and Liability Dollarization." Manuscript, International Monetary Fund, Washington, DC.

Kaufmann, D., A. Kraay, and P. Zoido-Lobaton. 1999. "Aggregating Governance Indicators." World Bank Policy Research Working Paper 2195, Washington, DC.

Kiyotaki, Nobu, Kiminori Matsuyama, and Akihiko Matsui. 1992. "Toward a Theory of International Currency." *Review of Economic Studies* 60:283–307.

Kroszner, Randall. 1999. "Is It Better to Forgive Than to Receive? Evidence from the Abrogation of the Gold Clauses in Long Term Debt during the Great Depression." Manuscript, University of Chicago, Graduate School of Business.

La Porta, Rafael, Florencio Lopez-de-Silanes, Andrei Shleifer, and Robert Vishny. 1997. "Legal Determinants of External Finance." *Journal of Finance* 52:1131–50.

Lucas, Robert, and Nancy Stokey. 1983. "Optimal Fiscal and Monetary Policy in an Economy without Capital." *Journal of Monetary Economics* 12:55–93.

Rodrik, Dani. 2001. "Institutions Rule." NBER Working Paper, National Bureau of Economic Research, Cambridge, MA.

Rose, Andrew. 2002. "One Reason Countries Pay Their Debts: Renegotiation and International Trade." NBER Working Paper no. 8853, National Bureau of Economic Research, Cambridge, MA.

Rose, Andrew, and Mark Spiegel. 2002. "A Gravity Model of Sovereign Lending: Trade, Credit, and Default." Manuscript, University of California, Berkeley, and Federal Reserve Bank of San Francisco.

Tirole, Jean. 2002. "Inefficient Foreign Borrowing." Invited lecture, Latin American and Caribbean Economic Association, Madrid, October.

Wyplosz, Charles. 2001. "Financial Restraints and Liberalization in Postwar Europe." In *Financial Liberalization: How Far? How Fast?* ed. Gerard Caprio, Patrick Honohan, and Joseph Stiglitz. Cambridge: Cambridge University Press.

Original Sin

The Road to Redemption

Barry Eichengreen and Ricardo Hausmann

THE PRECEDING CHAPTERS have shown that original sin—the inability of emerging markets to borrow abroad in their own currencies—is both prevalent and problematic. It implies the absence of opportunities for international risk sharing. It prevents the benefits of international capital mobility from being reaped because it gives rise to a very significant increase in the volatility of debt-servicing capacity. One way of seeing this is to recall the comparison in chapter 1 (table 1.8) of the volatility of GDP growth in domestic and dollar terms. Deflating nominal GDP by the domestic consumption basket, one finds that growth is a little less than twice as volatile in developing as developed countries. But when domestic product is measured in constant U.S. dollar terms, which is what is relevant for debt-servicing capacity when countries borrow in dollars, the volatility of GDP growth in developing countries more than doubles again. As a result, the volatility of debt-servicing capacity of developing countries with original sin is nearly five times that of industrial countries that borrow abroad in their own currencies.[1]

Our empirical analysis suggests that domestic reforms, by themselves, are unlikely to quickly eliminate this problem, given that the quality of domestic institutions and policies goes only so far in explaining the prevalence of original sin. Within the class of emerging markets, there is little correlation between the quality of institutions and policies on the one hand and the prevalence of original sin on the other. Widely prescribed institutional reforms, in other words, seem to have relatively little impact on this specific problem. As a result, emerging markets are consigned to a situation of greater volatility than their advanced-industrial counterparts, making it correspondingly harder for them to sustain the mutually reinforcing processes of growth and institutional reform.

We have no quibble with arguments for robust institutions that guarantee the rule of law, strengthen property rights, and encourage responsible fiscal, monetary, and financial policies. We would certainly encourage countries to develop long-term fixed-rate domestic debt markets in local currency, in nominal terms where possible and inflation-indexed terms where not.[2] But the findings of the preceding chapter suggest that doing so may not solve the problem of original sin; in addition, an international initiative may be required.

Earlier chapters have provided us with the building blocks for this initiative. We have seen that the global portfolio is concentrated in the currencies of a few large countries and international financial centers. We have seen how transaction costs in a world of heterogeneous economies can explain this bias toward a small handful of currencies. We have also seen that markets in the currencies of the select few emerging economies that have achieved redemption from original sin tend to develop through debt issuance by nonresidents, who then swap their debt-service obligations into their currency of choice, allowing residents on the other side of the swap to offload their currency risk as if they had borrowed in local currency. We have suggested that the role of nonresidents may be related to their comparative advantage in separating currency risk from credit risk. And we have shown that this is something that the residents of countries with original sin may find more difficult to do, given that currency depreciation makes it harder for emerging-market borrowers to stay current on their foreign-currency-denominated obligations (in other words, because in their case currency risk creates credit risk).

Our proposal envisions the creation of a synthetic unit of account in which claims on a diversified group of emerging-market economies can be denominated, together with steps by the international financial institutions (IFIs) to develop a liquid market in claims denominated in this unit. As this new unit conquers space in the global portfolio, it will become possible for emerging-market borrowers to issue claims denominated in the underlying currencies and to place them on international markets. The result will be a more efficient international diversification of risks and a reduction in financial fragility.

We are not the first to offer proposals for increased international risk sharing as a response to problems of macroeconomic and financial instability. The World Bank has attempted to promote the development of insurance markets for terms-of-trade risk. Shiller (2003) has proposed that governments issue derivative securities that would permit GDP-per-capita swaps between countries as a way of diversifying country-specific macroeconomic risks.[3] Caballero (2003) has advocated the development of instruments indexed to the prices of the principal commodity exports of emerging-market borrowers. Berg, Borensztein, and Mauro (2002) have promoted the idea of GDP-linked bonds, the coupons on which would fluctuate with the growth of real GDP.[4] Our proposal is one more attempt, in this spirit, to help to complete incomplete financial markets.[5]

The Proposal

Our plan has four steps. Step 1 is to define an inflation-indexed basket of currencies of emerging and developing countries, which for convenience we refer to as the "EM index." Step 2 is for multilateral institutions such as the World Bank to issue debt denominated in this index. To avoid incurring a currency mismatch, they would convert a portion of their existing loans into claims denominated in the inflation-adjusted currencies of each of the countries included in the index so as to replicate the index in their pattern of lending. This would allow the bank to become part of the solution rather than an additional source of original sin. Step 3 would broaden and deepen the EM market by having G-10 sovereigns issue debt in this instrument and swap their currency exposure with countries whose currencies are included in the EM index. Step 4 would then encourage institutional investors and mutual funds to create products that add credit risk to the index as a way of further encouraging the development of the market.

Step 1: Develop an index based on a basket of emerging-market currencies. For developing countries to be able to borrow abroad in local currency, foreign investors will have to take a long position in those currencies. But it is hard to imagine many foreign investors managing portfolios that include the currencies of many small, poorly diversified economies. We therefore propose the creation of a unit of account made up of a portfolio of emerging-market and developing-country currencies.[6]

For illustrative purposes, we describe in tables 10.1 and 10.2 two such baskets, one that includes the twenty largest countries for which the IMF publication *International Financial Statistics* conveniently provides quarterly data on exchange rates and consumer price indexes since at least 1980, and another that includes the largest twenty-two countries with the same continuous data since 1993. We refer to these as the "EM 1980" and "EM 1993" indexes. We weight the constituent countries by GDP at purchasing-power parity in order to avoid setting weights in a manner that favors countries that do not behave prudently.[7] To deal with the temptation to debase the currency faced by net debtors borrowing in their own currencies, we index the debt to the consumer price level of each country.[8] Indexing to the CPI, like indexing to the dollar, allows countries with limited credibility to lengthen the maturity of their obligations. But indexing to the CPI has better properties from the point of view of macroeconomic stability: it is similar to indexing to the real exchange rate, which is a relative price.[9] While indexing to the CPI may be necessary to create a demand by foreign investors to hold claims denominated in the currencies of emerging markets, it is not obviously sufficient, given that many emerging markets already issue CPI-indexed claims, which have not found their way into the portfolios of foreign investors. This is the problem that the remainder of our proposal seeks to address.

Indexing to the CPI nonetheless gives the EM index several important characteristics. First, if the real exchange rate is stationary, the index will display long-run stability. Averaging over twenty countries enhances this stability still

Table 10.1. Composition of the emerging market
indexes for base years 1980 and 1993

	Weights	
	1980 index	1993 index
	20 countries	22 countries
Brazil	18.95	18.09
Korea, Republic	14.27	13.62
India	11.32	10.80
Mexico	8.79	8.39
Argentina	7.47	7.13
Indonesia	5.02	4.79
Turkey	4.81	4.59
South Africa	4.14	3.95
Thailand	4.12	3.94
Poland		3.29
Singapore	2.60	2.48
Malaysia	2.59	2.47
Israel	2.53	2.41
Colombia	2.37	2.26
Philippines	2.13	2.03
Chile	1.94	1.85
Venezuela	1.92	1.83
Pakistan	1.72	1.65
Peru	1.49	1.42
Czech Republic		1.27
Hungary	1.31	1.25
Uruguay	0.52	0.49
	100	100

further. Second, since the real exchange rate tends to appreciate in good times and depreciate in bad times, debt-service payments on these obligations are positively correlated with capacity to pay, which is the opposite of dollar debts. Third, the index has a long-run tendency to appreciate. To the extent that late-developing countries grow faster than advanced economies, this generates domestic inflation not offset by depreciation of the exchange rate (the Balassa-Samuelson effect), strengthening the real exchange rate and thereby raising the compensation received by foreign investors.[10]

Figure 10.1 shows the value of the two indexes along with the yen-dollar and German mark–dollar exchange rates.[11] Historically, the two EM inflation-adjusted currency baskets are less volatile against the dollar than are the yen and the mark. For example, it is striking that in the period of the Asian and Russian crises, the EM index actually depreciates against the dollar by less than the mark. (We return to the reasons for this relative stability below.) This low volatility suggests, other things equal, that claims denominated in the EM index should be attractive to international investors.

Table 10.3 calculates the volatility of the two EM indexes vis-à-vis the dollar

Table 10.2. Emerging market 1980 and 1993 indexes

Period	EM-1980	Period	EM-1980	EM-1993
1980q1	100	1991q1	76.0	
1980q2	94.1	1991q2	74.8	
1980q3	90.1	1991q3	75.4	
1980q4	87.0	1991q4	77.3	
1981q1	85.5	1992q1	75.8	
1981q2	88.8	1992q2	74.0	
1981q3	88.2	1992q3	72.9	
1981q4	87.9	1992q4	73.4	
1982q1	94.2	1993q1	74.9	100.0
1982q2	96.1	1993q2	74.8	99.9
1982q3	103.9	1993q3	74.7	100.1
1982q4	106.0	1993q4	74.3	100.2
1983q1	108.6	1994q1	74.7	100.4
1983q2	109.8	1994q2	75.0	100.2
1983q3	109.9	1994q3	66.0	88.4
1983q4	112.7	1994q4	66.4	86.8
1984q1	111.5	1995q1	66.7	85.6
1984q2	111.0	1995q2	62.9	81.8
1984q3	113.0	1995q3	62.9	81.9
1984q4	117.0	1995q4	64.5	82.9
1985q1	117.9	1996q1	63.1	81.6
1985q2	121.3	1996q2	63.0	81.6
1985q3	117.3	1996q3	61.9	80.8
1985q4	114.6	1996q4	61.7	80.9
1986q1	110.6	1997q1	61.3	80.6
1986q2	109.2	1997q2	60.9	80.4
1986q3	109.7	1997q3	64.2	85.5
1986q4	109.2	1997q4	75.0	102.2
1987q1	108.2	1998q1	74.7	98.0
1987q2	109.2	1998q2	82.8	106.4
1987q3	105.3	1998q3	75.0	98.3
1987q4	104.9	1998q4	68.8	91.6
1988q1	101.5	1999q1	72.7	97.3
1988q2	101.9	1999q2	71.2	95.2
1988q3	99.5	1999q3	75.1	99.4
1988q4	95.8	1999q4	70.9	94.6
1989q1	89.7	2000q1	70.6	93.8
1989q2	125.8	2000q2	72.8	95.9
1989q3	97.8	2000q3	73.4	96.7
1989q4	112.6	2000q4	75.3	99.0
1990q1	95.2	2001q1	78.8	103.5
1990q2	80.9	2001q2	79.5	104.2
1990q3	76.6	2001q3	80.3	106.2
1990q4	76.6	2001q4	78.9	104.3

Note: Index value per U.S. dollars, quarterly.

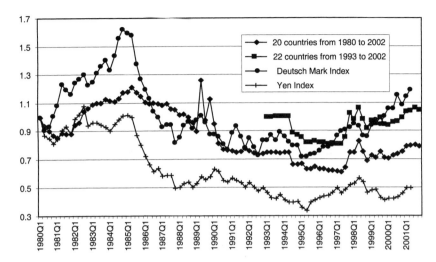

Figure 10.1 Exchange rates vis-à-vis the dollar: the EM indexes, the yen, and the mark

for various subperiods and shows that their volatility is generally in line with that of other major currencies. Table 10.4 shows their average return, their volatility, and their correlation with real private consumption in eight advanced economies (where many important international investors reside). The indexes exhibit trend appreciation of about 2 percent per annum, volatility of 10 to 13 percent, and a negative correlation with real private consumption growth in the advanced economies. These characteristics suggest that the index should be an attractive form of diversification for institutional and retail investors in the advanced economies.[12]

The reduction in volatility associated with moving from a single emerging-market currency to a portfolio of such currencies is related to more than pure diversification. That is, it is related to more than offsets in random, uncorrelated shocks to real exchange rates. In addition, there are structural reasons why one should expect negative correlations among the real exchange rates of the countries constituting the index. Many of the countries in question are on opposite sides of the same markets. While some export oil or coffee, others import those commodities. Therefore a positive shock to one is a negative shock to another. Even when different countries export the same commodities, they are affected in opposite ways when shocks are to commodity supply. A frost in Brazil's coffee-growing regions is a negative shock to Brazil but a positive shock to other coffee producers. An aggregate of emerging-market real exchange rates is thus more stable than the individual components.[13]

In sum, the basket we are proposing has three characteristics—trend appreciation, low volatility, and a negative correlation with consumption growth

Table 10.3. Exchange rate changes vis-à-vis the U.S. dollar

	1981–2001	1981–93	1993–2001
EM 1980			
Mean	1.6	2.5	0.2
Standard deviation	12.4	13.5	10.1
EM 1993			
Mean			0.5
Standard deviation			10.6
German mark			
Mean	0.1	2.0	−3.3
Standard deviation	13.8	15.5	9.8
Yen			
Mean	4.1	6.4	0.0
Standard deviation	14.4	14.6	13.5

Table 10.4. EM indexes: Average return, standard deviation, and correlation with real private consumption

	EM index 80 (1980–2001)			EM index 93 (1993–2001)		
	Avg. return	St. dev.	Consumption correlation	Avg. return	St. dev.	Consumption correlation
Canada	1.56	10.9	−14.5	1.49	10.5	−33.4
France	2.58	13.6	−25.9	2.92	10.2	−36.4
Germany	0.73	14.3	12.5	3.14	10.5	−14.5
Italy	4.22	14.0	−27.5	3.36	11.1	15.8
Spain	4.50	12.9	−62.0	4.30	10.5	−65.4
Japan	−3.12	13.9	4.3	0.13	11.8	34.3
United Kingdom	2.45	12.2	−35.3	−0.24	11.8	−21.4
United States	0.27	11.3	−23.4	−0.71	11.6	−25.5

Note: Correlations with real consumption: For France, Germany, Italy, and Spain, this covers 1980–98. For Canada, United Kingdom, United States, and Japan, this covers 1980–2001. A negative number indicates that the returns tend to be high when real private consumption is low.

in industrial countries—that should make it attractive for global investors. The question is how to create a liquid market in claims denominated in this index. The answer begins with step 2.

Step 2: Have the World Bank and other IFIs issue debt denominated in the EM index. By borrowing in the currencies that compose the EM index, the IFIs would gain the ability to extend loans to the countries issuing those currencies in inflation-adjusted local-currency terms without incurring balance-sheet mismatches themselves. And by issuing high-grade debt securities denominated in a basket of EM currencies, the IFIs would provide investors with a claim on a more stable unit than could be achieved by issuing in an individual currency.[14]

As noted in chapter 9, the process of escaping from original sin has been led, in many cases, not by residents but by foreigners and often by IFIs issuing obligations denominated in the currencies of these countries. We have argued that this pattern reflects the need to separate credit risk from currency risk and the difficulty that the residents of countries with original sin have in doing so themselves. Foreigners, in contrast, can issue instruments with currency risk that is uncorrelated with credit risk.

We therefore propose that the nonconcessional windows of the World Bank and other IFIs should issue debt in the index described above.[15] Their AAA rating allows them to access institutional investors. These bonds would be attractive as a result of the trend appreciation of the EM index, its relatively low volatility, and its negative correlation with consumption in the countries in which they are marketed. To be sure, they would be less attractive initially insofar as they would be relatively illiquid. However, given the mandate of the IFIs to foster economic growth and stability, not to mention their self-interest in the development of this market, explained below, it can be argued that the IFIs should subsidize issuance until sufficient liquidity develops to make the new bonds easily tradable.[16]

The argument that it is in the self-interest of the IFIs to develop the capacity to lend to their clients in local-currency inflation-indexed terms runs as follows. At present, the World Bank and other IFIs lend in dollars to finance projects relevant to the borrowers' development needs. All lending by the World Bank and the regional development banks (RDBs) is in dollars, other major currencies, and special drawing rights (which are themselves a basket of major currencies).[17] This means that IFI lending creates a currency mismatch in the balance sheets of the corporations whose investment projects are funded by these institutions. It similarly creates a mismatch for governments by loaning in dollars to fund schooling, transport, water, and energy projects whose costs are ultimately paid through local-currency-denominated taxes and service charges.

For nonconcessional lending, this practice of dollar lending has a clear explanation. The development banks borrow on international capital markets in the major currencies. By lending in those same currencies, they neatly match the currency denomination of their assets and liabilities.[18]

However, the concessional windows of these institutions—the International Development Agency (IDA) and the Poverty Reduction and Growth Facility of the IMF and its equivalent in the RDBs—are not financed through borrowing on capital markets. Rather, they are funded by grants from the high-income countries.[19] This makes it hard to argue that the reason for denominating these loans in dollars is to permit the development banks to avoid incurring currency mismatches. In this context, lending in dollars and special drawing rights is more difficult to rationalize.

Hausmann and Rigobon (2003) show that one result of the practice of denominating concessional loans in dollars is that repayments to the IDA have undesirable cyclical characteristics. IDA loans become more burdensome precisely when it is harder for countries to pay, that is, when the dollar value of the GDP of the borrowing countries declines significantly. Compare this with a situation in which IDA lending is denominated in inflation-indexed local-currency units of each country. In this case, the dollar value of debt service would decline (rise) when exchange rate depreciates (strengthens). Occasions on which a borrowing country was forced to suspend its repayment to IDA might then become less frequent because the tendency for the exchange rate to collapse at the same time output fell (making it doubly difficult to repay dollar debts) would no longer be relevant for debt-servicing capacity. This improved outcome might even be achieved without any additional subsidization of concessional loans, insofar as its improved risk characteristics caused the net present value of the IDA portfolio to rise rather than fall.[20]

Note that foreign currencies would maintain their function as means of payment. Borrowing countries would still receive loans and repay the World Bank in dollars. The only difference is that the unit of account on which those payments were based would now be inflation-indexed local currency.[21]

Hausmann and Rigobon propose that the concessional window of the World Bank—the IDA—should move rapidly in this direction by converting all dollar- and special-drawing-rights-denominated loans into inflation-indexed local currency. Our proposal is directed to the nonconcessional window of the World Bank—the International Bank for Reconstruction and Development—and would imply moving in the same direction, albeit more gradually. The problem with moving quickly is that, as just noted, the bank finances its nonconcessional lending by borrowing on international capital markets. If the bank were to re-denominate its loans into inflation-indexed currencies of emerging markets while continuing to borrow in dollars, it would incur a currency mismatch. The solution to this is for the International Bank for Reconstruction and Development to begin funding itself by issuing EM-denominated debt. Because this market would be relatively illiquid initially, this part of the adjustment would take time. Hence the argument for moving more gradually.

Note that the World Bank would not be required to take on additional currency risk if it began funding itself by issuing EM-denominated debt. By converting some of its already-outstanding loans to EM members into inflation-indexed local-currency loans, it could exactly match the currency composition of the asset and liability sides of its balance sheet.

RDBs such as the Inter-American Development Bank, the European Bank for Reconstruction and Development, the Asian Development Bank, and the African Development Bank lend only to subsets of the countries whose currencies are included in the EM index, as the latter is a globally balanced index. This would appear to make it more difficult for them to align the currency composition of the asset and liability sides of their balance sheets if they started borrowing in EMs. In fact, however, it would still be relatively straightforward for them to off-load the currency exposure associated with not lending to members of the EMs basket that are not in their region. They could do so by swapping currency exposures among themselves or with the World Bank. Each RDB would then have nicely matched EM-denominated debts and EM-denominated assets.[22] The RDBs would thereby eliminate the currency mismatch generated by their own lending, and at the same time become part of the solution rather than a source of original sin.[23]

Once issuance by the World Bank and the RDBs reached significant levels, claims denominated in the EM index would form part of standard global bond indexes such as the Lehman Global Bond Index. This would then increase the demand for EM bonds by institutional fixed-income investors with a mandate to form portfolios that track the index.[24]

It is important to emphasize that we are *not* proposing that developing countries should issue debt in EMs. This would not help to solve the problem of original sin, since it would just substitute exchange rate risk vis-à-vis the EM for exchange risk vis-à-vis the dollar. Currency risk would not be significantly diminished, because any one emerging-market currency would account for only a fraction of the EM basket.

Instead, we are proposing changes that would allow countries to denominate their obligations in constant units of their domestic consumption basket. That is, they would become able to issue domestic-currency-denominated bonds indexed to their consumer price indexes. The World Bank and RDBs would aggregate the loans of the countries making up the EM index in order to create a basket of loans with the same currency composition as the EM bonds that they themselves issue. Institutional investors would not do this for them from day 1, because private markets would initially be lacking in liquidity. But by taking steps to render the market more liquid, the IFIs would be paving the way for private financial institutions to take over the task.

It is important to emphasize that by adopting this strategy the World Bank and its regional counterparts are not assuming additional balance-sheet risk. Nor are they undertaking additional lending. To be clear, we are not proposing an expansion in the scale of their operations. The only effect of the initiative would be to repackage currency risk already on their books and place it with international investors through the issuance of EM-denominated debt. Emerging markets that borrow from the World Bank, for their part, would be able to off-load the currency risk currently associated with their debt-service obligations. Insofar as the result is an improvement in the capacity of countries borrowing from the bank to keep current on their external obligations, the credit risk in the World Bank's loan portfolio could in fact decline, other things equal.[25]

The cost to the World Bank of funding a loan denominated in inflation-indexed local-currency terms will depend on the yield that investors demand on EM-denominated World Bank bonds. This will differ from the yield on dollar-denominated World Bank bonds for three reasons. First, it will depend on the expected change in the exchange rate between the dollar and the EM index over the life of the bond. (Recall that we have argued that the EM index will tend to appreciate against the dollar due to the Balassa-Samuelson effect, so on average this factor should reduce the interest cost to the bank.) Second, it will depend on the risk premium that the foreign investor would demand for holding EM currency risk. And, third, it will depend on the liquidity premium that investors will demand due to the lower tradability of the new instrument.

It is hard to assert ex ante how large these last costs will be. New instruments often have to be priced at a discount until investors gain familiarity with them and secondary markets develop liquidity. On the other hand, the reduction in risk and the expected appreciation of the EM index might in fact result in no additional interest rate cost for the World Bank. The substantial gap between the interest rate on World Bank loans and the opportunity cost of borrowing for client countries suggests that the bank might still be able to make attractively priced loans to its clients and recover any additional cost if it turns out that there is one. Even if there is a residual cost over and above this, the bank might wish to absorb it. In other words, the bank could decide on some degree of more favorable pricing in order to encourage borrowing countries to participate in the scheme on the grounds that it has an interest in solving the problem of original sin that threatens the stability of the international financial system.[26]

Step 3: Have G-10 countries issue debt denominated in the index. If this effort succeeds in creating space in the global portfolio for EM debt, there will then be an opportunity for other high-grade nonresidents to develop the market further. The governments of the United States, Euroland, Japan, the United Kingdom, and Switzerland, the issuers of the five major currencies, are natural candidates to do so. (In what follows, we refer to them as the G-10 countries for short.) The debt denominated in their currencies is significantly greater than the debt issued by their residents (as documented in chapters 1 and 9). They are at the opposite end of the currency-of-denomination spectrum from emerging markets, which should make some portfolio diversification toward EMs relatively attractive. More broadly, they are not immune from the systemic consequences of original sin, giving them an interest in solving the problem.

Thus, these countries could issue EM debt in order to further transform the structure of the global portfolio. Following issuance, they may wish to swap out of some or all of the EM currency exposure in order to avoid adding an inconvenient currency mismatch to their own fiscal accounts.[27] To do this, they would negotiate currency swaps with the countries whose currencies make up the index. In turn, this would allow emerging markets to swap out of (to hedge) their dollar exposures. Eventually, these swaps could be intermediated by the investment banks, although in the initial stages the World Bank may have to organize them.[28]

It is useful to consider the performance risk associated with these swaps. Emerging markets would pay into the swaps when their currencies were strong, while getting money from them when their currencies were weak. Since real appreciation (depreciation) tends to occur in good (bad) times, the performance risk will be concentrated in good times. In times of crisis, when their currencies weaken significantly, emerging markets would be receiving net income from their swaps. This minimizes the relevance of ability to pay for performance risk, which is the opposite of what happens with dollar debts.

A swap can be thought of as an exchange of bonds between the two final parties to the transaction. Hence, if the emerging market were to default on its swap obligation, that is, on the bond that it issued, then the industrial country would simply take back the bond that it had committed to the swap. Default risk would be limited to the change in value of the two bonds since the time they were issued. Again, performance risk would be limited.

The net cost of borrowing for the G-10 countries, after taking into account the swap, might actually be less than borrowing in their own currencies. The swap would entail a transfer of resources from the country that is most anxious to pay in order to hedge its currency exposure to the country that is most indifferent about the transaction. In other words, the first country would be especially willing to pay for the privilege of concluding the transaction, while the second one would be relatively indifferent and could therefore negotiate more favorable terms. Since countries suffering from original sin would be particularly anxious to pay for the privilege of off-loading their currency exposures, the G-10 countries could presumably obtain relatively attractive terms.

However, the swap may be expensive to organize. If the cost of the swap exceeds the benefit to EM member countries of hedging their currency exposures, then the transaction may not take place. Anticipating this outcome, G-10 countries may not be willing to issue EM debt in the first place. A solution to this problem would be for EM member countries to commit to swap their exposures with G-10 countries at a preannounced price. G-10 governments could then exercise this de facto put option in the event that they did not find a more attractive swap alternative in the market.

The development of a private market in swaps will depend on the existence of liquid long-term fixed-rate bond markets in local currency. These exist in some emerging markets and not in others. While our initiative will facilitate the development of local markets, the RDBs could accelerate the process by issuing instruments denominated in the (inflation-indexed) currencies of individual member countries in order to help create a benchmark long-term bond that would be devoid of sovereign and convertibility risk. The existence of a market in these claims would encourage investment banks to create and price the relevant swaps.

Step 4: Further develop the EM index market. Imagine that as a result of the preceding steps a market develops in claims denominated in the EM index. It is reasonable to think that institutional investors and mutual funds will then create products that add credit risk to the index. They will be able to do so by buying local-currency debt of the countries in the index. This will facilitate the development of these markets, further helping to erode original sin. It is conceivable that once the market has developed sufficiently, the role of industrial country governments and international institutions can be scaled back, as has happened with the issuance by nonresidents of debt denominated in the currencies of the Czech Republic, Hong Kong, Poland, Slovakia, and South Africa (see table 9.10).

Additional Issues

Moral Hazard

Dollar-denominated debts have a value that cannot be influenced by the monetary and exchange rate policies of the borrower. The same cannot be said about debts denominated in local currency. This might create an incentive for borrowers to allow their currencies to depreciate in order to reduce their debt burdens.

We have framed our proposal in inflation-indexed terms precisely in order to address worries about inadequate monetary credibility and opportunistic behavior. While the nominal exchange rate can be influenced by the monetary authorities, it is not clear that the same is true of the real exchange, especially in the medium term (which is what is relevant to medium- and long-term debts). To put the point another way, debasing the currency would eventually accelerate inflation. Indexation protects the investor from this consequence.

In addition, it is not obvious that countries with original sin, which are the targets of this initiative, would manipulate their currencies in practice. As documented in chapter 1, countries that suffer from original sin exhibit fear of floating. They accumulate international reserves and allow little volatility in their exchange rates.[29] Of course, as these countries are freed from original sin as a result of our initiative, they might exhibit less fear of floating and exercise more monetary discretion. Investors could then become more reluctant to hold securities denominated in EMs. Recall, however, that EM securities would be denominated in a composite of the currencies of a significant number of countries, whose exchange rates are imperfectly correlated with one another. Consequently, much of this exchange risk would be diversified away. In addition, greater exchange rate flexibility and the absence of original sin would reduce the incidence of currency collapses, reassuring investors worried mainly about extreme outcomes. To the extent that there is still the fear of short-term gaming by borrowers to save on their debt service, amounts to be paid can be indexed to the average dollar value of the inflation-indexed local currency over a certain period, say a quarter or a semester. This would further reduce the incentive to manipulate the exchange rate for opportunistic reasons.

Additional Issues for the World Bank and Other IFIs

We have argued that our proposal involves few if any financial risks for the World Bank and other IFIs. The IFIs would not assume additional currency risk and would benefit from the reduction in credit risk caused by the denomination of the debt in a unit that better tracks the borrowers' capacity to pay.[30] To be sure, there still could be pecuniary costs. In particular, it is unclear in step 2 what interest rates investors will demand in order to purchase these bonds initially and how difficult it will then be to develop a liquid market. And it is unclear in step 3 how costly it will be to develop swap markets.

We will not know these costs absent an effort to implement the plan. However, it is possible for the IFIs to specify an upper limit on the financial burden that they are willing to assume and to lose nothing if costs turn out to exceed that limit. For example, the World Bank could first agree with countries whose currencies are included in the EM index on the spread over prevailing dollar rates that they would be willing to pay in order to convert their debt into inflation-indexed local-currency terms. Adjusted for whatever portion of the cost that the World Bank was willing to subsidize in the interest of market development (including zero), this would determine the coupon that the bank offered on its bonds. The feasibility of the initiative would then hinge on whether there existed a demand for World Bank bonds at the corresponding price. If there were no market, no debt would be issued, and nothing would be lost.

The same point applies to issuance by G-10 countries. But if things ever got to this stage, a market in World Bank–issued EM bonds would already exist, making it easier to price the EM risk and to anticipate the implications of EM-denominated issuance for the required rate of return on G-10 debt. Uncertainty would then be limited to the price of the swap (which can be resolved before any debt is issued by negotiating an international agreement among EM members to swap currency exposures with G-10 countries at an agreed price, as noted above). If such an agreement is feasible, debt is issued. If not, no debt is issued, and implementation stops.

The history of international capital markets is a history of some markets that took off and of others that did not. It is also a history of markets that took off due to international initiatives. For example, markets in developing-country bonds did not take off in the third quarter of the twentieth century; in practice, the market was dominated by syndicated loans. Following the debt crisis of the 1980s, however, the Brady Plan jump-started this market by converting preexisting loans into tradable securities.[31] Similarly, inflation-indexed U.S. Treasury bonds (TIPS) did not exist until the late 1990s, despite the obvious advantages of inflation-indexed securities. The markets, left to their own devices, did not solve this problem; solving it required action by the U.S. Treasury. But following the Treasury's initial issuance of such securities, the market in TIPS has become quite active and liquid. If the analysis in this chapter is correct, then the value of developing an equivalently deep market in EMs would be large, both for the World Bank and its member countries. This implies that they should be willing to invest something in the development of the market. And it is not clear that the market would develop without their intervention.

Possible Distributional Consequences

There is a temptation to think that if an initiative involving international debts benefits a certain set of countries, then those benefits must come at the expense of other countries. In this context, it is tempting to think that if developing countries that borrow on international capital markets benefit from converting dollar loans into inflation-indexed local-currency units, then the developed countries that lend on international capital markets must necessarily lose from the operation. In this section we suggest that this implication need not follow.

One way of thinking about the distributional consequences for debtor and creditor countries of converting dollar-denominated debts into local-currency terms is in terms of uncovered interest parity. If there are no deviations from uncovered interest parity—that is, if the change in the exchange rate is exactly offset by the interest differential between loans denominated in dollars and local currency—then there are no distributional consequences of converting dollar loans into local-currency obligations. In a world of ex ante uncovered interest parity, in other words, there are no ex ante winners and losers; there is only the improvement in risk sharing associated with increased portfolio diversification. If countries are risk averse, then they all benefit from this diversification.

On the other hand, if deviations from uncovered interest parity are possible, the conversion can have distributional consequences. The question is whether these are desirable or undesirable. If the borrower's exchange rate depreciates by more than the interest rate differential, then the borrower (in this case, the emerging market) gains and the lender (in this case, the advanced country) loses when debts are denominated in the borrower's currency. Conversely, borrowers that experience an unanticipated appreciation would pay more when their debts are denominated in local currency than when their debts are denominated in dollars. In this instance they would lose, and the advanced countries on the other side of the transaction would gain. If unexpected (real) exchange rate appreciations occur when times are unexpectedly good and unexpected real depreciations occur when times are unexpectedly bad, as seems plausible, countries then benefit when times are bad and pay an extra cost when times are good.[32] This pattern clearly has desirable risk-sharing characteristics.[33]

Note that the additional income insurance enjoyed by emerging markets as a result of this scheme does not come mainly from off-loading currency risk onto international investors. Rather, it comes from the more efficient sharing of risk among the countries whose currencies make up the EM index. International investors, for their part, would only be taking on the residual aggregate risk in the index.

Adverse Selection

Another possible objection is that countries with good credit will not want to be part of an index that also includes countries with poor credit. Because countries with creditworthiness problems could have depreciating real exchange rates, including them in the EM index could make the latter less attractive to international investors, raising the required rate of return. This could create an adverse selection problem where only countries with poor credit would participate, causing the EM market to collapse.

In practice, it is not clear that this objection holds water. Countries with poor credit ratings exhibit a variety of macroeconomic problems, to be sure, but this does not mean that their real exchange rates will necessarily weaken further, which is what could make their inclusion in the EM index less appealing to international investors. If they experienced an earlier crisis, that experience will already have caused their exchange rates to fall. If the currency has overshot, then there may be an expectation of recovery and trend appreciation.[34] In any case, the credit risk of these countries would not directly affect the cost of funds to the World Bank (since this depends on the creditworthiness of the industrial countries providing the World Bank capital that guarantees the bonds).

Why Not Concentrate on Other Forms of Hedging?

Our initiative seeks to provide a form of insurance. In this respect it is not unique. There is a long history of proposals designed to enable emerging markets to self-insure through the establishment of stabilization funds or by accessing derivatives markets. (See Newbery and Stiglitz 1981; Hausmann, Powell, and Rigobon 1993; Inter-American Development Bank 1995.) These are potential alternatives to our proposal. But self-insurance does not reduce the total risk facing a country; it only alters the time profile. Self-insurance through the creation of stabilization funds is also susceptible to political pressures to appropriate the resources of the fund for opportunistic (electoral) purposes. Moreover, hedging through markets is limited by the (non)existence of long-term, liquid futures and options markets in the items that are relevant to country risk: oil, coffee, copper, and so forth. In practice, these markets are liquid only at relatively short horizons, typically less than two years. They insure against only price risk, not quantity risk. And other shocks, both real (such as earthquakes, hurricanes, floods, drought) and financial (such as sudden stops in capital flows), can be insured against in this way only to a limited extent.

Our approach can be thought of as an effort to more fully share the resulting real exchange rate risk across countries. Real exchange rate risk is an encompassing measure of economic risk that incorporates real shocks, terms-of-trade shocks, and financial shocks. Better diversification of welfare-impacting risks can therefore be achieved through financial initiatives that share real exchange rate risk more thoroughly than is possible by hedging in commodity-price derivatives markets.[35]

Problems with Calculating the EM Index

Accurate measurement of inflation is critical for the development of a market in inflation-indexed bonds. This suggests that responsibility for measuring the inflation rate cannot simply be delegated to the borrower, who may have an incentive to report biased estimates. Outside monitoring of the procedures used in this calculation may be required. The International Monetary Fund is the obvious entity to engage in such monitoring. The IMF currently operates a Data Dissemination System and a Special Data Dissemination Standard for countries active on international financial markets. A precondition for adherence to this standard is the timely release of methodologically sound data on variables like inflation. Thus, it would be relatively straightforward to ask the IMF to vet the methodologies that countries use when calculating CPI inflation and to audit their correct application.[36]

Concluding Remarks

International financial integration has not worked as promised. Capital account liberalization was supposed to stimulate growth in the developing world by channeling scarce capital to deserving economies and facilitating international risk sharing. Instead, private financial markets have been an engine of instability, and since 1998 debt flows to developing countries have become negative.

The condition we refer to as original sin is central to these problems. Unhedged aggregate dollar liabilities—an unavoidable condition when a country unable to borrow in its own currency incurs a net foreign debt—played a key role in the Asian, Russian, and Latin American crises that soured international investors on emerging markets. But even where the impact is not so severe, it is clear that the inability of emerging markets to borrow abroad in their own currencies weakens their economic performance. Original sin renders their economies more volatile, their financial systems more fragile, and their fiscal position less solvent, in turn making it more difficult to finance the sustained investment in strengthening institutions and policies necessary for economic development and growth. Efforts to reconcile economic stability with international capital mobility and to promote sustained economic growth—which are the ultimate goals of the effort to develop a new international financial architecture—are unlikely to succeed absent a solution to this problem.

The evidence is strong that original sin will not go away anytime soon as a result of the standard recipe of macroeconomic prudence and institution building. Efforts to strengthen national policies and institutions will help, but neither cross-country nor time-series evidence suggests that they will suffice to ameliorate the problem over the horizon relevant for practical policy decisions. And even if some countries do succeed in achieving redemption from original sin through initiatives taken at the domestic level, they will only raise the bar for the others, insofar as the addition of one more currency to the global portfolio reduces the diversification benefits of adding yet another.

Thus, the best way for a large group of countries representing over 80 percent of the GDP of the developing world to escape original sin is for the international policy community to commit to an initiative to develop a debt market in a basket of developing country currencies. This chapter has sketched how they might go about this.

Notes

We have benefited from extensive discussions of earlier versions of this paper at seminars at the Inter-American Development Bank and the International Monetary Fund in Washington, DC, UBS-Warburg in Milan, and the Kennedy School of Government at Harvard University. We are grateful to Alesia Rodriguez for research assistance and Roberto Rigobon, Ugo Panizza, and Andrew Wong for discussions.

1. As expressed in their real GDP in local-currency units. Measured in constant dollar terms instead of domestic units, the volatility of GDP growth also rises in developed countries, but this is not relevant to debt-servicing capacity, our focus here, since these countries borrow in their own currencies. Another way of making the point is to say that original sin makes the real exchange rate (the relative price at which local currency is converted into dollars) matter for ability to pay. We return to this in what follows.

2. Indeed, the advantages of developing these markets feature prominently in our discussion below.

3. To the extent that GDP per capita is correlated with the real exchange rate, the proposal developed in this chapter achieves a similar result but with an index that is easier to calculate.

4. To the extent that GDP fluctuations are strongly correlated with real exchange rate movements, especially in bad times, these instruments may be seen as imperfect substitutes for our proposal. There are several differences. First, the Berg et al. proposal (2002) adjusts only the interest coupon and not the principal, meaning that it really does not solve the balance-sheet problem proper. For example, in Argentina's recent crisis, real GDP declined by less than 20 percent at its trough, while dollar GDP declined by over 60 percent. Second, while GDP growth and real exchange rates are correlated, the correlation is not perfect. The bulk of the collapse in the capacity to pay in bad times comes from the decline in the real exchange rate, not in the growth of GDP in constant local-currency units. Using real GDP involves using the secondary instead of the primary source of the collapse of the capacity to pay. Third, the calculation of GDP is much more

convoluted and can be done only at lower frequencies (quarterly at best) and with greater error (it requires several surveys of production and of prices instead of just the calculation of one price index).

5. But, in contrast to these earlier schemes, we base our initiative on an analysis of why the markets in question do not exist and attempt to learn as much as possible from the few exceptional cases where they have in fact developed, in order to identify the most natural way of promoting their self-sustaining growth.

6. As argued by Shiller (2003), new markets typically need new indexes to synthesize relevant information, whether it is the S&P 500, the CPI, or the Lehman Global Bond Index.

7. As would happen if we weighted them by the market dollar value of GDP or the value of foreign debt. In particular, the second criteria would favor heavily indebted countries, while the first would favor those with overvalued currencies.

8. We thus calculate the index as a weighted basket of inflation-indexed national currencies. For each country in the basket, we take an index of its end-of-period nominal exchange rate and divide by the consumer price index (CPI) of the same month. Note that the calculation of the real exchange rate would in addition multiply this ratio by the U.S. CPI. We do not take this last step. The implications are discussed below. Note that, to the extent that U.S. inflation is low and stable, our index resembles a basket of real exchange rates.

9. We say similar rather than identical because the bilateral real exchange rate is usually calculated by dividing the nominal exchange rate (in terms of domestic currency per dollar) by the local CPI and multiplying by the CPI of the United States. Here we are not taking this last step. The implications of this are discussed below.

10. The EM index appreciates vis-à-vis the dollar over time if the sum of the real exchange rate appreciation of the underlying currencies plus U.S. inflation is positive. This means that the index will appreciate, even if the real exchange rate depreciates, as long as this depreciation is less than U.S. inflation. If these countries are expected to see real appreciation, and U.S. inflation expectations are in the neighborhood of 2 percent, then trend appreciation should be a robust characteristic of the index.

11. The indexes are presented on a per dollar basis, so that increases in the index imply depreciations.

12. The stability of these real exchange rate baskets is not specific to our choice of countries. Hausmann and Rigobon (2003) calculate similar baskets for the eighty-eight borrowers of the International Development Agency (IDA), which is the concessional window of the World Bank. (This means that Hausmann and Rigobon's broader index is dominated by the poorest countries, whereas our indexes here are tailored to emerging markets.) They show that while the typical inflation-indexed currency of the eighty-eight IDA countries has a standard deviation of 15.6 percent, a portfolio of all eighty-eight countries weighted by their debt to IDA is just 3 percent. Hausmann and Rigobon also show that the volatility of an index limited to claims on a random sample of either half or a fourth of the members of IDA (forty-four or twenty-two countries) would have a volatility of 4.4 percent and 5.8 percent, respectively.

13. The more countries that are included, other things equal, the more stability we should expect. In the limit (when all countries are included), the real exchange rate would not fluctuate, since the real exchange rate of the world as a whole is constant, by

definition. Moreover, the inflation-indexed local currency is just the value of the domestic consumption basket, which is itself much more diversified than the export basket, and hence is also more stable.

14. In a world of costless transactions, an investor could create an implicit index by himself. Individuals could in theory create an S&P or a NASDAQ-based portfolio by themselves. In practice transaction costs imply that it is more efficient for somebody to create the portfolio and sell shares in it. In addition, an attempt to replicate the EM index privately by purchasing the underlying instruments in the market would involve buying securities that have much more credit risk than the AAA-rated IFIs, as no EM member is AAA rated.

15. IFIs usually operate through two main windows: a nonconcessional window that is funded by borrowing in international capital markets using their capital base as collateral, and a concessional window that is funded with fiscal resources of donor governments. In the case of the World Bank, the nonconcessional window is known as the International Bank for Reconstruction and Development and the concessional window is called the International Development Agency. See also below.

16. Moreover, since the World Bank would calculate the index, it would have a fiduciary responsibility to its investors in assuring that there is no opportunistic manipulation of the estimates of exchange rates or the CPI by member countries. This will impart more credibility to the index.

17. In what follows, we refer to these alternatives as dollar lending for short.

18. To put the point another way, they lend in dollars because, absent an initiative of the sort we develop here, original sin prevents them from issuing debt in the currencies of their borrowers.

19. They are then supplemented by reflows from their own lending operations.

20. Hausmann and Rigobon (2003) show that the currency risk of the portfolio of inflation-indexed local-currency IDA loans between 1985 and 2000 would have been low, given the low and often negative correlations among real exchange rate movements of IDA countries. This is the same pattern that holds for our EM index, as noted above. In addition, they show for IDA that the value of the inflation-indexed local-currency portfolio would exceed the value of the dollar portfolio if the sum of the U.S. inflation plus the real appreciation of the IDA basket of currencies exceeds 1.37 percent. U.S. inflation has been running at approximately 2 percent. If this rate is maintained going forward, there would be scope for some long-run real depreciation of the basket while still generating a larger net present value. However, if developing countries' income levels exhibit a trend toward convergence—as has been the case in China, India, East Asia, and eastern Europe, the Balassa-Samuelson effect would imply that they should also exhibit some trend appreciation. In this case, the move to local-currency inflation-indexed lending should generate an even larger expected repayment stream, even better risk characteristics, and an even lower volatility in the total dollar value of the portfolio (given the low volatility of the basket).

21. In other words, while dollars and other foreign currencies would be delivered, the amount of the obligation would be related to the inflation-indexed local-currency value of the debt.

22. Conceivably, if the issuance of EM debt by the World Bank is very large, the bank might be unable to hedge the resulting currency exposure by converting some of its old

loans into the member currencies of the index because the required amounts would exceed the volume of loans in its books to at least some of the EM members. But the bank could still hedge its excess exposure to that currency by arranging a swap with another IFI—say an RDB—that would similarly wish to convert its dollar loans to local currency. Alternatively, the World Bank could purchase inflation-indexed local-currency government obligations or ask an investment bank to offer it a hedge. All these operations would have the beneficial effect of reducing the currency mismatch of the respective countries.

23. Hausmann and Rigobon (2003) simulate the impact on the IDA portfolio of converting IDA loans into inflation-indexed local currency in the 1985–2000 period. They find that diversification implies a very large reduction in the overall currency risk of the portfolio of IDA. In addition, debt service becomes less procyclical and less correlated with the real exchange rate, moving the debt burden to states of nature where the capacity to pay is larger. Monte Carlo simulations show that under the counterfactual the same shocks to output, inflation, and the real interest rate are associated with a more predictable evolution of the debt to GDP ratio than under dollar-based lending.

24. In fact, some coordination between issuance and adjustment of the index should be feasible, as suggested to us by Andrew Wong.

25. In addition, there would be no additional convertibility risk, as countries' payments would be made in the same currencies used at present.

26. In addition, differential pricing could be justified by the fact that borrowing in local-currency inflation-indexed terms involves less credit risk for the World Bank.

27. That is to say, they may not want debt service denominated in EM currencies when their tax revenues were denominated in domestic currency.

28. In particular, the World Bank's AAA rating would allow it to provide greater assurances to the treasuries of developed countries.

29. In addition, Hausmann, Panizza, and Rigobon (2003) show that at short horizons, real exchange rate changes in developing countries exhibit negative skewness and excess kurtosis as would be the consequence of trying to maintain unsustainably appreciated exchange rates. They also show that at five-year horizons these two characteristics disappear, as would be expected from the endogenous nature of the medium-term real exchange rate.

30. To avoid currency risk they would have to make sure that they are able to match the issuance of debt in EMs with the conversion of existing loans to EM member countries into inflation-indexed local currency. Any temporary gap can be hedged by either buying a claim on that government in that denomination or swapping the currency exposure with it.

31. At the beginning, the market seemed to value the enhancements that were embedded in the Brady bonds to make them more attractive, but by 1996 it was clear that the market could see through these enhancements and countries started to exchange the Brady bonds for Global bonds with no enhancements.

32. We can think in terms of real exchange rate changes in this context because the local-currency-denominated claims in question are inflation indexed.

33. In practice, the World Bank and other IFIs do not set the interest rates on their loans so as to make the interest rate differential between loans denominated in different currencies differ by the expected rate of depreciation. Generally, they set the same inter-

est rate on loans to all borrowers in order to recover their costs and achieve an agreed profit target. This means that the interest rate is not determined to ensure uncovered interest rate parity. Some countries benefit from this practice (they enjoy lower interest rates on their World Bank loans than they might be charged otherwise), while other countries do not (the interest rate they are charged by the bank is higher than warranted by their country risk, since it is used to defray the additional costs associated with bank loans to other riskier countries). For example, there is the sense at the time of writing that China's real exchange rate will have a tendency to appreciate. China should now find that the cost of borrowing from the World Bank in dollars is much cheaper than the cost perceived by a country that is anticipating a real depreciation. Under current arrangements, in other words, China receives a subsidy, while other countries are penalized. Under the new regime, these winners and losers would change places.

34. This was the historical behavior of real exchange rates in East Asia and Russia in 1999 and Mexico in 1995: these countries underwent crises that caught the markets by surprise. Large unexpected real depreciations were followed by large and to a large extent expected real appreciations. An exception was Brazil. In spite of its successful management of the transition to a floating regime in the midst of a currency crisis in January 1999, the real exchange rate did not recover, but instead felt further pressure in 2001–2. By contrast, Ecuador, a country with less commendable policies, has undergone massive appreciation since the 1999 crisis. This provides further evidence for the idea that the future course of the real exchange rate is difficult to predict.

35. The downside is that the real exchange rate is a country-specific variable, and hence is more prone to more moral-hazard problems, as discussed above.

36. It should be pointed out that the EM index will be dominated by the currencies of countries that have access to international financial markets and consequently draw the bulk of their debt from private sources. Poorer countries whose debt is mostly from official concessional multilateral or bilateral sources should have their debts redenominated in inflation-indexed local currency, following Hausmann and Rigobon (2003). Countries in the EM index have two salient characteristics. First, they have a level of institutional development such that official entities can be trusted to perform such tasks as calculating a CPI, especially if they know that the World Bank will be auditing their activities. Second, they have a level of income such that the CPI is composed of a large and highly diversified basket of goods and services, so that the estimates of the CPI are unlikely to be affected by errors in any individual price measurement.

References

Berg, Andrew, Eduardo Borensztein, and Paulo Mauro. 2002. "Reviving the Case for GDP-Indexed Bonds." IMF Working Paper no. 02-211, International Monetary Fund, Washington, DC, December.

Caballero, Ricardo. 2003. "On the International Financial Architecture: Insuring Emerging Markets." NBER Working Paper no. 9570, National Bureau of Economic Research, Cambridge, MA, March.

Hausmann, Ricardo, Ugo Panizza, and Roberto Rigobon. 2003. "The Long-Run Real Exchange Rate Volatility Puzzle." Manuscript, Harvard University, Cambridge, MA.

Hausmann, Ricardo, Andrew Powell, and Roberto Rigobon. 1993. "An Optimal Spending Rule Facing Oil Income Uncertainty (Venezuela)." In *External Shocks and Adjustment Mechanisms*, 113–71. Washington, DC: Inter-American Development Bank.

Hausmann, Ricardo, and Roberto Rigobon. 2003. "IDA in UF: On the Benefits of Changing the Currency Denomination of Concessional Lending to Low-Income Countries." Manuscript, World Bank, Washington, DC.

Inter-American Development Bank. 1995. *Overcoming Volatility: Economic and Social Progress Report 1995*. Washington, DC: Inter-American Development Bank.

Newbery, David, and Joseph Stiglitz. 1981. *The Theory of Commodity Price Stabilization: A Study in the Economics of Risk*. Oxford: Clarendon Press.

Shiller, Robert. 2003. *The New Financial Order: Risk in the 21st Century*. Princeton, NJ: Princeton University Press.

Contributors

Michael D. Bordo is director of the Center for Monetary and Financial History at Rutgers University and a research associate at the National Bureau of Economic Research.

Luis Felipe Céspedes is a senior economist in the research department of the Central Bank of Chile.

Marcos Chamon is an economist at the International Monetary Fund.

Roberto Chang is professor of economics at Rutgers University.

Giancarlo Corsetti is Pierre Werner Chair, and joint chair for the Robert Schuman Centre for Advanced Studies and the Economics Department at the European University Institute.

Barry Eichengreen is the George C. Pardee and Helen N. Pardee Professor of Economics and Political Science at the University of California, Berkeley.

Marc Flandreau is professor of economics at the Institut d'Études Politiques de Paris.

Ricardo Hausmann is professor of the practice of economic development at Harvard University.

Olivier Jeanne is a senior economist at the research department of the International Monetary Fund.

Bartosz Maćkowiak is junior professor in the economics department at Humboldt University in Berlin.

Christopher M. Meissner is lecturer in the faculty of economics and politics at the University of Cambridge, fellow of King's College, and a faculty research fellow at the National Bureau of Economic Research.

Ugo Panizza is an economist in the research department of the Inter-American Development Bank.

Angela Redish is professor of economics at the University of British Columbia.

Nathan Sussman is senior lecturer in the department of economics at the Hebrew University.

Andrés Velasco is the Sumitomo Professor of International Finance and Development at Harvard University.

Jeromin Zettelmeyer is a senior economist at the research department of the International Monetary Fund.

Index

Cobb-Douglas production function, 81
Colombia, 241
commercial banks, 109, 134, 144, 164
commitment mechanism, 122
commodity price fluctuations, 3
Confederate states, U.S., 129
consumer price index (CPI), 52, 206–7, 268, 282, 285n16, 287n36
consumption smoothing, 13
contagion, 215n22
convertibility, 126, 143, 277, 286n25
corporate debt, 122, 132, 141, 202
corporate paper, 132
country risk premium, 49
country size, 34, 48, 234, 248–51, 262
CPI. *See* consumer price index
credit crunch, 96, 98, 101–2, 107, 110, 112–16, 118
credit market imperfections, 70, 85
credit ratings, 7, 28, 30, 35, 240, 281
creditworthiness, 7, 28, 30, 37, 142, 163, 281
Crimean War, 176
crises, 3, 4, 10, 28, 30, 35, 66n2, 89n1, 91n24, 95, 98–99, 101, 118, 123–24, 144, 154, 190–91, 218, 230, 269, 282; self-fulfilling, 8, 96, 97, 104, 107
cross-border bank claims, 18
currency: crises, 68, 70, 77, 81, 85, 89n1, 104, 116, 122, 148, 287n34; denomination, 7, 9, 11n3, 15, 65, 85, 164, 173, 273; depreciation, 4, 267; exposures, 20–21, 275, 277; mismatches, 4, 11n3, 13, 27, 104, 109, 118n2, 119n4, 123, 134, 148, 200, 213n1, 214n14, 252, 268, 273, 274–76, 286n22; pegs, 70, 190, 199, 202; risk, 20, 48, 122, 253–54, 267, 273, 275–76, 279, 280, 285n20, 286n30; union, 22
current account of the balance of payments, 4, 70, 81, 83–86, 88, 89n3, 91n22, 95, 243
Czech Republic, 23, 252, 254, 278

debt: crises, 30, 149, 279; default, 45n11, 48, 72, 90n7, 95, 100, 122, 155, 186–87, 192–97, 200–203, 212–14, 218, 221–27, 230n1, 240, 243, 253, 263n4, 277; denomination, 7, 9, 14, 226; dollar, 9, 35, 50, 57, 64, 74, 77, 79, 98, 100, 108, 122, 124–25, 139, 141, 143, 145, 201, 204, 218, 219–21, 226–27, 229, 252, 269, 274, 277; domestic, 25, 109, 123–25, 135, 136, 139, 141, 145–47, 156, 175, 179, 182, 191, 204–5, 209, 233, 266; external, 5, 6, 7, 13–14, 37, 123–24, 135–36, 138–39, 141, 144–45, 147, 150, 219; foreign, 4, 7, 8, 11n3, 13, 26–27, 30, 33–34, 36, 45n7, 95–96, 105, 123–25, 128, 134, 138, 142, 145–46, 148, 154–56, 179, 186, 190–92, 194, 199, 201–3, 208, 209–10, 214n13, 282, 284n7; funded, 128–29, 132–33; hard-currency, 144; indexed, 5, 209, 236, 263n4; internal, 136, 138–39, 145; international, 4, 191, 215n17, 280; long-term, 35, 78, 84, 91n19, 123–24, 148, 190, 278; maturity, 70, 81–82, 84; monetization, 101; private, 9, 25, 190–92, 202, 244; public, 25–26, 28, 30, 45n10, 69, 73, 75, 79, 81–82, 85, 88, 90n6, 91n19, 101, 125, 133–34, 136, 138–39, 147, 164, 173, 205, 240; repayments, 53, 98; service, 4, 29, 30, 34–35, 227, 240, 274, 278, 286n27; sovereign, 8, 123, 134, 141, 150, 190–91, 202–3, 205; structure, 194–95, 212–13
debt-servicing capacity, 246, 266, 274, 283n1
deflation, 74–75, 79, 85, 90n13, 134
demand, domestic, 101, 105
Denmark, 123, 149n1, 156, 252
derivative instruments, 192, 210
devaluation, 49, 61, 68–70, 73–79, 81, 83–85, 90nn12–13, 91nn17–18, 91nn20–21, 104, 105, 128, 199, 200, 202, 213, 214n11; real, 56–58, 62; risk, 190, 201, 218, 253, 263n4
developing countries, 3, 5, 6, 8, 10, 13, 15, 20, 23, 28, 29–30, 35–36, 45n10, 191, 235, 250, 257, 263n2, 266–69, 280, 282–83, 286n29
Diamond-Dybvig model, 99
discount window, 116, 119n10
diversification, 150, 156, 249–50, 263–64n15, 271, 280, 282–83, 286n23
dollar. *See* U.S. dollar
dollar-denominated securities, 129
dollarization, 9, 49, 60, 66n1, 70, 79, 104–5, 122, 192, 200, 202, 204, 208, 210–11, 214n5, 218–19, 224
dollar liabilities, 9, 35, 114, 117, 282
domestically issued debt, 132–33, 137, 139
domestic-currency debt, 11n3, 25, 26, 123, 124, 137, 141, 142, 144, 190, 193, 196, 201–6, 208–9, 214n15, 214n17, 215n19
domestic-currency external sovereign debt, 8, 123